VISUAL BASIC 2005 EXPRESS:
NOW PLAYING

VISUAL BASIC 2005 EXPRESS

NOW PLAYING

by Wallace Wang

NO STARCH PRESS

San Francisco

Printed on recycled paper in the United States of America

1 2 3 4 5 6 7 8 9 10 – 09 08 07 06

No Starch Press and the No Starch Press logo are registered trademarks of No Starch Press, Inc. Other product and company names mentioned herein may be the trademarks of their respective owners. Rather than use a trademark symbol with every occurrence of a trademarked name, we are using the names only in an editorial fashion and to the benefit of the trademark owner, with no intention of infringement of the trademark.

Microsoft® Visual Basic® 2005 Express © Microsoft Corporation. "Microsoft" is a registered trademark of Microsoft Corporation in the United States and/or other countries and is used by No Starch under license from owner. *Visual Basic 2005 Express: Now Playing* is an independent publication which is not affiliated with, nor has it been authorized, sponsored, or otherwise approved by Microsoft Corporation.

Publisher: William Pollock
Managing Editor: Elizabeth Campbell
Cover Design: Octopod Studios
Developmental Editor: Peter Spear
Technical Reviewer: Dan Mabbutt
Copyeditor: Lisa Theobald
Compositor: Riley Hoffman
Proofreader: Nancy Riddiough
Indexer: Ted Laux

For information on book distributors or translations, please contact No Starch Press, Inc. directly:

No Starch Press, Inc.
555 De Haro Street, Suite 250, San Francisco, CA 94107
phone: 415.863.9900; fax: 415.863.9950; info@nostarch.com; www.nostarch.com

The information in this book is distributed on an "As Is" basis, without warranty. While every precaution has been taken in the preparation of this work, neither the author nor No Starch Press, Inc. shall have any liability to any person or entity with respect to any loss or damage caused or alleged to be caused directly or indirectly by the information contained in it.

Library of Congress Cataloging-in-Publication Data

```
Wang, Wally.
  Visual Basic 2005 Express : now playing / Wallace Wang.
    p. cm.
  Includes index.
  ISBN 1-59327-059-3 (cd-rom)
1.  Microsoft Visual BASIC. 2.  BASIC (Computer program language)  I. Title.
QA76.73.B3W367435 2006
005.2'768--dc22
                                    2005025145
```

This book is dedicated to everyone who didn't have the "right" education, test scores, or job skills, but wound up succeeding at their chosen goal anyway. If you want to learn or do anything in your life, such as learn to program a computer, go ahead and do it and don't let anyone ever tell you otherwise.

BRIEF CONTENTS

CONTENTS IN DETAIL

PART I
LEARNING THE VB EXPRESS USER INTERFACE

1
YOUR FIRST VISUAL BASIC PROGRAM   13

2
UNDERSTANDING THE VISUAL BASIC EXPRESS
INTERFACE   27

3
WORKING WITH PROJECTS
41

4
DESIGNING A USER INTERFACE
49

5
WRITING AND EDITING BASIC CODE
59

6
GETTING HELP
71

PART II
DESIGNING A USER INTERFACE

7
UNDERSTANDING CONTROLS AND PROPERTIES 79

8
USING THE APPEARANCE PROPERTIES 87

9
USING THE LAYOUT AND BEHAVIOR PROPERTIES 101

13
OFFERING CHOICES WITH RADIO BUTTONS
AND BOXES   159

14
ACCEPTING AND DISPLAYING TEXT IN TEXT BOXES
AND LABELS   177

15
ACCEPTING A RANGE OF NUMERIC VALUES   187

16
DESIGNING A FORM WITH LAYOUT CONTROLS   197

17
DISPLAYING DIALOG BOXES   211

PART IV
WRITING BASIC CODE

18
USING VARIABLES AND CONSTANTS
231

19
MATHEMATICAL OPERATORS
247

25
CREATING PROCEDURES AND FUNCTIONS 345

26
UNDERSTANDING OBJECT-ORIENTED PROGRAMMING 355

27
COMMENTS, ERROR HANDLING, AND DEBUGGING 375

PART V
ENHANCING YOUR VISUAL BASIC PROGRAMS

28
CONNECTING TO FILES AND DATABASES 395

29
PRINTING DATA FROM YOUR PROGRAM 413

30
ADDING THE FINISHING TOUCHES TO YOUR PROGRAM 425

INDEX 435

ACKNOWLEDGMENTS

The wonderful people at No Starch Press always make book writing a fun and enjoyable experience. Perhaps the most important person involved in the creation of this book is William Pollock, who came up with the idea and asked me, "Hey, do you want to do a book about Visual Basic?" Usually when Mr. Pollock asks me to do anything, I'll do it—except if he asks to borrow money.

Two other extremely important people include Dan Mabbutt and Elizabeth Campbell, both of whom worked long hours with cramped fingers and bleary eyes as they worked tirelessly to ensure that this manuscript was as complete and error-free as possible.

Additional thanks go to Steve Schirripa (who appears on HBO's hit show *The Sopranos*) and Don Learned (www.laffspot.com) for giving me my break in performing at the Riviera Comedy Club (www.rivierahotel.com) in Las Vegas. Also a big thanks go to all the stand-up comedians I've had the pleasure of working with over the years, including Dobie Maxwell, Darrell Joyce, Larry Omaha, Dante, Kip Addotta, Bob Zany, Gerry Bednob, Patrick DeGuire, Russ Rivas (www.laffscomedy.com), and Leo "the Man, the Myth, the Legend" Fontaine.

Final thanks go to my wife Cassandra and son Jordan, who put up with my long hours in front of the computer. My four cats, Bo, Scraps, Tasha, and Nuit, deserve special acknowledgment too for draping themselves in various positions around my computer, making it nearly impossible to use the keyboard and mouse, or look at the computer screen past their furry butts.

INTRODUCTION

Programming can be fun. If you've ever used a computer and wondered how it worked, or better yet, wanted to make your computer do something better, or different—something that it couldn't do before—then you already have the mind of a programmer.

The only requirement to be a programmer is the desire to do it. You don't need a college degree, an aptitude for mathematics, or special schooling. All you need is a computer and the curiosity to learn programming.

People may want to learn how to program their computer for any number of reasons. Some people want to write computer programs for a career. Others want to create a new product that improves upon an existing program or even forges a new market altogether. Still others want to learn programming for the sheer mental exhilaration of doing so, in much the same way that people enjoy crossword puzzles and brain teasers. Whatever your reasons for learning to program, you'll find that plenty of people just like you have learned to program a computer. That means you can do so too.

A Programming Primer

A computer program is like a recipe that gives the computer step-by-step instructions to follow. Just as you can write a recipe in English, Spanish, Chinese, Arabic, or Swahili, so too can you write a computer program using any variety of programming languages you choose. Contrary to popular belief, there is no inherently "best" programming language just as there is no single "best" human language.

Like human languages, the best programming language depends entirely on circumstances. Just as you would probably want to learn Japanese if you wanted to talk to people in Tokyo, so might you want to choose one programming language over another based on what you want to do. Some programming languages are designed to be easy to learn, others are designed for calculating mathematical formulas, and still others are designed for manipulating text. If you write the same program in two different languages, you'll find that one language will be easier to use than another, although no language will be best for writing all types of programs every time.

When learning to program a computer, you actually need to learn three related, but different, tasks:

How to solve a particular problem. If you want to write a program to predict the winners of a horse race, you need to know what data you need and what steps to follow to predict winning race horses. If you want to write a video game, you need to know the goal of the game, the rules to restrict the player's actions, and what obstacles will get in the player's way. If you don't know what problem you want to solve and how to solve it, the computer will never know how to solve it either.

How to use a particular programming language. Once you know what problem you want to solve, you need to choose a specific programming language to use. That means learning what commands are available in your chosen programming language and how to type those commands to tell the computer what to do step by step. In this book, you'll be learning the Visual Basic programming language.

How to use a specific program to help you write programs in your chosen programming language. To type program commands, you need to use an editor, which acts like a simple word processor that lets you write, edit, and save your programming instructions in a file. When you're done using the editor to type your program commands into a file, you need another program called a compiler, which turns your programming commands into a special file that can run by itself on other computers. To write programs in the Visual Basic language, you need to use Microsoft Visual Basic 2005 Express (hereafter referred to as Visual Basic Express), which is known as an *Integrated Development Environment (IDE)* since it includes both an editor and a compiler.

But before you start learning anything about Visual Basic Express or the Visual Basic programming language, take some time to learn the general principles behind all computer programming. Once you understand how computer programming works, you can better understand how to write a program using any programming language, including Visual Basic.

The Principles of Writing a Computer Program

A computer program is nothing more than a long list of instructions that tells the computer what to do, what to display on the screen, and what to do with data it receives from the user. The more complicated your program, the more instructions you'll need to write in order to make your program work. A simple program, one that displays your name on the screen, might only require a handful of instructions, while a more complicated program, such as Microsoft Windows, could take several million instructions.

The key to programming is to write the fewest number of instructions that do the maximum amount of work as possible. The more instructions you write, the longer it will take and the more likely you may make a mistake. So rather than attempt to write one huge, monolithic program at one sitting, programmers divide a large program into several smaller ones. Once they write and test each small program, they put them together, like building blocks, to create a much larger program.

When you break a large program into several smaller ones, you can either store them in a single file on your hard disk, or store them in separate files. The advantage of storing everything in a single file is that you only have to look for one file when you want to edit or modify a program. The disadvantage of storing everything in a single file is that the longer your program gets, the harder it can be to find anything, much like trying to read a novel printed on a single scroll of paper.

For that reason, most programmers not only divide a large program into several smaller ones, but they also store the smaller programs in separate files. Separate files provide several advantages over storing everything in a single file:

- Smaller files are easier to edit, read, and ultimately understand.
- Separate files let different programmers work on the same program.
- Separate files isolate you from other parts of your program, which can prevent you from messing up other parts of your program by mistake.

KEY POINTS TO REMEMBER

No matter what computer, operating system, or programming language you use, the general principles of programming remain the same:

- Break a large program into smaller parts
- Make each part of a program as short and simple as possible (to make it easier to write, understand, and modify later)
- Keep each part of your program separate and isolated as much as possible (to keep one part of your program from accidentally messing up another part of your program)

The Principles of Programming Languages

The only language that computers understand is something called *machine code*, which consists of nothing more than instructions written as a series of zeroes and ones, such as:

1110 0110 1100 0001

1010 0000 1001 0111

0101 1110 0011 0110

One problem with machine code is that it's extremely difficult to understand just what each command really tells the computer to do. Another problem is that one misplaced 0 or 1 can give the computer a completely different command than you intended, and trying to find your mistake buried in a page full of zeroes and ones can be nearly impossible.

For that reason, few people program in machine code. To simplify programming, computer scientists created another programming language called *assembly language*. Assembly language replaces multiple lines of cryptic machine code with a single line of assembly language commands that can look very different, but be as equally confusing:

```
title   Hello World
; This program displays "Hello, World!"

dosseg
.model small
.stack 100h

.data
say_hello db 'Hello, World!',0dh,0ah,'$'

.code
main  proc
        mov     ax,@data
        mov     ds,ax

        mov     ah,9
        mov     dx,offset say_hello
        int     21h

        mov     ax,4C00h
        int     21h
main  endp
end   main
```

Unfortunately, computers don't understand assembly language either; they only understand machine code. To convert assembly language programs into machine code, computer scientists have created special programs called *assemblers*, which convert assembly language into machine code. Basically, every programming language is designed to make it easy for humans to write programs without going through the tedium and nuisance of learning machine code.

While somewhat simpler to understand then machine code, assembly language is still too complicated for most people to understand. So to make programming easier, computer scientists have invented computer languages that are much easier for people to read, write, and understand. As a result, programs that accomplish the same task, but written in different languages, can look drastically different:

```
; LISP
(DEFUN HELLO-WORLD ()
            (PRINT (LIST 'HELLO 'WORLD)))
```

The above example uses a programming language called LISP, which is designed for experimenting in giving computers artificial intelligence. The example below shows an equivalent program written in the popular C++ programming language.

```
#include <iostream>
int main()
{
    std::cout << "Hello, world!\n";
}
```

To convert different programming languages into machine code, computer scientists have written special programs called *compilers*. A compiler translates a program, written in one language, into machine code. To compile your Visual Basic programs into machine code, you need to use the Visual Basic Express program.

The Philosophy Behind Programming Languages

Computer scientists have designed every programming language to solve one particular type of problem. While every programming language is great for solving the one type of problem they were designed for, every programming language is also mediocre at solving most other types of problems, and horribly inefficient at solving a handful of other types of problems. That's why there is no one "best" programming language. The "best" programming language is the one that makes it easy for you write your program as quickly and easily as possible, so what might be the "best" language for you might be the worst language for writing someone else's programs.

The philosophical design behind each programming language determines:

- The number and type of built-in commands available (known as *keywords*)
- The way you combine commands together (known as *syntax*)

Keywords act like bricks that you can combine together to create a program, as shown in Figure 1. By combining keywords you can create instructions, called *statements*, which tell the computer to do something useful.

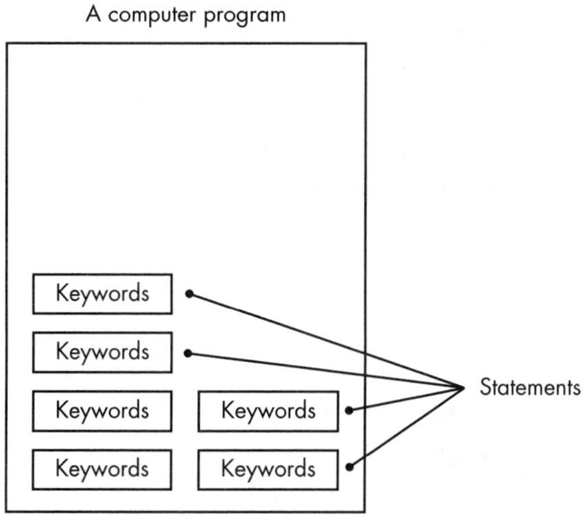

Figure 1: Keywords act like building blocks that you can combine to create a program.

Table 1 lists all the keywords available in the Visual Basic programming language.

NOTE *The boldfaced keywords are considered obsolete, although Visual Basic still recognizes them as valid. These obsolete keywords still exist so Visual Basic Express can still run programs written in older versions of the Visual Basic programming language.*

Table 1: Keywords Provided by the Visual Basic Programming Language

AddHandler	AddressOf	Alias	And
AndAlso	Ansi	As	Assembly
Auto	Boolean	ByRef	Byte
ByVal	Call	Case	Catch
CBool	CByte	CChar	CDate
CDec	CDbl	Char	CInt
Class	CLng	CObj	Const
CShort	CSng	CStr	CType
Date	Decimal	Declare	Default
Delegate	Dim	DirectCast	Do
Double	Each	Else	ElseIf
End	Enum	Erase	Error
Event	Exit	False	Finally
For	Friend	Function	Get
GetType	**GoSub**	GoTo	Handles
If	Implements	Imports	In
Inherits	Integer	Interface	Is
Let	Lib	Like	Long
Loop	Me	Mod	Module
MustInherit	MustOverride	MyBase	MyClass
Namespace	New	Next	Not
Nothing	NotInheritable	NotOverridable	Object
On	Option	Optional	Or
OrElse	Overloads	Overridable	Overrides
ParamArray	Preserve	Private	Property
Protected	Public	RaiseEvent	ReadOnly
ReDim	REM	RemoveHandler	Resume
Return	Select	Set	Shadows
Shared	Short	Single	Static
Step	Stop	String	Structure
Sub	SyncLock	Then	Throw
To	True	Try	TypeOf
Unicode	Until	**Variant**	When
While	With	WithEvents	WriteOnly
Xor	#Const	#ExternalSource	#If...Then...#Else
#Region	-	&	&=
*	*=	/	/=
\	\=	^	^=
+	+=	=	-=

Keywords may let you build any type of program, but using keywords alone to build a large program can be like building a skyscraper one brick at a time. It's possible, but not very practical. So instead of relying solely on keywords to build a program, you can combine keywords into miniature programs that you can reuse as bigger, more powerful building blocks, called *functions*. A function performs a unique task that a single keyword can't do, such as calculating the square root of a number or changing all characters from lowercase to UPPERCASE.

Many programming languages, including Visual Basic, come with a library of pre-written functions so you don't have to create them all over again. In addition to writing instructions using keywords, you can also use functions to build programs of greater complexity and power as shown in Figure 2.

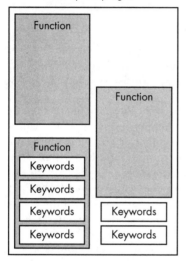

Figure 2: Functions allow you to create larger, more powerful building blocks for putting together a program.

Most programming languages provide libraries of prewritten, general-purpose functions for solving common tasks, but you can also create your own functions to solve tasks that are unique to your particular program.

No matter which programming language you use, the idea is always the same: Build your program one step at a time using a combination of keywords and functions to create statements that tell the computer what to do.

The Philosophy Behind the BASIC Programming Language

Every programming language provides a way to create building blocks out of different combinations of smaller building blocks (keywords), which in turn can be used to create larger and more powerful building blocks in a never-ending cycle. What makes the BASIC programming language unique is that it's specifically designed to make programming easy.

If you review the previous programming language samples that display the words "Hello, world" on the screen, you'll notice that most languages use less-than-intuitive abbreviations and symbols to tell the computer what to do. In contrast, the BASIC language uses complete English words as shown below, which makes BASIC a much easier programming language to learn and understand:

```
PRINT "Hello World!"
```

The Philosophy Behind Visual Basic

Visual Basic combines the simplicity of writing programs with the simplicity of designing them. Essentially, every program consists of two parts:

- A user interface
- Instructions that make your program do something useful

The user interface provides a way to get data from the user and display information back to the user. A user interface can be as simple as a printer that types messages on a piece of paper, but more often, the user interface consists of information displayed on a computer screen.

Once your program receives data from the user interface, it can then manipulate that data and display any new results back to the user interface. In the early days of computers, the user interface consisted of levers that programmers flipped to feed data into the computer and blinking lights that the computer flashed on and off to send data back to the programmers.

Later, computers replaced mechanical switches with keyboards that let you type commands into the computer (input) and receive data back from the computer (output) printed on a long scroll of paper. In this case, the user interface consisted of a keyboard and a printer.

Modern computers now let you give data to a computer (input) through multiple devices such as a keyboard, mouse, scanner, or even a video camera, although the keyboard is still the most common way to give data to a computer.

Getting data back out of the computer has improved. Instead of waiting for the computer to print messages on a scroll of paper, today's computers display information directly on the computer screen. Initially, computers just displayed messages in plain text at the bottom of the screen, but as computer graphics got more powerful, the user interface gradually transformed from displaying plain text on a screen to displaying formatted text in different colors and sizes in boxes or windows that can appear on the screen.

One big problem with user interfaces is that they took time to create. So not only did programmers have to write commands to make their program solve a problem, but they also needed to write additional commands to create a user interface so people could use their programs. So creating a user interface for your program essentially means you have to accomplish two things when writing a program:

- Write instructions to tell a computer how to solve a specific problem, step by step.
- Write instructions to tell the computer how to accept data from the user and then display it back to the user again.

To solve both problems, Visual Basic makes programming easier in two ways. First, Visual Basic uses the BASIC programming language, which is very easy for people to learn, understand, and write. Second, instead of forcing you to write instructions to create a user interface, Visual Basic provides prebuilt parts, called controls, that you can paste together to create a user interface that works with a minimal number of instructions.

How Visual Basic Works

Most programs can be divided into two parts, a user interface and the "brains" of the program that manipulates data. Creating a program in Visual Basic therefore requires two separate steps. One step involves designing your user interface and the second step involves writing BASIC code to make your program manipulate and respond to any data that it receives through that user interface.

Some people create the user interface first and then write BASIC code to make it all work. Others write BASIC code to tell the computer what to do and then design a user interface to allow others to interact with the program. Either way is correct just as long as you create a program that works and does something useful.

Just remember that the user interface allows your program to communicate with the outside world, for instance with a person pressing buttons or clicking the mouse, or even another computer sending data across the Internet to your program. Your BASIC code allows your program to respond to any information retrieved from the user interface as shown in Figure 3.

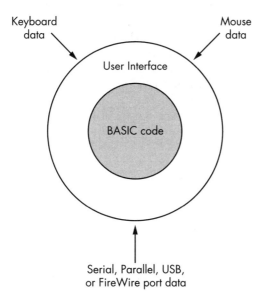

Figure 3: The user interface communicates with the outside world while your BASIC code provides instructions that tell the computer what to do.

How This Book Is Organized

The first part of this book teaches you how to understand, use, and customize the Visual Basic Express user interface. After all, you can't write a Visual Basic program until you learn how to use the Visual Basic Express menus and commands. This part of the book introduces you to using Visual Basic Express so you'll be comfortable writing your own programs later.

The second part of this book explains how to design a user interface using Visual Basic Express. To design a user interface in Visual Basic Express, you need to learn how to place and customize common user interface items in a window.

The third part of the book introduces you to the specific user interface controls you can use to design your user interface, such as buttons, checkboxes, and pull-down menus. You'll also learn how to use BASIC code to make your user interface work.

The fourth part of this book focuses on writing BASIC code that makes your program do something useful.

The fifth and final part of the book includes additional information to make your programs more interesting or useful, from connecting to database files to displaying pictures and playing sound.

By dividing information about using Visual Basic Express into five distinct sections, this book makes it easy for you to jump to the section that contains the information you need at any given time. If you thought that programming was too difficult, think again. With the help of this book and a copy of Visual Basic Express, you may find yourself writing programs that you never dreamed you could ever create before.

On the Companion CDs

Throughout the book, you'll notice the film icon in the margin (shown here to the left). This indicates that this section of text is associated with a movie file on the first CD. The movie's filename is below the icon. Go to the first CD and run the movie file to see a programming concept come to life! You'll also find source code examples on the CD that you can run and modify to suit your needs.

On the second CD, you'll find a full working version of Microsoft® Visual Basic® 2005 Express! For information on system requirements and support, please see "What's on CD2?" on the last page of this book.

PART I

LEARNING THE VB EXPRESS USER INTERFACE

1

YOUR FIRST VISUAL BASIC PROGRAM

To help you learn Visual Basic, this chapter guides you, step by step, through the process of creating your first Visual Basic program. This will give you hands-on experience and introduce you to using Visual Basic Express. Creating this sample program will demonstrate the different features of Visual Basic Express so you can see how easy it is to write and edit a Visual Basic program. You'll learn:

- How to create, edit, and save a Visual Basic program
- How to design a user interface (what your user sees)
- How to write BASIC code
- How to use shortcuts in Visual Basic Express to make programming easier

NOTE   *You must install Visual Basic Express on your computer before working through the examples in this chapter.*

Step 1: Create a Visual Basic Project

Before you can create a Visual Basic program, you must first create a *project* and decide where you want to store it. A project consists of multiple files that represent different parts of your entire Visual Basic program. To keep your project organized, Visual Basic Express creates a new folder and crams all the files that make up your Visual Basic program into it.

NOTE *A project folder is a storage area that holds all the parts of your program.*

How to Create a New Project in Visual Basic Express

To create a new project:

1. Launch Visual Basic Express. As you'll see, the Visual Basic Express screen divides information into separate areas, as shown in Figure 1-1. One area lists all the recent projects you've edited, one lists different articles about Visual Basic, and one provides links to additional help for learning to use Visual Basic.

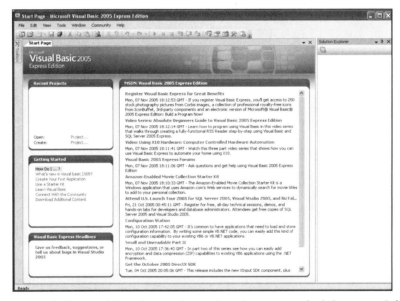

Figure 1-1: The Visual Basic Express Getting Started screen provides links to tutorials for learning Visual Basic.

2. Choose File ▸ New Project. (Note that the keystroke combination CTRL+N appears next to the New Project command. You could press the CTRL key and then the N key to choose the New Project command, just as you choose it from a submenu.) The New Project dialog box appears, as shown in Figure 1-2.

3. Click the Windows Application icon. By default, Visual Basic Express gives your new project a generic name, such as WindowsApplication1.

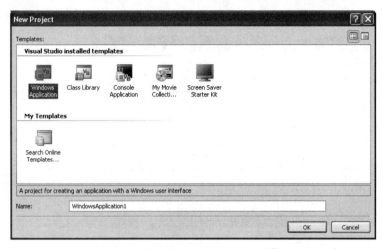

Figure 1-2: The New Project dialog box lets you create different types of programs.

4. Click in the Name text box, enter **MyFirstProgram**, and click OK. Visual Basic
    Express displays a single window, called a *form,* on the screen (see Figure 1-3). This
    form is the start of your program's *user interface,* the way your user will interact with
    your program.

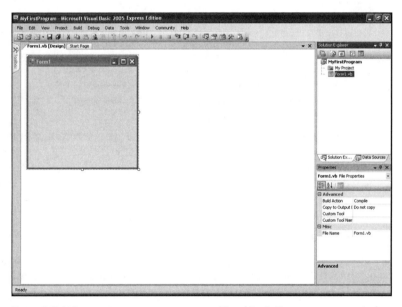

Figure 1-3: When you create a new program, Visual Basic Express creates a single
window (form) to help you begin creating your user interface.

5. Choose File ▶ Save All to open the Save Project dialog box, as shown in Figure 1-4.

Figure 1-4: The Save Project dialog box lets you save your Visual Basic program to a specific drive and folder on your computer. (The drive and directory displayed in the Location text box may differ on your computer.)

6. Click the Browse button. The Project Location dialog box appears (Figure 1-5).

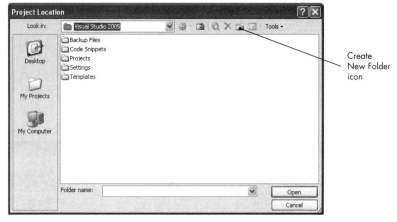

Figure 1-5: The Project Location dialog box lets you choose where to save your Visual Basic program.

7. Click in the Look In list box and choose the drive where you want to save your project, such as C:\.

8. (Optional) Click an existing folder where you want to store your Visual Basic project, or click the Create New Folder icon to create a new folder for your project.

9. Click Open. The New Project dialog box appears again, displaying the drive and folder that you specified as the place to save your project.

10. Click Save to save your project to the drive and folder that you specified.

Visual Basic Express saves your project in a folder with the same name as your project name. For example, if you called your project MyFirstProgram, Visual Basic Express stores your entire project in a folder called MyFirstProgram (see Figure 1-6).

Step 2: Design a User Interface

Once you've created a project, you'll need to create a user interface for your program. The three most common elements of a user interface are:

- Windows (called *forms*)
- Pull-down menus
- Buttons and boxes

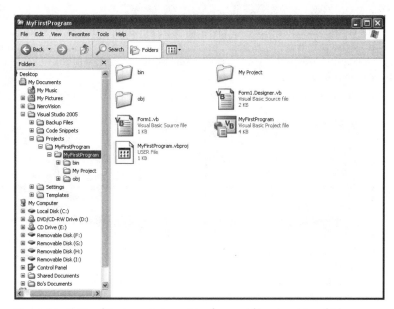

Figure 1-6: A Visual Basic project consists of several files stored in a folder.

NOTE *In this example, you will create three buttons (Save, Open, and Exit) and one text box, but no pull-down menus. The Save button will save text to a file; the Open button will open that file and display its contents in the text box; and the Exit button will stop the program from running.*

To create a user interface for your program, follow these steps:

1. *Mouse over* (that is, move the mouse pointer over) the Toolbox tab. The Toolbox window should slide into view, as shown in Figure 1-7.

How to
Design
a User
Interface

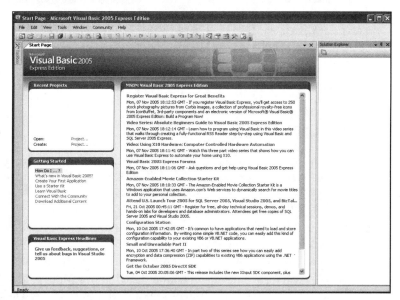

Figure 1-7: The Toolbox displays all the different items, known as controls, that you can place on a form.

2. Double-click the TextBox icon (in the vertical list at the left of the screen) and move the mouse pointer away from the Toolbox window. Visual Basic should display the text box, with handles on the left and right sides and an Action Button in the upper-right corner, as shown in Figure 1-8. (If you don't see handles around the text box, click on it.)

3. Click the Action Button. A pop-up menu appears, as shown in Figure 1-9.

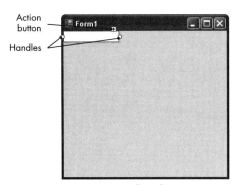

Figure 1-8: Handles allow you to resize a control while the Action Button lets you customize a control.

Figure 1-9: The Action Button of a text box lets you specify whether the text box can hold multiple lines of text.

4. Click the MultiLine check box then click anywhere away from the pop-up menu. Visual Basic Express should display the text box with additional handles around all corners and edges of the box, as shown in Figure 1-10.

5. Drag the bottom right corner handle of the text box until the text box fills up most of the form, as shown in Figure 1-11.

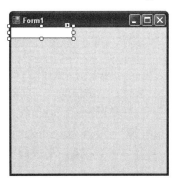

Figure 1-10: Once you specify that a text box can hold multiple lines, additional handles appear to let you resize both the width and the height of the text box.

Figure 1-11: Drag the corner of the text box so that it fills most of the form.

6. Double-click the Button icon in the Toolbox window. Visual Basic should display a button on the form, with handles at each corner.

7. Repeat step 6 two more times until you've drawn three buttons on the form.

8. Mouse over each form button, hold down the left mouse button, and drag the three buttons to the bottom of the form, as shown in Figure 1-12. (Or, click each button and then press the arrow keys on your keyboard to move the button.)

9. Click the button at the bottom-left corner of the form and press F4. The Properties window appears in the bottom-right corner of the screen.

10. Scroll in the Properties window to the Text property (Figure 1-13), then click the Text property and enter **Save**. This displays the word *Save* on the button.

Figure 1-12: Drag the three buttons to move them in a row along the bottom of the form.

Figure 1-13: The Properties window lets you change the behavior and appearance of an object.

11. Click the middle button and press F4 to display the Properties window.

12. Click the Text property and enter **Open** to display the word *Open* on the button.

13. Click the button at the bottom-right corner of the form and press F4 to display the Properties window, then click in the Text property and enter **Exit**. The word *Exit* should appear on the button. All buttons should appear, as shown in Figure 1-14.

14. Choose File ▸ Save to save the changes you've made to your form.

Figure 1-14: The Text property determines what text appears on a button.

Step 3: Write BASIC Code

How to
Write
BASIC
Code

Your program's user interface won't do anything until you write BASIC code to make it work. BASIC code consists of programming commands that tell the computer, step by step, what to do. To write code for your user interface, follow these steps:

1. Double-click the button that displays the word *Exit*. Visual Basic Express should display the Code window (Figure 1-15), with four lines. Here's what each line does:

    Public Class Form1   Defines the start of all the BASIC code stored in Form1.

    Private Sub Button3_Click   Defines the start of the event procedure that runs whenever the user clicks the button named Button1. An *event procedure* is a set of instructions that run whenever a certain event occurs, such as the user clicking the mouse.

    End Sub   Defines the end of the event procedure that runs whenever the user clicks Button3.

    End Class   Defines the end of all the BASIC code stored in Form1.

Event
procedure

Figure 1-15: The Code window displays the BASIC code needed to make your user interface respond to the user.

2. Type the command **End** between the Private Sub and the End Sub lines, so that the event procedure looks like this:

```
Private Sub Button3_Click(ByVal sender As System.Object, ByVal e As_
System.EventArgs) Handles Button3.Click
        End
End Sub
```

The End command runs whenever the user clicks Button3. Because Button3 is labeled the *Exit* button, clicking the Exit button runs the End command, which stops your program.

NOTE   *The first two lines of the code in step 2 should actually appear as a single line beginning with* `Private Sub` *and ending with* `Handles Button3.Click`*. Due to a limit on how wide code can extend on this page, BASIC code that appears as a single line on your computer may appear on two separate lines in this book. When you see an underscore character (_) at the end of a line, the line with the underscore character and the next line are actually a single line of code.*

3.   Click the Form1.vb [Design] tab just below the icon bar to view your user interface again, then double-click the Save button. Visual Basic Express should display the Code window again as well as the event procedure for the Save button.

4.   Right-click in the middle of the Save button event procedure. A pop-up menu should appear, as shown in Figure 1-16.

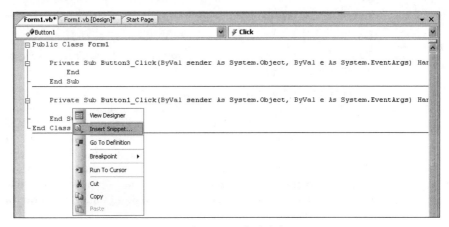

Figure 1-16: A pop-up menu appears when you right-click the mouse.

5.   Choose Insert Snippet. An Insert Snippet pop-up window appears (Figure 1-17). This menu lets you choose prewritten BASIC code related to different tasks such as Math or Processing Drives, Folders, and Files.

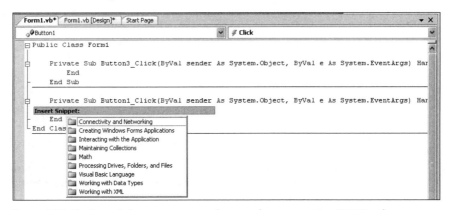

Figure 1-17: The Insert Snippet pop-up menu lets you choose prewritten BASIC code.

6.   Double-click Processing Drives, Folders, And Files. Another pop-up menu appears, displaying all the different code snippets from which you can choose, such as Copy a File or Create a Folder, as shown in Figure 1-18.

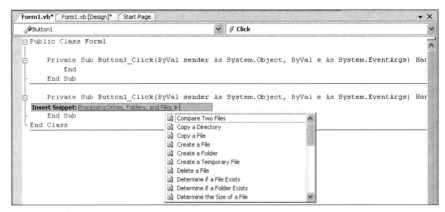

Figure 1-18: After you choose a category from the Insert Snippet pop-up menu, another menu appears listing specific code snippets you can use.

7. Scroll down the list of code snippets then double-click Write Text To Files. Visual Basic Express should automatically insert the code snippet in the event procedure, as shown in Figure 1-19. The highlighted portion of the code snippet represents the part you may wish to modify. In this example, the code snippet tells the computer to save the phrases *Text 1* and *Text 2* in a file named test.txt whenever the user clicks a button named Button1 which displays the text *Save*. For this example, you won't modify the highlighted code, but in your own programs, you would probably want to modify the highlighted code to have it do something more interesting than store *Text 1* or *Text 2* in the test.txt file.

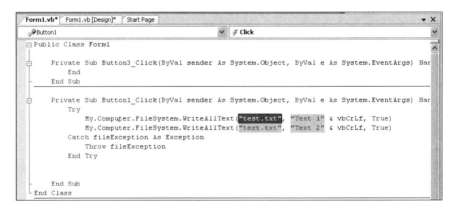

Figure 1-19: Visual Basic automatically inserts code snippets for you to modify if you wish.

8. Click the Form1.vb [Design] tab to view your user interface, then double-click the Open button. You should see the Code window and the event procedure for the Open button.

9. Right-click in the middle of the Open button event procedure. A pop-up menu should appear.

10. Click Insert Snippet. Another pop-up menu appears.

11. Double-click Processing Drives, Folders, And Files. Another pop-up menu appears.

12. Scroll down the list, and then double-click Read Text From A File. Visual Basic Express should insert the code snippet for the Open button (Figure 1-20). This code snippet tells the computer to store the text in the file test.txt temporarily in a storage bin named allText.

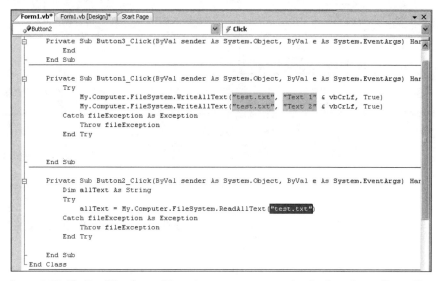

Figure 1-20: The Read Text from a File code snippet appears within the Open button (Button2) event procedure.

13. Type **TextBox1.Text = allText** at the bottom of the Open button event procedure, as shown here:

```
Private Sub Button2_Click(ByVal sender As System.Object, ByVal e As_
System.EventArgs) Handles Button2.Click
        Dim allText As String
        Try
            allText = My.Computer.FileSystem.ReadAllText("test.txt")
        Catch fileException As Exception
            Throw fileException
        End Try
        TextBox1.Text = allText
End Sub
```

The TextBox1.Text = allText command tells the computer to take all the text stored in the storage bin allText and copy it into the Text property of TextBox1. This displays all the text in the text box you drew earlier on your user interface.

14. Choose File ▶ Save All to save all the BASIC code you've typed so far.

Step 4: Run Your Program

Running a
Visual Basic
Program

Now that you've designed your user interface and written some BASIC code, the final step is to run your program to make sure that it works. To do so:

1. Choose Debug ▶ Start Debugging. Your program should appear as shown in Figure 1-21.

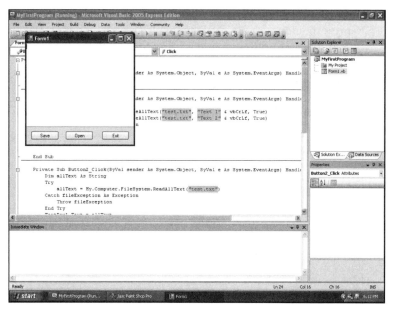

Figure 1-21: Run your program to see if it works.

2. Click the Save button. This tells your program to run the Save button event procedure, which stores the text *Text 1* and *Text 2* in the file test.txt.

NOTE *When you click the Save button, you won't see anything happening on the screen.*

3. Click the Open button. Your program should display *Text 1* and *Text 2* within the text box of your program, as shown in Figure 1-22.

Figure 1-22: Clicking the Open button displays the text saved in the test.txt file.

4. Click Exit. Your program should stop running and return you to the Visual Basic Express main window. (You can also stop your program, in case it crashes or freezes, by switching back to Visual Basic Express and choosing Debug ▶ Stop Debugging, or by pressing CTRL-ALT-BREAK.)

5. (Optional) Choose Build ▶ Build to create an *executable* version of your program that you can copy and distribute to others for them to run.

NOTE *If your program doesn't work exactly as you expected, you can examine what it may be doing wrong, a process known as* debugging.

Where to Go from Here

The goal of this chapter has been to introduce you to the steps needed to create a program and to demonstrate some of the Visual Basic Express features that will help you write programs quickly and easily. Once you understand how to create a Visual Basic program (including designing the user interface and writing BASIC code) and how the Visual Basic Express program works (such as letting you change user interface controls through the Properties window and adding prewritten code through the Insert Snippet feature), you're ready to learn more about the detailed steps involved in creating a program.

Anyone can learn to program, since programming just takes planning, patience, and persistence. With the help of Visual Basic Express, you may find that programming is not only easier than you think, but also fun and challenging at the same time.

KEY FEATURES TO REMEMBER

Here are key features to remember about creating a Visual Basic project:

- A project contains multiple files that all work together to create a single program.
- Visual Basic Express offers multiple ways to choose the same command, such as choosing either File ▸ New Project or pressing CTRL-N.

Here are the key features to remember about designing a user interface:

- A form displays a window on the screen.
- The Toolbox contains items, called *controls*, that you can drag or double-click to place on a form.
- A control provides a visual way for the user to give or receive information from the computer, such as a button, a pull-down menu, or a check box.
- Every user interface control has properties that you can change to modify each control's behavior and appearance.

Here are the key features to remember when writing BASIC code:

- You need to write BASIC code to make the elements of your user interface work.
- The End command stops your program from running.
- The Insert Snippets feature can automatically paste commonly used chunks of BASIC code in your program for you to modify later if you wish.
- Every form can display two tabs: one for displaying the user interface and the other for displaying your BASIC code.

Here are key features to remember when running a program:

- Every program needs a command that the user can choose to make it stop running.
- The Debug ▸ Stop Debugging command is another way to stop your program from running, especially if it freezes up.
- When your program works perfectly, you can create an executable version of it by choosing the Build ▸ Build command.

2

UNDERSTANDING THE VISUAL BASIC EXPRESS INTERFACE

To write programs in Visual Basic, you need to learn both the Visual Basic language and the Visual Basic Express user interface. You'll use Visual Basic Express to design your program's user interface (windows, pull-down menus, buttons, check boxes, and so on) and write commands in Visual Basic that will make your program work.

The Visual Basic Express user interface provides all the tools you need to create a Visual Basic program—from creating a file, to designing a user interface, to writing BASIC code. You'll find commands for creating a Visual Basic program in pull-down menus, toolbars, and windows.

Understanding Pull-Down Menus

Visual Basic Express displays every available command in its many pull-down menus and submenus, as shown in Figure 2-1, though you'll need to use only a fraction of these commands at any one time. Sometimes these menus will display dimmed commands, which are ones that are unavailable at that time. For example, until you choose the Cut or Copy command, you won't be able to choose Paste, so the Paste command will appear dimmed.

NOTE   *A list of commands in a computer language is often called* code. *We'll refer to a list of Visual Basic commands as* BASIC code *or just* code.

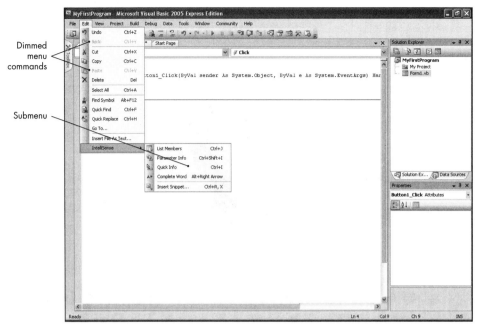

Dimmed
menu
commands

Submenu

Figure 2-1: Pull-down menus list every possible command and sometimes organize related commands in submenus while temporarily dimming commands that are unavailable at the moment.

When writing a Visual Basic program, you'll need to:

- Organize the files that make up your Visual Basic project.
- Design a user interface.
- Write BASIC code.

Table 2-1 lists the names of the pull-down menus that contain the various commands, the type of commands accessible from the menu, and a summary of what each command can do.

NOTE *When designing your user interface, a Format pull-down menu may suddenly appear then disappear when you switch to the code window. By selectively hiding and displaying pull-down menu titles, Visual Basic Express avoids displaying unavailable commands.*

Table 2-1: Description of the Pull-Down Menus in Visual Basic Express

Menu Title	Type of Commands	Command Summary
File	Organize your Visual Basic program.	Open, save, or print files that make up your Visual Basic program. Also includes the Exit command for quitting Visual Basic Express.
Edit	Design a user interface and write BASIC code.	Copy, delete, and paste parts of your user interface or parts of your BASIC code. Also includes commands for undoing and redoing a previous action, searching and replacing text, and selecting your entire user interface or BASIC code.
View	Organize your Visual Basic program.	Change the appearance of the interface such as opening and closing windows and toolbars.

(continued)

Table 2-1: Description of the Pull-Down Menus in Visual Basic Express (continued)

Menu Title	Type of Commands	Command Summary
Project	Organize your Visual Basic program.	Organize the different parts of a project such as adding new files to your Visual Basic program.
Build	Organize your Visual Basic program.	Convert your Visual Basic program into an executable file that you can sell or give away to others.
Debug	Write BASIC code.	Examine your BASIC code to look for errors.
Data	Organize your Visual Basic program.	Specify a file containing additional data (such as a database) to use in your Visual Basic program.
Format	Design a user interface.	Align and adjust the appearance of your user interface. (This pull-down menu only appears when you're designing a user interface in Design mode.)
Tools	Organize your Visual Basic program.	Customize the appearance of the Visual Basic Express user interface and performs additional administrative tasks.
Window	Organize your Visual Basic program.	Organize the different parts of the Visual Basic Express interface, such as its user interface or BASIC code.
Community	Design a user interface and write BASIC code.	Provide links to various Visual Basic help sites on the Internet. (Requires an Internet connection.)
Help	Design a user interface and write BASIC code.	Provide additional explanations for accomplishing tasks with the Visual Basic Express interface or examples for using specific Visual Basic language commands.

Hands-on Tutorial: Using Pull-Down Menus

Under-
standing
Pull-Down
Menus

Here's a look at how to use these menus.

1. Load Visual Basic Express. The initial start page and pull-down menus appear.
2. Hold down the ALT key. Notice that a single letter is underlined in each menu title, such as File or Edit, as shown in Figure 2-2. You can use ALT to open pull-down menus in case your mouse doesn't work, or if you prefer to use the keyboard instead of the mouse to choose commands.

Figure 2-2: The ALT key provides an alternative way to choose a menu without using the mouse.

3. Press ALT again (or press the ESC key). Notice that when you press ALT a second time, the underlining disappears from the menu titles.
4. Press ALT then type **F** and then **N**. This opens the File menu and chooses the New Project command. A New Project dialog box appears.
5. Click OK, and Visual Basic Express should create a blank project for you.
6. Click the View menu, and a list of commands appears. Menus typically display three different types of items, as shown in Figure 2-3:

    Commands   Clicking a command causes something to happen immediately.

Submenu titles   A submenu title has a black arrow at the right. When you click a submenu title, a submenu pops up listing additional available commands.

Ellipsis titles   An ellipsis title appears with an ellipsis (. . .) next to it. When you click an ellipsis title, a dialog box appears, letting you choose additional options.

7. Click Toolbox to open the Toolbox window. Choose View ▶ Other Windows (click the View menu and then click Other Windows). A submenu pops up.

8. Choose Project ▶ Add Windows Form to open the Add New Item dialog box.

9. Click Cancel.

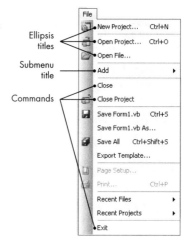

Figure 2-3: The three types of commands found on pull-down menus.

Understanding Toolbars

Toolbars display the same commands as the pull-down menus, except that they display the commands as icons rather than names. (They may look like Egyptian hieroglyphics but they really are icons.) Think of toolbars as shortcuts that provide quick, one-click access to commonly used commands.

Visual Basic Express provides three ways to help you decipher what each toolbar icon means:

• Move the mouse pointer over a toolbar icon and wait for a *tooltip* to appear, as shown in Figure 2-4.

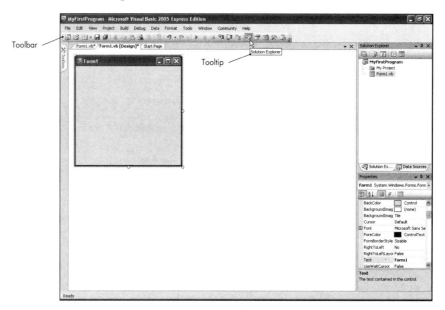

Figure 2-4: Tooltips provide a simple and fast way to identify icons that appear on a toolbar.

- Click a pull-down menu and memorize the icon that appears to the left of each command.
- View the complete list of toolbar icons and their accompanying commands by customizing your toolbars.

Deciphering Toolbar Icons

To decipher a toolbar icon through tooltips, mouse over a toolbar icon. Within a few seconds, a tooltip pops up, listing the command that the icon represents, as shown in Figure 2-4. To make the tooltip disappear, just move the mouse away.

Displaying and Hiding Toolbars

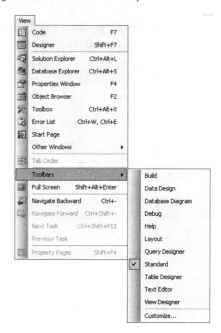

Normally, Visual Basic Express displays only the Standard toolbar, showing icons representing the most commonly used commands from the File, Edit, View, and Debug menus. However, Visual Basic Express can also show you additional toolbars that contain icons representing other commands. To display (or hide) a toolbar, follow these steps:

1. Choose View ▸ Toolbars. A submenu appears, listing all the available toolbars. A check mark appears next to any toolbar that's currently displayed, as shown in Figure 2-5.
2. Click to the left of the toolbar that you want to display (to add a check mark next to it) or hide (to remove the check mark).

Figure 2-5: Visual Basic Express displays a check mark next to any toolbar that's currently visible.

Customizing Toolbars

Toolbars display the most common commands, but you may want to add a command that you use more often or eliminate a command or two that you rarely use at all. To customize a toolbar, follow these steps:

1. Make sure the toolbar you want to customize is visible by following the two steps in the "Displaying and Hiding Toolbars" section.
2. Click the Toolbar Options button that appears on the far right of the toolbar. An Add or Remove Buttons menu appears, as shown in Figure 2-6.
3. Click Add Or Remove Buttons. Another pop-up menu appears.
4. Click the name of the toolbar you want to customize, such as Standard. A menu appears, listing all icons you can add or remove from that particular toolbar.
5. Click next to the icon that you want to display (to put a check mark next to it) or hide (to remove a check mark).

Hands-on Tutorial: Using Toolbars

Under-
standing
Toolbars

Toolbars provide convenient one-click access to commonly used commands. Here's a quick introduction to the power of toolbars:

1. Load Visual Basic Express. The start page appears.
2. Click the New Project icon. A New Project dialog box appears.
3. Click OK. Visual Basic Express displays a blank form as the start of your project.

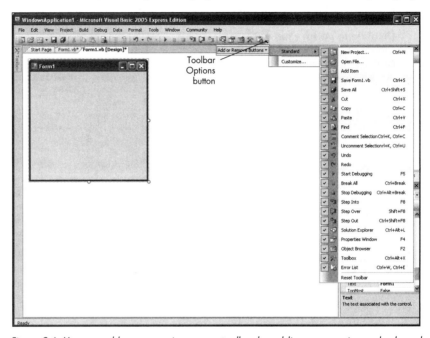

Figure 2-6: You can add or remove icons on a toolbar by adding or removing a check mark next to the different commands.

4. Click the Toolbar Options button on the far right side of the Standard toolbar. An Add or Remove Buttons menu appears.
5. Mouse over the Add or Remove Buttons menu. A submenu appears.
6. Mouse over Standard. A list of commands appears with check marks.
7. Click the first five check boxes to clear the check marks. Notice that as you clear a check mark from a command, Visual Basic Express removes that icon from the Standard toolbar.
8. Click Reset Toolbar and Visual Basic Express should restore your toolbar to its original appearance.

Because you aren't likely to use all the commands stored on a toolbar, consider customizing your toolbar by adding or removing icons. If you mess things up too badly, you can always choose the Reset Toolbar command to restore a toolbar to its original appearance.

Working with Windows

Manipu-
lating
Windows

Visual Basic Express displays additional information about your program in separate windows that appear on the sides of the screen. The three most common windows are the Solution Explorer, the Toolbox, and the Properties window, all shown in Figure 2-7.

- The Solution Explorer window lists all the files that make up your Visual Basic program. You can use it to quickly switch to a different file to edit or modify.
- The Toolbox window displays controls you can choose to create a user interface.
- The Properties window displays detailed information about each control, such as a radio button or check box, that makes up your user interface.

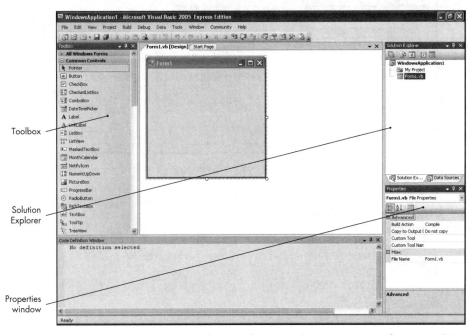

Figure 2-7: Windows display additional information about certain parts of your Visual Basic program.

Most windows can appear in one of four ways on the screen, as shown in Figure 2-8:

Docked   The window appears in a fixed location on one side of the screen

Floating   The window can appear anywhere on the screen

Auto Hide   The window appears as a tab but pops out completely when you mouse over its tab

Tabbed Document   The window appears on the tabbed interface in the middle of the screen

Making a Window Float

A *floating window* appears in the middle of the screen, where you can move and resize it. To create a floating window, follow these steps:

1.   Click the Window Position button on the window that you want to convert into a floating window. A pop-up menu appears, as shown in Figure 2-9.

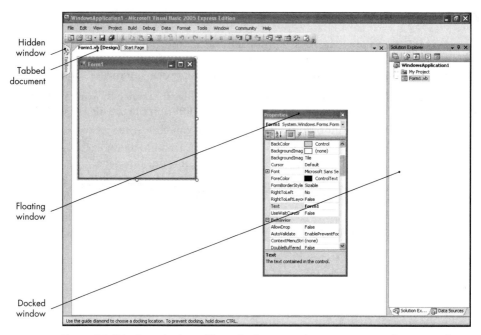

Figure 2-8: Windows display additional information about certain parts of your Visual Basic program.

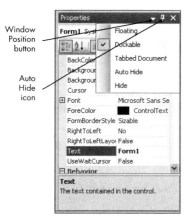

Figure 2-9: The Window Position button lets you choose how you want a window to appear.

2. Click Floating. Your window should now be floating.

NOTE *If the Floating option is dimmed, click the Auto Hide icon and then try step 1 again.*

3. (Optional) Mouse over one edge of the window and drag the mouse to resize the window.

4. (Optional) Mouse over the window title bar and drag the mouse to move the window to a new location.

NOTE *If a window appears docked, you can also mouse over the window's title bar and drag the mouse to make the window float.*

Docking a Window

Docked windows attach to a side of the screen. If you dock two or more windows on the same side of the screen, they can appear side by side or stacked. To turn a floating or tabbed document window into a docked window, follow these steps:

1. Right-click the title bar or tab of the window you want to dock to open a pop-up menu.

NOTE   *To convert an auto hidden window into a floating window, click the Menu button and click Auto Hide. Then repeat step 1.*

2. Click Dockable, then mouse over the window title bar and drag the mouse. Visual Basic Express should display a *Dock Diamond*, with arrows showing you where you can dock your window, as shown in Figure 2-10.

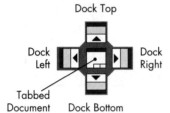

Figure 2-10: Use the Dock Diamond to choose the location for a window you want to dock.

3. Drag the window to the part of the screen where you want to dock it. (The Dock Diamond moves along with the mouse pointer.)
4. Mouse over one of the Dock Diamond arrows. Visual Basic Express highlights the screen to show you where your docked window will appear.
5. Release the mouse button to dock the window.

NOTE   *If you mouse over the circle in the middle of the Dock Diamond, you can make your window appear as a tabbed document.*

Tucking Windows Out of Sight with Auto Hide

Floating and docked windows always appear on the screen. While this can be convenient for easy access, such windows can clutter the screen. To solve this problem, you can Auto Hide a window.

When you Auto Hide window it appears as a tab on one side of the screen. When you mouse over the tab, the window pops into view. As soon as you move the mouse away from the window, the Auto Hide feature tucks the window back out of sight.

NOTE   *The Auto Hide feature works only with docked windows. If a window appears as a floating or tabbed document window, you'll have to convert it to a docked window before you can turn on Auto Hide.*

To convert a docked window into an Auto Hide window, follow these steps:

1. Click the Auto Hide icon on the window's title bar. The window appears as a tab on one side of the screen, as shown in Figure 2-11.
2. Mouse over the window tab to make the window appear.
3. To turn off Auto Hide, just click the Auto Hide icon again.

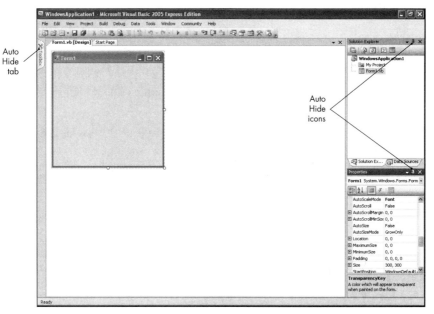

Figure 2-11: The Auto Hide icon lets you turn the Auto Hide feature on or off for a docked window.

Displaying a Window as a Tabbed Document

By default, most windows appear as small as possible to avoid blocking your view of the screen. Unfortunately, this sometimes make it difficult to find what you need. To solve this problem, you can display a window as a *tabbed document*. Not only does a tabbed document window fill up most of the computer screen, but it also allows you to find the window quickly by clicking its tab.

To turn a window into a tabbed document, do one of the following:

- To turn a docked window into a tabbed document, click the Window Position button and click Tabbed Document.

- To turn a floating window into a tabbed document, right-click the window title bar and then click Tabbed Document.

- To turn an Auto Hide window into a tabbed document, click the Auto Hide button to turn off the Auto Hide feature, then click Menu and click Tabbed Document.

Visual Basic Express displays your window as a tabbed document, as shown in Figure 2-12.

To convert a tabbed document window into a floating or dockable one:

1. Right-click the window tab. A pop-up menu appears, as shown in Figure 2-13.
2. Click Floating or Dockable. Visual Basic Express turns your tabbed document into a floating or dockable window.

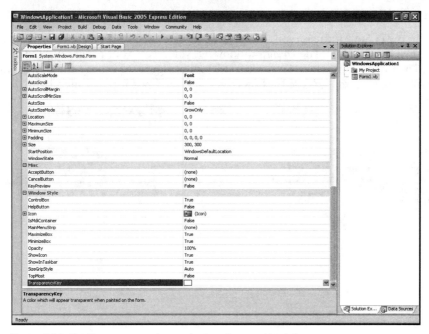

Figure 2-12: The Properties window is displayed as a tabbed document.

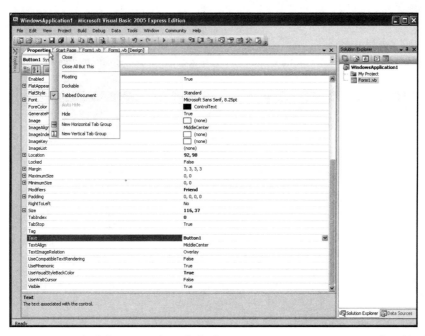

Figure 2-13: Right-clicking a window tab displays a pop-up menu so you can turn the tabbed document into a floating or dockable window.

Using Tabbed Groups

In the center of the screen, Visual Basic Express displays the Design window and the Code window. The Design window lets you create your program's user interface. The Code window lets you enter BASIC code. Figure 2-14 shows the Design window for a file, while Figure 2-15 shows the Code window for that same file.

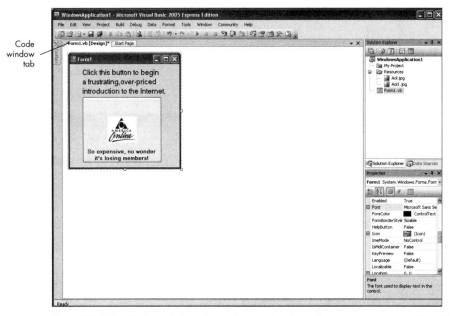

Figure 2-14: The Design window shows the user interface of your program stored in a file.

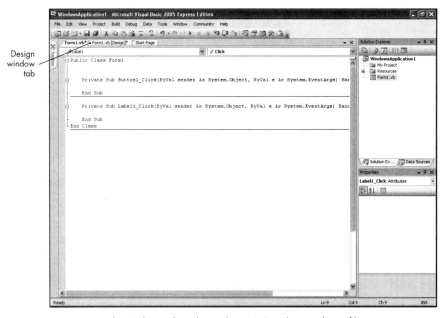

Figure 2-15: The Code window shows the BASIC code stored in a file.

To save space, Visual Basic Express normally displays the Design and Code windows as tabbed documents in the middle of the screen. To view the Design window for a file, click the tab that contains the filename followed by the word *[Design]*. To view the Code window for a file, click the tab that contains the filename that you want to open.

NOTE *If a tab does not appear for a file's Code window, right-click a filename in the Solution Explorer window then choose View Code.*

By clicking the tabs, you can alternately view the Design or Code window for each file that makes up your Visual Basic program. However, if you want to view two or more windows simultaneously, you can create an additional horizontal or vertical tab group.

To create either a horizontal or vertical tab group, follow these steps:

1. Right-click any tab. A pop-up menu appears, as shown in Figure 2-16.

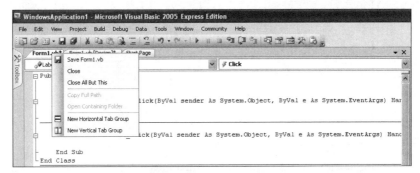

Figure 2-16: A pop-up menu appears when you right-click a tab.

2. Click either New Horizontal Tab Group or New Vertical Tab Group to display your chosen tab in a separate grouping, as shown in Figures 2-17 and 2-18.

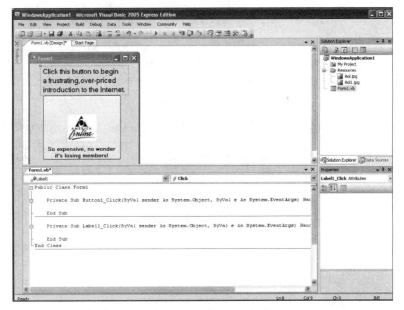

Figure 2-17: By displaying a tab on a new horizontal tab group, you can view two windows at the same time.

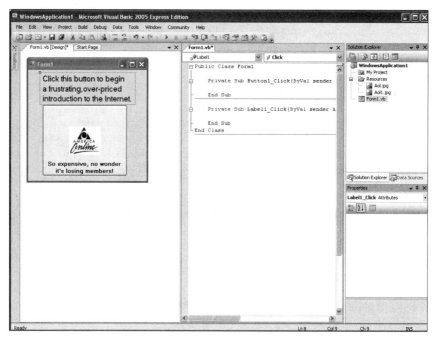

Figure 2-18: When grouped vertically, windows appear side by side.

3. Right-click any tab. A pop-up menu appears. Notice that a new command appears that reads either *Move to Next Tab Group* or *Move to Previous Tab Group*. As soon as you move all the tabs from one group to another, you should see all of your windows as a single tabbed group again.

KEY FEATURES TO REMEMBER

The purpose of the Visual Basic Express interface is to help you design the appearance of your program and write BASIC code to make it work.

- Pull-down menus contain every possible command available.

- Toolbars act as shortcuts that give you access to commonly used commands without having to use the pull-down menus.

- Windows provide additional information about a part of your program. Windows can appear docked, floating, temporarily hidden, or as tabbed documents.

- Tabbed groups let you rearrange tabs so you can see two or more windows simultaneously.

3

WORKING WITH PROJECTS

A Visual Basic *project* is a folder that contains all the files
that make up a single program. Although a trivial Visual
Basic program can consist of a single file, most Visual Basic
projects are likely to consist of a dozen, 100, or even 1,000
separate files.

One file in your project might contain the design of your user interface. A
second file might contain the BASIC code that takes data from the user interface
and calculates a result. A third file might contain BASIC code that tells your
program how to print data. By storing and isolating the different functions of
your program in separate files, you can gradually build a complicated program,
one piece at a time.

Managing Files

Managing files means knowing how to create, edit, and delete the multiple files
that make up a single Visual Basic program. Most Visual Basic programs consist
of one or more of the following file types:

1. **Forms**   A form file consists of a window that makes up your program's user
    interface and the BASIC code needed to retrieve and display data through
    the user interface. Most Visual Basic programs contain at least one form file.

NOTE *Although Visual Basic Express displays a form as a single file in the Solution Explorer Window, a form file actually consists of three physical files on your hard disk. One file contains the user interface, a second contains the BASIC code to make your user interface work, and a third is a resource file with information about making your form work with the .NET framework. All three files work together to create the illusion of a single form file when displayed in Visual Basic Express.*

2. **Modules** Module files are optional and are used to hold BASIC code separately from a form file. By storing BASIC code in a module file, you can create libraries of code that you can share among other programs just by copying the module file to a different Visual Basic project.

3. **Class** Class files are optional and contain BASIC code for defining objects to organize the way your program works—a technique known as *object-oriented programming* (discussed in more detail in Chapter 26). Essentially, object-oriented programming lets you organize programs into independent chunks or objects.

NOTE *A simple Visual Basic program may consist of nothing but form files, but a typical Visual Basic program is more likely to contain dozens of form, module, and class files.*

Creating a New Project

To create a Visual Basic program, you must first create a project. To create a new project, open the New Project dialog box (Figure 3-1) either choose File ▶ New Project, click the New Project icon on the Standard toolbar, or press CTRL-N. The three main types of programs you can create are represented as icons in the New Project dialog box: Windows Application, Class Library, and Console Application.

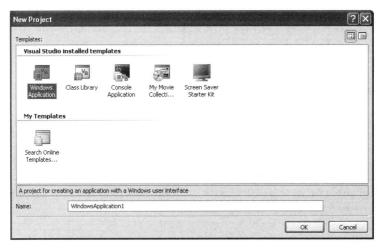

Figure 3-1: The New Project dialog box lets you enter a name for your program and define the type of program you want to create.

- A Windows application is a typical Windows program that uses windows, pull-down menus, and buttons in its user interface—such as a game or a word processor. (This book focuses exclusively on teaching you how to create a Windows application, although you can apply the same principles to create either a class library or a console application.)

- A Class library is designed to hold BASIC code used to define objects (as discussed further in Chapter 26).

- A console application is a program that does not display a Windows user interface. Many programmers create console applications for programs that won't interact with people or programs that allow them to test certain program features without having to go through the trouble of creating a user interface.

NOTE   *Although Visual Basic Express lets you create a Class library or a Console application, this book focuses exclusively on teaching you how to create Windows applications.*

To create a new Windows application:

1. Click the Windows Application icon (see Figure 3-1).
2. Click in the Name text box and type a name for your Visual Basic program (you can change this name later).
3. Click OK to display a single window (a form), as shown in Figure 3-2.

New Project icon

Form

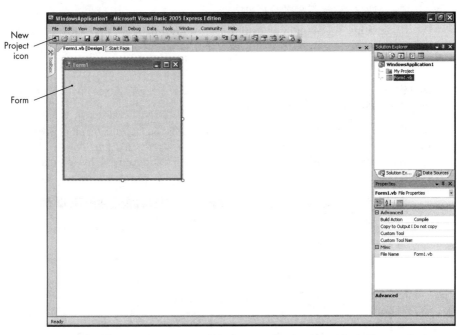

Figure 3-2: When you create a new Windows application, Visual Basic Express displays a single form as a starting point for creating a user interface.

Adding Files to a Project

Understanding Visual Basic Projects

Once you've opened or created a project, you may want to add another file to your project. You can add either a new file or one from another Visual Basic project.

Adding a New File to a Project

To add a new file to a project, follow these steps:

1. Choose Project ▸ Add New Item; click the Add New Item icon on the Standard toolbar; or press CTRL-SHIFT-A. An Add New Item dialog box appears (Figure 3-3).

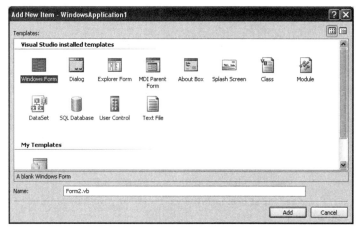

Figure 3-3: The Add New Item dialog box lets you choose what type of file you want to add to an existing project.

2. Click either the Windows Form, Class, or Module icon, then click in the Name text box and enter a name for your new file.

3. Click Add.

NOTE *You can actually add several different types of files to a project, but we focus on teaching you how to add form, module, and class files.*

Each time you add a file to a project, Visual Basic Express displays the name of your newly added file in the Solution Explorer window and on a tab. To see a list of all the files that make up your Visual Basic program click the Active Files icon, as shown in Figure 3-4.

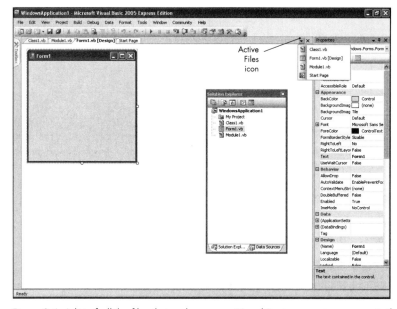

Figure 3-4: A list of all the files that make up your Visual Basic program appears in three places: on tabs, in the Solution Explorer window, and when you click the Active Files icon.

The name of each form file may appear on two tabs. One tab displays the user interface and the word *[Design]*. The second tab displays any BASIC code and appears only when you start writing BASIC code to make your user interface work. If an asterisk (*) appears next to a filename on a tab, that means the file has been changed but not yet saved.

Adding an Existing File to a Project

To add an existing file to a project:

1. Choose Project ▸ Add Existing Item, or press CTRL-D. An Add Existing Item dialog box appears.
2. Click the filename you want to add. You may need to switch to a different drive or folder, or click the Files of Type list box, to find the file you want.
3. Click Add. Visual Basic Express adds your chosen files and displays them in the Solutions Explorer window.

NOTE *You can select multiple files by holding down the CTRL key as you click each filename.*

Deleting Files from a Project

By deleting a file from a project that you no longer need you can make your final program smaller. To do so:

1. Choose View ▸ Solution Explorer, or press CTRL-R. The Solution Explorer window appears.
2. Right-click the file you want to delete. A pop-up menu appears.
3. Click Delete. A dialog box appears, asking if you want to permanently delete the chosen file.
4. Click OK or Cancel. (If you click OK, Visual Basic Express permanently deletes the chosen file, so make sure you really want to do this.)

Saving the Files in a Project

Once you create and add files to a project, you should save your files. You can save the file under its current name; save a copy of a file under a different name and, optionally, in a different folder; or save all the files that make up a single project.

When you choose the Save command, Visual Basic Express saves the currently displayed file. The Save command appears under the File menu and displays the name of the currently displayed file. For example, if you're working on a file named Form1.vb, the Save command will appear under the File menu as Save Form1.vb.

To save a different file, you must first switch to that file by:

- Clicking the tab that contains the name of the file you want to save.
- Double-clicking the icon that appears to the left of the filename in the Solution Explorer window.

Saving a Single File

Saving a single file is useful when you've made changes to that file and you want to save those changes right away. To save a single file, choose one of the following:

- Choose File ▶ Save. (Remember, the Save command under the File menu always includes the name of the currently displayed file such as Save Module1.vb or Save Form1.vb.)
- Click the Save icon on the Standard toolbar.
- Press CTRL-S.

Copying a File

You may have a file stored in one project and decide you want to reuse it in another project. To do so, you can save a copy of the current file under a different name and directory, like so:

1. Choose File ▶ Save As. A dialog box appears, asking you for a name and folder in which to store the copy of the file.

NOTE   *Visual Basic Express displays the name of the current file within the Save As command; so, for example, to save a file named MyForm.vb, the Save As command actually appears as Save MyForm.vb As.*

2. Click in the File Name text box and enter a name for your file.
3. Click in the Save In list box and then click the folder in which you want to save the file, then click Save.

Saving All Files in a Project

Rather than require you to save files individually, Visual Basic Express offers a Save Project command, which saves all the files that make up a single project. This can be useful once you've changed multiple files because you don't have to save each file individually.

To save all the files that make up a project, follow these steps:

1. Choose File ▶ Save All; click the Save All icon on the Standard toolbar; or press CTRL-SHIFT-S. Visual Basic Express saves all the files in your project.

   If you have not saved your project previously, continue with steps 2 through 3. Visual Basic Express displays a Save Project dialog box, as shown in Figure 3-5.

Figure 3-5: The Save Project dialog box lets you specify the name of a project along with a folder in which you'll store your project files.

2. Click in the Name text box and enter a name for your project. Whatever name you enter automatically appears in the New Solution Name text box.

3. Click the Browse button and then click the folder in which you want to save your project, then click Save.

Closing and Opening a Project

Once you've finished working on a project, you have to close it. To close a project, choose File ▶ Close Project. (If you choose File ▶ Close, you'll close just the currently displayed file.) If you haven't saved your changes before closing a project, a dialog box pops up and gives you one last chance to do so.

To open a saved project, you can choose File ▶ Open Project; click the Open Project icon on the Standard toolbar; press CTRL-SHIFT-O; or choose File ▶ Recent Projects and then click the project you want to open. You should see an Open Project dialog box, in which you can choose the drive, folder, and project file you want to open.

When opening a recently viewed project, it's faster to choose File ▶ Recent Projects and then click the name of the last project you recently opened.

NOTE *If you exit Visual Basic Express and rename or move files in a project using another program (like Windows Explorer), Visual Basic Express may not know what to do with the moved or renamed files. You can always add that file back to your project by using the steps outlined in the section "Adding an Existing File to a Project" on page 45.*

KEY FEATURES TO REMEMBER

A project folder defines a single Visual Basic program. When you create a new Visual Basic program, you must create a new project file. Every time you edit an existing Visual Basic program, you can edit the files stored inside a project folder.

- A Visual Basic program consists of one or more files. By storing different parts of your program in separate files, you can build a complicated program one piece at a time.

- A project keeps all the separate files, which make up a Visual Basic program, organized in a single folder.

- You can copy files from one project and reuse them in another.

4

DESIGNING A USER INTERFACE

The *user interface (UI)* allows your program to interact with the "outside world," such as a human user or another computer. Although UIs can vary drastically in appearance (think of the vast difference between a word processor's UI and a computer game's UI), the purpose is the same: to send and receive data to and from the outside world.

Creating a User Interface

A typical user interface consists of one or more forms, pull-down menus, or controls (such as buttons, check boxes, and labels), as shown in Figure 4-1.

To create a user interface in Visual Basic Express, you first create a form, which appears on the screen as a window. You then place pull-down menus, buttons, boxes, and other controls on the form using the Toolbox.

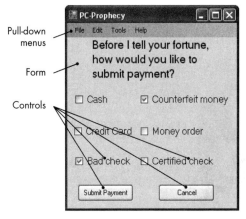

Pull-down menus

Form

Controls

Figure 4-1: A typical user interface consists of a form, pull-down menus, and controls.

Creating and Deleting a Form

When you create a new project, Visual Basic Express automatically creates a single form for your UI. To create more forms, follow these steps:

1. Choose Project ▶ Add Windows Form. An Add New Item dialog box appears.
2. Click in the Name text box and type a descriptive filename for your form.
3. Click Add. Visual Basic Express displays a blank form.

If you create a form and later decide you don't need it anymore, you can delete it by:

*   Clicking a form name in the Solution Explorer window and pressing DELETE (or the DEL key).
*   Clicking a form name in the Solution Explorer window and choosing Edit ▶ Delete.
*   Right-clicking a form name in the Solution Explorer window and choosing Delete.

NOTE *When you delete a form, Visual Basic Express asks you if you're sure you want to delete the form. Click Yes to delete or No to cancel the deletion. If you delete a form, you won't be able to retrieve it later if you change your mind.*

Viewing a Form in the Design Window

Visual Basic Express normally displays only one file at a time. If your project consists of multiple files, Visual Basic Express lists all the project files in the Solution Explorer window and in a tabbed interface at the top of the main window, as shown in Figure 4-2.

The Design window displays one form at a time where you can add, delete, and modify controls. To view a form in the Design window, choose one of the following:

*   Click the tab that contains the form name followed by the word *[Design]*.
*   Click the form name displayed in the Solution Explorer window and then choose View ▶ Designer.
*   Click the form name in the Solution Explorer window then press SHIFT-F7.
*   Right-click the form name in the Solution Explorer window then choose View Designer.

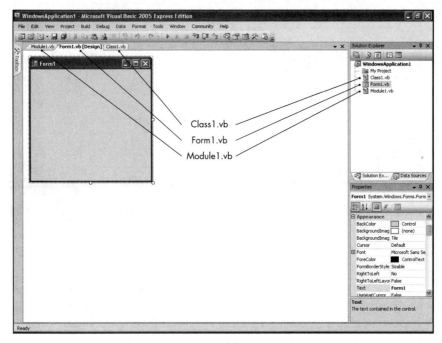

Figure 4-2: The Solution Explorer window lists all the files that make up a single Visual Basic Express program; files are also shown on the tabs in the main window.

Viewing the Toolbox

The Toolbox window lists the different types of user interface controls you can add to a form. To display the Toolbox window, choose one of the following (see Figure 4-3):

- Mouse over the Toolbox tab on the left side of the screen.
- Click the Toolbox icon on the Standard toolbar.
- Choose View ▶ Toolbox.
- Press CTRL-ALT-X.

The Toolbox organizes the user interface controls as follows:

All Windows Forms   Displays an alphabetical list of every control available

Common Controls   Displays only those controls you're most likely to use

Containers   Displays controls that are used to organize and arrange other controls

Menus & Toolbars   Displays controls used to create pull-down menus and toolbars that list commonly used icons or commands

Data   Displays controls used to retrieve data from a database

Components   Displays controls that perform a specific function without being visible, such as a timer or control that monitors the serial port

Printing   Displays controls for creating a dialog box for printing a file

Dialogs   Displays controls for creating a variety of commonly used dialog boxes, such as Open File or Color

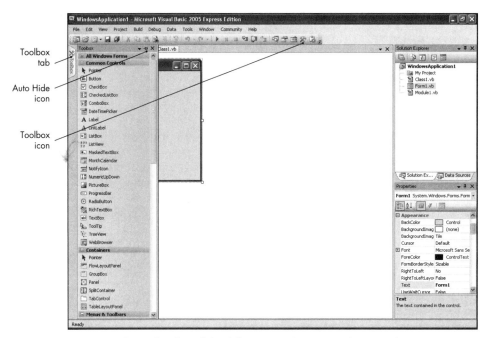

Toolbox
tab

Auto Hide
icon

Toolbox
icon

Figure 4-3: The Toolbox lists all the different controls you can place on a form.

To view the different categories in the Toolbox, click the plus sign (+) that appears next to a category name (such as Data or Components). To hide a category, click the minus sign (–) next to each category name.

Normally, the Toolbox automatically tucks itself out of sight and appears only when you want to see it. To keep the Toolbox visible at all times click the Auto Hide icon (see Figure 4-3). To make it disappear, click Auto Hide again.

Adding Controls on a User Interface

To place a control from the Toolbox on to a form, you can double-click the control in the Toolbox or click the control you want to add, mouse over your form, and then click the mouse.

NOTE *When you double-click a control in the Toolbox, Visual Basic Express automatically places your chosen control on the currently displayed form. You can reposition the control later.*

Moving Controls on a User Interface

To move or resize a UI control on a form you can do one of the following:

- Drag the control with the mouse.
- Press the up/down and right/left arrow keys.
- Type the exact X and Y coordinates where you want the control to appear.

Moving a Control by Dragging the Mouse

The fastest way to move a control is to drag it with the mouse. To do so:

1. Mouse over the control. The mouse pointer turns into a four-way pointing arrow.

2. Hold down the left mouse button. Handles appear on the corners of your chosen control.

3. Drag the mouse to move the control to its new location.

To help you align multiple controls on a form, Visual Basic Express displays *snaplines* that appear when you align one control with another. Blue snaplines appear when the edges of two controls align. Red snaplines, as shown in Figure 4-4, appear when the text that appears on different controls aligns.

Moving a Control by Pressing the Arrow Keys

The up/down and right/left arrow keys move a control slowly, but they can be useful for making minor adjustments to a control's position on a form. To use them to adjust the placement of a control:

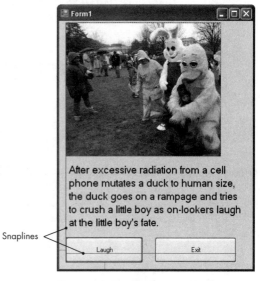

Snaplines

Figure 4-4: Snaplines automatically appear to help you align the edges or text captions of one control with another.

1. Click the control you want to move. Handles appear on the control's corners.

2. Press the up/down or right/left arrow keys to move the control. To move a control faster, hold down CTRL and then press the up/down or left/right arrow key. This moves a control to the next snap position where Visual Basic Express thinks you might want to move a control, such as into the corner of a form or aligned next to an existing control.

Typing the Exact X and Y Coordinates of a Control

If you want to place controls precisely on a form, you can enter exact *X and Y coordinates*, measured in pixels, into the Size property in the Properties window. The X coordinate defines the distance from the left edge of a form to the right edge of a control. The Y coordinate defines the distance from the top of the form to the top of a control, as shown in Figure 4-5.

Entering X and Y coordinates can be especially handy when you want to align multiple controls precisely, either a fixed distance from each other or from the edge of a form.

To move a control by entering X and Y coordinates, follow these steps:

1. Click the control you want to move. Handles appear around its corners.

2. Press F4 to open the Properties window then scroll down to the Location property, which displays two numbers, such as 38, 149. The first number represents the X coordinate, and the second number represents the Y coordinate. These numbers represent the location of the control's top-left corner.

3. Click the Location property and enter new values for the X and Y coordinates, making sure you type a comma (**,**) between the two values. Or, click the plus sign

that appears to the left of the Location property and then enter separate values in the X and Y properties.

4. Press ENTER. Visual Basic Express moves your chosen control to its new location.

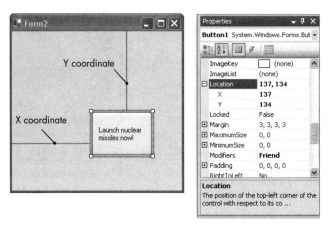

Figure 4-5: The X and Y coordinates let you precisely place a control on a form.

Moving Multiple Controls at Once

Visual Basic Express lets you move groups of controls rather than moving individual controls, one at a time. Before you can move multiple controls at the same time, you must select the controls you want to move by following these steps:

1. Select the controls you want to move by choosing one of the following methods:

    • Hold down the CTRL or SHIFT key and click each control that you want to move.

    • Click and drag the mouse to draw a dotted rectangle around the controls you want to select, as shown in Figure 4-6. Release the left mouse button when you're done selecting all the controls you want. Visual Basic Express displays handles around each selected control.

2. Move the mouse pointer over any of your selected controls until the pointer turns into a four-way arrow.

3. Drag the mouse or press the arrow keys to move your selected controls.

Resizing Controls on a User Interface

When you place a control on a form, you may still need to resize it so that it appears exactly the way you want. You can resize a control in three ways:

    • Click the control and drag its handles.

Figure 4-6: By dragging the mouse, you can select multiple controls.

- Click the control, hold down the SHIFT key, and press the up/down or right/left arrow keys.

- Enter specific Width and Height values into the Properties window.

NOTE *You may not be able to resize all types of controls on a form. For example, Visual Basic Express won't let you resize a label control to prevent you from making a label too small to display any text inside.*

To enter specific Width and Height values, measured in pixels, in the Properties window, follow these steps:

1. Click the control you want to resize.
2. Press F4 to display the Properties window, then scroll down the Properties window until you see the Size property, as shown in Figure 4-7.
3. Click the Size property and enter the Width value, a comma, and the Height value. Or, click the plus sign that appears to the left of the Size property to display the Width and Height properties separately. (In Figure 4-7, the plus sign has been clicked so you can see these two properties.) Play around with the values by making them larger or smaller until the size of the control looks right to you.

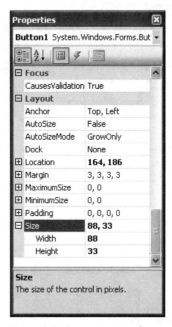

Figure 4-7: You can enter values directly in the Size property or in the separate Width and Height properties.

Changing the Properties of a Control

When you create a UI control, such as a button, Visual Basic displays a generic version of that control. While functional, generic controls often look dull (see Figure 4-8).

A generic user interface   A customized user interface

Figure 4-8: Until you change the properties of a control, they have a generic appearance.

To change the properties of a control, display the Properties window by clicking the control that you want to modify and pressing F4, choosing View ▶ Properties Window, or clicking the Properties Window icon on the Standard toolbar.

Properties can define a control's appearance (background color, text, or font), layout (size, location, or minimum and maximum size), or its connection to any external data. Although most controls share similar properties, each control has unique properties that allow the control to be customized. To change a property, you may need to do one of the following:

- Type a value, such as a number or text.
- Click a list box to choose from a fixed set of values.
- Click an ellipsis (. . .) button to display a dialog box to choose an item such as a file or a font.

Figure 4-9 shows the three different ways to change a property of a control in the Properties window.

When you select a UI control, the Properties window displays all the properties available for your chosen control. Every control type (such as a button, text box, or radio button) has a dozen or more different properties. To help you find the properties you want, the Properties window can sort all available properties either by category or alphabetically (see Figure 4-10).

Sorting properties by *category* can help you find a group of properties that affect specific behavior of a control, such as the layout category, which groups all properties related to the position and size of a control.

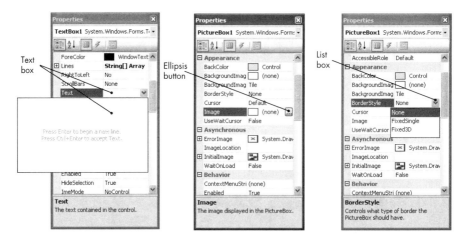

Figure 4-9: Visual Basic Express provides three different ways to change the properties of a control in the Properties window.

Click the expand/collapse icon (the plus or minus sign) to the left of each category name to view or hide properties.

NOTE   *Sorting properties alphabetically can help you find a specific property if you know the property name but don't know in which category it might be located.*

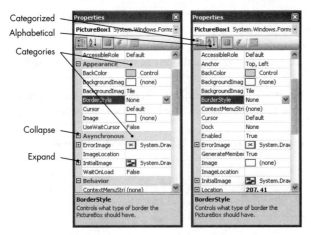

Categorized
Alphabetical
Categories
Collapse
Expand

Figure 4-10: The Properties window can organize properties by category or alphabetically.

Deleting Controls on a User Interface

To delete a control, follow these steps:

1. Click the control you want to delete, such as a button or a check box. Visual Basic Express should display handles around the control.
2. Press the DEL (DELETE) key on your keyboard; click the Cut icon on the Standard toolbar, choose Edit ▶ Cut, press CTRL-X; or choose Edit ▶ Delete.

If you delete a control by mistake, you can retrieve it by pressing CTRL-Z.

Hands-on Tutorial: Designing a User Interface

Creating and Designing a User Interface

Follow these steps to familiarize yourself with the way forms, controls, and the Toolbox work, as you create and modify controls through the Properties window:

1. Load Visual Basic Express, then press CTRL-N to create a new project. A New Project dialog box appears. Click OK and a blank form appears.
2. Choose View ▶ Toolbox. The Toolbox appears. Click the Auto Hide icon. Notice that the Toolbox stays fixed in place and the blank form slides over to the right so you can see the entire form.
3. Double-click the Button control. Notice that Visual Basic Express automatically creates a button in the upper-left corner of the form.
4. Click the RadioButton control and mouse over the form. Notice that the mouse pointer turns into a crosshair and a radio button icon, as shown in Figure 4-11.
5. Click anywhere on the form. Visual Basic Express draws the radio button on your form.
6. Hold down the CTRL key and press the up/down and left/right arrow keys. Notice that each time you press an arrow key, the RadioButton control moves around the form.

7. Mouse over the Button control, hold down the left mouse button, and drag the mouse to one side of the RadioButton control. Snaplines should appear between the Button and the RadioButton controls. Release the mouse button.

8. Click the Button control and press F4 to view the Properties window for the Button control.

9. Double-click the Text property (which currently displays *Button1*), type **Exit**, and press ENTER. Notice that the text you enter in the button's Text property appears on the button.

10. Click the downward-pointing arrow in the BackColor property. A window appears with three tabs (see Figure 4-12).

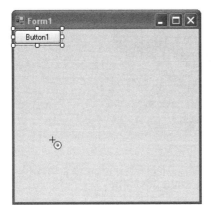

Figure 4-11: The mouse pointer displays a crosshair and the control that you chose from the Toolbox.

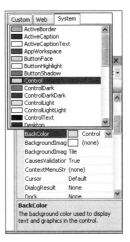

Figure 4-12: The BackColor property lets you choose from different colors organized by categories: Custom, Web, and System.

11. Click the Web tab and then click Red. The color of the Button control changes to red.

12. Click in the Size property, enter a Width and Height value (such as 125, 70), and press ENTER. The Button control immediately changes size.

13. Choose File ▶ Close Project. A Close Project dialog box appears, asking you to save your current project. Click Discard.

KEY FEATURES TO REMEMBER

The user interface provides a way to give your program information and retrieve new information back out again.

- A form displays a window on the screen.
- The Toolbox contains controls, such as menus or buttons, that you can place on a form.
- Once you place a control on a form, you can always move or resize that control later.
- The Properties window lets you customize each control to modify its appearance.

5

WRITING AND EDITING BASIC CODE

Once you've designed your user interface, your next step is to write instructions in BASIC to make your user interface do something with the data it retrieves from the user. You'll write and edit your code in the *Code window.* The Code window acts like a simple word processor, where you can type, edit, and search the code that tells your program what to do.

You can store code in one or more files. To open a file and view its code in the Code window (as shown in Figure 5-1), you can:

- Click the tab that contains a filename.
- Click a filename displayed in the Solution Explorer window and then choose View ▶ Code.
- Click a filename displayed in the Solution Explorer window and press F7.
- Right-click a filename displayed in the Solution Explorer window and then choose View Code.

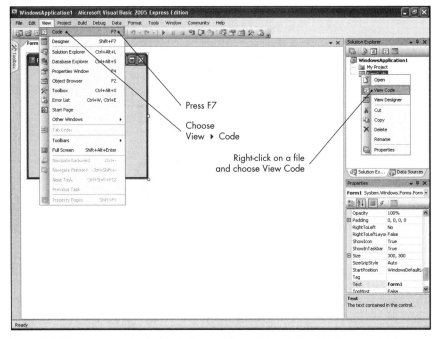

Figure 5-1: You can open the Code window to edit BASIC code in a file in several different ways.

Viewing BASIC Code in the Code Window

The Code window lets you see your code, but the more code you create, the less likely the Code window will be able to display it all. To show more code in the Code window:

- Increase the size of the Code window.
- Temporarily hide parts of your code from view.

Increasing the Code Window Size

Normally, the Code window fills only part of your computer screen so Visual Basic Express can display other items of the UI, such as the Standard toolbar or the Solution Explorer window. To see more of the Code window (and more of your code), you can expand it to fill the entire screen (Figure 5-2). Once expanded as such, most of the Visual Basic Express UI, such as the Standard toolbar, will disappear.

To toggle the Code window's size from normal (fills just part of the screen) to expanded (full screen), choose View ▶ Full Screen or press SHIFT-ALT-ENTER.

Hiding BASIC Code Temporarily

Expanding the size of the Code window can help you see more of your BASIC code, but the Code window may still overwhelm you with multiple lines of code that clutter up your screen. To make editing code easier, Visual Basic Express automatically draws horizontal lines between separate parts of your BASIC code. (These lines don't affect the way your BASIC code works; they're just a visual aid to help you identify the different parts of your code.)

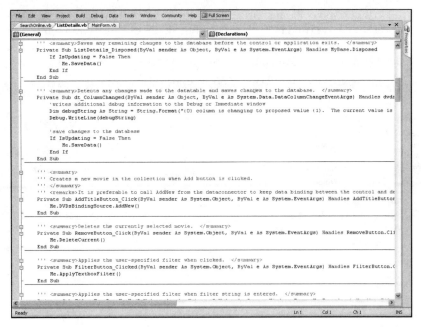

Figure 5-2: You can see more BASIC code when you expand the Code window to fill the entire screen.

Visual Basic code consists of miniature programs, called *procedures*, that perform a single task. Because your program might contain hundreds of different procedures, you can *collapse* or *expand* procedures from view. Normally, the Code window displays all procedures expanded so you can see all the BASIC code, as shown in Figure 5-3.

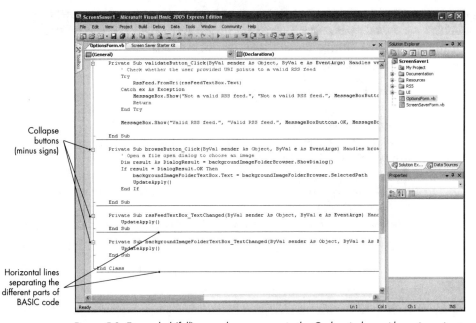

Collapse
buttons
(minus signs)

Horizontal lines
separating the
different parts of
BASIC code

Figure 5-3: Expanded (full) procedures appear in the Code window with a minus sign to the left of the procedure name.

When you collapse a procedure, the Code window displays only the first line of the procedure—so you know it's there—but all the details are hidden so you have more room to look at the rest of your code. Figure 5-4 shows how collapsing procedures can make the Code window appear less cluttered and easier to read.

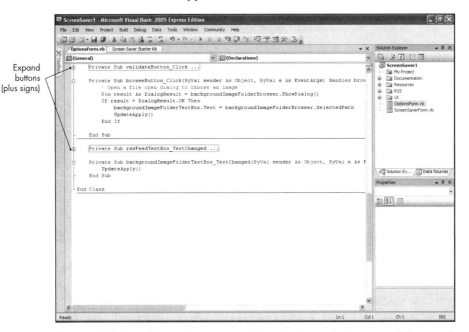

Figure 5-4: Collapsed procedures appear with a plus sign and a box around the procedure name.

Hands-on Tutorial: Viewing BASIC Code in the Code Window

This tutorial will show you how you can manipulate the Code windows to help you view your code, using a sample program provided by Visual Basic Express.

1. Load Visual Basic Express, then press CTRL-N to open a New Project dialog box.
2. Click the Screen Saver Starter Kit icon and click OK. Visual Basic Express displays the Starter Kit: Screen Saver page.
3. Right-click the ScreenSaverForm.vb file in the Solution Explorer window. A pop-up menu appears. Click View Code to show the Code window.
4. Scroll through the Code window and click the collapse buttons (minus signs) next to different chunks of the code. Notice how the Code window temporarily hides most of the code from sight.
5. Click the expand button (plus sign) of any bit of code you previously collapsed.
6. Choose View ▶ Full Screen. Notice how the Code window expands to fill the entire screen.
7. Choose View ▶ Full Screen again. Notice how the Code window shrinks back in size to show the rest of the Visual Basic Express UI.
8. Choose File ▶ Close Project. A Close Project dialog box appears. Click Discard.

Typing BASIC Code

Typing BASIC code into the Code window is much like typing text in a word processor. You can type BASIC code into the Code window in three ways:

- Manually
- Using the *IntelliSense* feature to help you type BASIC commands
- By pasting in a prewritten code snippet

The problem with typing BASIC code manually is that you have to know both the proper order to type each BASIC command (known as *syntax*), as well as which BASIC commands to use in which order to accomplish a particular task. If you enter the syntax incorrectly, Visual Basic Express won't understand your command. (Part IV of this book explains more about using various BASIC commands.)

To help you learn the syntax of a BASIC command, Visual Basic Express offers *syntax prompts* that appear on the screen as you type. For even more help with writing complete BASIC commands to accomplish particular tasks, Visual Basic Express offers *IntelliSense Code Snippets*, which contain prewritten BASIC code that you can customize.

NOTE *You don't need to use either syntax prompts or the IntelliSense Code Snippet features, but they can make writing a Visual Basic program faster while reducing the chance of misspelling a command.*

Using Syntax Prompts

Visual Basic Express's syntax prompts appear automatically as soon as you start typing a BASIC command in the Code window (Figure 5-5). By viewing the syntax prompt, you can see how to type the rest of your BASIC command correctly.

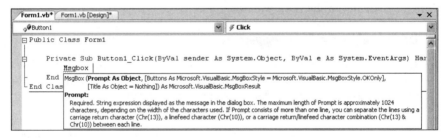

Figure 5-5: As you type, a prompt displays the proper syntax to use for that BASIC command.

Syntax prompts may initially appear confusing, but the more you use Visual Basic Express, the more you'll begin to understand what they're telling you.

NOTE *Sometimes the syntax prompt feature may display the syntax to a BASIC command that you don't want to use. To ignore the prompt, just keep typing and it will go away.*

Using AutoCorrect

If you misspell a command while writing a program, your computer won't understand your command and will likely prevent your program from working. To avoid this problem, Visual Basic Express includes an *AutoCorrect* feature that can display a list of valid commands as you type. With AutoCorrect, you can just click the command you want to use rather than type out its entire name and risk misspelling it. To use AutoCorrect:

1. Type a BASIC command. As you type, AutoCorrect displays a pop-up menu that lists commands that would fit into your code, as shown in Figure 5-6. Once you select a valid command from the AutoCorrect pop-up menu, the syntax prompt window may appear in order to guide you in typing the rest of a command.

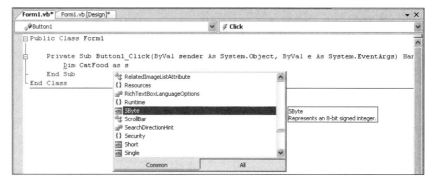

Figure 5-6: AutoCorrect displays a list of valid BASIC commands that you can insert in your program.

2. Scroll through the list until you find the command you want. As soon as you type one or more letters, AutoCorrect displays only those BASIC commands that contain all the letters you typed. For example, if you type the letter *S*, AutoCorrect will show all the BASIC commands that begin with the letter *S*.

3. Double-click the command you want, or highlight it with the up/down arrow keys and then press ENTER. Visual Basic Express will finish typing the chosen BASIC command in the Code window.

Using IntelliSense Code Snippets

Code snippets provide prewritten BASIC code that you can use to accomplish a variety of tasks. All you have to do is choose the task you want to accomplish, insert the working code into your program, and modify the code to fit your program.

To insert an IntelliSense code snippet into your program:

1. Right-click in the Code window where you want to insert a code snippet. A pop-up menu appears, as shown in Figure 5-7.

Figure 5-7: To access an IntelliSense code snippet, you need to choose the Insert Snippet command.

2. Choose the Insert Snippet command to open an Insert Snippet menu listing different tasks, such as Math or Processing Drives, Folders, and Files (Figure 5-8).

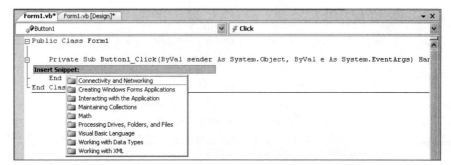

Figure 5-8: Visual Basic organizes IntelliSense code snippet into different categories.

3. Double-click the category corresponding to the type of task you need. For example, if you want to open or delete a file, you would choose the Processing Drives, Folders, and Files category. The IntelliSense feature displays another menu that lists specific tasks, as shown in Figure 5-9.

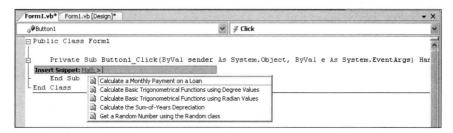

Figure 5-9: Once you choose an IntelliSense category, choose a specific task.

4. Double-click a specific task. Visual Basic Express inserts your chosen code snippet into the Code window (Figure 5-10), then highlights the part of the BASIC code that you need to modify in order to customize it for your program.

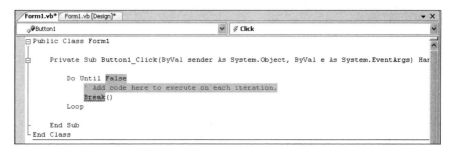

Figure 5-10: An IntelliSense code snippet contains generic BASIC code to accomplish a task.

5. Edit the highlighted part of the IntelliSense code snippet to customize it.

NOTE *If you accidentally insert the wrong IntelliSense code snippet, you can remove it immediately choosing Edit ▶ Undo or by pressing CTRL-Z.*

Hands-on Tutorial: Writing BASIC Code

Using the
Code
Window

Writing BASIC code involves typing one command after another in the order in which you want them to run. In this tutorial, you'll test out different features of Visual Basic Express that can save you time when you start writing your own programs.

1. Load Visual Basic Express, then press CTRL-N to open a New Project dialog box.

2. Click the Windows Application icon and then click OK.

3. Choose View ▶ Toolbox. The Toolbox appears.

4. Double-click the Button control and move your mouse away from the Toolbox. If the Auto Hide command is not selected, the Toolbox disappears, and the Button control is revealed on the form.

5. Double-click the Button control. Visual Basic Express displays the Code window with the BASIC code already written for you, as shown in Figure 5-11.

Figure 5-11: Double-clicking a control opens the Code window.

```
Public Class Form1
    Private Sub Button1_Click(ByVal sender As System.Object, ByVal e As_
System.EventArgs) Handles Button1.Click

    End Sub
End Class
```

6. Move the cursor in between the `Private Sub` and the `End Sub` lines and right-click the mouse. A pop-up menu appears.

7. Click Insert Snippet. Another pop-up menu appears.

8. Double-click Visual Basic Language. Another pop-up menu appears.

9. Scroll down the list in the pop-up menu and then double-click For...Next Statement. Visual Basic Express inserts a For...Next code snippet into the Code window, which looks like this:

```
Public Class Form1
    Private Sub Button1_Click(ByVal sender As System.Object, ByVal e As_
System.EventArgs) Handles Button1.Click
        For index As Integer = 1 To 10
            ' Add code to be executed on each iteration.
        Next
    End Sub
End Class
```

10. Move the cursor to the end of the `For index As Integer = 1 To 10` line and press ENTER to create a blank line immediately below this line.

11. Type **MsgBox (**. Notice that Visual Basic displays a syntax prompt to show you the proper way to use the `MsgBox` command.

12. Finish typing **MsgBox(index)** so the entire BASIC code looks like this:

```
Public Class Form1
    Private Sub Button1_Click(ByVal sender As System.Object, ByVal e As_
System.EventArgs) Handles Button1.Click
        For index As Integer = 1 To 10
          MsgBox(index)
            ' Add code to be executed on each iteration.
        Next
    End Sub
End Class
```

13. Press F5 to run your BASIC code. A window entitled *Form1* with a button in the upper-left corner appears.

14. Click the button. A message box appears, displaying the number *1*.

15. Keep clicking OK. Notice that each time you click OK, the message box displays a higher number. When the message box displays *10*, click OK once more and the message box will disappear.

16. Click in the Close box (the bright orange box with an X in it at the top-right corner of the Form1 window).

17. Choose File ▶ Close Project. A Close Project dialog box appears. Click Discard.

Navigating in the Code Window

The more code your program contains, the more you'll have to scroll through the Code window to find the one line of code that you want to edit. To make viewing your BASIC code easier, use one of the shortcut keystroke combinations shown in Table 5-1.

Table 5-1: Navigational Keystrokes

Keystroke combination	Description
HOME	Moves cursor to beginning of line
END	Moves cursor to end of line
CTRL-left arrow	Moves cursor left one word at a time
CTRL-right arrow	Moves cursor right one word at a time
CTRL-PGUP	Moves cursor up to previous procedure
CTRL-PGDN	Moves cursor down to next procedure
CTRL-HOME	Moves cursor to top of a file
CTRL-END	Moves cursor to bottom of a file

In addition to these keystroke shortcuts, Visual Basic Express offers two alternatives for moving the cursor to another part of the Code window:

Quick Find   Searches for specific text

Go To Line Number   Jumps to a specific line number of the Code window

Searching for Text with the Quick Find Command

If you know a particular word or phrase that you want to find in your code, you can search for it using the Quick Find command. Not only can Quick Find search the code displayed in the Code window, but it can also search all the files that make up your Visual Basic project. To use Quick Find command:

1. Press CTRL-F or choose Edit ▸ Quick Find. The Find and Replace dialog box appears, as shown in Figure 5-12.
2. Click in the Find What text box and enter the text you want to find. Make sure to spell the text correctly.
3. Click in the Look In list box and choose the location you want to search, such as Current Project or Current Document.
4. (Optional) Click the plus sign to the left of the Find Options label. The Find and Replace dialog box expands to display additional options, as shown in Figure 5-13.

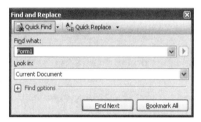

Figure 5-12: The Find and Replace dialog box lets you search your Visual Basic files for particular text.

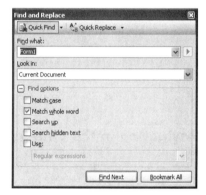

Figure 5-13: Additional options in the Find and Replace dialog box let you search for whole words or case-sensitive words.

5. (Optional) Click any additional options you want to use for your search, such as Match case or Search up.
6. Click Find Next. Visual Basic Express searches until it finds (and highlights) the first occurrence of the search text you typed in Find What text box in step 2. Click the Find Next button again to search for the next occurrence of your text.
7. Click the Close box of the Find and Replace dialog box to make it go away.

Jumping to a Specific Line Number

You can also tell the Code window to display a specific *line number* in your code. The first line of code that appears in the Code window is line 1, the second is line 2, and so on.

NOTE   *Visual Basic Express counts all lines whether they have text in them or not, so a blank line counts as one line.*

To jump to a specific line in the Code window:

1. Choose Edit ▶ Go To. A Go To Line dialog box appears, as shown in Figure 5-14. The dialog box displays the total number of lines that you can view in the Code window. In Figure 5-14, the total number of lines of code is 341.

Figure 5-14: The Go To Line dialog box tells you the total number of lines of code in the Code window and lets you type a line number to which you want to jump.

2. Type a line number, such as 45 or 223.
3. Click OK. Visual Basic Express moves the cursor to the chosen line number.

Hands-on Tutorial: Navigating in the Code Window

To see how you can manipulate the Code window to help you view BASIC code, this tutorial guides you through loading a sample program provided by Visual Basic Express.

1. Load Visual Basic Express, then press CTRL-N to open the New Project dialog box.
2. Click the Screen Saver Starter Kit icon and click OK. Visual Basic Express displays the Starter Kit: Screen Saver page.
3. Right-click the ScreenSaverForm.vb file in the Solution Explorer window. A pop-up menu appears.
4. Click View Code. The Code window appears.
5. Press CTRL-END. The cursor jumps to the end of the Code window.
6. Press CTRL-HOME. The cursor jumps to the beginning of the Code window.
7. Choose Edit ▶ Go To. A Go To Line dialog box appears.
8. Type a line number, such as 83 or 102, and then press ENTER. Visual Basic Express moves the cursor to the chosen line number.
9. Choose Edit ▶ Quick Find. The Find and Replace dialog box appears.
10. Type Private in the Find What text box and click Find Next. The Code window highlights the first *Private* word it finds.
11. Click the Find Next button multiple times. Notice that each time you click, a different area of the code containing the word *Private* is highlighted in the Code window.
12. Press ESC or click the Close box of the Find and Replace dialog box to make the dialog box go away.
13. Choose File ▶ Close Project. A Close Project dialog box appears, then click Discard.

KEY FEATURES TO REMEMBER

In the Code window, you can view, write, and edit BASIC code for your program.

- Visual Basic Express stores BASIC code in multiple files.
- You can expand the Code window to fill an entire screen so you can see more BASIC code at one time.
- You can selectively collapse or expand parts of your BASIC code to view only the portion(s) of your code you want to edit.
- Syntax prompts help you use BASIC commands correctly.
- AutoCorrect shows you a list of valid BASIC commands you can use as you type.
- IntelliSense Code Snippets allow you to insert prewritten code into your program.
- The Code window provides a variety of different ways to move the cursor to different parts of a file.

6

GETTING HELP

Although Microsoft aims to make Visual Basic Express easy to use, especially for beginning programmers, not everyone can start using Visual Basic Express right away. So to help you learn how to use both Visual Basic Express and the Visual Basic language itself, you need to learn how to get the type of help you need, when you need it.

Browsing the Contents

Getting Help
with Visual
Basic Express

Finding help in a computer help system is often a paradox: you may know what you don't understand, but you don't know how to find the answer. To solve this problem, Visual Basic Express offers several ways to look for help.

One way is to browse through the help Contents, which you can use to explore and stumble across useful nuggets of information, much like browsing through an encyclopedia in a library. You may never know what you'll find, but chances are good you'll find something new and interesting.

To browse the Help Contents, follow these steps:

1. Choose Help ▶ Contents, or press CTRL-ALT-F1. A window appears, displaying the Contents panel on its left-hand side. A Filtered By list box contains the words *Visual Basic Express*, as shown in Figure 6-1.

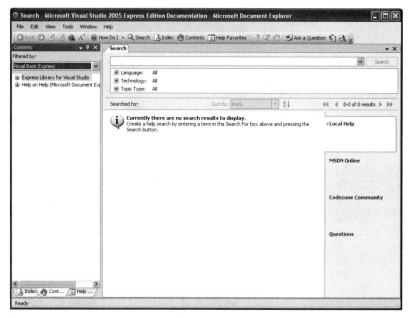

Figure 6-1: The Visual Basic Express filter forces the Contents panel to show help about Visual Basic only.

2. Click the plus sign in the Contents panel to the left of *Express Library for Visual Studio.* (Visual Studio is Microsoft's name for both the Visual Basic Express program and all the additional programs that help you create applications for Windows.) A list of additional topics appears.

3. Click the plus sign in the Contents panel to the left of the words *Visual Basic Express.* A list of Visual Basic Express topics appears.

4. Click the plus sign to the left of any topic that you want to browse, such as Visual Basic Reference. Repeat this step until you see a topic without a plus sign that you'd like to view.

5. Click a topic. Help for your topic appears in the right-hand panel (Figure 6-2).

6. Click the Close box to make the help window go away.

Searching for Help

By browsing through various topics, you will eventually find the help you want, but this can be cumbersome and time-consuming. As a faster alternative, you can search for a particular word or phrase for which you want help.

One drawback to searching for specific words, however, is that a word may mean one thing to you but something else to Visual Basic Express. For example, if you search for *print functions,* you'll get entirely different results than if you search for *print commands.*

In Visual Basic's vocabulary, the word *function* specifies a built-in BASIC program, such as ABS or COS, which calculates specific values. Similarly, its vocabulary treats the word *command* as a more generic term to describe any BASIC code. Until you know Visual Basic's vocabulary, searching can often bombard you with irrelevant results.

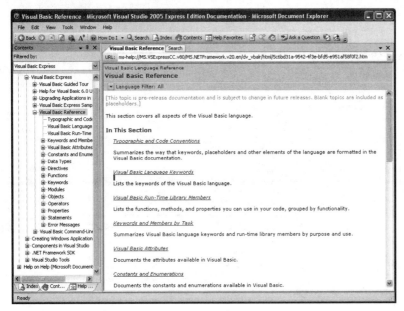

Figure 6-2: You may need to browse through several topics before you can find help for a specific one.

NOTE   To search through all available help, you need an Internet connection so that Visual Basic Express can access the latest help files from Microsoft's website.

To search for a word or phrase:

1. Choose Help ▸ Search, or press CTRL-ALT-F3. A window appears, displaying the Search for text box. Click in the Search For text box and enter a word or phrase.

2. Click Search or press ENTER. A list of help topics appears (Figure 6-3), organized in three categories: Local Help, MSDN Online, and Codezone Community. Local Help contains the help files stored on your computer. MSDN Online and Codezone Community contain help stored on websites on the Internet.

3. (Optional) Click a different source on the right side of the window, such as MSN Online or Codezone Community, to view different help topics.

4. Click the Back or Forward buttons or scroll down to view different help topics.

5. Click a help topic. Your chosen help topic appears in the right pane.

6. Click the Close box to make the window go away.

Looking in the Index

Once you understand the terminology used by Visual Basic Express, you may find it faster to use the Index. Like a book index, the Visual Basic Express Index lists Visual Basic Express commands alphabetically. If you know just what you're looking for, you can jump to the Index and find help on that particular word or command without wading through a list of possibly irrelevant topics.

To use the Index:

1. Choose Help ▸ Index, or press CTRL-ALT-F2. A window appears displaying the Index panel (Figure 6-4).

Back button

Forward button

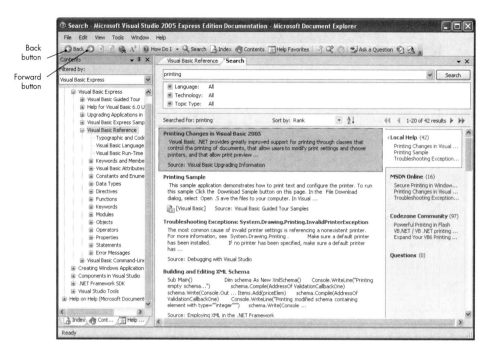

Figure 6-3: Visual Basic displays help from three different sources: Local Help, MSDN Online, and Codezone Community.

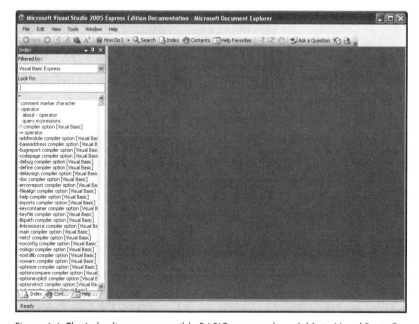

Figure 6-4: The Index lists every possible BASIC command available in Visual Basic Express.

2. Scroll down the Index or type a letter or two in the Look For text box. As you type, the Index displays only those commands that include the letters you've typed.

3. Double-click a topic. Visual Basic Express displays help for your chosen topic in the right panel of the window.

4. Click the Close box to make the window go away.

Using the How Do I Feature

To learn how to perform common tasks, you can browse through the Visual Basic Express *How Do I help system*, which provides sample BASIC code that accomplishes a particular task.

1. Choose Help ▶ How Do I, or press CTRL-F1. A window appears, with a selection of topics, as shown in Figure 6-5.

Figure 6-5: The How Do I window organizes answers to common questions by topic.

2. Click a topic, such as Learning the Visual Basic Language. Additional topics appear along with a list of topics that might answer your question.

3. Click a topic. Visual Basic Express displays help for your chosen topic.

4. Click the Close box to make it go away.

Using Dynamic Help

Browsing through the different help systems can be cumbersome because you either have to know the particular Visual Basic word to search for or you have to browse through multiple topics until you find the answer to your question. Alternatively, you can use *Dynamic Help*.

Dynamic Help is context sensitive: the list of topics changes based on what you're doing at a particular time. So if you're designing a user interface, Dynamic Help lists only those help topics related to designing your user interface. Once you switch to writing BASIC code, Dynamic Help displays help topics related to writing BASIC code.

To use Dynamic Help, follow these steps:

1. Choose Help ▶ Dynamic Help, or press CTRL-ALT-F4. The Dynamic Help window, as shown in Figure 6-6, appears in the bottom-right corner of the screen.
2. Click a help topic. A window appears, displaying help for your chosen topic.
3. Click the Close box to make the window go away.

As you change tasks within Visual Basic Express, the Dynamic Help window displays a different list of help topics. Figure 6-7 shows two different lists of help topics displayed in the Dynamic Help window. The Dynamic Help window on the left appears after you create a button as part of your user interface. The one on the right appears when you open the Code window to write or edit BASIC code.

Figure 6-6: The Dynamic Help window lists help topics based on what you're doing.

Figure 6-7: The Dynamic Help window constantly changes the list of help topics displayed.

Using the Help Toolbar

KEY FEATURES TO REMEMBER

Visual Basic Express provides help in many different ways, based on what you need to know at the time.

- The Contents act like a table of contents that organizes help into topics.
- Searching within help lets you look for a specific word or phrase.
- The Index lets you find help by looking up a specific word.
- The How Do I feature provides sample BASIC code for solving specific problems.
- Dynamic Help changes its list of help topics based on what you're doing when you choose help.

PART II

DESIGNING A USER INTERFACE

7

UNDERSTANDING CONTROLS
AND PROPERTIES

Every Visual Basic user interface consists of two types of
items: forms and controls. A *form* dictates the size and
appearance of a window. *Controls* display specific parts of
a user interface, such as radio buttons, check boxes, scroll
bars, and text boxes.

To create a user interface, you must create a form and fill it with controls.
When you first create controls and arrange them on a form, you'll have a
generic, unfinished UI, like the one shown in Figure 7-1. To customize the
appearance of your UI, you must modify the *properties* of your form and controls
which define both the appearance and behavior of forms and controls, such as
size, background color, and text that appears on the control. By modifying
properties, you can create a custom UI, as shown in Figure 7-2.

When creating a UI in Visual Basic, you'll basically take these steps:

1. Create a form or add a control to an existing form.
2. Choose the form or control you want to modify.
3. Modify the properties of your selected form or control.

Figure 7-1: An unfinished user interface

Figure 7-2: Modifying the properties of a form and controls can give you a finished user interface.

Using the Toolbox

To create controls, you must use the Toolbox, which lists all the different user interface controls you can place on a form, as shown in Figure 7-3.

To display the Toolbox, either choose View ▶ Toolbox; press CTRL-ALT-X; or click the Toolbox icon in the Standard toolbar.

NOTE   *To keep the Toolbox visible at all times, you can either click the Auto Hide icon in the Toolbox or choose Window ▶ Auto Hide.*

To hide a category, click the minus sign at its left; to display a category, click the plus sign. By hiding categories that you don't need to see, you can display more controls that you might need in the Toolbox, as shown in Figure 7-4.

Understanding Properties

Once you've placed controls on a form, you need to customize each control's properties to define its size, position, color, and the text that appears on it. Although every control contains dozens of properties, you need to modify only a handful to customize that control.

Opening the Properties Window

The Properties window lets you view and modify the properties for a single control. To open it to view a control's properties, follow these steps:

1. Click the control you want to examine, such as a button, a check box, or a form. Visual Basic Express highlights the chosen control.
2. Either choose View ▶ Properties Window, press F4, or click the Properties Window icon in the Standard toolbar.
3. Click the property that you want to change.

Auto Hide
icon

Figure 7-3: The Toolbox lists
every control you can place on a
form to create a user interface.

Figure 7-4: Hiding Toolbox
categories helps you easily
find the controls you want.

Viewing a Control's Properties

To help you view the different properties for a control, the Properties window can display the list of properties alphabetically (click the Alphabetical icon in the Properties window), or by category (click the Categorized icon). Table 7-1 lists the common categories of properties and how each affects a control.

Table 7-1: Common Property Categories Found in Most User Interface Controls

Category Heading	Properties
Appearance	Defines the control's appearance, such as its background color, image, font, and text alignment.
Behavior	Defines how a control acts when the user mouses over it or presses the TAB key. Behavior properties affect only how a control *looks*. You must write BASIC code to determine what the control *does* when the user clicks it.
Data	Specifies where to retrieve information from a database file that appears in the user interface control.
Design	Defines the control's name and whether you can move or resize the control while editing your Visual Basic program.
Layout	Defines the size and position of the control on a form.

Editing a Control's Properties

To modify a control, you must change one or more of its properties in the Properties window. You can change a property in three ways, as shown in Figure 7-5.

Ellipsis (. . .)   Displays a dialog box for choosing multiple options

List box   Lists a fixed number of valid options

Text box   Allows you to type characters such as a number or text

Clicking an ellipsis displays a dialog box that lets you choose multiple options at once. For example, Figure 7-6 shows a Font dialog box that appears if you click the ellipsis in the Font property.

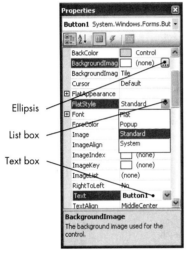

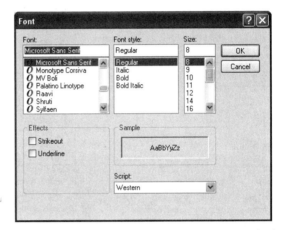

Figure 7-5: The three ways to change properties in the Properties window

Figure 7-6: Clicking the ellipsis in the Font property displays a Font dialog box.

Clicking a list box in a property displays a list of only the valid options you can choose. Clicking a text box lets you type and edit text to appear in a property, such as the Name or Text property. If a property holds a large amount of text, double-clicking that property or clicking the downward-pointing arrow that appears to the right of the property can display a pop-up window that lets you view the text, as shown in Figure 7-7.

NOTE   *The pop-up window in which you can type text won't automatically wrap your words as you type, so you will need to press ENTER when you want text to start on a new line. When you're done typing text in this window, click the mouse anywhere away from the window or press CTRL-ENTER. (For more on this window, see Chapter 8.)*

Understanding Common Properties

Every control contains a *Name* property that uniquely identifies it. When you create a new control, Visual Basic Express gives it a generic name, such as Button1 or Label3. You should give each control a unique, descriptive name that identifies its purpose or the type of data it holds. Naming a control TextBox21 won't tell us the type of data that control might hold, but a name like FirstName would help identify that control's purpose and the type of data it will hold.

NOTE *The name you enter in the Name property has no effect on how your program looks or acts; the Name property is there for your convenience in identifying controls. It can be especially useful when writing BASIC code because event procedures contain both the name of the event (such as a mouse click) and the name of the control that needs to deal with the event.*

The *Text* property, the second most common property, determines what text appears on a control such as a radio button, check box, or in the title bar of a form, as shown in Figure 7-8. Your typing in the Text property of a control appears directly on the control in your user interface.

Not all controls contain a Text property, but those that do also include a *Font* property, which defines the font type, size, and style (boldface or italics) for any text stored in the Text property.

Figure 7-7: If a property holds a large amount of text, such as the Text property, a pop-up window may appear when you double-click the property.

Most controls also include Size and Location properties. The *Size* property defines the height and width of a control. The *Location* property determines the position of a control on a form as defined by the X and Y properties. The *X* property measures how far from the left edge of a form a control appears, while the *Y* property measures how far from the top of a form a control appears.

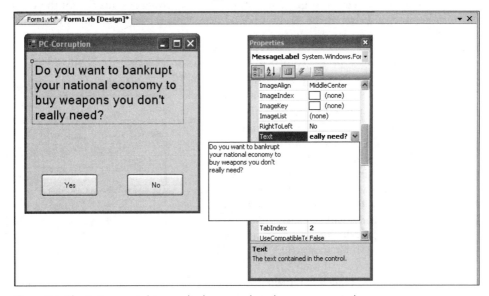

Figure 7-8: The Text property lets you display a word or phrase on a control.

NOTE *By comparing the X and Y properties of two different controls, you can make sure they are exactly aligned with one another or spaced a fixed distance apart from each other.*

Once you customize a control's properties, you may want to use the *Locked* property, stored under the Design category of the Properties window. When the Locked property value is True, Visual Basic Express won't let you move or modify a control. Only when the Locked property is False can you move or modify the control. The Locked property has no effect on the way your program looks or behaves; it's solely for your convenience in designing your program's user interface.

Defining the Tab Order of Controls

Users typically interact with a program through the mouse or the keyboard. While more people are likely to use the mouse to point and click the buttons and check boxes that appear on your user interface, users should also be allowed to choose and select buttons, check boxes, and radio buttons using the keyboard.

Users can press two keys to navigate through a user interface: the TAB key and the arrow keys. The user presses the TAB key to highlight a UI control and the SPACEBAR to toggle the currently highlighted UI controls, such as a radio button or check box.

The order in which the TAB key highlights UI controls is known as the *tab order,* and the property that controls the tab order is *TabIndex,* located under the Behavior category of the Properties window.

When your program runs, the first control highlighted is the one with a TabIndex property of 0. If the user presses the TAB key, the control highlighted is the one with its TabIndex property set to 1. The next control highlighted is the one with a TabIndex value set to 2, and so on. If you press the TAB key enough times to cycle through all the controls on a form, you'll eventually highlight the control with a TabIndex value of 0, followed by the control with a TabIndex value of 1, and so on.

While you could edit each control's TabIndex property by first selecting that control, typing a new value into the TabIndex property, and then selecting another control again, it's faster to edit multiple controls' TabIndex properties directly on the form. To view and edit the tab order of multiple controls on a form, follow these steps:

1. Choose View ▸ Tab Order. Visual Basic Express displays the value of each control's TabIndex property directly on every control, as shown in Figure 7-9.

2. Click each control's TabIndex property (the number displayed in the upper-left corner of each control) to change its value. Each time you click a control's TabIndex number, the number increments by 1. (It's a good idea to make sure every control has a different TabIndex value. If two controls contain identical TabIndex values, Visual Basic Express decides which control gets highlighted first, which may not be the order you want.)

3. Choose View ▸ Tab Order to hide the values of each control's TabIndex property.

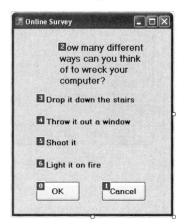

Figure 7-9: You can view and edit the tab order of a user interface by choosing View ▸ Tab Order.

Hands-on Tutorial: Playing with Controls and Properties

To design a user interface in Visual Basic, you need to understand how to create and arrange controls on a form and how to modify the properties of each form and control you create. Here's an example.

1. Load Visual Basic Express and press CTRL-N to open the New Project dialog box, then click OK to create a new project with a single form.

2. Choose View ▶ Toolbox. The Toolbox appears. Choose Window ▶ Auto Hide to keep the Toolbox visible at all times. (If a check mark already appears next to the Auto Hide command, skip this step.)

3. Double-click the Button control in the Toolbox. Visual Basic Express draws a button control on the displayed form.

4. Click the CheckBox control in the Toolbox, move the mouse to the center of the displayed form, and click the left mouse button. Visual Basic Express draws a check box control in the center of the displayed form.

5. Click the RadioButton control in the Toolbox, mouse over to the bottom-right corner of the displayed form, and click the left mouse button. Visual Basic Express draws a radio button control in the bottom-right corner of the displayed form.

6. Click the collapse button at the left of the Common Controls category of the Toolbox. Notice that the Toolbox hides the controls displayed under the Common Controls category.

7. Choose View ▶ Tab Order. Visual Basic Express displays the TabIndex values of each control on the form.

8. Click the TabIndex number of the check box control in the center of the form until the value displays *0*, then click the TabIndex number of the button control in the upper-left corner of the form until the value displays *1*. The TabIndex values should appear as shown in Figure 7-10.

9. Choose View ▶ Tab Order to hide each control's TabIndex number.

10. Click the check box in the center of the form. Visual Basic Express highlights the check box.

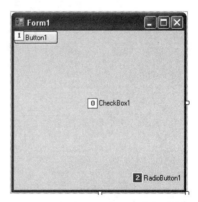

Figure 7-10: The center control should have a TabIndex value of 0 so it appears highlighted when your program first runs.

11. Press F4 to open the Properties window, then click the Text property in the Properties window and type any text, such as **My own check box**, and press ENTER. (Notice that whatever text you type into the Text property appears on the check box control.)

12. Press F5 to run your program. Your user interface appears on the screen.

13. Press TAB. The button in the upper-left corner of the form is highlighted.

14. Press TAB. The radio button in the bottom-right corner of the form is highlighted.

15. Press SPACEBAR. Notice that this toggles the radio button on.
16. Press TAB. The check box in the center of the form is highlighted.
17. Press ALT-F4 to stop your program from running, then choose File ▶ Close Project. A Close Project dialog box appears. Click Discard.

KEY FEATURES TO REMEMBER

Forms are windows that typically hold one or more controls. Controls are predesigned parts that you can use to create a user interface. Common types of controls include buttons, check boxes, and radio buttons. To customize the appearance of each control, you need to modify the properties of each control.

- Designing a user interface is a three-step process: First, you create a form; then you place controls on that form; and, finally, you modify the properties of each control on that form.
- Controls and properties let you customize a user interface for your Visual Basic program.
- Properties define the behavior and appearance of a control or form.
- The Toolbox lets you choose which controls to use for your user interface.
- Changing properties may require clicking an ellipsis, clicking a list box, or typing text into a text box.
- The Name and Locked properties exist solely for your convenience in designing your Visual Basic program.

8

USING THE APPEARANCE
PROPERTIES

The Appearance category of the Properties window defines
how a specific control appears on the user interface. All
the properties that define a control's appearance appear
in the Properties window under the Appearance category,
as shown in Figure 8-1. The various properties under
the Appearance category can be used to make a control
aesthetically pleasing but do not affect the way your
program works.

While not all controls share the same number and types of properties
under the Appearance category, most controls offer properties that define
the following:

- Text
- Colors
- User interaction
- Pictures

Figure 8-1: The Properties window can organize and display all Appearance properties of a control.

Properties for Modifying Text

Every program's user interface needs to display information to the user, and the most common way to do so is through text. To display text in a Visual Basic program, you modify the *Text* property of a user interface control, such as a button, a check box, or even a form. For example, Figure 8-2 shows the text *The answer is four* displayed in the Text property of a form, a label, a radio button, and a button.

Typically, the Text property describes a control's purpose. For example, the Text property of a form might display the name of the program (such as PC-scanner) and the Text property of a button describes the command that button represents (such as Cancel or Close).

To display text on a form you use the *Label* control. Labels can give the user instructions for using the user interface or describe the type of information that should be typed into a nearby text box, as shown in Figure 8-3.

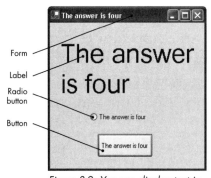

Figure 8-2: You can display text in any object that has a Text property.

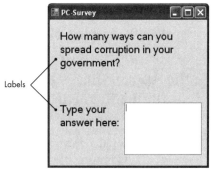

Figure 8-3: A label can identify the purpose of the user interface or that of a text box.

An object's Text property contains the actual text that appears on your user interface. A collection of one or more characters is often referred to as a *string of text* or just a *string*. In addition, several other properties can be used to affect the appearance of your text, as listed in Table 8-1.

Table 8-1: Properties That Modify the Appearance of the Text Property

Property	Description
Font	Defines the font, font size, and other characteristics of the string stored in the Text property.
Text	Contains the string to appear on the user interface.
TextAlign	Defines where the text appears in relation to the user interface object. The six choices are TopLeft, TopCenter, TopRight, MiddleLeft, MiddleCenter, MiddleRight, BottomLeft, BottomCenter, and BottomRight.

Modifying the Text Property

Anything stored in the Text property appears on your user interface. You can modify the Text property at *design time* (when you're creating your user interface) or at *run time* (when your program is actually running).

Modifying the Text Property at Design Time

To change the Text property at design time, use the Properties window. On some controls, such as buttons or check boxes, the Text property lets you type only a single line of text in the Properties window. For other controls, such as labels and text boxes, the Text property lets you choose to either type all your text as a single line, or to type text in a small pop-up window that appears when you click a downward-pointing arrow in the Text property, as shown in Figure 8-4.

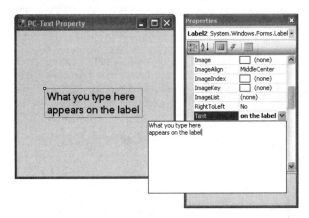

Figure 8-4: For typing and editing long strings of text, the Text property can display a pop-up window.

To display the pop-up window of the Text property:

1. Click the control you want to modify, such as a label or a text box.
2. Open the Properties window by pressing F4 or choosing View ▶ Properties Window.
3. Click the Text property. A downward-pointing arrow appears to the right of the Text property box. (If you don't see a downward-pointing arrow, the Text property for your chosen object won't display a pop-up window.)
4. Click the arrow. A small pop-up window appears.
5. Type or edit your text within this pop-up window. To force text to appear on separate lines, press ENTER to start each new line.

6. Press CTRL-ENTER or click anywhere outside the pop-up window to stop editing the Text property.

Modifying the Text Property at Run Time

To change the Text property at run time, you must use BASIC code. While you'll learn more about BASIC code later in this book, the general BASIC code required for modifying the Text property looks like this:

```
ControlName.Text = "New text"
```

where *ControlName* is the name of the user interface control, such as Button1, and *New text* is any text you want to appear in that particular user interface control.

Changing the Text Property Font

The *Font* property determines the appearance of any text stored in the Text property. Some of the more common properties to change under the Font property include Name (the font name); Size (the font size); Bold (boldface font); Italic (italic font); Strikeout (text that appears with a line through it); and Underline (underlined text).

You can modify the Font property through a dialog box or through the Properties window. To modify the Font property through a dialog box, follow these steps:

1. Click the user interface control that you want modify.
2. Open the Properties window by pressing F4 or choosing View ▸ Properties Window.
3. Click the ellipsis button (. . .) that appears to the right of the Font property. A Font dialog box appears, as shown in Figure 8-5.
4. Make any changes you want in the Font dialog box and click OK when you're done.

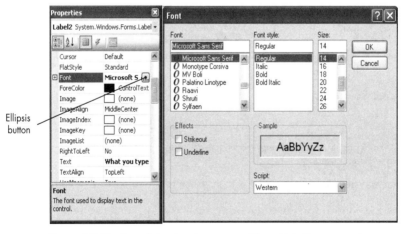

Figure 8-5: The Font dialog box lets you modify multiple Font properties.

Although the Font dialog box offers an easy way to change multiple Font properties, you can also change the individual Font properties directly within the Properties window by following these steps:

1. Click the user interface control you want to modify then open the Properties window by pressing F4 or choosing View ▸ Properties Window.

2. Click the plus sign to the left of the Font property. The Font property expands to display all the separate properties available for modification, as shown in Figure 8-6.

3. Change one or more properties. When you're done, click the minus sign to the left of the Font property to collapse all the separate Font properties.

Figure 8-6: Expanding the Font property in the Properties window can reveal all the separate properties you can modify.

Aligning Text Within an Object

The *TextAlign* property lets you align text in different positions within the physical boundary of a user interface control, such as a button (Figure 8-7). This property has no effect on the way your user interface works; it simply gives you more ways to make your UI aesthetically pleasing. To modify the TextAlign property:

1. Click the user interface control you want to modify then open the Properties window by pressing F4 or choosing View ▶ Properties Window.

2. Click the downward-pointing arrow next to the TextAlign property. A menu appears, displaying all the different positions you can choose (see Figure 8-7).

3. Click a new position to align your text.

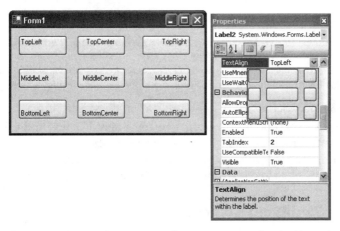

Figure 8-7: The TextAlign property allows more options for displaying the contents of the Text property.

Hands-on Tutorial: Modifying Text Properties

The Text property is one of the most important and commonly used properties. This tutorial shows you how to modify the Text property of a form and a control using both the Properties window and BASIC code:

1. Load Visual Basic Express and press CTRL-N to open the New Project dialog box.

2. Click OK and Visual Basic Express should create a blank form. Click the form and press F4 to open the Properties window.

3. Click the Text property in the Properties window and enter a string, such as **This is my form**. Press ENTER; the string you typed should appear in the form's title bar.

4. Choose View ▸ Toolbox. The Toolbox appears.

5. Click the TextBox control, mouse over your form, and click the left mouse button. Visual Basic Express should display a text box control on your form.

6. Double-click the text box control to display the Code window with the following BASIC code:

```
Public Class Form1
    Private Sub TextBox1_TextChanged(ByVal sender As System.Object, ByVal e As_
System.EventArgs) Handles TextBox1.TextChanged

    End Sub
End Class
```

Move the cursor in between the lines Private Sub and End Sub and then type **Me.Text = TextBox1.Text** so the BASIC code now looks like this:

```
Public Class Form1
    Private Sub TextBox1_TextChanged(ByVal sender As System.Object, ByVal e As_
System.EventArgs) Handles TextBox1.TextChanged
        Me.Text = TextBox1.Text
    End Sub
End Class
```

NOTE   *As you type, Visual Basic Express displays pop-up menus that list possible commands for you to choose. The Me keyword refers to the blank form initially created by Visual Basic Express, so the entire BASIC statement Me.Text = TextBox1.Text says to take the text stored in the text box named TextBox1 and display it in the Text property of the currently displayed form.*

7. Press F5. Your user interface should appear on the screen.

8. Click the Text box on the form and type some text. The text in the form's title bar should automatically change to display what you type.

9. Press ALT-F4 to stop your program from running, then choose File ▸ Close Project. A Close Project dialog box appears. Click Discard.

Properties for Modifying Colors

Controls have two properties to define colors that appear: *BackColor* and *ForeColor*. The BackColor property defines the color that fills the entire control; the ForeColor property defines the color of text stored in the Text property of a control, as described in Table 8-2.

Table 8-2: Properties That Modify Colors of a Control

Property	Description
BackColor	Defines the color that appears on the background of a control
BorderColor	Defines the color of the border around the control
BorderSize	Defines the thickness of the border
ForeColor	Defines the color of the string displayed in the Text property

NOTE *For best results, the ForeColor and BackColor values should contain contrasting colors, such as black and white. If you don't choose two contrasting colors, your text may be nearly impossible to read.*

Changing the BackColor and ForeColor Properties

To change the ForeColor and BackColor properties, follow these steps:

1. Click the user interface control you want to modify.

2. Open the Properties window by pressing F4 or choosing View ▶ Properties Window.

3. Click the ForeColor or Back-Color property. A downward-pointing arrow appears.

4. Click the downward-pointing arrow. A window appears displaying three tabs: Custom, Web, and System. Each provides a palette of colors from which you can choose, as shown in Figure 8-8.

5. Click the Custom, Web, or System tab.

6. Click a color. Visual Basic Express displays the text or background in the chosen color.

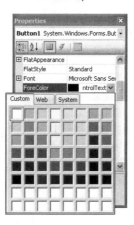

Figure 8-8: Clicking the ForeColor or BackColor property displays a palette of additional colors.

Properties for Defining User Interaction

When the user mouses over a control, the control can change its appearance, change the mouse pointer's appearance, or both. Changing the control or mouse pointer's appearance can alert the user to the existence of a particular control on the user interface. For example, many web pages change the mouse pointer from an arrow to a pointing hand when the user mouses over a hyperlink. Table 8-3 lists properties that alter the control or mouse pointer's appearance.

NOTE *Changing the mouse pointer or control's appearance can make it easier for a user to navigate your UI, but doing so isn't always necessary.*

Table 8-3: Properties That Define the Appearance of the Control or Mouse Pointer

Property	Description
Cursor	Defines the appearance of the mouse pointer when the user moves it over the control
FlatStyle	Defines how the control appears when the user moves the mouse pointer over it

Changing the Mouse Pointer

The *Cursor* property defines the appearance of the mouse pointer when it's over a control. To define the Cursor property, follow these steps:

1. Click the user interface control you want to modify.
2. Open the Properties window by pressing F4 or choosing View ▸ Properties Window.
3. Click the Cursor property. A downward-pointing arrow appears.
4. Click the downward-pointing arrow. Visual Basic Express displays a list of mouse pointer icons from which you can choose, as shown in Figure 8-9.
5. Click the mouse pointer icon that you want to use.

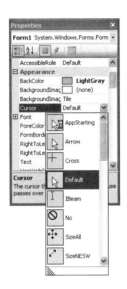

Figure 8-9: The Cursor property offers a variety of different icons you can use to change the appearance of the mouse pointer.

NOTE *The mouse pointer won't change its appearance over your control until you run your program by pressing F5.*

Changing the Appearance of a Control

The *FlatStyle* property defines the appearance of a control when the user mouses over it. To define the FlatStyle property, follow these steps:

1. Click the user interface control you want to modify.
2. Open the Properties window by pressing F4 or choosing View ▸ Properties Window.
3. Click the FlatStyle property. A downward-pointing arrow appears. Click this arrow to see a drop-down menu of options that include Flat, Popup, Standard, and System. Figure 8-10 shows the appearance of each of the different FlatStyle values. Click the value that you want.

NOTE *With some controls, such as a button, you won't see any difference in appearance between the Standard and System values for the FlatStyle property. With others, such as a check box or radio button, changing the FlatStyle property to System could affect their alignment.*

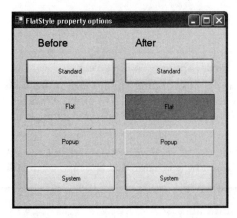

Figure 8-10: The FlatStyle property
defines how the control appears when
the mouse pointer appears over it.

Hands-on Tutorial: Modifying the Appearance of a Control

Using the
Appearance
Properties

Controls define the way users interact with your program, so it's important to know how they can provide visual feedback for your users. In this tutorial, you'll learn how to create visual cues to alert a user to click a button.

1. Load Visual Basic Express, then press CTRL-N to display the New Project dialog box. Click OK to display a blank form.

2. Choose View ▶ Toolbox. The Toolbox appears.

3. Click the Button control, mouse over the form, and click where you want to place the button control.

4. Press F4 to open the Properties window and click the FlatStyle property. A downward-pointing arrow appears. Click this arrow and choose Flat.

5. Click the Cursor property and downward-pointing arrow appears. Click the arrow and pop-up window appears that displays different cursor styles.

6. Scroll down this list and click the Hand cursor style.

7. Double-click the button control on your form to display the Code window and the following BASIC code:

```
Public Class Form1
Private Sub Button1_Click(ByVal sender As System.Object, ByVal e As System.EventArgs)_
Handles Button1.Click

    End Sub
End Class
```

8. Move the cursor in between the Private Sub and End Sub lines and type **Me.BackColor** =. You should see a pop-up window listing different options from which you can choose, such as Color.Aqua or Color.Blue, as shown in Figure 8-11.

9. Double-click a color you want, such as Color.Red. Visual Basic Express adds your chosen color in the Code window, as shown here:

```
Public Class Form1
Private Sub Button1_Click(ByVal sender As System.Object, ByVal e As System.EventArgs)_
Handles Button1.Click
```

```
        Me.BackColor = Color.Red
    End Sub
End Class
```

10. Press F5 to run your program. Your UI appears on the screen.

11. Mouse over the button control; the mouse pointer should turn into a hand icon (because of the Cursor property changes made in step 6) and the button should change to a dark gray color (because of the FlatStyle property changes made in step 4).

12. Click the button. The form changes color based on the color you chose in step 9.

13. Choose File ▶ Close Project. A Close Project dialog box appears. Click Discard.

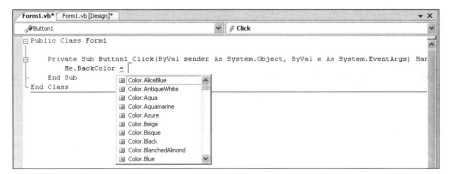

Figure 8-11: Visual Basic Express lets you double-click a color instead of forcing you to type it.

Properties for Modifying Images

To make a control look more interesting, you can display an image *inside* it. You can choose any one of four possible properties to display an image inside a control. (You cannot specify two of these properties at one time.)

- BackgroundImage
- Image
- ImageIndex
- ImageKey

Although each property can display images, each offers different features that may determine which property you want to use to display an image. Table 8-4 lists properties that define how an image appears within a control.

Table 8-4: Common Properties That Modify Images on a Control

Property	Description
BackgroundImage	Displays a graphical image inside a control. If the image is larger than the control, only a portion of the image is visible. If the image is smaller than the control, its position depends on the value of the BackgroundImageLayout property (see next).
BackgroundImageLayout	Defines how an image appears within a control. The possible values are None, Tile, Center, Stretch, and Zoom.
Image	Displays a graphical image inside a control, like the BackgroundImage property. The main difference is that you can specify the position of the image using the ImageAlign property (see next).

(continued)

Table 8-4: Common Properties That Modify Images on a Control (continued)

Property	Description
ImageAlign	Aligns an image, as specified by the Image property, in one of nine positions, such as TopLeft or BottomRight.
ImageIndex	Defines a graphical image previously stored in the ImageList control by its numeric position in the ImageList control.
ImageKey	Defines a graphical image previously stored in the ImageList control by filename.
TextImageRelation	Defines how both a graphical image and the text stored in the Text property appear in relation to one another inside a control.

Using the BackgroundImage Property

The main advantage of the Background-Image property is that you can use it with the BackgroundImageLayout property to display your image in various positions, such as Tiled, Stretched, Zoomed, or Centered. Figure 8-12 shows the different ways the Background-ImageLayout property can display a graphical image. To display an image using the BackgroundImage property, follow these steps:

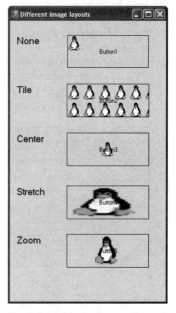

Figure 8-12: The BackgroundImageLayout property defines how an image appears within a control.

1. Click the user interface control that you want to modify, such as a button or a check box.

2. Open the Properties window by pressing F4 or choosing View ▸ Properties Window then click the BackgroundImage property. An ellipsis (. . .) button appears.

3. Click the ellipsis button. A Select Resource dialog box appears. (If a list of images appears above the Import button, you can click the image you want and skip to step 7.)

4. Click the Import button. An Open dialog box appears.

5. Navigate to and then click the graphical image you want to use. To select multiple images, hold down the CTRL key and click each image you want. You may need to switch to a different drive or directory to find the image files you want to use.

6. Click Open. The Select Resource dialog box appears again, as shown in Figure 8-13.

7. Click OK. Visual Basic Express displays your chosen image inside the control you selected in step 1.

8. (Optional) Click the BackgroundImageLayout property. A downward-pointing arrow appears. Click the arrow and choose a display option such as Tile or Zoom. Visual Basic Express displays your image in your chosen style.

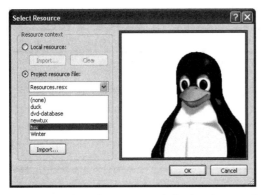

Figure 8-13: The Select Resource dialog box lets you choose and add an image.

Using the Image Property

The *Image* property works like the BackgroundImage property, except that in order to align an image within a control, you use the ImageAlign property instead. The *ImageAlign* property lets you specify a position for a graphical image in one of nine possible locations inside a control, as shown in Figure 8-14.

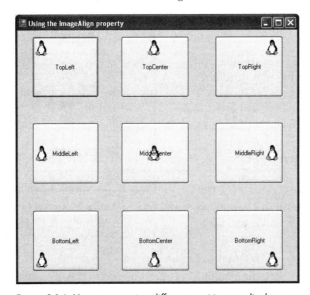

Figure 8-14: You can use nine different positions to display a graphical image inside a control.

NOTE   *If the image is larger than the control, you may not see any difference when you choose a different position for the image through the ImageAlign property.*

To display an image using the Image property, follow these steps:

1. Click the user interface control you want to modify then open the Properties window by pressing F4 or choosing View ▶ Properties Window.

2. Click the Image property. An ellipsis (. . .) button appears. Click the ellipsis button and a Select Resource dialog box appears. (If a list of images appears above the Import button, you can click the image you want and skip to step 6.)

3. Click the Import button. An Open dialog box appears.

4. Click the graphical image you want to use. To select multiple images, hold down the CTRL key and click each image you want. You may need to switch to a different drive or directory to find the image files you want to use.

5. Click Open. The Select Resource dialog box appears again.

6. Click OK. Visual Basic Express displays your chosen image inside the control you selected in step 1.

7. (Optional) Click the ImageAlign property. A downward-pointing arrow appears. Click this arrow and pull-down menu appears and displays the nine positions from which you can choose for positioning your image within the control, as shown in Figure 8-15. Visual Basic Express displays the image in the position you choose.

Figure 8-15: Click a position in which your image will appear inside a control.

KEY FEATURES TO REMEMBER

Most controls offer a variety of properties under the Appearance category of the Properties window. These properties let you define how a control looks when your program runs.

- Many user interface controls include a Text property for displaying text on your UI.

- You can modify the Text property of any user interface control through the Properties window (at design time) or through BASIC code (at run time).

- The Font property can modify the appearance of text on a user interface control.

- Most controls let you define three different colors: a background color (BackColor), foreground color (ForeColor), and border color (BorderColor).

- The Cursor and FlatStyle properties let you change the appearance of the mouse pointer or control while your program is running.

- The four different properties that can display an image in a control are BackgroundImage, Image, ImageIndex, and ImageKey.

9

USING THE LAYOUT AND
BEHAVIOR PROPERTIES

You can always use your mouse to draw a control on a form, but to place a control on a form precisely, you can enter specific values in the various *Layout* properties which determine the physical *position* of a control on a form.

The *Behavior* properties define how the control *acts* when your program is running, such as when the user drags or right-clicks the mouse or presses TAB. While you don't need to change Behavior properties for a control, doing so can make your user interface easier to use and more responsive.

Changing the Layout Properties

The two basic Layout properties are *Location* and *Size*. Location properties define where a control appears on a form, and Size properties define the width and height of a control. If you use the mouse to move or resize a control, Visual Basic Express adjusts the values stored in the Location and Size properties automatically, but you may still want to enter specific values if you need to place a control in a precise position or make it a specific size on a form. Table 9-1 lists the more common Layout properties you may want to modify for your controls.

Table 9-1: Properties That Modify the Layout of a Control

Property	Description
Anchor	Ties one side of a control to a fixed position near one side of a form, so if the user resizes a form, the control moves at the same time.
Dock	Either pins a control along the entire length of one side of a form or fills the entire form completely.
Location	Defines the X and Y positions of a control on a form, where X is measured in pixels from the left edge of a form to the left edge of a control and Y is measured in pixels from the top of a form to the top of a control.
MaximumSize	Defines the maximum width and height you can resize a control.
MinimumSize	Defines the minimum width and height you can resize a control.
Size	Defines the width and height of a control.

To type a value into the Location or Size properties, follow these steps:

1. Click the control that you want to modify, such as a label or a text box.
2. Open the Properties window by pressing F4 or choosing View ▸ Properties Window.
3. Click the plus sign that appears to the left of the Location or Size property. The Properties Window displays the X and Y or the Width and Height properties in separate rows, as shown in Figure 9-1.

Figure 9-1: You can modify the Location and Size properties by typing two values either directly into the Location or Size property or into the X and Y or Width and Height properties separately.

4. Enter a value into the fields of the properties you want to modify, such as the X or Height property. You can type two values into the Location and Size properties if you separate them with a comma, so to specify both an X and a Y property of a control, enter the X, Y values directly into the Location property field.
5. Press ENTER. Visual Basic Express changes your control so you can see how it looks.

Docking a Control

Typically, the Location property defines where a control appears on a form. However, you can override the Location property by using the *Dock* property instead. The Dock property places a control along the entire length of one side of a form, such as the top or left side, or so that it fills up the entire form. If the user resizes a form, all docked controls automatically adjust along with the new size of the form. The six different values for the Dock property are:

Left   Control appears on the entire left side of a form
Right   Control appears on the entire right side of a form
Top   Control appears along the entire top side of a form
Bottom   Control appears along the entire bottom of a form
Fill   Control expands to the same size as the form
(None)   Docking for a control is turned off

If you dock two or more controls, none of your docked controls will overlap each other. For example, if you dock one control along the bottom and a second to the left, the left-docked control will expand along the entire left side of the form without overlapping the first docked control, as shown in Figure 9-2.

The Dock property is set to (None) by default. To set it to a different value, follow these steps:

Figure 9-2: Multiple docked controls will not overlap each other.

1.   Click the control that you want to modify, such as a label or a text box.

2.   Open the Properties window by pressing F4 or choosing View ▶ Properties Window.

3.   Click the Dock property. A downward-pointing arrow appears. Click the arrow and Visual Basic Express displays the positions in which you can dock a control, as shown in Figure 9-3.

4.   Click a position at which to dock your control. Visual Basic Express docks your control accordingly.

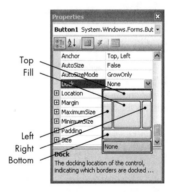

Figure 9-3: To define the Dock property for a control, click the position you want.

Anchoring a Control

If you place a control on a form and the user resizes that form while your program is running, your user interface (as shown in Figure 9-4) could appear skewed and unbalanced (as shown in Figure 9-5).

To keep your user interface looking balanced and proportional, *anchor* your controls. Anchoring keeps a control docked along one or more sides of a form, even if the user resizes a window. For example, if the right edge of a control is anchored exactly 1 inch from the right side of a form, it will always remain exactly 1 inch from the right side of the form, no matter how the user resizes the form while the program is running.

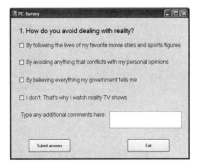

Figure 9-4: Before the user resizes a form, every control is in place.

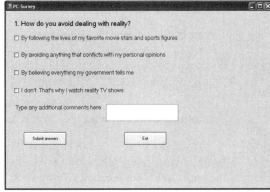

Figure 9-5: After resizing, a form can look unbalanced with empty spaces around it.

You can anchor a control along the top, left, right, or bottom of a form. If you anchor a control to one edge of a form, the control will move in the direction of that edge of the form when the user resizes it, as shown in Figures 9-6 and 9-7.

Figure 9-6: Before resizing a form with a text box anchored to the right and a radio button anchored to the bottom

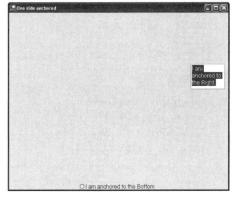

Figure 9-7: Resizing a form to increase its size moves the text box to the right and the radio button down to the bottom, creating an unbalanced window.

If you anchor a control to two sides of a form, the control moves in *both* directions when the user resizes it. For example, if you anchor a control to the bottom and right edges of a form, resizing the form moves the control toward the bottom and right edges of the form as the form changes in size. Anchoring a control along two adjoining edges—such as top, right or bottom, right—maintains the control's original size while moving the control as the user resizes the form.

To anchor a control, follow these steps:

1. Click the control that you want to modify, such as a label or a text box.
2. Open the Properties window by pressing F4 or choosing View ▸ Properties Window then click the Anchor property. A downward-pointing arrow appears.

3. Click the downward-pointing arrow to display the four different anchors you can define for a control, as shown in Figure 9-8.

NOTE *You won't be able to see how anchoring affects a control until you actually run your program and resize the form on which the control appears.*

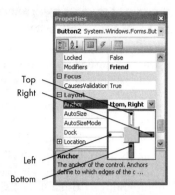

Top
Right
Left
Bottom

Figure 9-8: A gray bar means that the control is anchored to that side of the form.

Defining the MaximumSize and MinimumSize

If the user resizes a form in which controls are anchored, there's a good chance that an anchored control can either stretch or shrink too much. To prevent this from happening, use the *MaximumSize* and *MinimumSize* properties to specify how much a control can change in size. By setting one or both of these properties, you can either keep yourself from accidentally changing the size of a control while you're designing your user interface (at design time) or keep a control from changing its size while your program runs (at run time).

The MaximumSize and MinimumSize properties consist of *Width* and *Height* properties. When Width and Height of MaximumSize are set to zero (0), there is no limit on a control's maximum size. Likewise, if the Width and Height of MinimumSize property are set to zero (0), there is no limit on a control's minimum size.

To define the MaximumSize or MinimumSize properties, follow these steps:

1. Click the user interface control that you wish to modify.
2. Open the Properties window by pressing F4 or choosing View ▶ Properties Window then click the plus sign to the left of the MaximumSize or MinimumSize property. The Properties Window expands to show the Width and Height properties, as shown in Figure 9-9.
3. Enter values for Width and Height. (You may want to examine the Size property to determine the current Width and Height properties for your control, and then estimate how much larger or smaller you want it to grow or shrink.)

Figure 9-9: The MinimumSize and MaximumSize properties can be found in the Layout category of the Properties window.

Hands-on Tutorial: Anchoring Controls

By anchoring controls, you can keep your user interface consistent and visually pleasing no matter how much the user resizes a form. This tutorial shows you how different anchoring positions can effect a control.

1. Load Visual Basic Express, then press CTRL-N to display the New Project dialog box. Click OK.

2. Choose View ▶ Toolbox. The Toolbox appears. Choose Window ▶ Auto Hide to keep the Toolbox visible at all times.

3. Click the Button control in the Toolbox, mouse over the form, and click the left mouse button. Visual Basic Express draws a button control on your form.

4. Press F4 to open the Properties window then click the Anchor property. A downward-pointing arrow appears. Click the arrow and the Anchor layout appears with the top and left anchors highlighted in gray.

5. Click the anchors so that only the right anchor appears gray (see Figure 9-10).

6. Press F5. Your user interface appears.

7. Mouse over the right side of the form so that the mouse pointer turns into a two-way arrow. Hold down the left mouse button and drag the mouse to resize the form. Notice that as you resize the form, the button remains a fixed distance from the right side of the form.

8. Press ALT-F4 to stop your program.

9. Click the button control, press F4, and click the Anchor property. A downward-pointing arrow appears.

Figure 9-10: A gray bar shows that a control is anchored to the right side of a form.

10. Click the arrow to display the Anchor layout, then click the left anchor so that the left and right anchors appear gray.

11. Press F5 to display your user interface, then mouse over the right side of the form until the mouse pointer turns into a two-way arrow. Hold down the left mouse button and drag the mouse to resize the form. Notice that with the button anchored to the left and right sides of the form, resizing the form stretches the button.

12. Press ALT-F4 to stop your program, then choose File ▶ Close Project. A Close Project dialog box appears. Click Discard.

Changing the Behavior Properties

Behavior properties define how user interface controls respond when the user either presses certain keys or clicks the control with the mouse. Changing the Behavior properties of any control is purely optional but can make your user interface easier to use. Table 9-2 lists some of the more common behavior properties found in user interface controls.

Table 9-2: Properties That Modify the Behavior of a Control

Property	Description
AutoSize	Defines whether the control will automatically resize when its contents get larger or smaller.
ContextMenuStrip	Defines a menu to display when the user right-clicks the control.
Enabled	Defines whether the control appears dimmed or not. When a control appears dimmed, it's still visible but the user cannot choose it.
Visible	Defines whether the control appears visible or hidden on a form.

Defining the AutoSize Property

The *AutoSize* property can be set to True or False. When set to True, it allows a control to expand or shrink depending on its contents, such as when text is entered inside a label control. When set to False, the AutoSize property keeps the control a fixed size no matter how much or how little data appears inside, as shown in Figure 9-11.

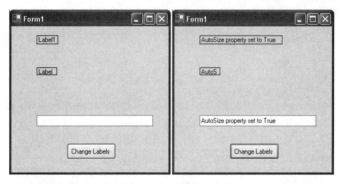

Figure 9-11: The label control at the right has its AutoSize property set to True, which allows it to expand to display its entire contents. The label directly underneath the first label has its AutoSize property set to False, which means that it remains a fixed size.

To define the AutoSize property for a control, follow these steps:

1. Click the control you want to modify, such as a text box or a button then open the Properties Window by pressing F4 or choosing View ▸ Properties Window.
2. Click the AutoSize property. A downward-pointing arrow appears. Click the arrow and a pop-up menu appears.
3. Click either True or False.

Defining the ContextMenuStrip Property

The *ContextMenuStrip* property defines the name of the menu that appears when the user right-clicks a control. To use it, you must first add a ContextMenuStrip control to your form, then create a menu, define a name for your menu, and then add the name of your newly created menu to the ContextMenuStrip property.

NOTE *The ContextMenuStrip property lets you choose the name of a ContextMenuStrip, so you must add at least one ContextMenuStrip to your user interface.*

To add and create a ContextMenuStrip control to your form, follow these steps:

1. Double-click the ContextMenuStrip control in the Toolbox (in the Menus & Toolbars category). Visual Basic Express displays the ContextMenuStrip control beneath your currently displayed form and a context menu at the top of your form, as shown in Figure 9-12.

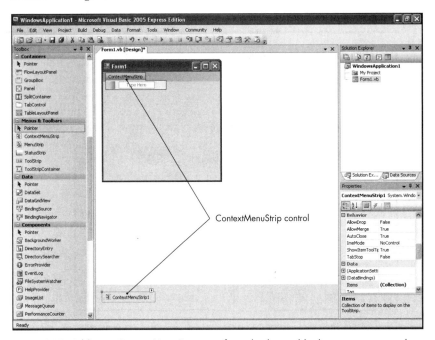

Figure 9-12: Adding a ContextMenuStrip to a form displays a blank context menu at the top of the form so you can create your menu.

2. Open the Properties window by pressing F4 or choosing View ▶ Properties Window. Click the Name property, and type a name for your context menu.

3. Click in the text box in the context menu that says *Type Here*, and type a command. Then press ENTER.

4. Repeat step 3 for each additional command you want to add to your context menu.

NOTE *The context menu commands do nothing until you write BASIC code to make them work.*

Once you have added a ContextMenuStrip to your form and typed commands in it, you can make it appear when the user right-clicks a control such as a button or check box. To define a context menu to appear on a control, follow these steps:

1. Click the control that you want to display a context menu, then open the Properties window by pressing F4 or choosing View ▶ Properties Window.

2. Click the ContextMenuStrip property. A downward-pointing arrow appears. Click the arrow to display a list of available context menu names.

3. Click the name of the context menu you want to appear. Now, when your program runs and the user right-clicks the control you chose in step 1, your context menu should appear, as shown in Figure 9-13.

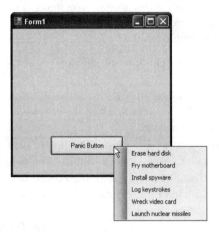

Figure 9-13: Right-clicking a control displays the context menu defined by its ContextMenuStrip property.

Disabling a Control with the Enabled and Visible Properties

If you want a control to appear dimmed or invisible to prevent the user from choosing it at that particular moment, you have two options:

- Change the control's Enabled or Visible property through the Properties window.
- Change the control's Enabled or Visible property using BASIC code.

Using the Properties Window to Change the Enabled and Visible Properties

The *Enabled* property defines whether a control appears normal or dimmed. The *Visible* property defines whether a control appears normal or invisible. To define these properties for a control, follow these steps:

1. Click the control that you want to modify, such as a text box or radio button then open the Properties window by pressing F4 or choosing View ▶ Properties Window.
2. Click the Enabled or Visible property. A downward-pointing arrow appears. Click the arrow to display a pop-up menu.
3. Click either True or False. When the Enabled property is set to False, the control appears dimmed when your program runs. When the Visible property is set to False, the control appears invisible when your program runs.

To change a control's Enabled or Visible property using BASIC, specify the control name followed by the Enabled or Visible property set to True or False, like so:

```
Button1.Enabled = False
Button2.Visible = False
```

The first BASIC command dims a control named Button1. The second command hides a control named Button2.

Hands-on Tutorial: Dimming and Hiding Controls

To dim and hide controls while your program is running, you need to use BASIC. This tutorial gives you some practical experience in seeing how you can use BASIC to modify a control's properties while your program runs.

1. Load Visual Basic Express, then press CTRL-N to display the New Project dialog box. Click OK.

2. Choose View ▸ Toolbox to display the Toolbox then choose Window ▸ Auto Hide to keep the Toolbox visible at all times. (Skip this step if a check mark does not appear in front of the Auto Hide command.)

3. Click the button control in the Toolbox, mouse over the form's center, and click the left mouse button. Visual Basic Express draws a button control on the form.

4. Click the button control in the Toolbox again, move the mouse anywhere underneath the first button, and click the left mouse button. Visual Basic Express draws a second button control on the form.

5. Double-click the ContextMenuStrip control under the Menus & Toolbars category of the Toolbox to display the ContextMenuStrip control at the top of your form.

6. Click in the Type Here text box of the ContextMenuStrip control, type **Dim button**, then click in the Type Here text box that appears directly underneath. Next, type **Hide button** and click in the Type Here text box that appears directly underneath.

7. Type **Show button** and press ENTER. Your ContextMenuStrip should now look like the one shown in Figure 9-14.

Figure 9-14: The ContextMenuStrip control now contains three commands.

8. Double-click the Dim Button command in the ContextMenuStrip to display the Code window.

9. Type `Button2.Enabled = False` in between the `Private Sub` and `End Sub` lines, so that the code looks like this:

```
Public Class Form1

    Private Sub DimbuttonToolStripMenuItem_Click(ByVal sender As_
System.Object, ByVal e As System.EventArgs) Handles_
DimbuttonToolStripMenuItem.Click
        Button2.Enabled = False
    End Sub
End Class
```

10. Choose View ▸ Designer to display your user interface, including the Context-MenuStrip.

11. Double-click the ContextMenuStrip1 control that appears at the bottom of the screen to display the context menu strip on your form. (Skip this step if the context menu strip is already visible at the top of your form.)

12. Double-click the Hide Button command in the ContextMenuStrip to display the Code window again, then type **Button2.Visible = False** in between the Private Sub and End Sub lines so that the code looks like this:

```
Public Class Form1

    Private Sub DimbuttonToolStripMenuItem_Click(ByVal sender As_
System.Object, ByVal e As System.EventArgs) Handles_
DimbuttonToolStripMenuItem.Click
        Button2.Enabled = False
    End Sub

    Private Sub HidebuttonToolStripMenuItem_Click(ByVal sender As_
System.Object, ByVal e As System.EventArgs) Handles_
HidebutonToolStripMenuItem.Click
        Button2.Visible = False
    End Sub
End Class
```

13. Choose View ▸ Designer to view your user interface once more then double-click the ContextMenuStrip1 control that appears at the bottom of the screen to display the context menu strip on your form. (Skip this step if the context menu strip is already visible at the top of your form.)

14. Double-click the Show Button command in the ContextMenuStrip to display the Code window again, then type **Button2.Enabled = True** and **Button2.Visible = True** on two lines in between the Private Sub and End Sub lines so that the code looks like this:

```
Public Class Form1

    Private Sub DimbuttonToolStripMenuItem_Click(ByVal sender As_
System.Object, ByVal e As System.EventArgs) Handles_
DimbuttonToolStripMenuItem.Click
        Button2.Enabled = False
    End Sub

    Private Sub HidebuttonToolStripMenuItem_Click(ByVal sender As_
System.Object, ByVal e As System.EventArgs) Handles_
HidebutonToolStripMenuItem.Click
        Button2.Visible = False
    End Sub

    Private Sub ShowbuttonToolStripMenuItem_Click(ByVal sender As_
System.Object, ByVal e As System.EventArgs) Handles_
ShowbutonToolStripMenuItem.Click
        Button2.Enabled = True
        Button2.Visible = True
    End Sub
End Class
```

15. Choose View ▸ Designer to view your user interface once more, then click the button that displays the text *Button1* and press F4 to open the Properties window.

16. Click the ContextMenuStrip property in the Behavior category. A downward-pointing arrow appears. Click the arrow to display a pop-up menu.

17. Click ContextMenuStrip1 then press F5. Your user interface appears.

18. Right-click the button control that displays the text *Button1*. The pop-up menu that you created with the ContextMenuStrip control should appear.

19. Click Dim Button. The second button control on the form should appear dimmed.

20. Right-click the Button1 button control and click the Hide Button command. The second button should disappear.

21. Right-click the Button1 button control and click the Show Button command. The second button should appear again.

22. Press ALT-F4 to stop your program from running then choose File ▸ Close Project. A Close Project dialog box appears. Click Discard.

KEY FEATURES TO REMEMBER

Layout and Behavior properties define both the placement of controls and the ways they work on the user interface.

- The Layout properties define the physical placement of controls on a form.

- The Behavior properties define how the control works when your program runs. You'll need to write BASIC to change most of the Behavior properties.

- Anchoring a control keeps it fixed to one or more sides of a form when the user resizes the form. Docking expands a control so it fills up one side of a form.

- The Location and Size properties define the physical placement and dimensions of a control on a form.

- To use the ContextMenuStrip property, you must first add a ContextMenuStrip control to a form and create a menu to appear when the user right-clicks a control.

- Setting the Enabled property to False dims a control. Setting the Visible property to False makes a control invisible. Eventually, you will have to use BASIC code to set both properties to True so users can choose those controls.

10

DESIGNING THE WINDOWS OF
A USER INTERFACE

To display a user interface, your Visual Basic program needs
to contain at least one window, called a *form*. Once you've
created one or more forms, you can fill them with user interface controls such as buttons, boxes, and pull-down menus.

Forms are like containers that display the different parts of a program's user
interface. A form can fill the entire screen (as a *maximized* window) or take up just
part of the screen. You can resize and move forms around the screen or hide them
altogether (a *minimized* window).

Creating and Deleting a Form

When you create a new project, Visual Basic Express creates one form for you
automatically. To create additional forms, follow these steps:

1.   Choose Project ▸ Add Windows Form. An Add New Item dialog box appears.
2.   Click the Name text box and enter a name, such as PasswordWindow, for
     your form, then click Add. Visual Basic Express displays a blank form.

To add an existing form from another project, follow these steps:

1.   Choose Project ▸ Add Existing Item to display the Add Existing Item
     dialog box.

2. Hold down CTRL and click each of the form files you want to add, then click Add. Visual Basic Express adds the form(s) to your project.

To delete a form, follow these steps:

1. Choose View ▶ Solution Explorer. Visual Basic Express highlights the Solution Explorer window.
2. Right-click the form you want to delete. A pop-up menu appears.
3. Choose Delete. A dialog box appears, warning that if you delete the form file, you won't be able to retrieve it. Click OK to delete the form or click Cancel to keep it.

Displaying a Form

A Visual Basic program can consist of dozens of different forms. However, only the initial form created by Visual Basic will appear when your program runs; you must tell Visual Basic Express when to display any additional forms that you've created. A Visual Basic program can display a form at one or more of the following times:

- As the *first window* that allows the user to do something
- As *another window* that makes up your user interface and appears while your program runs

Displaying a Startup Form

If your program contains two or more forms, the first form, which Visual Basic Express automatically creates every time you create a new project, will appear first. You can designate a different form to appear first as follows:

1. Choose Project ▶ Properties. The Properties window appears for your project.
2. Click Application on the left side of the window then click the Startup Form list box and choose the name of the form you want to appear first when your program runs, as shown in Figure 10-1.
3. Click the Close box to make this Application Properties window go away.

Showing and Hiding a Form

If your program contains multiple forms, you'll need to write BASIC code to tell it when to display and remove the forms on the screen. The three BASIC commands to use for displaying and removing forms from the screen are: Show, Close, and Hide. (You'll learn more about writing BASIC code in Part IV of this book.)

To use one of these commands first specify the name of the form you want to show or hide followed by a command, like so: Form4.Show (which simply tells your program to display *Form4* on the screen). To remove a form from the screen and remove it from your computer's memory, use the Close command, like so: Form4.Close. To hide a form temporarily but still retain it in memory, use the Hide command like so: Form4.Hide.

By temporarily hiding a form, you can quickly display it again with the Show command. If you use the Close command and then use Show, your program may need a few seconds to load and then display the form. As a general rule, if speed is crucial, use the Hide command to remove a form from view. To prevent your program from gobbling up chunks of memory by hiding multiple forms, use Close instead.

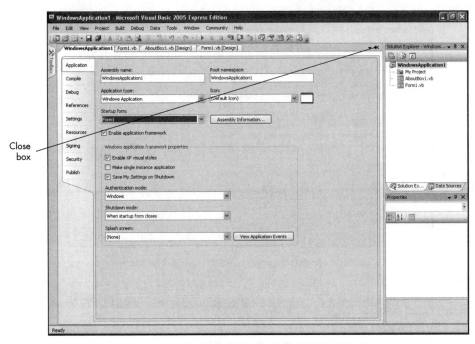

Close
box

Figure 10-1: The Startup Form list box lets you choose which form should appear when your program starts, such as the Form1.vb or the AboutBox1.vb file.

Hands-on Tutorial: Showing and Hiding a Form

Adding
Forms to a
Visual Basic
Project

This tutorial shows you how to use the Show and Close commands to create and display forms while your program runs.

1. Load Visual Basic Express, then press CTRL-N to display the New Project dialog box. Click OK to display a blank form.

2. Choose View ▶ Toolbox to display the Toolbox then choose Window ▶ Auto Hide to keep the Toolbox fixed in place. (Skip this step if a check mark does not appear in front of the Auto Hide command.)

3. Click the Button control in the Toolbox, mouse over the form, and left-click the mouse. A button control appears on your form.

4. Choose Project ▶ Add Windows Form. An Add New Item dialog box appears, as shown in Figure 10-2.

5. Click the About Box icon and then click Add. The AboutBox form appears, as shown in Figure 10-3.

6. Double-click the OK button in the bottom-right corner of the AboutBox form. The Code window appears. Near the bottom of the Code window, the command Me.Close tells your program to use the Close command to close the AboutBox form when the user clicks the OK button.

7. Click the Form1.vb [Design] tab. Your first form appears with the button control you created in step 3. Double-click the Button control to display the Code window.

Figure 10-2: The Add New Item dialog box lets you add a blank form or a variety of form templates.

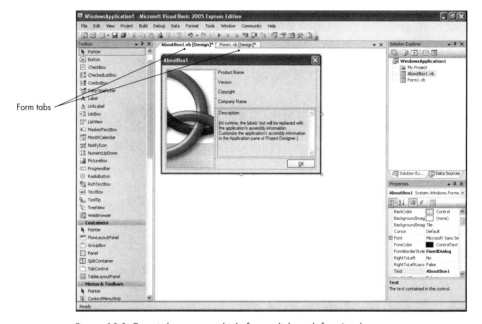

Figure 10-3: To switch among multiple forms click each form's tab.

8. Type **AboutBox1.Show()** in between the Private Sub and End Sub lines, like so:

```
Public Class Form1

    Private Sub Button1_Click(ByVal sender As System.Object, ByVal e As_
System.EventArgs) Handles_
Button1.Click
        AboutBox1.Show()
    End Sub
End Class
```

9. Press F5. *Form1* appears on the screen with a button. Click the button to run the AboutBox1.Show command you typed in step 8. The AboutBox form appears.

10. Click the OK button to run the Me.Close command that you viewed in step 6. The AboutBox form disappears.

11. Press ALT-F4 to stop your program from running, then choose File ▶ Close Project. A Close Project dialog box appears. Click Discard.

Defining a Form's Layout

By using the BASIC commands Show, Hide, and Close, you can make your program display and hide forms as it runs. If you change certain properties in the *Layout* category, you can also specify where on your screen you want a form to appear (such as in the middle of the screen or off to one side). You can also set the window's initial appearance (minimized, maximized, or normal) as well as both the extent to which a user can resize a form. Table 10-1 lists some of the more common properties you can modify.

Table 10-1: Common Properties for Modifying a Form

Property	What It Does
AutoSize	When set to True, the user cannot resize the form so that it hides any controls, such as buttons or text boxes.
FormBorderStyle	Defines the appearance of a form's title bar.
MaximizeBox	Displays (or hides) the maximize icon in the upper-right corner of the form.
MaximumSize	Defines the largest size (width and height) the form can be resized, even when the user clicks the maximize icon in the upper-right corner of the form.
MinimizeBox	Displays (or hides) the minimize icon in the upper-right corner of the form.
MinimumSize	Defines the smallest size (width and height) the form can be resized.
Opacity	Ranges in value from 100% (completely visible) to 0% (invisible). By entering values between 0 and 100, you can make a form and any controls on it appear transparent.
Size	Defines the initial width and height of a form. Both the Width and Height properties can be defined separately.
StartPosition	Defines the position on the screen where the window appears.
WindowState	Defines whether the form initially appears minimized, maximized, or normal, which is the size of the form defined by the Size property.

Defining the Position of a Form

To control where a form pops up on the screen, you define its StartPosition property. You have five options:

Manual   The form initially appears in the upper-left corner of the screen. Each time the user closes or hides the form, it reappears the next time in the last position in which it appeared before it was closed or hidden from view.

CenterScreen   Displays the form in the center of the screen.

WindowsDefaultLocation   Displays the form at the default location defined by Microsoft Windows.

WindowsDefaultBounds   Displays the form at the default location and size defined by Microsoft Windows.

CenterParent   Centers the form inside another form designated as the *parent* form.

To change the StartPosition property of a form, follow these steps:

1. Click the form you want to modify. Be sure to click only the form, not any controls displayed on it. You should see handles around your form.
2. Press F4 to open the Properties window.
3. Click the StartPosition property. A downward-pointing arrow appears.
4. Click the downward-pointing arrow. A pop-up menu with different options appears, as shown in Figure 10-4.
5. Click the option you want to use, such as Center-Parent or CenterScreen.

Figure 10-4: The StartPosition property displays a pop-up menu of different options.

Defining a Form's Controls

You have various additional ways to control the appearance of a form. Forms can display one or more of the following, as shown in Figure 10-5:

Control box   Appears as an icon to the left of the caption in the title bar. Clicking the control box displays a pull-down menu that gives you another way to resize, move, minimize, maximize, or close a window.

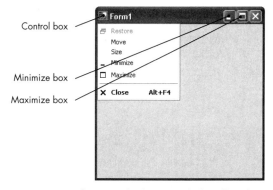

Minimize box   Minimizes a form so that it appears in the Windows Taskbar.

Maximize box   Maximizes a form to fills the screen.

Figure 10-5: A form can display controls that allow the user to adjust the size of a form while the program is running.

By default, the ControlBox, MinimizeBox, and MaximizeBox properties are set to True to display these controls on a form. To keep the user from minimizing or maximizing a form, set the value of MinimizeBox and MaximizeBox properties to False.

To change one or more of these properties, follow these steps:

1. Click the form you want to modify. Be sure to click only the form, not any controls displayed on it. You should see handles around your form.
2. Press F4 to open the Properties window then click the ControlBox, MinimizeBox, or MaximizeBox property in the Window Style category of the Properties window. A downward-pointing arrow appears. Click the arrow to display a pop-up menu.
3. Click True or False.

Defining a Form's Appearance

When a window initially appears on screen, it can appear in one of the following ways:

Minimized　As a button on the Windows Taskbar, usually at the bottom of the screen.

Normal　In the same size in which it was created. While Visual Basic Express creates every form the same size, you can resize the form or change its Size properties.

Maximized　The form fills the entire screen.

To change these properties, modify the WindowState property. By default, the WindowState property of every form is set to Normal. To change this property:

1. Click the form you want to modify. Be sure to click only the form, not any controls displayed on it. You should handles around your form.
2. Press F4 to open the Properties window then click the WindowState property in the Layout category of the Properties window. A downward-pointing arrow appears.
3. Click the arrow to display a pop-up menu, then, from the menu, select Normal, Minimized, or Maximized.

Defining a Form Size

The Size property lets you define both the form's width and height, although you can expand the Size property to display the Width and Height properties separately, as shown in Figure 10-6. Both Width and Height measure a form's size in pixels.

It's usually faster to resize a form by moving the mouse pointer over one edge or one corner of a form until the mouse pointer turns into a two-way arrow, then hold down the left mouse button and drag the mouse to resize your form. Once you define a form's initial size, you can use Width and Height to enter higher or lower values until the form is exactly the size you want.

To keep your form a certain minimum or maximum size, you can modify the MinimumSize and MaximumSize properties, which specify the minimum and maximum sizes a form can be resized. Both properties can be expanded in the Properties window to let you specify the minimum and maximum Width and Height properties separately. Or, you can set a form's AutoSize property to True, in which case the user can resize a form only to the extent that all controls on the form remain visible.

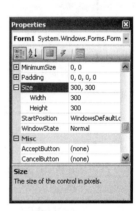

Figure 10-6: The Size property can expand to show the Width and Height properties separately.

To set the Width and Height values of the Size, MinimumSize, and MaximumSize:

1. Click the form you want to modify, clicking only the form, and not any controls displayed on it. You should see handles around your form.
2. Press F4 to open the Properties window then click the plus sign that appears to the left of the Size, MinimumSize, or MaximumSize property in the Layout category of the Properties window. The Properties window displays Width and Height properties under the parent property.
3. Click in the Width or Height property and enter a new value.

Making a Form Transparent

To create special effects, you can modify a form's Opacity property, which accepts values from 0 to 100. With an opacity value of 100, a form completely covers up anything it overlaps on the screen; with an opacity of 0, the form and any controls on it are invisible. By defining a value between 0 and 100, you can create forms that appear transparent, allowing items underneath to be visible through them. To change the Opacity:

1. Click the form you want to modify, clicking only the form, and not any controls displayed on it. You should see handles around your form.
2. Press F4 to open the Properties window then click the Opacity property in the Windows Style category of the Properties window.
3. Enter a value between 0 and 100. The next time your program runs, you should see the transparent effect on your form.

Aligning Controls on a Form

Aligning Controls on a Form

A form defines a window for your user interface, but you still need to fill it with *user interface controls*, such as buttons and text boxes. While you can place controls on a form haphazardly, it's usually best to align them. Figure 10-7 shows the difference between a user interface with aligned controls and one with controls placed haphazardly.

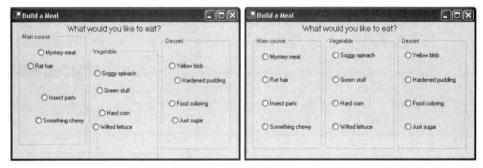

Figure 10-7: Aligning controls on a form can make your user interface look more professional, like the form on the right.

Visual Basic Express provides two ways to help you align your user interface controls:

Guides   Appear when you move controls near each other

Format menu   Contains commands to align multiple controls simultaneously

Using Guides

To help you align controls with one another on a form, Visual Basic Express automatically displays *horizontal* or *vertical guides* (also called *snaplines*) when you move one control in line with another, as shown in Figure 10-8. To view guides, follow these steps:

1. Mouse over a control. The mouse pointer turns into a four-way pointing arrow.
2. Hold down the left mouse button and drag the mouse near another control on the form. As soon as the two controls appear aligned horizontally or vertically, Visual Basic Express displays a respective horizontal or a vertical guide.
3. Release the left mouse button.

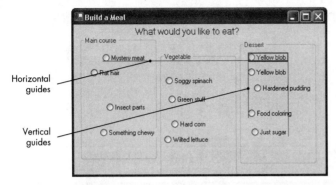

Horizontal guides

Vertical guides

Figure 10-8: When you move one control in line with another one, Visual Basic Express displays guides to help you align the two controls.

Aligning Controls with the Format Menu Commands

How about aligning three or more controls on a user interface? You could align them one at a time, but a faster way is to align them all simultaneously using the Format menu:

1. Click the control to which you want all the other controls to align. This control will stay in one place and never move.

2. Hold down SHIFT and click any other controls that you want to align with the control you clicked in step 1. Notice that each additional control you click appears with a black handle in its upper-left corner, as shown in Figure 10-9.

3. Choose Format ▶ Align. A pop-up menu appears.

4. Choose Lefts, Centers, Rights, Tops, Middles, or Bottoms, as shown in Figure 10-10. Visual Basic Express aligns your controls automatically, as shown in Figure 10-11.

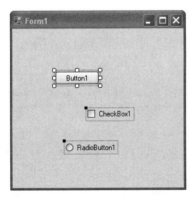

Figure 10-9: A black handle appears on any additional controls you click while holding down the SHIFT key.

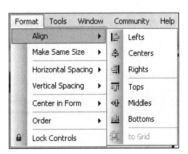

Figure 10-10: Choosing Format ▶ Align displays a submenu of additional options for aligning controls.

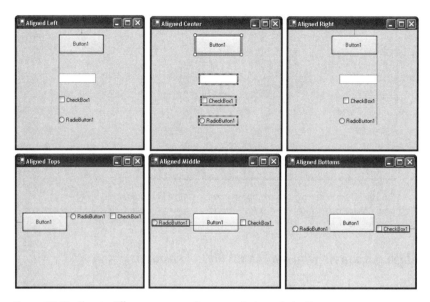

Figure 10-11: The six different ways to align controls through the Format menu

Resizing Controls

If your user interface needs to display two or more copies of the same control, you may want them to appear the same size. While you could enter the same values into each control's Size property, a faster way is to resize them automatically as follows:

1. Click a control, such as a button. This control won't change in size, but any additional controls you choose will resize to the width or height of this control.
2. Hold down the SHIFT key and click additional controls then choose Format ▶ Make Same Size. A pop-up menu appears.
3. Choose Width, Height, or Both (resizes both the width and height) to automatically resize all your chosen controls.

Grouping Controls

Rather than move controls individually, you can move them as a *group* to preserve the alignment of multiple controls with each other. To do so:

1. Click the first control you want to move to display handles around it.
2. Hold down SHIFT and click each additional control you want to move. Each time you select another control, Visual Basic Express displays handles around it.
3. Mouse over any of the controls you chose in step 1 or 2. The mouse pointer turns into a four-way pointing arrow.
4. Hold down the left mouse button and drag the mouse to move all your selected controls, then release the mouse button when you're happy with their position.
5. Click anywhere outside any of your selected controls to remove the handles from the controls you selected.

Locking Controls

Once you've aligned and placed controls on your user interface, you may want to lock them in place so you don't accidentally resize or move them. To lock a single control:

1. Click a control that you want to lock then press F4 to open the Properties window.
2. Click the Locked property in the Design category of the Properties window. A downward-pointing arrow appears. Click the arrow and a pop-up menu appears.
3. Click True or False.

If you want to lock multiple controls, it can be cumbersome to lock controls one by one. You can lock multiple controls simultaneously by following these steps:

1. Hold down SHIFT and click each control you want to lock.
2. Choose Format ▸ Lock Controls. An icon appears in the upper-left corner of each chosen control. In Figure 10-12, only one control has been locked.

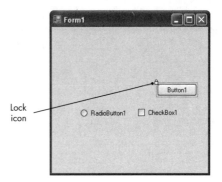

Figure 10-12: A lock icon appears on the control that's been locked.

To *unlock* all previously locked controls, choose Format ▸ Lock Controls again. Choosing the Format ▸ Lock Controls command on a control toggles the Locked property of all controls; so if you change the Locked property of a button to True and then choose Format ▸ Lock Controls, the Locked property of that button is now set to False.

KEY FEATURES TO REMEMBER

Forms define the windows that make up your program's user interface.

- You need to designate one form as the Startup form, which is the first form that appears when the user launches the program.
- You can use BASIC code to make forms appear and disappear while your program is running.
- By modifying a form's properties, you can modify the way the form appears on the screen when your program runs.
- Visual Basic Express provides guides to help you align controls on a form.
- You can lock controls in place to keep from accidentally modifying them.

PART III

GETTING AND DISPLAYING DATA ON A USER INTERFACE

11

WRITING EVENT PROCEDURES

Most Visual Basic programs display a user interface on the screen and then wait for the user to take some action. Once the user takes action, such as clicking a button, a pull-down menu command, or a check box, the program runs a short program called an *event procedure*, which tells the computer, step by step, how to respond to the user's action.

An *event* is something that the user does, such as click the mouse over a control, and a *procedure* is a term that programmers use to describe a short program. An event procedure is just a short program that tells the computer how to respond when the user interacts with a particular control.

When you initially create a user interface control, such as a button or a text box, that control contains empty event procedures that do nothing. To make a control do something, you need to write an event procedure—some code in the BASIC language—for every event to which you want the control to respond. Although each control can theoretically respond to dozens of different events, Table 11-1 lists the more common events that a user will likely perform.

Table 11-1: Common Events

Event	What happens
Click	The user clicks the mouse while pointing at a control.
CheckedChanged	The user clicks a radio button or check box.
SelectedIndexChanged	The user selects a choice displayed in a list or combo box.
TextChanged	The user edits text inside a text box.

When the user takes an action, your program tries to determine two things:

- What happened (what *event* occurred)?
- Where did it happen (which *control* was affected)?

Once your program determines this information, it looks for an event procedure to tell it what to do. The name of the event procedure is a combination of the control name and the event. For example, the following empty event procedure combines the name of the button control (*Button1*) that the user clicked with the event (*Click*), so the complete event procedure name is Button1_Click, as shown here:

```
Private Sub Button1_Click(ByVal sender As System.Object, ByVal e As_
System.EventArgs) Handles Button1.Click

End Sub
```

The BASIC code that makes up an empty event procedure consists of several parts:

Private Every form stores both controls and event procedures. Because it's possible to give identical names to controls stored on different forms, the Private keyword restricts your event procedure from running unless the user clicks a control stored in the same form as this event procedure.

Sub Short for *subprogram*, a term used for one of the small programs that make up a larger program. The Sub keyword identifies the beginning of a subprogram. All event procedures are considered subprograms.

Button1_Click This identifies the name of the event procedure, the name of a control, and the specific event that must occur to make this event procedure run the code stored in it. In the preceding code example, no BASIC code is stored in the event procedure, so clicking the Button1 control will do nothing.

(ByVal sender As System.Object, ByVal e As System.EventArgs) This contains BASIC code that retrieves information on what event occurred (stored in the e variable) and to which control it happened (stored in the sender variable). This BASIC code is solely for the computer to use; you can ignore this code when writing your own Visual Basic programs.

Handles Button1.Click This tells you what event this particular event procedure handles. In this case, the event procedure runs only when the user clicks a button named Button1.

End Sub This defines the end of your subprogram or event procedure.

Creating Event Procedures

You can create an event procedure in two ways:

- Double-click any control on your user interface.
- In the Code window, select both the name of a control and the event to which you want it to respond.

NOTE *Once you create an event procedure, you must still add BASIC code inside it to tell it to do something. When you were writing BASIC code in the sample program in Chapter 1, you were actually writing event procedures.*

Creating an Event Procedure by Double-Clicking

Every control, such as a button or text box, can respond to dozens of different types of events, such as a user clicking a control (the *Click* event), changing text inside of a control (the *TextChanged* event), or changing the background color of a control (the *BackColorChanged* event). However, most controls only need one or two likely events. For example, when most people see a button on the screen, they know they'll probably click it. For this reason, the most common event that a button control needs to respond to is the Click event.

When you create an event procedure by double-clicking a control, Visual Basic Express creates the most common event procedure for that particular control. To create the most common event procedure for a control, follow these steps:

1. Choose View ▸ Designer to open the Design window and display your program's user interface.
2. Double-click a control in your user interface. Visual Basic Express opens the Code window and creates an empty event procedure for your control. Figure 11-1 shows an event procedure that tells the computer how to respond when the user clicks a button named *Button1*. At this point, you'll need to add BASIC code inside the event procedure to make it do something.

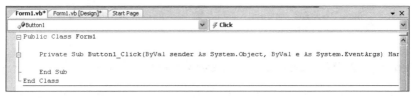

Figure 11-1: Double-clicking any control displays or creates an event procedure.

Creating Event Procedures for a Control

What if you need to create an event procedure that responds to a more obscure event, such as when the user presses a key or the mouse wheel? To create event procedures for less common events, follow these steps:

1. Choose View ▸ Code to display the Code window then click the Class Name list box and click the name of a control, as shown in Figure 11-2.

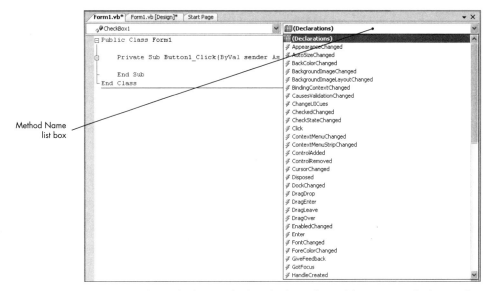

Figure 11-2: The Class Name list box displays the names of all controls displayed on a form.

2. Click the Method Name list box and click an event to which you want the control to respond (see Figure 11-3). Visual Basic Express creates an empty event procedure for your chosen control and event. At this point, you need to add BASIC code to make this event procedure do something.

Figure 11-3: The Method Name list box displays all possible events to which your chosen control can respond.

Writing BASIC Code into an Event Procedure

Until you type BASIC code into an event procedure, the procedure won't do anything in response to an event. You can add code inside an event procedure in three ways:

- Use prewritten code snippets.
- Type commands using the Visual Basic language.
- Combine these two methods by copying a code snippet into an event procedure and then modifying it with additional commands.

NOTE *At the simplest level, an event procedure can contain a single BASIC command.*

Using Code Snippets

To make programming as easy as possible, Visual Basic Express provides a library of prewritten *code snippets* which contain BASIC code to accomplish a specific task, such as calculating a mathematical result or accessing a file stored on your hard disk. Table 11-2 lists the library categories of code snippets available.

Table 11-2: Available Code Snippet Libraries

Library name	Examples of code snippets
Connectivity and Networking	Connects to a local area network (LAN) or the Internet; sends email
Creating Windows Forms Applications	Stores and retrieves data from the clipboard, plays sound, manipulates forms, stores and retrieves data from controls
Interacting with the Application	Accesses user settings, captures output from a console application, clears a console window
Maintaining Collections	Creates and manages different variations of collection data structures such as stacks, queues, and lists
Math	Calculates mathematical results such as trigonometric equations or interest payments
Processing Drives, Folders, and Files	Creates, copies, deletes, or determines whether a file exists
Visual Basic Language	Creates empty loops, If-Then statements, and other types of common programming statements
Working with Data Types	Converts numbers into a string; string manipulation
Working with XML	Manipulates and reads data stored in XML format

To insert a code snippet into an event procedure, follow these steps:

1. Right-click where you want to paste the code snippet in an event procedure, then click Insert Snippet. A list of code snippet library folders appears (Figure 11-4).

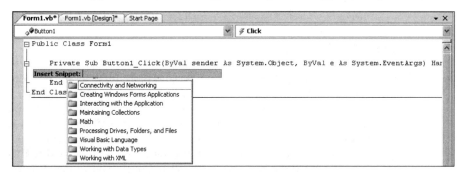

Figure 11-4: Visual Basic Express organizes code snippets into categories.

2. Double-click the library you want to use, such as Math or Interacting with the Application. A list of code snippets appears, as shown in Figure 11-5.

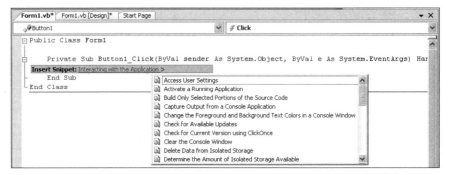

Figure 11-5: Once you double-click a library folder, you can double-click the code snippet you want to use.

NOTE *If you double-click some folders, such as Creating Windows Forms Applications or Maintaining Collections, you'll need to double-click a list of additional folders before you'll see any code snippets from which to choose.*

3. Double-click the code snippet you want to use. Visual Basic Express inserts your chosen code snippet into the event procedure and highlights part of the code snippet, as shown in Figure 11-6. At this point, you need to modify the highlighted part of the code snippet to customize the code for your program.

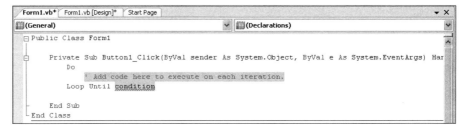

Figure 11-6: Highlighting shows you what part of the code snippet you'll need to customize.

Using BASIC Commands

Code snippets make programming faster and more reliable, since you're using proven code. However, Visual Basic Express, can't possibly provide all the code snippets that your program might need. As a result, you'll need to write some commands yourself.

The Visual Basic language is like a spoken language, such as English, Spanish, or Arabic. By stringing together words in any language, you can communicate a thought or an idea. It's the same with computer programming; by stringing together "words" from a programming language such as Visual Basic, you can create instructions for a computer to follow.

Just as human languages contain words, Visual Basic includes many *commands*. You can combine these commands in different ways to have your computer perform different tasks, from displaying a dialog box to calculating mathematical results. Table 11-3 lists some of the built-in commands available in the Visual Basic language.

Table 11-3: Some of the Built-in Commands in Visual Basic

Visual Basic command	What it does
Beep	Plays a single beep through the computer speaker
CStr	Converts a number into a string
End	Stops and exits the program
FileCopy	Copies a file
Len	Counts the number of characters in a string
MsgBox	Displays a message box with text in it
NPer	Calculates the number of payment periods needed based on both fixed periodic payments and a fixed interest rate
Rnd	Generates a random number
StrComp	Compares two strings to determine whether they're equal
TimeofDay	Returns or sets the current time on the computer clock
Today	Returns the current date

The End command is one of the more important BASIC commands, because you can use it to tell your program to exit and stop running, such as:

```
Private Sub Button1_Click(ByVal sender As System.Object, ByVal e As_
System.EventArgs) Handles Button1.Click
    End
End Sub
```

NOTE *Although users can always exit out of your program by clicking the close box of your program's user interface, it's usually better to provide an Exit command that users can choose, such as through an Exit or Quit command in a File pull-down menu or a button that users can click, clearly marked Exit or Quit.*

Hands-on Tutorial: Writing BASIC Commands

This tutorial shows you how to write BASIC code inside an event procedure.

1. Load Visual Basic Express and press CTRL-N to display the New Project dialog box. Click OK.
2. Choose View ▸ Toolbox to display the Toolbox, then choose Window ▸ Auto Hide to keep the Toolbox visible at all times.
3. Click the Button control in the Toolbox, mouse over the form, and click the left mouse button to create a button control on the form.
4. Repeat step 3 to create a second button control on the form.
5. Double-click the button control with the word *Button1* on it. The Code window appears, showing an empty event procedure for Button1.

6. Type `MsgBox ("Wipe out life on this planet in the name of profits?")` inside the event procedure, as shown here:

```
Private Sub Button1_Click(ByVal sender As System.Object, ByVal e As_
System.EventArgs) Handles Button1.Click
    MsgBox("Wipe out life on this planet in the name of profits?")
End Sub
```

7. Click in the Class Name list box in the Code window and choose Button2, as shown in Figure 11-7.

Figure 11-7: The Class Name list box lets you choose a control by name.

8. Click in the Method Name list box in the Code window and choose Click, as shown in Figure 11-8. Visual Basic Express creates an empty event procedure for Button2 in the Code window.

Figure 11-8: The Method Name list box lets you choose an event to go along with your control name to create a new empty event procedure.

9. Type `End` in this event procedure, like so:

```
Private Sub Button2_Click(ByVal sender As System.Object, ByVal e As_
System.EventArgs) Handles Button2.Click
    End
End Sub
```

10. Press F5. Your user interface appears with *Button1* and *Button2* on the form. Click Button1 to run the `Button1_Click` event procedure, which you created in step 6, and runs the `MsgBox` command to display the message *Wipe out life on this planet in the name of profits?* as shown in Figure 11-9.

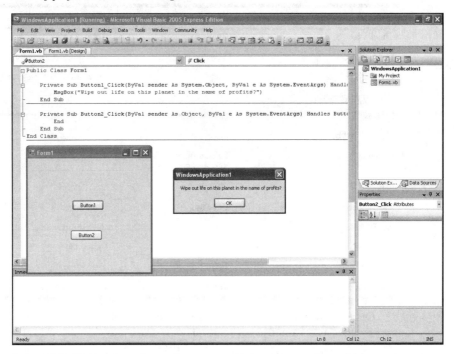

Figure 11-9: Clicking *Button1* runs the `Button1_Click` event procedure, which runs the `MsgBox` command.

11. Click OK in the message box to make it go away.

12. Click Button2 to run the `Button2_Click` event procedure, which you created in step 9, and runs the `End` command, which stops your program from running.

13. Choose File ▶ Close Project. A Close Project dialog box appears. Click Discard.

Retrieving Data from the User Interface

The whole purpose of any computer program is to get *data*, manipulate it, and then return some sort of *result*. A word processor accepts text as data, formats and checks your spelling, and then spits it out as a neatly printed document. A computer game accepts data in the form of a game controller or mouse movements, and based on the position of the cursor, displays different images on the screen such as a car driving off the road or a gun shooting at a monster.

Most event procedures get data from one or more user interface controls, such as text the user types into a text box, a radio button the user clicks to make a selection, or the mouse movement of dragging a scroll box's scroll bars. When a user's action provides data to a control, that control stores the data in one of its *properties*. For example, a text box stores data in its *Text* property, while a radio button and a check box store data in the *Checked* property.

Table 11-4 lists some user interface controls that accept data and shows where they store this information in specific properties.

Table 11-4: Properties That Store Control Information

Control	Property name	Data stored
Check box	Checked	True or False
Combo box	SelectedItem	Any string stored in the Items property
Combo box	Text	Any string that the user types in
Date/Time picker	Value	Date
List box	SelectedItem	Any string stored in the Items property
Masked text box	InputText	Any string
Month calendar	SelectionRange.Start and SelectionRange.End	Date
Numeric up down	Value	Any integer
Radio button	Checked	True or False
RichTextBox	Text	Any string
Scroll bars (horizontal and vertical)	Value	Any integer
Text box	Text	Any string
Track bar	Value	Any integer

Once the user stores data in a user control, you'll need to write BASIC code to retrieve that data from the control's property. You can either manipulate the control property directly or copy the data out of the control's property.

Hands-on Tutorial: Getting Data from a Control

Because your user interface will likely allow users to type or choose items, this tutorial shows you how to use BASIC code and properties to display information on your user interface and retrieve information that the user has input.

1. Load Visual Basic Express and press CTRL-N to display the New Project dialog box, then click OK to display a blank form.
2. Choose View ▶ Toolbox to display the Toolbox, then choose Window ▶ Auto Hide to keep the Toolbox visible at all times. (Skip this step if a check mark does not appear in front of the Auto Hide command.)
3. Click the Button control in the Toolbox, mouse over the form, and click the left mouse button to draw a button control on the form.
4. Click the TextBox control in the Toolbox, mouse over the form, and click the left mouse button to draw a text box on the form.
5. Double-click the Button1 control. The Code window appears.

6. Type **Button1.Text = TextBox1.Text** inside the event procedure, as follows:

```
Private Sub Button1_Click(ByVal sender As System.Object, ByVal e As_
System.EventArgs) Handles Button1.Click
      Button1.Text = TextBox1.Text
End Sub
```

7. Click the Class Name list box in the Code window and click KeyPress to create a Button1_KeyPress event procedure.

8. Type **End** inside this event procedure, like so:

```
Private Sub Button1_KeyPress(ByVal sender As Object, ByVal e As_
System.Windows.Forms.KeyPressEventArgs) Handles Button1.KeyPress
         End
End Sub
```

9. Pres F5. Your user interface appears.

10. Click the text box and type a word or two.

11. Click the Button1 control. Notice that whatever you typed in the text box in step 10 now appears inside the button because of the BASIC code you created in step 6.

12. Press any key. Your program stops running because of the End command you wrote in the Button1_KeyPress event procedure in step 8.

13. Choose File ▶ Close Project. A Close Project dialog box appears. Click Discard.

KEY FEATURES TO REMEMBER

Event procedures are miniature programs (procedures) that run when something happens (an event) to a user interface control. An event is a specific action taken by the user, such as clicking the mouse or pressing a key.

- The name of every event procedure consists of the control name and the event that occurs.
- Code snippets contain prewritten BASIC code to accomplish specific tasks.
- The Visual Basic language contains hundreds of built-in commands for accomplishing specific tasks, such as calculating interest payments, displaying dialog boxes, or retrieving the current date and time.
- Every Visual Basic program needs at least one event procedure that contains nothing but the End command. That way, the user can stop and exit the program.
- You can create an event procedure by double-clicking it or by choosing the name of a control in the Class Name list box and then choosing an event in the Method Name list box.
- You can create dozens of different event procedures for each control, although most controls need only one or two event procedures.
- Most user interface controls can retrieve and store information from the user in different properties, such as the Text or Value property.

12

DISPLAYING COMMANDS IN BUTTONS AND MENUS

Every program needs to provide *commands* that the user can choose to tell it what to do next. To display a command to the user, most programs use either buttons, pull-down menus, or ToolStrips.

Most programs use *buttons* to display a limited number of available commands, such as a dialog box that asks *Do you really want to delete this file?* and then offers two possible commands: Yes and No.

But while buttons make commands easy to find, only a limited number of buttons can appear at any given time before the user interface gets too cluttered. To display all possible commands, most programs use *pull-down menus* organized into categories such as File, Edit, Tools, and Window.

To provide fast access to commonly used commands, many programs also include icons or buttons stored in toolbars, or what Visual Basic Express calls a *ToolStrip*. ToolStrips can display commands as text, icons, or both. Figure 12-1 shows how commands can appear as buttons, pull-down menus, and ToolStrips on a user interface.

NOTE *After you create and display commands on your user interface through buttons, menus, or ToolStrips, you need to write BASIC code to make these controls do something. You'll learn about this later in the chapter.*

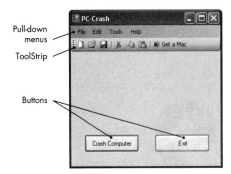

Pull-down menus

ToolStrip

Buttons

Figure 12-1: You can display commands to the user through buttons, menus, or ToolStrips.

Using Buttons

Buttons are a simple way to display commands on the user interface. Once you've drawn a button on a form, the two most important parts of the button to consider are:

The Text property   Displays the command name you want to display on the button

The Click event procedure   The BASIC code you write to make your program run the command displayed on the button

To make a button more noticeable, you can access the Properties window and change both the FlatStyle property and the MouseOverBackColor property, which is part of the FlatAppearance property. When the FlatStyle property is set to Flat, and the user mouses over the button, the button will change to the color specified by the MouseOverBackColor property. Figure 12-2 shows how the Text, FlatStyle, and MouseOverBackColor properties define a button's appearance.

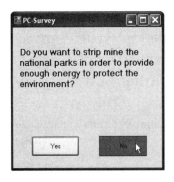

Figure 12-2: The Text property defines what appears on a button, and the FlatStyle and MouseOverBackColor properties work together to change a button's color when the mouse pointer moves over it.

Creating Pull-Down Menus

Creating Pull-Down Menus

Buttons are useful for displaying a limited number of commands, but when more than a handful of commands are available, those commands are often stored in pull-down menus. You can create two types of pull-down menus:

- Generic pull-down menus that can be modified
- Pull-down menus created from scratch

Because most programs need to offer commonly used commands, such as Cut, Copy, and Paste, Visual Basic Express can automatically create *generic pull-down menus* for these functions. All you have to do is customize them with additional commands.

Menu titles appear in the *menu bar* at the top of pull-down menus and display the different categories of commands available, such as File, Edit, View, and Help. *Menu commands* appear directly underneath each specific menu title, such as the commands Cut, Copy, and Paste that usually appear on the Edit menu.

Creating Generic Pull-Down Menus

To create generic pull-down menus, follow these steps:

1. Double-click the MenuStrip control (under the Menus & Toolbars category in the Toolbox) to display a MenuStrip control under the currently displayed form and a blank pull-down menu at the top of the form (Figure 12-3).

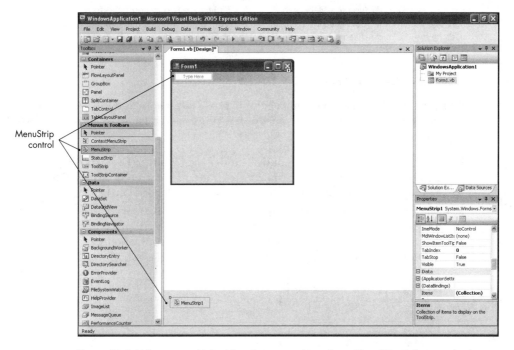

Figure 12-3: When you add the MenuStrip control to a form, Visual Basic Express displays a blank pull-down menu at the top of the form.

2. Right-click the MenuStrip control at the top of your form. (Be sure to right-click away from the Type Here text box.) A pop-up menu appears (Figure 12-4).

3. Click Insert Standard Items. Visual Basic Express automatically creates generic pull-down menus in a menu bar across the top of the currently displayed form, as shown in Figure 12-5. You can now add, delete, or rearrange each pull-down menu to customize it.

Figure 12-4: Right-clicking the MenuStrip control on your form displays a pop-up menu with the Insert Standard Items command.

Figure 12-5: A generic pull-down menu bar contains the typical commands found in File, Edit, Tools, and Help menus.

Creating a Pull-Down Menu from Scratch

While it's usually easier to create a generic pull-down menu and then modify it later, you may want to create your own pull-down menu from scratch so you don't have to edit a generic one. To do so:

1. Double-click the MenuStrip control (under the Menus & Toolbars category in the Toolbox) to display a MenuStrip control under the currently displayed form and a blank pull-down menu at the top of the form (see Figure 12-3).

2. Click in the pull-down menu Type Here text box, and enter the name of the first menu title you want, such as File. You should see new Type Here text boxes on the menu bar at the right of the last menu item, and at the bottom of the pull-down menu (see Figure 12-6).

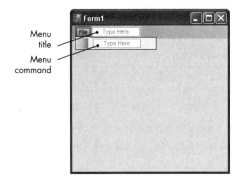

Figure 12-6: Once you enter your first menu title, Visual Basic Express displays text boxes where you can enter additional menu titles or commands.

3. Click in one of the Type Here text boxes, enter an appropriate menu title or command, and press ENTER.

4. Repeat step 3 for each menu title or command you want to create.

Editing Pull-Down Menus and Commands

Editing
Pull-Down
Menus

Once you've created pull-down menu titles, you may need to add new menu titles or commands or delete existing ones. For even fancier effects, you can add shortcut keys and icons to menu commands.

Deleting a Menu Title or Command

To delete a menu title or command:

1. Click the menu title or command you want to delete. Visual Basic Express highlights the chosen menu title or command. *Warning: If you delete a menu title, such as File or Edit, you'll also delete any commands that appear under that menu title.*
2. Right-click the highlighted menu title or command. A pop-up menu appears.
3. Click Delete.

   If you accidentally delete a menu title or command, you can retrieve it right away if you choose Edit ▶ Undo.

Adding a Menu Title

To add a new menu title to the menu bar:

1. Click a menu title. Visual Basic Express displays a Type Here text box at the far right of the menu bar, to the right of all the existing menu titles.
2. Click in the Type Here text box, enter a menu title, and press ENTER.
3. Repeat step 2 for each menu title you want to add.

Adding a Menu Command

To add a menu command:

1. Click the menu title where you want to add a new command. Visual Basic Express displays a Type Here text box at the bottom of the pull-down menu.
2. In the Type Here text box, enter a new menu command, and press ENTER.
3. Repeat step 2 for each additional command you want to add.

Adding a Submenu

While menu titles appear at the top of the pull-down menus and display the different categories of commands available, and menu commands appear directly under a specific menu title, *submenus* appear to the right of a menu command after it is clicked, as shown in Figure 12-7. To add a submenu:

1. Click a menu title where you want to add a submenu. Visual Basic Express displays the pull-down menu.
2. Click the command to which you want to add the submenu. Visual Basic Express displays a Type Here text box to the right of the chosen command, as shown in Figure 12-8.
3. Click in the Type Here text box and enter a command that will appear in the submenu, then press ENTER. Visual Basic Express displays another Type Here text box directly below that one.

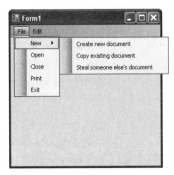

Figure 12-7: A submenu appears when the user clicks a menu command with an arrow next to it.

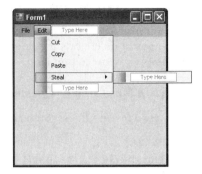

Figure 12-8: When you click a menu command, a Type Here text box appears to the right so you can create a submenu.

4.   Click in the new Type Here text box, and enter another command that will appear in your submenu, then press ENTER.

5.   Repeat step 4 for each additional command you want to add to the submenu.

NOTE   *You don't have to write BASIC code to make the menu command (that contains a submenu) work, because all it does is display a submenu on the screen.*

You can use submenus to hide commands so that they don't clutter up your user interface. While many programs may display submenus, submenus rarely display submenus within other submenus. Figure 12-9 shows submenus buried within other submenus; not a pretty sight.

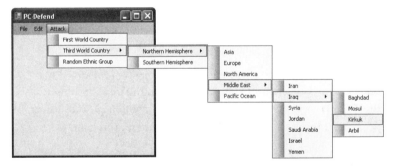

Figure 12-9: Burying submenus within submenus can make your program more difficult to use.

Editing Menu Titles and Commands

If you misspell a menu title or command name, you can always edit it later by editing and typing a new or modified title or command directly in the pull-down menu. To edit a menu title or command directly in the pull-down menu:

1.   Click the menu title you want to edit. To edit a menu command, click a menu title to display its list of menu commands, and then click the command you want to edit. Visual Basic Express highlights the chosen menu title or command.

2.   Click the highlighted menu title or command again. Visual Basic displays the chosen menu title or command highlighted in a text box. You can now edit the menu title or command directly in the menu or follow the next step.

3. Press F4 to open the Properties window then click in the Text property to edit the text.

Defining Hot Keys for Menu Titles and Menu Commands

Most users access pull-down menus with a mouse, but you can make commands on the pull-down menu *keyboard accessible*, especially for users who rely on keyboards more than a mouse and for users with disabilities that prevent them from using a mouse. A *hot key* provides a way to access a menu title or command via the keyboard.

If you look at most programs, the File menu shows the letter *F* underlined, and the Edit menu shows the letter *E* underlined. The underlined menu title means that you can access that menu's commands (that is, open the pull-down menu) by pressing the ALT key plus the underlined letter. So, for example, if you wanted to access the File menu, you would press ALT-F. If you wanted to access the Edit menu, you would press ALT-E.

While menu *title* hot keys let you display their pull-down menus by pressing the ALT key plus the underlined letter in the menu title, menu *command* hot keys let you choose a specific menu command just by typing the underlined letter, as long as the corresponding pull-down menu is open. For example, you can press ALT-E to open the Edit menu of most programs; in the menu, you'll see the Cut and Copy commands, with the underlined letters *t* and *C*; these represent the hot keys you press to access each command.

NOTE   *Don't confuse menu command hot keys with shortcut keys. You can use a menu command hot key only once you've displayed the menu on which your chosen command appears. Shortcut keys, such as CTRL-X for Cut or CTRL-V for Paste, allow you to choose a command without using the pull-down menus at all. You'll learn about shortcut keys in the section "Making Shortcut Keys" on page 147.*

For example, to choose the Copy command in the Edit menu, you could do the following, without involving the mouse:

1. Press ALT-E to display the Edit pull-down menu.
2. Type **C** to choose the Copy command.

As you're creating menu titles and commands, you can create hot keys for them by typing the *ampersand* character (&) in front of the letter that you want to turn into a hot key. For example, to turn the letter *F* into a hot key for the File menu title, you would type **&File** into the Type Here text box. To turn the letter *t* into a hot key for the Cut command, you would type **Cu&t** into the Type Here text box.

You can type the ampersand character while creating a menu title or command, or you can add it to a menu title or command by editing it after you've created it (see the preceding section, "Editing Menu Titles and Commands" on page 144).

Rearranging Menu Titles and Commands

Once you've created menu titles and commands, you may want to rearrange their positions on the menu bar or on the specific drop-down menu. To rearrange a menu title on the menu bar, follow these steps:

1. Mouse over the menu title you want to move, such as Edit, File, or Help.
2. Hold down the left mouse button and drag the mouse over another menu title. Visual Basic Express will move your chosen menu title to the left of the second

menu title. The mouse pointer displays a box under the mouse pointer to let you know that you are moving a menu title, as shown in Figure 12-10.

3. Release the mouse button.

Figure 12-10: Moving a menu title involves dragging a menu title to a new location on the pull-down menu bar.

To rearrange a menu command under a menu title, follow these steps:

1. Click the menu title that contains the menu command you want to move. The pull-down menu appears.

2. Move the mouse pointer over the menu command you want to move.

3. Hold down the left mouse button and drag the mouse over another menu command; Visual Basic Express displays a box around this menu command. Visual Basic Express will move your chosen menu command (the one you chose in step 1) *above* the menu command you highlight in this step.

4. Release the left mouse button to move the chosen command.

Adding Extra Features to a Pull-Down Menu

While most people are happy with default pull-down menus and commands, you may want to customize yours to make them look more professional, to better organize them, or to make them more accessible. For example, you may want to display menu commands with icons, display separator bars between menu commands, or display shortcut keys for choosing specific menu commands.

Adding Separator Bars

If you include a large number of commands in a pull-down menu, consider using *separator bars* to group related commands (see Figure 12-11). To create separator bars in a pull-down menu:

1. Click the MenuStrip control at the top of the displayed form.

2. Click the menu title where you want to add the separator bars to display your menu titles.

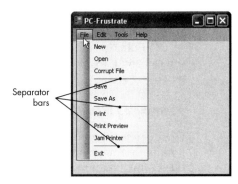

Separator bars

Figure 12-11: Separator bars can group related commands together.

3. Highlight a menu command with your mouse. Your separator bar will appear over this menu command.

4. Right-click the mouse. A pop-up menu appears (Figure 12-12).

5. Click Insert. A submenu appears.

6. Click Separator. Visual Basic Express displays a separator bar over the menu command you chose in step 3.

Making Shortcut Keys

Using pull-down menus can often get cumbersome if you're choosing the same commands repeatedly. To provide a faster way to access menu commands, many programs assign shortcut keys to commonly used commands. For example, in many programs, users can press CTRL-N to choose the New command, CTRL-O to choose the Open command, and CTRL-P to choose the Print command.

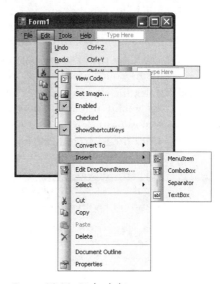

Figure 12-12: Right-clicking on a menu command displays a pop-up menu.

You can assign *shortcut key combinations* to any commands that users are most likely to need. To assign shortcut keys for a menu command, follow these steps:

1. Click the MenuStrip control at the top of the displayed form.

2. Open the Properties window by choosing View ▶ Properties Window, then click the Items property. An ellipsis button appears.

3. Click the ellipsis button. An Items Collection Editor window appears as shown in Figure 12-13.

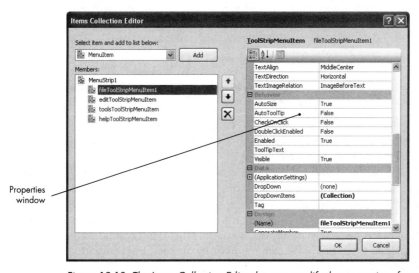

Properties window

Figure 12-13: The Items Collection Editor lets you modify the properties of your pull-down menus.

4. Click the name of the menu title that contains the command to which you want to assign a shortcut key. For example, to add a shortcut key to a command in a menu named FileToolStripMenuItem, you would click that menu title.

5. Click the DropDownItems property that appears in the Properties window of the Items Collections Editor. An ellipsis button appears.

6. Click the ellipsis button. The Items Collection Editor displays a list of all the menu commands displayed under the chosen menu title. Click a menu command to which you want to assign a shortcut key.

7. Click the ShortcutKeys property located under the Misc category of the Properties window in the Items Collection Editor. A downward-pointing arrow appears.

8. Click the downward-pointing arrow. A window appears with checkboxes for choosing the CTRL, SHIFT, or ALT modifier key plus a Key list box to choose a character, as shown in Figure 12-14.

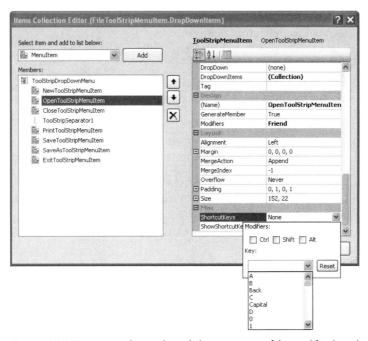

Figure 12-14: To create a shortcut key, click one or more of the modifier key check boxes and then choose a character.

9. Click one or more of the modifier check boxes. (If you click two or more check boxes, such as the CTRL and SHIFT check boxes, the user will have to hold down *both* modifier keys to use your shortcut.)

10. Click in the Key list box and choose a key. To create the shortcut key CTRL-P, for example, click the CTRL check box and choose the letter *P* in the Key list box.

11. Click OK. You may need to click OK twice to close the Items Collection Editor. The next time you run your program, you should see your shortcut key displayed on the pull-down menu. Users can now select the menu command either by clicking the command on the pull-down menu or by pressing the shortcut key combination you created.

NOTE   *You cannot assign the same shortcut key to two different menu commands.*

Adding Check Marks

A menu command may be used to toggle an item on or off. For example, a word processor might display a check mark next to a command to show that the command is currently active, as shown in Figure 12-15. To add a check mark to a menu command:

1. Click the MenuStrip control at the top of the currently displayed form.

2. Open the Properties window by choosing View ▸ Properties Window, then click the Items property. An ellipsis button appears.

3. Click the ellipsis button. An Items Collection Editor window appears (see Figure 12-13).

4. Click the name of the menu title containing the command to which you want to add a check mark. For example, to add a check mark to a menu named EditToolStripMenuItem, click EditToolStripMenuItem.

Figure 12-15: A menu command can display check marks to toggle a command on or off.

5. Click the DropDownItems property that appears in the Properties window of the Items Collections Editor. An ellipsis button appears.

6. Click the ellipsis button. The Items Collection Editor displays a list of all the menu commands displayed under the chosen menu title. Click a menu command for which you want to display a check mark.

7. Click the CheckOnClick property in the Behavior category of the Properties window. A downward-pointing arrow appears. Choose True to display a check mark or False to hide a check mark (Figure 12-16).

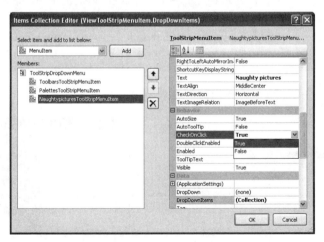

Figure 12-16: The CheckOnClick property lets a menu command display (True) or hide (False) a check mark.

8. Click OK. You may have to click OK twice to close the Items Collection Editor. The next time you run your program, you'll be able to click the menu command you chose in step 4 and toggle a check mark on and off.

Adding Icons

Many programs allow users to choose a command either from the pull-down menu or from a toolbar, which Visual Basic Express calls the *ToolStrip*. To save space, most toolbars display commands as icons. To help users learn which command each toolbar icon represents, that same icon often appears next to the corresponding command in a pull-down menu. Figure 12-17 shows how icons look when displayed next to menu commands.

Next to the Save command on some programs, you'll see an icon of a floppy disk which also appears on a toolbar. By displaying the same icon on both the toolbar and pull-down menu, users can choose either to invoke the Save command. To add an icon to a pull-down menu command:

Figure 12-17: Icons can appear next to menu commands.

1. Click the MenuStrip control at the top of the currently displayed form then open the Properties window choosing View ▸ Properties Window.

2. Click the Items property then click the ellipsis button that appears. An Items Collection Editor window appears (see Figure 12-13).

3. Click the name of the menu title that contains the command to which you want to add an icon.

4. Click the DropDownItems property that appears in the Properties window in the Items Collections Editor then click the ellipsis button that appears. The Items Collection Editor displays a list of all the menu commands displayed under your chosen menu title. Click the menu command for which you want to display an icon.

5. Click the Image property in the Appearance category of the Properties window, then click the ellipsis button that appears. A Select Resource dialog box appears.

6. Click Import. An Open dialog box appears.

7. Click the graphics files you want to use and click Open. (You may need to change drives and folders to find the graphics files you want.) Your chosen graphical image appears in the Select Resource dialog box, as shown in Figure 12-18.

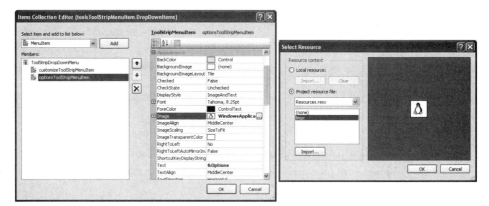

Figure 12-18: The Select Resource dialog box displays your chosen graphical image.

NOTE *If the graphical image you choose is too large, only a portion of the image will appear next to the pull-down menu command.*

8. Click OK to close the Select Resource dialog box. Click OK. You may have to click OK twice to close the Items Collection Editor.

If you create a ToolStrip to display commonly used commands (see the section "Making a ToolStrip" on page 152), use the same icon on your ToolStrip that you use in your pull-down menus. That way, users can associate a particular icon with a specific command, such as a printer icon that represents the Print command in a pull-down menu and in a ToolStrip.

Hands-on Tutorial: Creating Pull-Down Menus

Pull-down menus look nice, but they won't help users do anything until you write BASIC code to make them work. This tutorial guides you through creating a simple pull-down menu and adding BASIC code to it.

1. Load Visual Basic Express, then press CTRL-N to display the New Project dialog box. Click OK to display a blank form.
2. Choose View ▸ Toolbox to display the Toolbox, then choose Window ▸ Auto Hide to keep the Toolbox visible. (If no check mark appears in front of the Auto Hide command, you can skip this step.)
3. Double-click the MenuStrip located in the Menus & Toolbars category of the Toolbox to display the MenuControl at the top of the form and under the form as well.
4. Click in the Type Here text box on the MenuControl near the top of the form, and type **File**.
5. Click in the Type Here text box directly under the File menu title, type **Message**, and press ENTER.
6. Click in the Type Here text box directly under the Message command, type **Exit**, and press ENTER. Your pull-down menu should look like Figure 12-19.
7. Double-click the Message command that you created in step 5. (You may need to click the File menu first to display the Message command in the pull-down menu.) The Code window appears.
8. Type `MsgBox ("This message appears when you click the Message command.")` between the `Private Sub` and `End Sub` lines, as shown here:

Figure 12-19: Creating a pull-down menu with two commands.

```
Private Sub MessageToolStripMenuItem_Click(ByVal sender As System.Object, ByVal e As_
System.EventArgs) Handles MessageToolStripMenuItem.Click
        MsgBox("This message appears when you click the Message command.")
End Sub
```

9. Click the Class Name list box and choose ExitToolStripMenuItem, as shown in Figure 12-20.

Figure 12-20: The Class Name list box provides a quick way to choose another menu command to create an event procedure.

10. Click the Method Name list box and choose Click. The Code window creates an empty event procedure for the ExitToolStripMenuItem.

11. Type **End** between the `Private Sub` and `End Sub` lines, as shown here:

```
Private Sub ExitToolStripMenuItem_Click(ByVal sender As Object, ByVal e As_
System.EventArgs) Handles ExitToolStripMenuItem.Click
        End
End Sub
```

12. Press F5 to display your user interface with the pull-down menus you created.

13. Click the File menu to display the File pull-down menu, then click Message to run the `MsgBox` command that you typed in step 8. Click OK to make it go away.

14. Choose File ▶ Exit to stop your program, then choose File ▶ Close Project. (Be sure to click the File menu of the Visual Basic Express user interface and not the File menu of your program.) A Close Project dialog box appears. Click Discard.

Making a ToolStrip

Creating ToolStrips

A *ToolStrip* is a Visual Basic Express term for a toolbar that displays the most commonly used commands in a program. A ToolStrip can display eight types of items, as shown in Figure 12-21:

Buttons   Displays a graphical image as an icon.

Text   Displays a word or a phrase that the user can click.

Split buttons   Displays a downward-pointing arrow that can display a pop-up menu of additional commands.

Drop-down buttons   Displays a downward-pointing arrow that can display a pop-up menu of additional commands. Drop-down buttons are similar to split buttons but when your program runs, a Split button displays a vertical line between its icon and its downward-pointing arrow while a Drop-down button does not.

Separator bars   Displays a vertical line so you can group related ToolStrip commands. Separator bars are purely aesthetic and cannot be clicked by the user.

Combo boxes   Displays a list of options from which the user can choose, and allows the user to enter text instead.

Text boxes   Allows the user to enter text.

Progress bar   Displays a line of vertical green bars that moves from left to right to indicate the progress of a task.

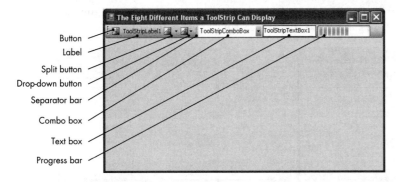

Button
Label
Split button
Drop-down button
Separator bar
Combo box
Text box
Progress bar

Figure 12-21: A ToolStrip can display eight different items.

NOTE *Once you create a ToolStrip, you still need to write BASIC code to make your ToolStrip items work.*

To create a ToolStrip, follow these steps:

1. Double-click the ToolStrip control under the Menus & Toolbars category of the Toolbox to display a ToolStrip control at the bottom of the screen and at the top of the currently displayed form, as shown in Figure 12-22.

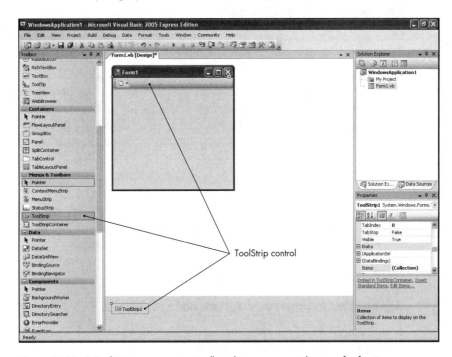

Figure 12-22: A ToolStrip can create a toolbar that appears at the top of a form.

NOTE *If you right-click the ToolStrip control at the top of your form, you can choose Insert Standard Items from the pop-up menu. This will fill your ToolStrip with icons that represent commonly used commands such as Save, Open, and Print, as shown in Figure 12-23.*

2. Click the Add ToolStrip button. A pop-up menu appears, listing all the different types of items you can add to your ToolStrip, as shown in Figure 12-24.

Add
ToolStrip
button

Figure 12-23: Visual Basic Express can create a standard ToolStrip filled with icons that represent familiar commands.

Figure 12-24: The Add ToolStrip button lets you quickly add items to your ToolStrip.

3. Click the type of item you want to add to your ToolStrip, such as Button or Label. Your chosen item appears in your ToolStrip.

Rearranging ToolStrip Commands

Editing
ToolStrips

Once you've added commands to a ToolStrip, you may want to rearrange them. To move a ToolStrip command to a new location:

1. Mouse over the ToolStrip command you want to move.
2. Hold down the left mouse button and drag the mouse pointer over another ToolStrip command to highlight that ToolStrip command.
3. Release the left mouse button. The ToolStrip command you chose in step 1 appears in its new location, pushing the other ToolStrip commands to the right.

Deleting ToolStrip Commands

To delete commands from a ToolStrip:

1. Right-click the ToolStrip command you want to delete. A pop-up menu appears.
2. Click Delete to delete the chosen command.

NOTE   *If you make a mistake, choose Edit ▶ Undo to retrieve your deleted command.*

Adding Items to Drop-Down Buttons and Split Buttons

Both the drop-down and split buttons display a menu of additional commands. To store a list of additional commands within them:

1. Create a drop-down or split button on a ToolStrip.
2. Click the downward-pointing arrow that appears to the right of the drop-down or split button to display a pull-down menu.

3. Mouse over the Type Here text box that appears directly under the drop-down or split button. Another downward-pointing arrow appears.

4. Click this downward-pointing arrow. A pop-up menu appears, listing all the items you can add to your drop-down or split button, as shown in Figure 12-25.

5. Click an item you want to appear, such as a MenuItem or TextBox.

6. Repeat steps 3 through 5 for each item you want to add.

Figure 12-25: A pull-down menu lets you choose the types of items you want to appear in a drop-down or split button.

Adding Options to a Combo Box

A *combo box* lets a user view and choose from a list of options. To fill a combo box with options, follow these steps:

1. Create a combo box on a ToolStrip or in the menu of a drop-down or split button.

2. Click the combo box that you want to fill with items and press F4 to open the Properties window.

3. Click the Items property under the Data category of the Properties window then click the ellipsis button that appears. A String Collection Editor dialog box appears, as shown in Figure 12-26.

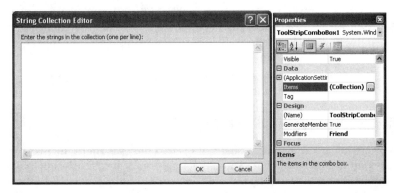

Figure 12-26: The String Collection Editor dialog box lets you enter items you want to appear inside a combo box.

4. Enter an item that you want to appear in your combo box and press ENTER.

5. Repeat step 4 for each additional item you want to add to the combo box.

6. Click OK. When you run your program, you'll see the item(s) in the combo box.

Adding a Text Box to a ToolStrip

One common reason for adding a text box in a ToolStrip is to give users a place to type a word or phrase for which they want to get help. To add a text box to a ToolStrip:

1. Click the ToolStrip on which you want to add a text box.
2. Click the Add ToolStrip button. A drop-down menu appears.
3. Click TextBox. A text box appears on your chosen ToolStrip.

NOTE *A ToolStrip text box stores its data in its Text property. To retrieve the data that a user types into a text box on a ToolStrip, you must specify both the name of the text box (such as ToolStripTextBox1) and the Text property, like so:*

```
ToolStripTextBox1.Text
```

Grouping Commands on a ToolStrip

If your ToolStrip contains a large number of commands, you may want to group related ones so users can find them more easily. In addition to placing commands next to each other on a ToolStrip (see the section "Rearranging ToolStrip Commands" on page 154), you may also want to include separator bars around a group of related commands.

Separator bars display a vertical line that divides ToolStrip commands. You can add separator bars while you're creating a ToolStrip or after you've added various commands to a ToolStrip. To add separator bars to an existing ToolStrip:

1. Click the ToolStrip control at the top of your form where you want to add a separator bar.
2. Click the Add ToolStrip button. A drop-down menu appears.
3. Click Separator. A separator bar appears on your ToolStrip.
4. Mouse over the separator bar, hold down the left mouse button, and drag the mouse to highlight a ToolStrip command. The separator bar will appear to the left of the ToolStrip command that you highlight.
5. Release the left mouse button over a highlighted ToolStrip command. Repeat steps 2 through 5 for each additional separator bar you want to add.

Adding a Progress Bar to a ToolStrip

A progress bar can provide visual feedback to the user about the progress of an action the computer is taking. For example, it might show how much time remains before the computer is done searching for a file on your hard disk. Table 12-1 lists some properties for modifying the appearance of a progress bar.

Table 12-1: Progress Bar Properties

Property	What it does
Maximum	Defines the value that fills up the entire progress bar. (The default is 100.)
Minimum	Defines the lowest value when the progress bar is completely empty. (The default is 0.)
Step	Defines the increment that the Value property increases each time the PerformStep() command runs.

(continued)

Table 12-1: Progress Bar Properties (continued)

Property	What it does
Style	Defines how the progress bar appears. The choices are Blocks, Continuous, and Marquee.
Value	Defines the current value of the progress bar, ranging from the Minimum and Maximum values, such as 0 to 100.

To add a progress bar to an existing ToolStrip, follow these steps:

1. Click the ToolStrip control at the top of your form, where you want to add a progress bar.
2. Click the Add ToolStrip button. A drop-down menu appears.
3. Click ProgressBar. A progress bar appears on your ToolStrip.
4. Mouse over the progress bar, hold down the left mouse button, and drag the mouse to highlight a ToolStrip command. The progress bar will appear to the left of the ToolStrip command that you highlight.
5. Release the left mouse button over the highlighted ToolStrip command.

Once you create a progress bar, you'll have to use BASIC code to show the progress bar filling up. To fill a progress bar, you can use the `PerformStep` command, like so:

```
ProgressBarName.PerformStep()
```

ProgressBarName is the name of your progress bar, such as ToolStripProgressBar1. Each time you run the `PerformStep()` command, the Value property of the progress bar increases by the amount defined by the Step property. As the Value property increases, the progress bar fills up until the value in the Value property equals or exceeds the value defined by the Maximum property of the progress bar.

Hands-on Tutorial: Creating ToolStrips

ToolStrips aren't necessary, but they can be convenient and give your program that extra level of polish to make it look and act like other professional programs. This tutorial guides you through creating a ToolStrip and writing code to make it work.

1. Load Visual Basic Express and press CTRL-N to display the New Project dialog box, then click OK to display a blank form.
2. Choose View ▶ Toolbox to display the Toolbox, then double-click the ToolStrip control in the Menus & Toolbars category of the Toolbox. A ToolStrip control appears at the top of the form and near the bottom of the screen.
3. Click the Add ToolStrip button (see Figure 12-27). A pop-up menu appears, listing all the different items you can add to your ToolStrip.

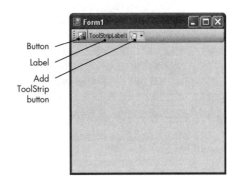

Figure 12-27: A ToolStrip containing a button and a label

4. Click Button. A button icon appears in the ToolStrip along with an Add ToolStrip button.

5. Click the Add ToolStrip button. A pop-up menu appears.

6. Click Label. A ToolStripLabel1 button appears on the ToolStrip, along with an Add ToolStrip button.

7. Double-click the button at the far left of the ToolStrip. The Code window appears.

8. Type **End** between the `Private Sub` and `End Sub` lines, like so:

```
Private Sub ToolStripButton1_Click(ByVal sender As System.Object, ByVal e As_
System.EventArgs) Handles ToolStripButton1.Click
        End
End Sub
```

9. Click the Class Name list box and choose ToolStripLabel1.

10. Click the Method Name list box and choose Click. The Code window displays the Click event procedure for ToolStripLabel1.

11. Type **MsgBox ("My ToolStrip works!")** between the `Private Sub` and `End Sub` lines, like so:

```
Private Sub ToolStripLabel1_Click(ByVal sender As Object, ByVal e As_
System.EventArgs) Handles ToolStripLabel1.Click
        MsgBox("My ToolStrip works!")
End Sub
```

12. Press F5. Your user interface appears.

13. Click the ToolStripLabel1 label on the ToolStrip. The `MsgBox` command, which you typed in step 11, runs. Click OK to make this message box go away.

14. Click the button on your ToolStrip. This runs the `End` command that you typed in step 8, which stops your program.

15. Choose File ▸ Close Project. A Close Project dialog box appears. Click Discard.

KEY FEATURES TO REMEMBER

The most common ways to display commands on a user interface are through pull-down menus, controls (such as buttons), or in ToolStrips along the edge of a window.

- Visual Basic Express can create generic pull-down menus and toolbars that you can customize, or you can create your own from scratch.
- Pull-down menus can include hot keys, check marks, separator bars, and shortcut keys to make choosing commands easier.
- ToolStrips can display icons that represent the most commonly used commands from your pull-down menus.

13

OFFERING CHOICES WITH RADIO BUTTONS AND BOXES

In the old days, programs forced users to *type* data. For example, the program might ask the user, "What is your gender?" Then the user would have to type *Male* or *Female*. If either word was misspelled, the computer would ask the user to retype an answer.

Rather than force users to type everything into a program, most programs today offer a list of choices from which the user can select. This ensures that the user will always choose a valid option, and it makes the program easier to use.

A program can offer choices to the user as:

- Radio buttons
- Check boxes
- List boxes
- Combo boxes

Using Radio Buttons

Radio buttons take their name from old-fashioned car radios that let you push buttons to choose one, and only one, radio station at any given time. In a computer program, radio buttons are best used for listing mutually exclusive options, such as the answer when the program asks for a person's gender (male or female), income range ($20,000–$50,000 or $50,001–$100,000), or marital status (married or single).

Any time two or more radio buttons appear on a form, Visual Basic Express treats all the radio buttons as a single group and allows only one radio button in that group to be selected at any given time, whether you have two or 200 radio buttons on a form.

Grouping Radio Buttons

If you want the user to be able to select more than one radio button on a form, you must divide the radio buttons into *groups* using the *GroupBox* control (found in the Containers category of the Toolbox). Visual Basic Express treats all radio buttons inside a GroupBox as a single group, and any radio buttons outside a GroupBox as a separate group, as shown in Figure 13-1.

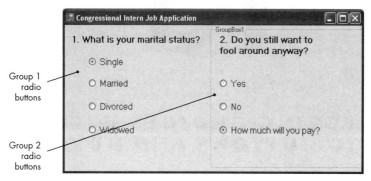

Figure 13-1: Radio buttons inside a GroupBox control are treated as a single group, while those that do not appear inside a GroupBox control are treated as a separate group.

You can group radio buttons on a form in two ways:

- Draw a GroupBox on a form, and then draw radio buttons inside the GroupBox.
- Draw radio buttons on a form, draw a GroupBox, and then move radio buttons inside the GroupBox.

Customizing a Radio Button

Radio buttons contain two unique properties that you need to use when you add them to a form, as shown in Table 13-1.

Table 13-1: Useful Radio Button Properties

Property	What it does
CheckAlign	Defines where the radio button appears relative to the string stored in its Text property
Checked	Holds a True or False value that determines whether the radio button is selected or unselected

The CheckAlign property defines the radio button's appearance in relation to the button text. The default appearance property, MiddleLeft, places the radio button to the left of the button text. Figure 13-2 shows the possible positions for the radio button.

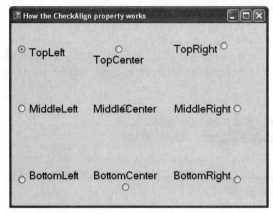

Figure 13-2: The CheckAlign property can display the radio button in nine different positions.

If you don't change the Font or Font Size of a radio button's Text property, choosing the TopLeft, TopRight, BottomLeft, and BottomRight values for the CheckAlign property may not appear to change anything. That's because the default font in a radio button doesn't leave much room to display the button in the up or down orientation, even if you choose a CheckAlign property such as TopLeft or BottomRight.

When you click a radio button's CheckAlign property in the Properties window, nine boxes appear in a drop-down menu, as shown in Figure 13-3. Click the box in the position that matches the alignment you want to use for your radio button.

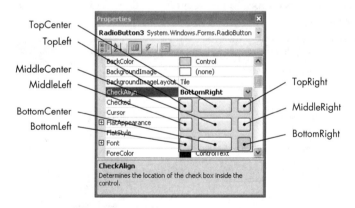

Figure 13-3: Clicking the CheckAlign property of a radio button displays different positions for your radio buttons.

A radio button's Checked property determines whether the button has been selected or not. A True value means that it has been selected, and displays a dot inside the button. A False value means the button has not been selected, and the button is empty.

By default, all radio buttons have a False value in their Checked property, although you can set the Checked property of one radio button in a group to True. Most likely, your program will display all radio buttons unselected (False) and wait until the user clicks the radio button to select it. Then you can use BASIC to determine which radio button the user clicked (has its Checked property set to True) so your program can take the appropriate action.

Hands-on Tutorial: Grouping Radio Buttons

If you want users to be able to choose two or more radio buttons on a form, you must divide your radio buttons into two or more groups. This tutorial shows you how to use the GroupBox control to create a group of radio buttons.

1. Load Visual Basic Express, then press CTRL-N to display the New Project dialog box. Click OK to display a blank form.
2. Choose View ▶ Toolbox to display the Toolbox, then choose Window ▶ Auto Hide to keep the Toolbox visible. (If a check mark does not appear in front of the Auto Hide command, skip this step.)
3. Click the GroupBox control in the Containers category of the Toolbox, then mouse over the form, and click the left mouse button to create a GroupBox control on the form.
4. Click the RadioButton control under the Common Controls category of the Properties window, move the mouse pointer anywhere *outside* the GroupBox control, and click the left mouse button.
5. Repeat step 4 two more times to create a total of three radio buttons *outside* the GroupBox control.
6. Repeat step 4 two times to create two radio buttons *inside* the GroupBox control. You should now have a total of three radio button controls outside the GroupBox control and two inside the GroupBox control, as shown in Figure 13-4.

Figure 13-4: Two radio buttons inside and three radio buttons outside the GroupBox

7. Press F5. Your user interface appears.
8. Click the two radio buttons inside the GroupBox control. Notice that each time you click a radio button inside the control, it has no affect on the appearance of any of the three radio buttons outside the control.
9. Click any of the radio buttons outside the GroupBox control. Notice that clicking a radio button outside the control has no affect on any of the radio buttons inside the control.
10. Press ALT-F4 to stop your program from running, then choose File ▶ Close Project. A Close Project dialog box appears. Click Discard.

Using Check Boxes

Check boxes display several options from which the user can choose. Unlike radio buttons, check boxes allow the user to make *multiple* selections in reply to a statement such as "Give all the reasons why you hate your computer," as shown in Figure 13-5.

Check boxes have three unique properties that you may wish to modify to customize their appearance, as shown in Table 13-2.

The CheckAlign property defines the appearance of the check box relative to the text that appears with the check box, as shown in Figure 13-6.

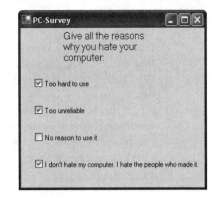

Figure 13-5: Multiple check boxes can be selected.

Table 13-2: Properties for Customizing a Check Box

Property	What it does
CheckAlign	Defines where the check box appears relative to the string stored in its Text property
Checked	Holds a True or False value that determines whether the check box is selected or unselected
CheckState	Displays the check box as Unchecked, Checked, or Indeterminate

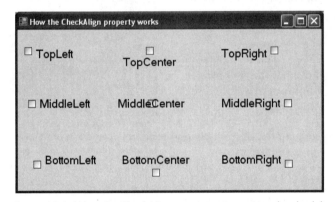

Figure 13-6: Ways the CheckAlign property can position the check box.

If you don't change the Font or Font Size of a check box's Text property, choosing the TopLeft, TopRight, BottomLeft, and BottomRight values for the CheckAlign property may not appear to change anything. The reason is that the default font in a check box doesn't leave much room to display the check box in top or bottom orientation, even if you choose a CheckAlign property such as TopLeft or BottomRight.

The Checked property defines whether the check box is checked or unchecked. If the value of the Check property is True, the check box is checked. If the Checked property is False, the check box is empty.

The CheckState property lets you display a check box in one of three states, *Unchecked, Checked,* or *Indeterminate,* as shown in Figure 13-7.

When the user clicks a check box, the check box toggles from a Checked to an Unchecked state; if the user clicks the check box again, it toggles from Unchecked to Checked. The user cannot click a check box to display an Indeterminate state.

If the user clicks a check box that displays the Indeterminate state, the check box displays an Unchecked state. Clicking the check box again displays a Checked state. Because few users are likely to understand what an Indeterminate appearance of a check box may be, it's generally not a good idea to use it in your programs.

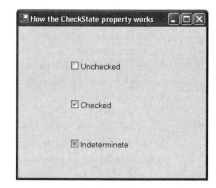

Figure 13-7: The three different Check-State values for a check box

When the CheckState property is set either to Checked or Indeterminate, the Checked property is automatically set to True. Only when the CheckState property is set to Unchecked will the Checked property be set to False.

Using List Boxes

Using List Boxes

The problem with both check boxes and radio buttons is that if a large number of options is available to the user, multiple check boxes and radio buttons can clutter the user interface. To solve this problem, you can offer multiple choices through a list box.

A *list box* displays each option on a separate line. If more options are available than the list box can display, the list box can scroll additional options into view if the user clicks the list box's scroll bar, as shown in Figure 13-8.

Table 13-3 lists some of the properties you may want to modify to customize the way your list boxes work.

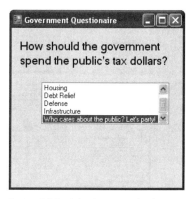

Figure 13-8: A list box can display multiple options in a box that can be scrolled to display more items.

Table 13-3: Properties for Modifying a List Box

Property	What it does
Items	Contains all the choices that appear in the list box
MultiColumn	Displays the contents of the list box in separate columns
SelectionMode	Defines how many items the user can select from the list box: None, One (default), MultiSimple, or MultiExtended
SelectedItem	Contains the item selected in a list box when the SelectionMode property is set to One
SelectedItems.Item	Stores a list of items the user selected when the SelectionMode property is set to MultiSimple or MultiExtended
Sorted	Sorts the items stored in the Items property in alphabetical order

Filling a List Box with Items

A list box initially appears empty until you enter items into the Items property. The order that you enter the items is the order in which they appear in the list box. To fill a list box, follow these steps:

1. Click the list box control you want to modify, then open the Properties window by choosing View ▶ Properties Window.
2. Click the Items property. An ellipsis button appears. Click the ellipsis button to display the String Collection Editor dialog box, as shown in Figure 13-9.

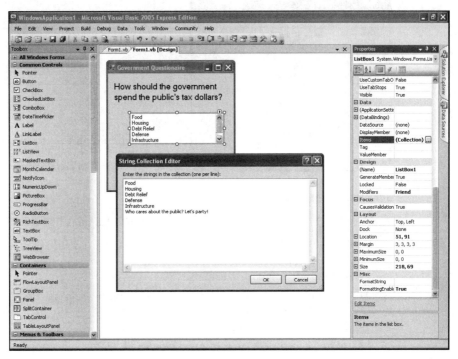

Figure 13-9: The String Collection Editor lets you type all the items you want to appear inside a list box.

3. Enter an item that you want to appear in the list box and press ENTER. Repeat this step for each additional item you want to appear.
4. Click OK. Visual Basic Express displays your items in the list box.

Displaying Items in a List Box

Normally, a list box displays items in a single column in the order in which you enter them into the String Collection Editor. However, you can sort items alphabetically or display them in multiple columns.

Sorting Items Alphabetically

When you sort items in a list box alphabetically, Visual Basic Express displays them in A-to-Z order, with items beginning with *A* at the top of the list box and items beginning with *Z* near the bottom. To sort a list box, change the Sorted property (under the

Behavior category in the Properties window) to True. If you don't want the list box to sort items alphabetically, set the Sorted property to False, which is its default value.

Displaying Items in Multiple Columns

Normally, if a list box contains more items than it can display, it lets the user scroll vertically through the list. However, if you set the list box's MultiColumn property to True, you can make the list box display items in multiple columns that users can scroll horizontally to view, as shown in Figure 13-10.

Figure 13-10: The MultiColumn property can display items in a list box in columns that you can view by scrolling horizontally.

Selecting Items in a List Box

The SelectionMode property provides defines how a list box allows users to select items:

None The user can view but not select items in the list box.

One The user can select only one item in a list box at a time. This is the default SelectionMode value for a list box.

MultiSimple The user can select multiple items by holding down CTRL and clicking each additional item.

MultiExtended Like MultiSimple, except that the user can select a range of items by holding down SHIFT to select two items and all items that appear in between.

Hands-on Tutorial: Retrieving One Item from a List Box

When the user clicks an item in a list box that has its SelectionMode property set to One, the list box stores their selection in the SelectedItem property. This tutorial shows you how to create a list box, fill it with some items, sort them, and retrieve the item the user clicked inside the list box.

NOTE *The SelectedItem property does not appear in the Properties window of a list box. You can only access the SelectedItem property using BASIC code.*

1. Load Visual Basic Express, press CTRL-N to display the New Project dialog box, then click OK to display a blank form.
2. Choose View ▶ Toolbox to display the Toolbox.
3. Click the ListBox control on the Toolbox, mouse over the form, and click the left mouse button. A list box control appears on your form.

4. Press F4 to open the Properties window and click the Items property under the Data category. Click the ellipsis button that appears to open the String Collection Editor dialog box.

5. Type **Oranges** in the String Collection Editor and press ENTER; type **Apples** and press ENTER; then type **Guano** and click OK. The three items should appear in your list box.

6. Click the Sorted property in the Behavior category of the Properties window. A downward-pointing arrow appears.

7. Click the downward-pointing arrow and click True. Notice that the list box now sorts your items in alphabetical order.

8. Choose View ▸ Toolbox to display the Toolbox again.

9. Click the Button control, move the mouse pointer under the list box on the form, and click the left mouse button. A button control appears under your list box.

10. Double-click this button. The Code window appears.

11. Type `MsgBox(ListBox1.SelectedItem)` between the `Private Sub` and `End Sub` lines, like so:

```
Private Sub Button1_Click(ByVal sender As System.Object, ByVal e As System.EventArgs)_
Handles Button1.Click
        MsgBox(ListBox1.SelectedItem)
End Sub
```

12. Press F5 to display your user interface, then click an item in the list box. The item appears highlighted. (Only one item at a time can appear highlighted in the list box, because the list box's SelectionMode property is set to One.)

13. Click the Button1 button to run the BASIC code you typed in step 11. A message box appears, displaying the item you clicked in the list box, such as Guano, as shown in Figure 13-11. Click OK to make the message box go away.

14. Press ALT-F4 to stop your program, then choose File ▸ Save All to display the Save Project dialog box.

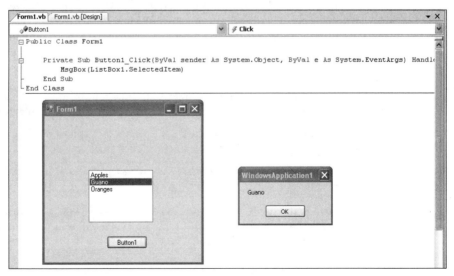

Figure 13-11: When the user clicks an item in ListBox1, the data is stored in the SelectedItem property of the list box.

15. Type **ListBoxExample** in the Name text box and click Save. Visual Basic Express saves your project (to be modified in the next tutorial in this chapter).

16. Choose File ▸ Close Project.

Hands-on Tutorial: Retrieving Multiple Items Using the SelectedItems.Item Property

If the SelectionMode property of a list box is set either to MultiSimple or MultiExtended, a user can select multiple items, which the list box stores in its SelectedItems.Item property. Visual Basic Express identifies each selected item by a number. The selected item at the top of the list box is assigned the number 0, the second from the top is assigned the number 1, and so on, as shown in Figure 13-12.

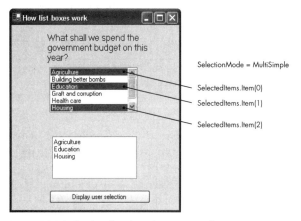

Figure 13-12: To identify selected items, Visual Basic Express assigns each selected item a number.

As Figure 13-12 shows, the first selected item is stored in the SelectedItems.Item(0) property, the second is stored in the SelectedItems.Item(1) property, and the third is stored in the SelectedItems.Item(2) property. The actual order in which the user selects items does not affect the numbers assigned to each item by the SelectedItems.Item property. The numbering assignments are based entirely on the order in which the items appear in the list box.

To retrieve an item stored in the SelectedItems.Item property, you need to use BASIC code. You'll find the following two BASIC commands particularly important:

ListBoxName.SelectedItems.Count   Returns the total number of items that the user selected in the list box.

ListBoxName.SelectedItems.Item(*index*)   Returns the selected item defined by the value of index.

ListBoxName is the name of your list box control, and *index* is the number of the selected item you want to retrieve, where the first selected item is numbered zero (0), the second is numbered one (1), and so on.

To retrieve multiple items from a list box, follow these steps (if you haven't created the list box tutorial earlier in this chapter, go back and do it now or you won't be able to complete the steps in this tutorial):

1. Choose File ▸ Recent Projects. A pop-up menu appears.
2. Click the ListBoxExample.vbproj file.
3. Double-click the Form1.vb file listed in the Solution Explorer window. Your user interface appears.
4. Click the list box on your form and press F4 to open the Properties window.
5. Click the SelectionMode property under the Behavior category of the Properties window. A downward-pointing arrow appears.
6. Click the downward-pointing arrow. A pop-up menu appears, listing None, One, MultiSimple, and MultiExtended.
7. Click MultiSimple or MultiExtended.
8. Click the TextBox control in the Toolbox, mouse over the form, and click the left mouse button to draw a text box on your form. You may need to move this text box on your form to make sure it doesn't overlap the list box or the button that already appears on your form.
9. Press F4 to open the Properties window and click the Multiline property under the Behavior category. A downward-pointing arrow appears.
10. Click the downward-pointing arrow and choose True. Handles appear around the text box.
11. Mouse over the handle in the bottom-right corner of the text box, hold down the left mouse button, and drag the mouse to increase the size of the text box. Your user interface should look similar to Figure 13-13.
12. Double-click the Button1 button on the form. The Code window appears.

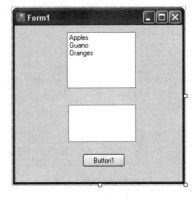

Figure 13-13: The appearance of your modified user interface includes one list box, one text box, and one button on a form.

13. Modify the Button1_Click event procedure so that it contains the following code:

```
Private Sub Button1_Click(ByVal sender As System.Object, ByVal e As_
System.EventArgs) Handles Button1.Click
        Dim i As Integer
        For i = 1 To ListBox1.SelectedItems.Count
            TextBox1.Text = TextBox1.Text & ListBox1.SelectedItems.Item(i - 1) & vbCr
& vbLf
        Next
End Sub
```

This event procedure first uses the ListBox1.SelectedItems.Count command to determine how many items the user selected. Next, it retrieves the first selected item and stores it in the text box named TextBox1. It repeats this step until all of the selected items from the list box are stored in the TextBox1 text box.

Don't worry if the BASIC code stored in the event procedure from step 13 looks confusing. The important point is that you need to use BASIC code to count the total number of selected items in a list box (using the `ListBox1.SelectedItems.Count` command) and then retrieve each selected item individually using the `ListBox.SelectedItems.Item(index)` property.

14. Press F5. Your user interface appears.

15. Hold down CTRL if you chose MultiSimple in step 7 or SHIFT if you chose MultiExtended in step 7, then click two items, such as Guano and Oranges. The list box highlights your two choices.

16. Click the Button1 button. The two choices you selected in step 15 now appear in the text box, as shown in Figure 13-14.

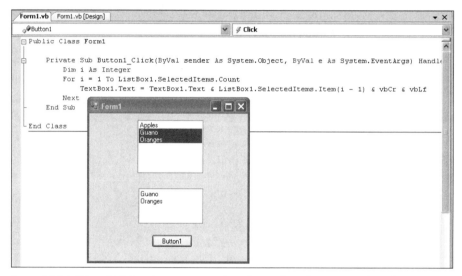

Figure 13-14: Write BASIC code to retrieve selected items from the ListBox.SelectedItems.Item property.

17. Choose File ▶ Save All.

18. Choose File ▶ Close Project.

Using a Checked List Box

A *checked list box* shares the same properties as a normal list box. It looks and acts like a normal list box except that it displays a check box in front of every item, as shown in Figure 13-15.

The main difference between the two is that a checked list box uses the Checked-Items.Item property to store the list of all the items that have a check mark. To retrieve items stored in the CheckedItems.Item property, you need to use BASIC code.

You'll find the following two BASIC commands particularly important:

CheckedListBoxName.`CheckedItems.Count`   Returns the total number of items that appear with a check mark in the checked list box.

CheckedListBoxName.`CheckedItems.Item(index)`   Returns the checked item defined by the value of index.

CheckedListBoxName is the name of your checked list box control and *index* is the number of the checked item you want to retrieve, where the first checked item is index zero (0), the second is index one (1), and so on.

Figure 13-15: A checked list box lets users select multiple items with a click of the mouse.

Hands-on Tutorial: Using a Checked List Box

This tutorial guides you through creating a checked list box and retrieving the items the user checked.

1. Load Visual Basic Express, then press CTRL-N to display the New Project dialog box. Click OK to display a blank form.

2. Choose View ▸ Toolbox to display the Toolbox, then choose Windows ▸ Auto Hide to keep the Toolbox visible at all times. (You can skip this step if a check mark does not initially appear in front of the Auto Hide command.)

3. Click the CheckedListBox control in the Toolbox, mouse over the form, and click the left mouse button. A checked list box appears on your form.

4. Press F4 to open the Properties window, and click the Items property under the Data category. An ellipsis button appears.

5. Click the ellipsis button. A String Collection Editor dialog box appears.

6. Type **Goldfish** and press ENTER; type **Dogs** and press ENTER; then type **Cats** and click OK. The checked list box should display the items you just typed.

7. Click the TextBox control in the Toolbox, mouse over the form, and click the left mouse button to draw a text box on your form.

8. Press F4 to open the Properties window and click the Multiline property under the Behavior category. A downward-pointing arrow appears.

9. Click the downward-pointing arrow and choose True. Handles appear around the corner and edges of the text box.

10. Mouse over the bottom-right corner of the text box, hold down the left mouse button, and drag the mouse to expand the size of the text box.

11. Click the Button control in the Toolbox, mouse over the form, and click the left mouse button. Your user interface should look similar to Figure 13-16.

Figure 13-16: A checked list box, a text box, and a button control on a form

12. Double-click the Button1 button. The Code window appears.

13. Type the following BASIC code in between the `Private Sub` and `End Sub` lines so the entire event procedure looks like the code shown here:

```
Private Sub Button1_Click(ByVal sender As System.Object, ByVal e As_
System.EventArgs) Handles Button1.Click
        Dim i As Integer
        For i = 1 To CheckedListBox1.CheckedItems.Count
            TextBox1.Text = TextBox1.Text & CheckedListBox1.CheckedItems.Item(i - 1)_
& vbCr & vbLf
        Next
End Sub
```

This event procedure first uses the `CheckedListBox1.CheckedItems.Count` command to determine how many items the user checked. Next, it retrieves the first checked item and stores it in the text box named TextBox1. It repeats this step until all of the checked items from the checked list box are stored in the TextBox1 text box.

14. Press F5. Your user interface appears.

15. Click one or more of the items in the checked list box control so a check mark appears in front of each item.

16. Click the Button1 control. The text box displays the checked items from the checked list box control, as shown in Figure 13-17.

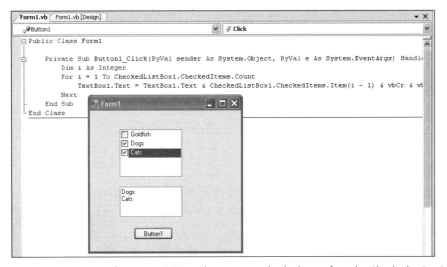

Figure 13-17: You need to write BASIC code to retrieve checked items from the CheckedListBox1 .CheckedItems.Item property.

17. Press ALT-F4 to stop your program from running.

18. Choose File ▶ Close Project. A Close Project dialog box appears. Click Discard.

Using Combo Boxes

Using Combo Boxes

Combo boxes combine the features of a list box with a text box. Like a list box, a combo box can display a list of multiple items for the user to select. Like a text box, a combo box displays a box where users can enter text. Figure 13-18 shows how a combo box lets users either select from an existing list of items or enter their own item.

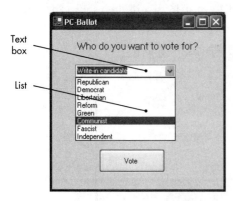

Text box

List

Figure 13-18: A combo box displays both a list and a text box so users can either click an item or type something in themselves.

Table 13-4 lists some of the properties you may want to modify to customize the way your combo boxes work.

Table 13-4: Properties for Modifying a Combo Box

Property	What it does
DropDownStyle	Defines how the combo box appears on a form. The choices are Simple, DropDown (default), and DropDownList.
Items	Contains all the items that appear in the combo box.
SelectedItem	Contains the item the user clicked in the combo box.
Sorted	Alphabetically sorts the items stored in the Items property.
Text	Contains the item the user typed into the combo box.

Filling a Combo Box with Items

A combo box appears empty until you type items into the Items property. The order that you type the items in is the order in which they appear in the combo box. To fill a combo box, follow these steps:

1. Click the combo box control you want to modify.
2. Open the Properties window by choosing View ▶ Properties Window.
3. Click the Items property. An ellipsis button appears. Click the ellipsis button to display the String Collection Editor dialog box (see Figure 13-9).
4. Type an item you want to appear in the combo box and press ENTER. Repeat this step for each additional item you want to include.
5. Click OK. Visual Basic Express displays your items in the combo box.

Changing the Appearance of a Combo Box

You can change both the overall appearance of a combo box and the width and height of the list that appears when the user clicks it. The DropDownStyle property, under the Appearance category of the Properties window, lets you create three types of combo boxes, as shown in Figure 13-19:

Simple   Displays a list that that always appears under the combo box.

DropDown   Displays a list of options only when the user clicks the downward-pointing arrow. Users can select an item or enter text directly into the combo box.

DropDownList Identical to the DropDown style except the user cannot enter anything into the combo box.

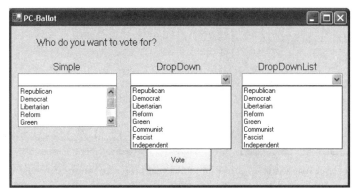

Figure 13-19: The three different styles for a combo box

Sorting Items in a Combo Box

By default, a combo box displays items in a single column in the order in which you entered them in the String Collection Editor. To sort items alphabetically, change the Sorted property, under the Behavior category in the Properties window, to True.

Hands-on Tutorial: Selecting Items in a Combo Box

With a combo box, the user can choose only one item, which the combo box stores in one of two properties:

Items Stores the item that the user clicks in the combo box list

Text Stores text the user types into the combo box

Because a user can type in or click an item to select it, a combo box needs to check both its Items and Text properties to see which contains data. This tutorial shows you how to check both the Items and Text properties of a combo box using BASIC code.

1. Load Visual Basic Express and press CTRL-N to display the New Project dialog box. Click OK to display a blank form.
2. Choose View ▶ Toolbox. The Toolbox appears.
3. Click the ComboBox control in the Toolbox, mouse over the form, and click the left mouse button to draw a combo box control on the form.
4. Press F4 to open the Properties window and click the Items property. An ellipsis button appears.
5. Click the ellipsis button. A String Collection Editor dialog box appears.
6. Type **Republican** and press ENTER.
7. Type **Democrat** and press ENTER.
8. Type **Reform** and click OK.
9. Choose View ▶ Toolbox to view the Toolbox again.
10. Click the Button control, mouse over the form, and click the left mouse button to create a button control on your form.

11. Double-click this button control. The Code window appears.

12. Type the following boldface code so the entire event procedure looks like this:

```
Private Sub Button1_Click(ByVal sender As System.Object, ByVal e As_
System.EventArgs) Handles Button1.Click
        If ComboBox1.SelectedItem = "" Then
            MsgBox(ComboBox1.Text)
        Else
            MsgBox(ComboBox1.SelectedItem)
        End If
End Sub
```

First, the event procedure checks to see if the SelectedItem property is empty. If it is, that means the user must have typed something in, so the event procedure displays a dialog box that contains the contents of the Text property. If the SelectedItem property isn't empty, the event procedure displays a dialog box that contains the contents of the SelectedItem property.

13. Press F5. Your user interface appears, displaying the combo box and the button on the form.

14. Click the downward-pointing arrow in the combo box. A list of items you typed in steps 6–8 appears.

15. Click an item, such as Democrat or Reform. The combo box displays your choice in the text box portion of the combo box.

16. Click the Button1 control. A message box appears, displaying the item you selected in step 15.

17. Click in the text box portion of the combo box and type **Communist**.

18. Click the Button1 control. A message box appears, displaying the word *Communist*.

19. Choose File ▸ Close Project. A Close Project dialog box appears. Click Discard.

KEY FEATURES TO REMEMBER

To provide choices to the user, your program can use a variety of different controls including radio buttons, check boxes, list boxes, and combo boxes. When your program needs to offer choices to the user, keep the following in mind:

- The Contents act like a table of contents that organizes help into topics.

- All radio buttons that appear on a form are treated as a single group. Only one radio button can be selected in a group. If you store radio buttons inside of a GroupBox control, Visual Basic Express treats those radio buttons as a single group.

- Check boxes provide multiple items from which the user can select.

- List boxes provide a list of items in a scrollable box. Checked list boxes display a check box in front of items in a list box.

- A list box stores a single selected item in its SelectedItem property. If the user selects multiple items, the list box stores these items in the list box's SelectedItems.Item property.

- A checked list box acts like a list box except it stores all checked items in its CheckedItems.Item property.

- Combo boxes let users either click an item or type something directly into the combo box. A combo box stores user input in either the Text or Items property.

14

ACCEPTING AND DISPLAYING TEXT IN TEXT BOXES AND LABELS

Programs often need to display information to the user as *text*—for instance, in error messages, like "The operating system has recovered from a serious error. Next time get a Mac." To display text on a user interface in a variety of fonts, sizes, and colors, you can use either a *label* or a *text box* control.

A label can only display text while a text box can display text *and* allow users to enter new data or edit existing data (such as a name, date, or telephone number). Text boxes can hold a single character to several thousand characters.

Using Labels

Using Labels

The label control displays anything stored in its Text property. You can modify the Text property either through the Properties window (at design time) or through BASIC code (at run time). To change the Text property of a label in the Properties window, follow these steps:

1. Click the label control you want to modify then open the Properties window by choosing View ▶ Properties Window.

2. Click the Text property. A downward-pointing arrow appears. Click the downward-pointing arrow to display a text box.

3. Type any text you want to appear in the label. You can press ENTER as you type to display text on multiple lines.

4. Press CTRL-ENTER or click outside the Text property text box. Visual Basic Express displays your label with the text you typed in step 3.

To change the Text property using BASIC code, define the name of the label you want to modify, its Text property, and the new text you want to store in it:

```
LabelName.Text = "New Text"
```

where `LabelName` is the name of your label control and `"New Text"` is the text you want to display in the label control. By using BASIC code to change a label's contents, you can create messages that change while your program runs. For example, Figure 14-1 shows some simple BASIC code that changes a label's contents when the user clicks a button named Button1.

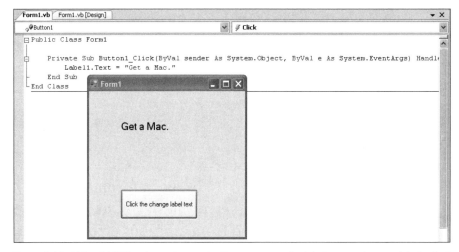

Figure 14-1: Using BASIC code to change the Text property of a label can make your labels display different messages as your program runs.

```
Label1.Text = "Get a Mac."
```

This BASIC code puts the string `"Get a Mac."` into the Text property of the Label1 control.

You can also modify the BorderStyle property, which gives you three choices for a border around your label, as shown in Figure 14-2:

None   The label boundaries are invisible; only the text stored in the label's Text property is visible. This is the default value.

FixedSingle   Displays a single border around the outline of the label.

Fixed3D   Displays the boundaries of the label as if the label were recessed into the window.

Figure 14-2: A label can appear in one of three different border styles: None, FixedSingle, or Fixed3D.

Using Link Labels

Using Link Labels

While a label simply displays text, a *link label* can display text as a *hyperlink* that users can click to run an event procedure that makes the program do something. A hyperlink can highlight all or part of the Text property. Hyperlinks make their presence known to a user in the following ways (see Figure 14-3):

- By appearing in color
- By appearing underlined
- By changing the mouse pointer into a hand icon when the user mouses over the link label

You might think of a link label as a variation on a button control that lets users click something to choose a command. Table 14-1 lists some of the properties you may need to modify to customize the appearance and behavior of a link label.

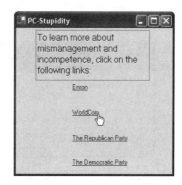

Figure 14-3: Users can identify a hyperlink in one of a few ways.

Table 14-1: Properties for Customizing the Appearance of a Link Label

Property	What it does
ActiveLinkColor	Defines the color that appears when the user clicks the link label.
LinkColor	Defines the initial color of any string stored in a link label's Text property.
LinkArea	Defines which part of the text stored in the Text property appears as a hyperlink.
LinkVisited	If set to True, the hyperlink appears in the color defined by the VisitedLinkColor. If set to False, the hyperlink appears in the color defined by the LinkColor property.
Text	Displays the string that appears in the link label.
VisitedLinkColor	Defines the color of text in the link label, if the LinkVisited property has been set to True.

Filling the Text and Links Properties

The Text property defines the string that appears inside a link label, which can be a single word or several thousand characters. The LinkArea property defines which part of the string stored in the Text property appears highlighted as a hyperlink. To fill in the Text property:

1. Create a LinkLabel control on a form, then open the Properties window by choosing View ▸ Properties Window.
2. Click the Text property. A downward-pointing arrow appears. Click the downward-pointing arrow to display a text box.
3. Type the string you want to appear inside the LinkLabel and click outside the text box when you're done to display your string inside the LinkLabel control.

Once you've filled in the Text property of a LinkLabel control, you can define the hyperlinks within the string by opening the Links property and following these steps:

1. Click the LinkLabel you want to modify, then open the Properties window by choosing View ▸ Properties Window.
2. Click the LinkArea property. An ellipsis button appears.
3. Click the ellipsis button to display a LinkArea Editor dialog box, then highlight the text you want to appear as a hyperlink, as shown in Figure 14-4.

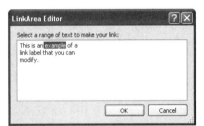

Figure 14-4: The LinkArea Editor lets you highlight the text to turn into a hyperlink.

4. Click OK. The LinkArea Editor dialog box goes away and the LinkLabel control highlights the text you selected as your hyperlink in step 3.

Once you've created text and defined a hyperlink, you need to write BASIC code to make the LinkLabel control actually do something when the user clicks a hyperlink.

Displaying Colors

Your hyperlinks initially appear in the color you defined in the LinkColor property. The ActiveLinkColor property defines the color a hyperlink appears when the user clicks it.

To make a hyperlink change color once a user clicks it, set its LinkVisited property to True and then change the color defined by the VisitedLinkColor property. To define the LinkColor, ActiveLinkColor, or the VisitedLinkColor properties, follow these steps:

1. Click the LinkLabel you want to modify, then choose View ▸ Properties Window.
2. Click the LinkColor, ActiveLinkColor, or VisitedLinkColor property. A downward-pointing arrow appears.
3. Click the downward-pointing arrow. A color palette appears with three tabs (Custom, Web, and System) as shown in Figure 14-5. Click the appropriate tab, then choose a color for your hyperlink.

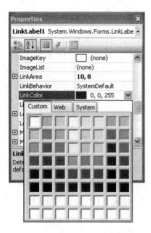

Figure 14-5: Choose a color for your hyperlink from the color palette.

Hands-on Tutorial: Playing with LinkLabels

Here's how to use both a Label and a LinkLabel control.

1. Load Visual Basic Express, then press CTRL-N to display the New Project dialog box. Click OK to display a blank form.

2. Choose View ▸ Toolbox to display the Toolbox, then choose Window ▸ Auto Hide to keep it visible. (Skip this step if there is no checkmark in front of the Auto Hide command.)

3. Click the Label control, mouse over the form, and click the left mouse button near the top of the form. A label control appears on your form.

4. Click the LinkLabel control, mouse over the form, and click the left mouse button underneath the label you created in step 3. A link label appears on the form.

5. Press F4 to open the Properties window and click the Text property, then click the downward-pointing arrow to display a pop-up containing the text *LinkLabel1*.

6. Erase the LinkLabel1 text and type **This is an example of a hyperlink.** Then press CTRL-ENTER. The link label control displays the text you just typed.

7. Click the LinkArea property under the Behavior category in the Properties window. Click the ellipsis button that appears to display the LinkArea Editor dialog box.

8. Highlight the word *example* and click OK, as shown in Figure 14-6. Notice that your link label control now highlights only the word *example* as a hyperlink.

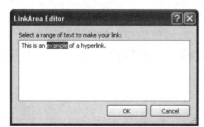

Figure 14-6: Highlighting part of the text inside a link label control

9. Double-click the link label control. The Code window appears.

10. Type `Label1.Text = "The label text has changed!"` between the `Private Sub` and `End Sub` lines, like so:

```
Private Sub LinkLabel1_LinkClicked(ByVal sender As System.Object, ByVal e As_
System.Windows.Forms.LinkLabelLinkClickedEventArgs) Handles LinkLabel1.LinkClicked
        Label1.Text = "The label text has changed!"
System.Diagnostics.Process.Start("www.nostarch.com")
End Sub
```

11. Press F5 to display your user interface, then click the word *example* in your link label. The text in your label should now display the text *The label text has changed!* If you have an Internet connection, click the link label to load your browser and display the No Starch Press website with all of its tasty books.

12. Press ALT-F4 to stop your program from running, then choose File ▸ Close Project. A Close Project dialog box appears. Click Discard.

Using Text Boxes

Text boxes display text and can let users enter new text or edit existing text using the arrow keys, DELETE, and BACKSPACE as well as Cut (CTRL-X), Copy (CTRL-C), and Paste (CTRL-V). Table 14-2 lists some of the properties you may want to modify in a text box.

Table 14-2: Properties for Customizing a Text Box

Property	What it does
MaxLength	Defines the maximum number of characters a text box can hold.
Multiline	Allows a text box to display more than one line of text.
PasswordChar	Replaces all characters in a text box with a predefined character such as an asterisk (*).
ReadOnly	Allows a text box to display text that the user can't edit.
ScrollBars	Defines whether horizontal and/or vertical scroll bars appear within the text box.
Text	Contains the string that appears inside the text box.
TextAlign	Aligns text in a box either Left, Center, or Right.
WordWrap	When set to True, text automatically wraps to fit within the text box. When set to False, the text scrolls to the right until the user presses ENTER to move the cursor to the next line.

Modifying the Behavior of a Text Box

You can control the behavior of your text box by changing its properties as listed in Table 14-2. For example, to make it act like a simple word processor that automatically wraps lines to fit the width of the text box, set the properties shown in Table 14-3.

Table 14-3: Properties for Turning a Text Box into a Word Processor

Property	Value
MultiLine	True
ScrollBars	Vertical
WordWrap	True

If you set the ScrollBars property to Vertical, users can type as much text as they want; they can click the vertical scroll bar to view any text that has scrolled out of sight.

Set WordWrap to False but keep MultiLine True and the text box will only display text on a new line when you press ENTER. Because text can scroll off both the right and bottom edges of a text box when WordWrap is False, you should also set the ScrollBars property to display both vertical and horizontal scroll bars, as listed in Table 14-4.

Table 14-4: Properties for Turning a Text Box into a Text Editor

Property	Value
MultiLine	True
ScrollBars	Both
WordWrap	False

Figure 14-7 shows how text boxes behave differently when the MultiLine, ScrollBars, and WordWrap properties are set to the values listed in Tables 14-3 and 14-4.

Figure 14-7: Text boxes behave differently with different property settings.

Hiding Text in a Text Box

If you want the user to enter text that won't be displayed on screen, such as a password, use the properties listed in Table 14-5 to hide anything that the user types in to a text box.

Table 14-5: Properties for Masking Text that Appears in a Text Box

Property	Value
MultiLine	False
PasswordChar	Any single character such as an asterisk (*)
WordWrap	False

When a user types text into a text box that has PasswordChar defined as a single character, the text box stores the text in its Text property. All text, including spaces, will appear as the character defined by the PasswordChar property, shown in Figure 14-8.

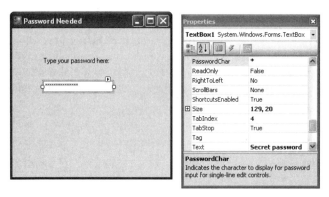

Figure 14-8: With the PasswordChar property defined as an asterisk (*),
the text box hides all text typed into a text box and displays only asterisks.

Using a Masked Text Box

Using
Masked
Text Boxes

Say you want users to type information in a specific format, such as a telephone number, Social Security number, or birth date. To force users to type data in a certain format, use a *masked text box*. A masked text box looks and acts like a normal text box, except that it accepts only numbers in a fixed format, such as that of a telephone number—(999) 123-4567. To create one, follow these steps:

1. Click the Masked Text Box control in the Toolbox, mouse over a form, and click the left mouse button to create a masked text box on your form. Then open the Properties window by choosing View ▶ Properties Window.

2. Click the Mask property, then click the ellipsis button to display the Input Mask dialog box, as shown in Figure 14-9.

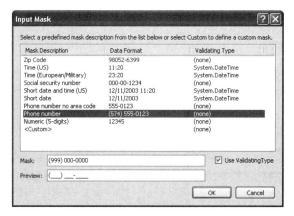

Figure 14-9: The Input Mask dialog box lets you choose
or customize your own format for accepting numbers.

3. Click one of the masks listed in the Mask Description list box. Visual Basic Express displays your chosen mask and format in the Mask and Preview text boxes.

4. Click OK. Visual Basic Express displays your mask in the masked text box control on your form.

When the user types a number into a masked text box, that number is stored in the Text property, including any characters that make up the mask. For example, if you defined a mask to be (999) 000-0000 and the user typed in 8001234567, the Text property would store the number as (800) 123-4567, including the punctuation.

Hands-on Tutorial: Playing with Masked Text Boxes

This tutorial shows you how to use masked text boxes.

1. Load Visual Basic Express, press CTRL-N to display the New Project dialog box, then click OK to display a blank form.
2. Choose View ▶ Toolbox to display the Toolbox, then choose Window ▶ Auto Hide to keep the Toolbox visible. (Skip this step if there is no checkmark in front of the Auto Hide command.)
3. Click the Label control, mouse over the form, and click the left mouse button near the top of the form. A label control appears on your form.
4. Click the TextBox control, mouse over the form, and click the left mouse button underneath the label you created in step 3. A text box appears on the form.
5. Click the MaskedTextBox control, mouse over the form, and click the left mouse button underneath the text box you created in step 4. A masked text box appears.
6. Press F4 to open the Properties window and click the Mask property, then click the ellipsis button that appears to display the Input Mask dialog box.
7. Click the Phone Number mask description (it displays space for an area code) and click OK. The masked text box displays your mask.
8. Click the Button control in the Toolbox, move the mouse pointer underneath the masked text box, and click the left mouse button to draw a button control on the form. Your user interface should look similar to Figure 14-10.

Figure 14-10: The appearance of the completed user interface

9. Double-click the Button1 control. The code window appears.
10. Type `Label1.Text = TextBox1.Text & MaskedTextBox1.Text` between the Private Sub and End Sub lines, like so:

```
Private Sub Button1_Click(ByVal sender As System.Object, ByVal e As_
System.EventArgs) Handles Button1.Click
        Label1.Text = TextBox1.Text & ": " & MaskedTextBox1.Text
End Sub
```

11. Press F5 to display your user interface, then click in the top text box and type your name, such as **Joe Smith**.

12. Click in the masked text box and type your phone number, such as **(123) 456-7890**. Notice that the numbers are automatically placed within the parentheses and on either side of the dash.

13. Click the Button1 control. The label at the top of your form displays the text box contents along with the masked text box contents using the BASIC code you typed in step 10.

14. Press ALT-F4 to stop your program from running, choose File ▶ Close Project, then Click Discard.

KEY FEATURES TO REMEMBER

Labels, link labels, and text boxes are three types of controls that can display text on the screen.

- Labels store text in the Text property. BASIC code can change the Text property of a label but the user cannot change the Text property while a program is running.

- Link labels can display hyperlinks embedded within ordinary text that the user can click to cause some action to occur.

- A text box can display data and allow a user to type and edit new data.

- A masked text box restricts the format of any numbers a user can type. Any numbers typed in a masked text box get stored in the Text property.

15

ACCEPTING A RANGE OF NUMERIC VALUES

Accepting numeric data from a user can be a challenge. Users could type a number into a text box, but they might type it with a comma (1,725) or without (1725). Too, you'll probably want to limit the range of acceptable values. For example, you wouldn't want the user to enter a negative number for *age* or a decimal number for *number of children in family*.

To make data entry easier for everyone, Visual Basic offers two types of controls that can accept a range of values. The first, *scroll bars*, let a user click an arrow or slide a *scroll box* to define a specific numeric value. The second, *calendar controls*, allow users to click a date rather than type a specific one.

Using Scroll Bars

While scroll bars are often used inside text boxes to allow users to scroll up and down or back and forth, they can appear separately to represent a range of values (see Figure 15-1).The movable box inside a scroll bar is known as a *scroll box*; the area inside the bar is the *scroll area*.

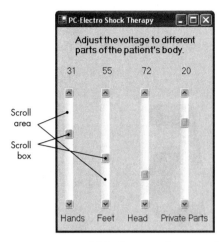

Scroll
area

Scroll
box

Figure 15-1: Users can choose a value by sliding a scroll box inside a scroll bar.

Table 15-1 lists the properties that can be modified to define the range of values a scroll bar can represent.

Table 15-1: Scroll Bar Properties

Property	What it does
LargeChange	Determines how far the scroll box moves, within the Minimum and Maximum property values, when the user presses the PAGE UP or PAGE DOWN key or clicks inside the scroll area. (The default is 10 pixels.)
Maximum	Defines the largest value that the scroll bar can return. (The default is 100.)
Minimum	Defines the smallest value the scroll bar can return. (The default is 0.)
SmallChange	Determines how far the scroll box moves, within the Minimum and Maximum property values, when the user presses an arrow key or clicks the arrows in the scroll bar. (The default is 1 pixel.)
Value	Stores the current value of the scroll bar, based on the current position of the scroll box. This value will always be between the Minimum and Maximum property values, such as 0 to 100.

You can create either *horizontal* and *vertical* scroll bars. The scroll bar controls appear under the All Windows Forms category in the Toolbox, as shown in Figure 15-2.

When the user drags the scroll box to the far left or top of a scroll bar, the scroll bar returns the value stored in its Minimum property. When the scroll box is moved to the far right or bottom of a scroll bar, the scroll bar returns a value stored in its Maximum property, as shown in Figure 15-3.

The SmallChange property defines how far the scroll box moves when the user presses an arrow key or clicks the scroll bar arrows. The LargeChange property defines how far the scroll box moves when the user presses the PAGE UP or PAGE DOWN key or clicks the scroll area of the scroll bar. To restrict a user's choice by a fixed number, such as counting by 2 (the only choices would be 2, 4, 6, and so on), set the SmallChange property to 2 and the LargeChange property to a multiple of 2.

Horizontal scroll bar control

Figure 15-2: Scroll bar controls appear under the All Windows Forms category in the Toolbox.

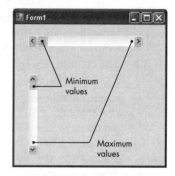

Minimum values

Maximum values

Figure 15-3: Identifying the Minimum and Maximum values for horizontal and vertical scroll bars

When the user chooses a value through the scroll bar, the value is stored in the scroll bar's *Value* property. To view a scroll bar's Value property while a program runs, you use BASIC code to transfer the scroll bar's Value property to the Text property of a label or text box.

The *TrackBar* control is a variation on the horizontal scroll bar. It shares the same properties (see Table 15-1) as a scroll bar and works much like a horizontal scroll bar, except that it displays a slider that moves in visible increments, as shown in Figure 15-4.

Figure 15-4: A TrackBar displays a fixed number of tick marks to which the slider can point.

Hands-on Tutorial: Creating Scroll Bars and TrackBars

Using Scroll Bars and TrackBars

A scroll bar often needs to display the current value on screen so the user can see their chosen value. In this tutorial, you'll draw both a horizontal scroll bar and a track bar.

1. Open a new project in Visual Basic Express, then choose View ▸ Toolbox to display the Toolbox. Choose Window ▸ Auto Hide to keep the Toolbox visible. (Skip this step if a check mark does not appear in front of the Auto Hide command.)

2. Click the plus sign that appears to the left of the All Windows Forms category at the top of the Toolbox.

3. Click the HScrollBar control in the Toolbox, move the mouse pointer near the top of the form, hold down the left mouse button, and drag the mouse to draw a horizontal scroll bar.

4. Click the Label control in the Toolbox, move the mouse pointer under the horizontal scroll bar you just created on the form, and click the left mouse button. A label control appears underneath the horizontal scroll bar control.

5. Double-click the horizontal scroll bar. The Code window appears.

6. Click the TrackBar control in the Toolbox, move the mouse pointer near the bottom of the form, hold down the left mouse button, and drag the mouse to draw the track bar approximately the same size as the horizontal scroll bar you created in step 3.

7. Click the Label control in the Toolbox, move the mouse pointer *underneath* the TrackBar control you just created on the form, and click the left mouse button. A label control appears on the form. Your user interface should look like Figure 15-5.

Figure 15-5: Two labels, a horizontal scroll bar, and a track bar on a form

8. Type **Label1.Text = HScrollBar1.Value** between the `Private Sub` and `End Sub` lines, as follows:

```
Private Sub HScrollBar1_Scroll(ByVal sender As System.Object, ByVal e As_
System.Windows.Forms.ScrollEventArgs) Handles HScrollBar1.Scroll
        Label1.Text = HScrollBar1.Value
End Sub
```

9. Click the Class Name list box in the Code window and choose TrackBar1.

10. Click the Method Name list box in the Code window and choose Scroll, as shown in Figure 15-6. The scroll event procedure for the TrackBar control appears.

11. Type **Label2.Text = TrackBar1.Value** between the `Private Sub` and `End Sub` lines, as follows:

```
Private Sub TrackBar1_Scroll(ByVal sender As Object, ByVal e As System.EventArgs)_
Handles TrackBar1.Scroll
        Label2.Text = TrackBar1.Value
End Sub
```

12. Press F5 to display your user interface then drag the scroll box to see how the value of the horizontal scroll bar changes.

13. Click the track bar, press the left and right arrow keys, and press the PAGE UP and PAGE DOWN keys to see how the value of the track bar control changes.

14. Press ALT-F4 to stop the program then choose File ▶ Close Project. Click Discard.

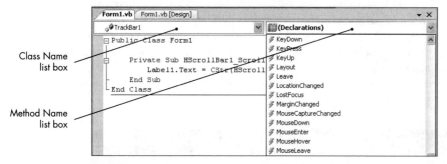

Class Name
list box

Method Name
list box

Figure 15-6: Creating an event procedure for the track bar control using the Class
Name and Method Name list boxes

Displaying Numbers with the NumericUpDown Control

Scroll bars and TrackBars can take up a lot of room. If space is limited, consider using a *NumericUpDown* control instead, which lets users click up and down arrows to choose a value, as shown in Figure 15-7.

Like scroll bars, the NumericUpDown control gives users a range of values from which to choose, and it offers these additional features:

- Numeric choices can include decimals and not just integers (whole numbers).
- Numeric choices can display a comma to make large numbers easier to read.
- The current value always appears inside the NumericUpDown control.

Table 15-2 lists the properties that you can modify to define the range of values a NumericUpDown control can represent.

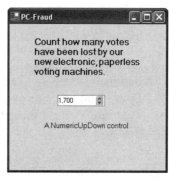

Figure 15-7: A NumericUpDown control lets a user click arrows until the appropriate number appears.

Table 15-2: NumericUpDown Control Properties

Property	What it does
DecimalPlaces	Defines whether you want the NumericUpDown control to display decimal places. (The default value is 0.)
Increment	Defines how numbers increase or decrease with each click of the up and down arrows. (The default value is 1.)
Maximum	Defines the largest value the NumericUpDown control can return. (The default value is 100.)
Minimum	Defines the smallest value the NumericUpDown control can return. (The default value is 0.)
ThousandsSeparator	Defines whether you want commas to appear in large numbers, such as 1,000,000. (The default value is False.)
Value	Contains the number currently displayed in the NumericUpDown control.

To have the NumericUpDown control display decimals, define the DecimalPlaces property to any value greater than 1 and change the Increment property to a decimal value, such as 1.5 or 2.75. For example, to display one decimal place, change the DecimalPlaces property to 1 and set the Increment property to a value with one decimal place, such as 0.5.

To retrieve the value displayed by the NumericUpDown control, you need to use BASIC code to access the Value property.

Hands-on Tutorial: Using the NumericUpDown Control

Using the Numeric-UpDown Control

In this tutorial, you'll create a NumericUpDown control to see how little space it requires compared to using a scroll bar.

1. Open a New Project in Visual Basic Express, then click OK to display a blank form.
2. Choose View ▶ Toolbox to display the Toolbox, then choose Window ▶ Auto Hide.
3. Click the NumericUpDown control in the Toolbox, move the mouse pointer near the top of the form, hold down the left mouse button, move the mouse, and then release the mouse button to draw the NumericUpDown control on the form.
4. Press F4 to open the Properties window, click the DecimalPlaces property, and type **2**.
5. Click in the Increment property and type **1.32**.
6. Click the Label control in the Toolbox, move the mouse pointer under the NumericUpDown control you just created on the form, and click the left mouse button. A label control appears underneath the NumericUpDown control.
7. Double-click the NumericUpDown control. The Code window appears.
8. Type `Label1.Text = NumericUpDown1.Value` between the `Private Sub` and `End Sub` lines, as follows:

```
Private Sub NumericUpDown1_ValueChanged(ByVal sender As System.Object, ByVal e As_
System.EventArgs) Handles NumericUpDown1.ValueChanged
        Label1.Text = NumericUpDown1.Value
End Sub
```

9. Press F5 to display your user interface, then click the up and down arrows of the NumericUpDown control to see how the value changes.
10. Press ALT-F4 to stop the program, choose File ▶ Close Project, then click Discard.

Choosing Dates

Many programs ask users to choose a date. While you can force a user to enter a date in a text box, it's often simpler to use the *MonthCalendar* and *DateTimePicker* controls to allow users to click a date (see Figure 15-8).

The DateTimePicker control works like a list box. It uses a minimal amount of space on a form and displays a calendar only when the user clicks it. It also lets users retrieve the current time as well as any date.

The MonthCalendar control lets users choose a single date or a range of dates. Unlike the DateTimePicker, it always appears full size on a form.

Figure 15-8: The DateTimePicker control compared to a MonthCalendar control.

Using the MonthCalendar Control

The MonthCalendar control is useful both when you want to display dates and when you want to allow users to select a range of dates. Table 15-3 lists some of the properties you can modify to customize its appearance and behavior.

Table 15-3: Properties for Customizing a MonthCalendar Control

Property	What it does
FirstDayOfWeek	Defines the first day that appears at the far left side of the calendar. (The default is Sunday.)
MaxDate	Defines the maximum date the user can select. (The default is 12/31/9998.)
MaxSelectionCount	Defines the maximum number of days a user can select. (The default is 7.)
MinDate	Defines the minimum date a user can select. (The default is 1/1/1753.)
SelectionRange	Contains the date or range of dates that the user selected.
ShowToday	Defines whether the calendar displays today's date at the bottom of the control. (The default is True.)
ShowTodayCircle	Defines whether today's date appears highlighted on the calendar. (The default is True.)
ShowWeekNumbers	Defines whether the calendar shows the numbers of each week in the left-hand column, where Week 1 defines the first full week of January, Week 2 defines the second week of January, and so on, until the last week of the year, labeled Week 52. (The default is False, which will not show week numbers.)
TodayDate	Displays the date to be marked as the current date. (The default is the current date as stored in your computer's clock.)

Once the user selects a date or a range of dates, you'll need to write BASIC code to determine which dates the user selected. The MonthCalendar control uses the Selection-Range.Start and SelectionRange.End properties to store the start and end dates of a selected range of dates. If the user selects a single date, these properties are the same.

Using the DateTimePicker Control

The DateTimePicker control allows users to display and select a single date, using a minimum amount of space. It displays a full month calendar only when the user clicks the control. Table 15-4 lists some of the properties you can modify to customize its appearance and behavior. (Once the user selects a date, you'll need to write BASIC code to retrieve the date stored in the DateTimePicker control's Value property.)

Table 15-4: Properties for Customizing a DateTimePicker Control

Property	What it does
MaxDate	Defines the maximum date the user can select. (The default is 12/31/9998.)
MinDate	Defines the minimum date a user can select. (The default is 1/1/1753.)
Value	Stores the current time and the date the user selected in a format such as 2/3/2006 3:21:07 PM.

Hands-on Tutorial: Selecting Dates with the DateTimePicker and MonthCalendar Controls

This tutorial shows how to create the DateTimePicker control to choose a single date and the MonthCalendar control to choose a range of dates.

1. Start a new Visual Basic Express project, then click OK to open a blank form. Choose View ▸ Toolbox to display the Toolbox, then choose Window ▸ Auto Hide to keep it visible.

2. Click the DateTimePicker control in the Toolbox, move the mouse pointer near the top of the form, hold down the left mouse button, move the mouse, and release the left mouse button to draw the DateTimePicker control near the top of the form.

3. Click the MonthCalendar control in the Toolbox, move the mouse pointer under the DateTimePicker control you just created on the form, and click the left mouse button. A MonthCalendar control appears on the form.

4. Click the Label control in the Toolbox, mouse over the form, and click the left mouse button underneath the Month-Calendar control. A label control appears on your form. Your user interface should look like Figure 15-9.

Figure 15-9: A DateTimePicker, Month-Calendar, and Label control on a form

5. Double-click the DateTimePicker control. The Code window appears.

6. Type **Label1.Text = DateTimePicker1.Value** between the Private Sub and End Sub lines, as follows:

```
Private Sub DateTimePicker1_ValueChanged(ByVal sender As System.Object, ByVal e As_
System.EventArgs) Handles DateTimePicker1.ValueChanged
        Label1.Text = DateTimePicker1.Value
End Sub
```

7. Click the Class Name list box and choose MonthCalendar1.

8. Click the Method Name list box and choose DateChanged. The code window creates en empty event procedure for the MonthCalendar control.

9. Type `Label1.Text = MonthCalendar1.SelectionRange.Start & "     " & MonthCalendar1.SelectionRange.End` between the `Private Sub` and `End Sub` lines, as follows:

```
Private Sub MonthCalendar1_DateChanged(ByVal sender As System.Object, ByVal e As_
System.Windows.Forms.DateRangeEventArgs) Handles MonthCalendar1.DateChanged
        Label1.Text = MonthCalendar1.SelectionRange.Start & "     " &_
MonthCalendar1.SelectionRange.End
End Sub
```

10. Press F5 to display your user interface, then click the downward-pointing arrow on the DateTimePicker control. A drop-down calendar appears.

11. Click a date. Notice that the label control near the bottom of the form now displays the date you chose. (Try experimenting with clicking the right and left arrows to change the month displayed in the DateTimePicker control.)

12. Click the MonthCalendar control, click a date, hold down the left mouse button, and drag the mouse to cover a range of dates. Notice that the label now displays the first and last dates you selected. (The maximum number of dates the user can select is defined by the MaxSelectionCount property of the MonthCalendar control. By default, the value of the MaxSelectionCount property is 7, so if you want users to be able to select a larger range, you'll have to modify the MaxSelectionCount property.)

13. Press ALT-F4 to stop the program, choose File ▸ Close Project, then click Discard.

KEY FEATURES TO REMEMBER

Scroll bars, TrackBars, and NumericUpDown controls are handy for giving users a range of numbers from which to choose. The MonthCalendar and DateTimePicker controls are useful for letting the user click a date rather they typing it into a text box.

- Scroll bars use the Value property to store the current position of the scroll box within the scroll bar.

- You'll need to use BASIC code to retrieve the Value property of a scroll bar and display it in another control, such as a label or text box, to make it visible to the user.

- A TrackBar acts like a horizontal scroll bar except it displays a slider that moves in discrete segments indicated by tick marks.

- The NumericUpDown control lets users choose from a range of values, including decimal values and values that include commas.

- The MonthCalendar control lets users select a single date or a range of dates.

- The MonthCalendar control stores the start date of a selected range in its SelectionRange .Start property and the end date of a selected range in its SelectionRange.End property. If the user selects only a single date, the SelectionRange.Start and SelectionRange.End properties will be identical.

- The DateTimePicker stores both the selected date and the current time in its Value property.

16

DESIGNING A FORM WITH LAYOUT CONTROLS

A well-organized user interface can make your program easier for people to use. To help you organize buttons, check boxes, list boxes, and other user interface controls on a form, Visual Basic Express provides a variety of special *layout controls* that can organize other controls on a form. These layout controls appear under the Containers category of the Toolbox.

You can add a layout control and then create additional ones such as buttons and check boxes inside the layout control. If you have created other controls, you can create a layout control and then move any existing controls inside a layout control. To add a *layout control* to a form, you simply click the control you want to use from the Toolbox, as shown in Figure 16-1.

NOTE *Layout controls simply organize other controls, such as text boxes or radio buttons that actually display text or offer choices to a user.*

Figure 16-1: All the layout controls are stored under the Containers category of the Toolbox.

Using Panels

Using the Panel and GroupBox Controls

Panels are like boxes that let you organize related controls into groups. While panels are normally invisible, you can change a panel's BorderStyle property to one of three settings, as shown in Figure 16-2.

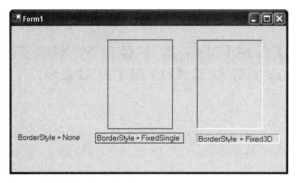

Figure 16-2: The BorderStyle property determines the appearance of the panel on a form.

These properties have the following characteristics:

None The panel appears invisible (default).

FixedSingle A single line appears around the panel edges.

Fixed3D The panel appears "pushed" into the form.

The *GroupBox* control acts like a panel but includes a Text property so you can enter descriptive text to identify the controls grouped inside it, as shown in Figure 16-3.

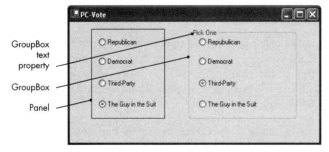

GroupBox text property

GroupBox

Panel

Figure 16-3: A GroupBox (at right) acts like a panel (at left) but adds a Text property that lets you identify its contents.

Using a FlowLayoutPanel

The *FlowLayoutPanel* looks and acts like a regular panel except that it automatically aligns any controls you place inside it. It can align controls in one of four ways, as defined by the FlowDirection property:

- LeftToRight
- TopDown

- RightToLeft
- BottomUp

Table 16-1 shows the order in which controls would appear on a form when the FlowDirection property is set to LeftToRight. The first control aligns at the top-left corner, and additional controls appear to the right. When there's no more room for additional controls, they appear in the next row down, starting from the left.

Table 16-1: LeftToRight FlowDirection Setting

1st control	2nd control	3rd control
4th control	5th control	

Table 16-2 shows how controls appear when the FlowDirection property is set to RightToLeft. The first control aligns in the top-right corner, and additional controls appear to the left. When there's no more room for additional controls, they appear in the next row down, starting from the right.

Table 16-2: RightToLeft FlowDirection Setting

3rd control	2nd control	1st control
	5th control	4th control

Table 16-3 shows how controls appear when the FlowDirection property is set to TopDown. The first control aligns in the top-left corner, and additional controls appear directly underneath it. When there's no more room for additional controls, they appear in the next column to the right, starting from the top.

Table 16-3: TopDown FlowDirection Setting

1st control	4th control
2nd control	5th control
3rd control	

Table 16-4 shows how controls appear when the FlowDirection property is set to BottomUp. The first control aligns at the bottom-left corner, and additional controls appear directly above it. When there's no more room for additional controls, they appear in the next column to the right, starting from the bottom.

Table 16-4: BottomUp FlowDirection Setting

3rd control	
2nd control	5th control
1st control	4th control

To create a FlowLayoutPanel control, follow these steps:

1. Double-click the FlowLayoutPanel control under the Containers category in the Toolbox. Your FlowLayoutPanel appears on the form. (You may want to move or resize it.)

2. Choose View ▸ Properties Window to open the Properties window, then click the FlowDirection property. A downward-pointing appears.

3. Click the downward-pointing arrow and choose an option such as BottomUp or RightToLeft.

4. Add a control, such as a radio button or check box, *inside* the FlowLayoutPanel control. The FlowLayoutPanel control should automatically align your control according to the way you defined the Flow-Direction property in step 3. Figure 16-4 shows the default FlowDirection value of LeftToRight.

5. Repeat step 4 for each additional control you want to display inside the FlowLayout-Panel control.

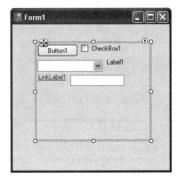

Figure 16-4: Multiple controls aligned automatically inside a FlowLayoutPanel control.

Using a TableLayoutPanel

Using the TableLayout-Panel Control

One problem with the FlowLayoutPanel is that it doesn't offer you much control over the spacing between controls, which are all crammed together (see Figure 16-4). If you want more control over the placement of your controls, use the TableLayoutPanel control, which divides a normal panel into rows and columns that intersect to form *cells*.

When you place a control inside a cell, the TableLayoutPanel centers it within the cell. You can create or delete additional rows and columns and adjust the size of your rows and columns as well. Table 16-5 lists four properties that you can modify to customize a TableLayoutPanel control.

Table 16-5: TableLayoutPanel Control Properties

Property	What it does
CellBorderStyle	Defines the appearance of the lines that divide the TableLayoutPanel into rows and columns. (The default is None, which makes the TableLayoutPanel invisible.)
ColumnCount	Defines the number of columns in the TableLayoutPanel control. (The default is 2.)
ColumnStyles	Defines the size and position of a column.
RowCount	Defines the number of rows in the TableLayoutPanel control. (The default is 2.)
RowStyles	Defines the size and position of a row.

The TableLayoutPanel is normally invisible because its CellBorderStyle property is set to None. If you want users to see its borders, change the CellBorderStyle to a value such as Single or InsetDouble. (The different appearances of the CellBorderStyle can be subtle, so experiment with different values until you find one that you like.)

To create a TableLayoutPanel control:

1. Double-click the TableLayoutPanel control under the Containers category in the Toolbox. Visual Basic Express draws a TableLayoutPanel on the form. (You may want to move or resize it later.)
2. Click the CellBorderStyle property and choose an option, such as Single or Outset.
3. Add a control, such as a radio button or check box, inside a cell of the TableLayout-Panel. The TableLayoutPanel should automatically center your control inside the cell, as shown in Figure 16-5.
4. Repeat step 3 for any additional controls.

Changing the Size of Rows and Columns

If a row or column is too big or too small, you can change its size using either the mouse or the Properties window. To resize a column or a row using the mouse:

1. Click the TableLayoutPanel control that you want to modify, then mouse over a column or row border so the mouse pointer turns into a two-way pointing arrow, as shown in Figure 16-6.

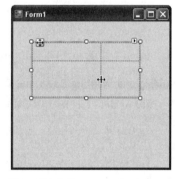

Figure 16-5: Controls appear centered within each cell of a TableLayoutPanel control.

Figure 16-6: You can resize a row or column in a TableLayoutPanel using the mouse.

2. Hold down the left mouse button and drag the mouse until you're happy with the size of the row or column.

To resize a row or column to a specific size, use the Height or Width property of a row or column in the Properties window. To do so:

1. Click the TableLayoutPanel control that you want to modify.
2. Open the Properties window by choosing View ▸ Properties Window.
3. Click the Columns or Rows property. An ellipsis button appears. Click the ellipsis button to display a Column and Row Styles dialog box, as shown in Figure 16-7.
4. Under the Member column, click the row or column that you want to resize.
5. Click a radio button in the Size Type group to choose one of the following:

   Absolute   Resizes a row or column based on the pixel size you type in. (Be careful, because it's possible to define a height or width so small that controls stored inside that row or column can appear truncated.)

Percent   Defines the row or column size as a percentage of the entire TableLayout-Panel control size.

AutoSize   Resizes the row or column based on the largest size of a control stored in that row or column.

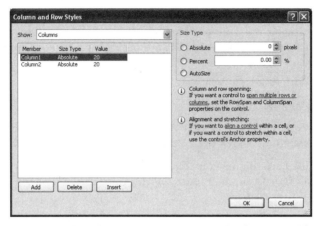

Figure 16-7: The Column and Row Styles dialog box lets you modify your rows and columns in the TableLayoutPanel.

6.   Click OK. Visual Basic Express resizes your chosen row or column.

Adding and Deleting Rows and Columns

To add or delete rows and columns inside a TableLayoutPanel control:

1.   Click the TableLayoutPanel that you want to modify. An Actions button appears in the top-right corner.

2.   Click the Actions button. An Actions menu appears, as shown in Figure 16-8.

3.   Click Add Column, Add Row, Remove Last Column, or Remove Last Row. Visual Basic Express adds or deletes a column to the right or a row at the bottom of the TableLayoutPanel. Note that if you delete a row or column that contains any controls inside it, such as a radio button or text box, Visual Basic Express will delete those controls, too. (If you click Edit Rows And Columns, the Columns and Rows Styles dialog box appears as shown in Figure 16-7.)

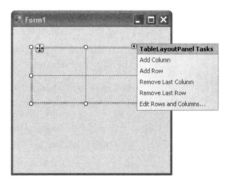

Figure 16-8: Click the Actions button to display an Actions menu, where you can add or remove a row or column.

You can also add or delete rows and columns using the Column and Row Styles dialog box by following these steps:

1.   Click the TableLayoutPanel that you want to modify, then open the Properties window by choosing View ▸ Properties Window.

2. Click the Columns or Rows property. An ellipsis button appears. Click the ellipsis button to display the Column and Row Styles dialog box (see Figure 16-7).

3. Choose one of the following:

    - Click the Add button to add a row at the bottom or a column to the right of the TableLayoutPanel.
    - Click a row or column you want to delete and then click Delete. (Note that deleting a row or column will also delete any controls stored inside that row or column.)
    - Click a row or column and click Insert. This will add a *row above* the currently selected row or a *column* to the *left* of the currently selected column.

4. Click OK.

Once you've created a TableLayoutPanel, you can either drag existing controls or create new controls directly inside a TableLayoutPanel. For a quicker way:

1. Click the TableLayoutPanel where you want to add a control.

2. Double-click any control in the Toolbox. Your chosen control appears in an empty cell starting from the upper-left corner. (If all rows are filled with controls, this step will automatically add a new row to your TableLayoutPanel.)

Using a TabControl

Creating Tabbed Interfaces with the TabControl

If you cram too many controls on a form, the forms can look disorganized and cluttered. To avoid this problem, use a *TabControl*, so that each tab contains and displays a different set of controls, as shown in Figure 16-9.

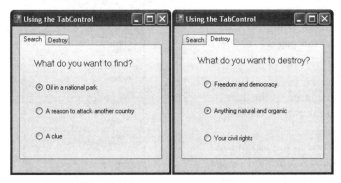

Figure 16-9: The TabControl lets you display multiple groups of controls in the same physical space.

Creating a TabControl

To create a TabControl:

1. Double-click the TabControl in the Toolbox. Visual Basic Express draws a TabControl on the form.

2. (Optional) Click the Alignment property under the Behavior category of the Properties window, and choose where you want your tabs to appear: Top (the default value), Bottom, Right, or Left.

3. Click the TabPages property. An ellipsis button appears. Click the ellipsis button to display the TabPage Collection Editor dialog box, as shown in Figure 16-10.

Up button
Down button

Figure 16-10: The TabPage Collection Editor lets you rearrange and modify individual tab pages.

4. Click a tab page, such as TabPage1, in the Members list box.
5. Click the Text property in the properties list at the right of the dialog box.
6. In the right column, type the text that you want to appear on your tab.
7. Repeat steps 4 to 6 to modify the text that appears on each tab.
8. Click OK. Your tab control appears with any changes you made to the Text properties of each tab page.

Selecting a TabControl or Individual Tab Pages

Once you've created a TabControl, you can modify the entire TabControl or just the individual tab pages. To select the entire TabControl, you can use one of two methods:

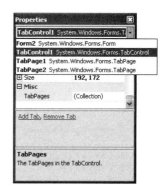

*   Click a tab displayed in the Tab-Control to highlight the entire TabControl.
*   Click the list box at the top of the Properties window and choose the name of the TabControl you want to modify, as shown in Figure 16-11.

Figure 16-11: The Properties window list box lets you select a control by name.

To select an individual tab page, do one of the following:

*   Click a tab to display the tab page you want to view, then click inside the tab page.
*   Click a tab to select the entire TabControl, press F4 to open the Properties window, and click the TabPages property under the Misc category. When an ellipsis button appears, click it to display the TabPage Collection Editor. Click the tab page you want to edit, and the Property window for that tab page appears in the TabPage Collection Editor.
*   Click the list box at the top of the Properties window and click the name of the tab page you want to modify.

Adding and Deleting Tabs

When you first create a TabControl, it automatically displays two tabs. To add or delete additional tabs, do the following:

1. Click any tab on the TabControl that you want to modify. An Actions button appears in the top-right corner.
2. Click the Actions button. An Actions menu appears, as shown in Figure 16-12.
3. Click Add Tab or Remove Tab. (If you click the Remove Tab command, Visual Basic Express removes the currently highlighted tab and all of its contents.)

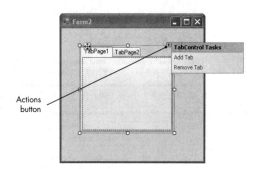

Figure 16-12: The Actions menu lets you quickly add or remove tabs.

Rearranging Tabs

After creating a TabControl and placing different controls on your tab pages, you may want to rearrange the tabs. (Rearranging tabs does not affect any controls stored on that tab page; it simply moves the tab position that appears to the user.)

To rearrange tabs:

1. Click any tab that's part of the TabControl you want to modify. (Be sure to select the entire TabControl and not just an individual tab page.)
2. Open the Properties window, click the TabPages property, then click the ellipsis button that appears to open the TabPage Collection Editor dialog box (see Figure 16-10).
3. Click the tab you want to move, then click the up and down arrow buttons to move it.
4. Click OK. Visual Basic Express displays the new arrangement of your tabs.

Using a SplitContainer

Using the Split-Container Control

A *SplitContainer* consists of two panels in which you can place controls. You can customize the appearance of each panel, hide a panel from view, and even resize both panels with the mouse as your program runs, as shown in Figure 16-13.

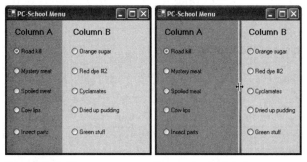

Figure 16-13: The user can resize the panels of a SplitContainer while the program runs.

Creating a SplitContainer

A SplitContainer's two panels can appear either side by side or stacked on top of one another. Visual Basic Express refers to the *left* or *top* panel as *Panel1* and the *right* or *bottom* panel as *Panel2*. When you create a SplitContainer, you may want to modify the properties listed in Table 16-6.

Table 16-6: SplitContainer Properties

Property	What it does
BorderStyle	Defines the border of the SplitContainer: None, FixedSingle, or Fixed3D. (The default is None, which makes the borders of the SplitContainer invisible when your program runs.)
FixedPanel	Defines whether Panel1 or Panel2 remains a fixed width or height no matter how much the user may resize the form. (The default is None.)
IsSplitterFixed	Defines whether the *splitter*, which divides the panels, remains fixed in place. (The default is False so the user can move the splitter while the program runs.)
Orientation	Defines whether the splitter appears vertical or horizontal.
Panel1Collapsed, Panel2Collapsed	Defines whether the panel initially appears collapsed or not. (The default is False.)
Panel1MinSize, Panel2MinSize	Defines the minimum size of Panel1 or Panel2.
SplitterDistance	Defines how far from the left or top the splitter initially appears, measured in pixels.
SplitterIncrement	Defines how far the splitter moves when the user drags it with the mouse, measured in pixels. (The default is 1.)
SplitterWidth	Defines the width of the splitter, measured in pixels. (The default is 4.)

Once you have drawn a SplitContainer on a form, you can draw additional controls (such as buttons or check boxes), inside either of its panels. Visual Basic Express treats all radio buttons inside the same panel as members of the same group, which means only one radio button in a panel can be selected at any given time.

When modifying a SplitContainer's properties, you must select the entire SplitContainer and not just one of its panels. To select a SplitContainer, do one of the following:

- Drag the mouse to draw a dotted-line rectangle over *both* of the SplitContainer's panels, as shown in Figure 16-14. Release the left mouse button to highlight the entire SplitContainer.
- Click the list box of the Properties window and choose the name of the Split-Container (not the panel of the SplitContainer), as shown in Figure 16-15.

Customizing Panels in a SplitContainer

In addition to modifying properties for your SplitContainer, you can also modify properties for either Panel1 or Panel2. To do so:

1. Click the panel you want to modify in a SplitContainer.
2. Open the Properties window, then modify any properties for your chosen panel, such as the BackColor property.

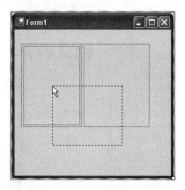

Figure 16-14: Drag the mouse over both panels of a SplitContainer to select both panels.

Figure 16-15: Use the list box of the Properties window to select the entire SplitContainer or just one of its panels.

NOTE You can change the BackColor properties of both Panel1 and Panel2 of a SplitContainer so that, for example, one panel appears with a red background and another appears in yellow. This can make the individual panels easier to see.

Hands-on Tutorial: Understanding Different Layout Controls

The purpose of a layout control is to help you organize other controls, such as radio buttons, check boxes, and text boxes. This tutorial guides you in creating different layout controls so you can see how they appear in a user interface.

1. Open a new project then click OK to display a blank form.
2. Click the TabControl under the Containers category of the Toolbox, mouse over to the upper-left corner of the form, hold down the left mouse button, and drag the mouse so the TabControl fills up most of the form.
3. Click the TableLayoutPanel under the Containers category of the Toolbox, mouse over the TabControl, and click the left mouse button. A TableLayoutPanel appears on TabPage1 of the TabControl you created in step 2.
4. Click the RadioButton control in the Toolbox, mouse over the TableLayoutPanel, and click the left mouse button. A radio button control appears inside the Table-LayoutPanel.
5. Repeat step 4 to add another radio button inside the TableLayoutPanel. Notice that the new control automatically aligns itself within the row and column of the TableLayoutPanel. Your user interface should look like Figure 16-16.
6. Click the TabPage2 tab of the TabControl. (You may have to click it twice.) The TabControl displays the blank TabPage2 page.
7. Click the SplitContainer under the Containers category of the Toolbox, mouse over the TabPage2 page of the TabControl, and click the left mouse button. A SplitContainer appears.
8. Press F4 to open the Properties window of the SplitContainer then click the Border-Style property. A downward-pointing arrow appears. Click the arrow and choose FixedSingle.
9. Click the RadioButton control in the Toolbox, mouse over the left panel of the SplitContainer, and click the left mouse button to create a radio button.

10. Repeat step 9, but this time click in the right panel of the SplitContainer. Your user interface should look like Figure 16-17.

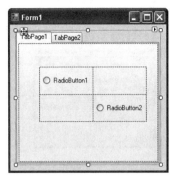

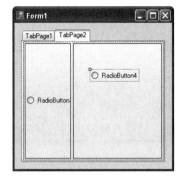

Figure 16-16: A TableLayoutPanel inside a TabControl

Figure 16-17: A SplitContainer inside a TabControl

11. Press F5. Your user interface appears, displaying TabPage1 of the TabControl.

12. Click the TabPage2 tab. The SplitContainer appears inside the TabPage2 page of the TabControl.

13. Mouse over the vertical line dividing the SplitContainer until the mouse pointer turns into a two-way pointing arrow.

14. Hold down the left mouse button and drag the mouse to resize the two panels of the SplitContainer. (If you make the panels of the SplitContainer too small, part of the radio button can be hidden from view.)

15. Press ALT-F4 to stop your program, then choose File ▸ Close Project. Click Discard.

Editing Layout Controls

When you create a layout control (such as a panel, GroupBox, TabControl, or SplitContainer), you may need to move or resize it on a form or even delete it altogether. Fortunately, all layout controls work the same, so moving or deleting a panel is no different than moving or deleting a GroupBox or TabControl.

Docking a Layout Control

Because layout controls help organize controls on your user interface, consider using the Dock property to lock the layout control to a specific part of a form so that, no matter how a user resizes a form, the layout control remains in a fixed location. The six different Dock property options are:

- Top
- Left
- Right
- Bottom
- Fill
- None

When a layout control's Dock property is set to Top or Bottom, the layout control remains the same height but its *width* changes if the user resizes the form, as shown in Figure 16-18. When the Dock property is set to Right or Left, the layout control remains the same width but its *height* changes when the user resizes the form. If the Dock property is set to Fill, the layout control fills the entire form and changes both its *width* and *height* if the user resizes the form. (The default Dock property value for a SplitContainer is Fill.)

If the Dock property is set to None, the layout control remains the same size no matter how large or small the user resizes a form.

To define the Dock property for a layout control:

1. Click the layout control you want to dock. When selecting a SplitContainer, be sure to select the *entire* SplitContainer and not just one of its panels.
2. Open the Properties window, then click the Dock property under the Layout category. A downward-pointing arrow appears.
3. Click the downward-pointing arrow. A chart appears, showing the options available for docking, as shown in Figure 16-19.
4. Click a docking location. Visual Basic Express docks your chosen layout control.

Figure 16-18: A TabControl docked to the top of a form.

Figure 16-19: The Dock property lets you visually choose a location in which to dock a control on a form.

Moving a Layout Control

If you set the Dock property of a layout control to None, you can move the control anywhere inside a form. (If the Dock property is *not* set to None, you won't be able to move a layout control.) When you move a layout control, you also move any controls stored inside it. To move a layout control:

1. Click the layout control you want to move. If you're selecting a SplitContainer, be sure to select the entire SplitContainer and not just one of its panels. Visual Basic Express highlights your chosen layout control and displays a Move button in the upper-left corner, as shown in Figure 16-20.
2. Mouse over the Move button. The mouse pointer turns into a four-way arrow.
3. As you hold down the left mouse button, move the mouse to move the layout control to a new position inside the form.
4. Release the left mouse button when you're happy with the control's new location.

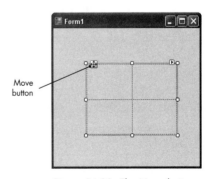

Figure 16-20: The Move button appears as a four-way pointing arrow when you select a layout control.

Deleting a Layout Control

When you delete a layout control, you also delete any controls stored inside it, so make sure you really want to do this before you delete the layout control. To delete a layout control, follow these steps:

1. Click the layout control you want to delete. If you're selecting a SplitContainer, be sure to select the entire SplitContainer and not just one of its panels. Visual Basic Express highlights your chosen layout control.

2. Press DELETE. Visual Basic Express deletes the chosen layout control and any controls stored inside it.

NOTE *If you make a mistake, press CTRL-Z to retrieve your previously deleted layout control and any controls stored inside it.*

KEY FEATURES TO REMEMBER

Visual Basic Express offers a variety of layout controls to organize the appearance of your user interface.

- Panels and GroupBoxes act like boxes in which you can store other types of controls, such as radio buttons or check boxes. Unlike a panel, a GroupBox includes a Text property to display text that you can use to describe the contents of the GroupBox.

- The FlowLayoutPanel and the TableLayoutPanel can automatically arrange any controls you place inside either type of panel.

- A TabControl lets you group different controls in the same physical location, but you can display only one group of controls at a time.

- A SplitContainer displays two panels that the user can resize while your program runs.

- The Dock property can dock a layout control to one side of a form.

- When you delete a layout control, you also delete any controls stored inside it.

17

DISPLAYING DIALOG BOXES

Most programs require that users respond to questions. These might be simple yes/no questions like "Do you really want to delete your file?", or they might be questions with a fixed list of options, such as "Which printer do you want to use?"

When requesting additional information from the user, programs usually display a *dialog box*, which poses a question and provides multiple choices for the user. More complicated dialog boxes, like the typical Print dialog box found in most programs, may display other choices, such as the size of print margins and the orientation of the printed page.

Because dialog boxes are so common in user interfaces, Visual Basic Express provides several built-in dialog boxes that you can use in your own programs. To incorporate them into your programs, all you need to do is write BASIC code to display the dialog box, customize the dialog box by changing a few properties, and retrieve the user's answer. (Dialog boxes won't actually do anything until you write the code to make them work.)

The five dialog box types that Visual Basic Express provides appear under the Dialogs category of the Properties window, as shown in Figure 17-1.

They are:

OpenFileDialog Displays an Open dialog box to let the user choose a file to open.

SaveFileDialog Displays a Save dialog box to let the user type a filename under which data is to be saved.

FolderBrowserDialog Displays a Browse For Folder dialog box to let the user either create a new folder or choose an existing one.

FontDialog Displays a Font dialog box so users can choose a font.

ColorDialog Displays a Color dialog box so users can pick a color.

Figure 17-1: The Dialogs category of the Toolbox displays all the dialog boxes you can include in your program.

Creating and Displaying a Dialog Box

To add a dialog box to your program, you first add the *dialog box control* to the form, then you write BASIC code to make the dialog box appear and retrieve the user's choices.

To add a dialog box control to a form, double-click the name of the dialog box you want to add, such as the OpenFileDialog control. Visual Basic Express displays the dialog box control at the bottom of the Design window, as shown in Figure 17-2.

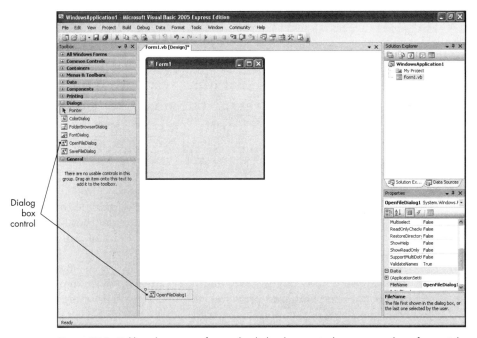

Figure 17-2: Unlike other types of controls, dialog box controls appear under a form, at the bottom of the Design window.

Once you've added a dialog box control to a form, you need to write the BASIC code to display it. The command to display a dialog box combines the dialog box control's name with the ShowDialog command, like so, where *DialogBoxName* is the name of dialog box you want to display.

```
DialogBoxName.ShowDialog()
```

Hands-on Tutorial: Opening and Using a Color Dialog Box

This tutorial shows you how to display a Color dialog box and retrieve the color the user's choice of color from that dialog box.

1. Start a new project, then click OK to display a blank form.
2. Choose View ▶ Toolbox to display the Toolbox, then choose Window ▶ Auto Hide to keep it visible.
3. Double-click the ColorDialog control under the Dialogs category of the Toolbox. The ColorDialog control appears under your blank form.
4. Click the Button control in the Toolbox, mouse over the center of the form, and click the left mouse button to create a button on the form.
5. Double-click the Button1 control on the form. The Code window appears.
6. Type the lines **ColorDialog1.ShowDialog()** and **Button1.BackColor = ColorDialog1.Color** between the Private Sub and End Sub lines, like so:

```
Private Sub Button1_Click(ByVal sender As System.Object, ByVal e As System.EventArgs)_
Handles Button1.Click
        ColorDialog1.ShowDialog()
        Button1.BackColor = ColorDialog1.Color
End Sub
```

7. Press F5 to display your user interface, then click the Button1 control. A Color dialog box appears, the result of the ColorDialog1.ShowDialog() command you typed in step 6.
8. Click a color and click OK. The Button1 control changes to the color you just chose because of the Button1.BackColor = ColorDialog1.Color command you typed in step 6.
9. Press ALT-F4 to stop your program, choose File ▶ Close Project, then click Discard.

Using the Open and Save Dialog Boxes

The Open and Save dialog boxes display a list of files located within a folder. The Open dialog box lets users choose an existing file, while the Save dialog box lets users enter a name of a file to save. Table 17-1 lists some of the properties you can modify to customize both types of dialog boxes.

Table 17-1: Properties for Customizing Open and Save Dialog Boxes

Property	What it does
Filter	List the filename descriptions and filters that define specific types of files to display, such as only files that end with the .exe or .txt file extensions.
FilterIndex	Defines which filter to use, as defined by the Filter property.
InitialDirectory	Defines the directory displayed in the Open dialog box.
FileName	Contains the directory and filename that the user selected. Also contains the text that initially appears in the File Name text box of the Open dialog box.

Defining Filters

Filters determine the types of files that appear in either the Open or Save dialog box. To display all files, leave the Filter property blank or define a filter that displays all files.

If you want the Open dialog box to display only files with a certain file extension, you must define that file extension in the filter. For example, to display only files with a .txt file extension, use this filter: (*.txt). To display only files with a .exe file extension, use this filter: (*.exe).

Each filter consists of a filter description and the filter itself. Filter descriptions identify the type of files the filter displays in the Files Of Type list box in the Open dialog box, as shown in Figure 17-3. Typical filter descriptions might be:

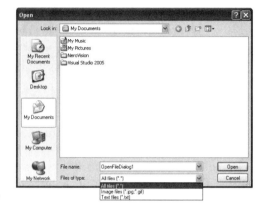

- All files (*.*)
- Image files (*.jpg;*.gif)
- Text files (*.txt)

When defining the Filter property of an Open dialog box, you must specify the filter description, followed by a separator bar and then the filter, like so:

Figure 17-3: The Filter property and the Filter Index properties display data in an Open dialog box.

```
Filter description | Filter
```

For example:

- `All files (*.*) | (*.*)`
- `Text files (*.txt) | (*.txt)`
- `Image files (*.jpg;*.gif) | (*.jpg;*.gif)`

You can modify the Filter property of an Open or Save dialog box by changing it in the Properties window or by using BASIC code.

To modify the Filter property in the Properties window:

1. Click the OpenFileDialog or SaveFileDialog control.
2. Open the Properties window by choosing View ▶ Properties Window, then click the Filter property in the Properties window and enter the name of your filter. For example:

```
All files (*.*) | (*.*) | Image files (*.jpg;*.gif) | (*.jpg;*.gif) | Text files
(*.txt) | (*.txt)| Word documents (*.doc) | (*.doc) | Pirated music (*.mp3) | (*.mp3)
```

To modify the Filter property using BASIC, use the following format:

```
DialogBoxName.Filter = "Type your filter here"
```

where `DialogBoxName` is the name of your Open or Save dialog box, and `"Type your filter here"` is the actual filter.

For example, to display a filter in a Save dialog box, you could use the following BASIC code:

```
SaveFileDialog1.Filter = "All files (*.*) | (*.*) | Image files (*.jpg;*.gif) |
(*.jpg;*.gif) | Text files (*.txt) | (*.txt) | Word documents (*.doc) | (*.doc) | Pirated
music (*.mp3) | (*.mp3)"
```

The FilterIndex property defines which filter the Open dialog box uses when it first appears. The FilterIndex property contains a number: 1 represents the first filter stored in the Filter property, 2 represents the second filter, and so on.

Now, suppose you created the following filter:

```
Image files (*.jpg;*.gif) | (*.jpg;*.gif) | Text files (*.txt) | (*.txt)
```

A FilterIndex of 1 would use the Image files (*.jpg;*.gif) | (*.jpg;*.gif) filter and a FilterIndex value of 2 would use the Text files (*.txt) | (*.txt) filter.

Hands-on Tutorial: Retrieving a Filename from a Dialog Box

1. Creating
an Open
File Dialog
Box to
Select a
Single File;
2. Selecting
Multiple
Files in an
Open File
Dialog Box

When used with the Open dialog box, the FileName property stores the name of the file the user last selected. When used with the Save dialog box, it stores the name of the file the user entered. This tutorial shows you how to retrieve the name of the file that the user selected in an Open dialog box as well as the filename the user typed into a Save dialog box.

1. Start a new project then click OK to display a blank form.

2. Choose View ▸ Toolbox to display the Toolbox, then choose Window ▸ Auto Hide to keep the Toolbox visible.

3. Double-click the OpenFileDialog control under the Dialogs category of the Toolbox. The OpenFileDialog control appears under your blank form.

4. Double-click the SaveFileDialog control under the Dialogs category of the Toolbox. The SaveFileDialog control appears under your blank form.

5. Click the Button control in the Toolbox, mouse over the center of the form, and click the left mouse button to create a button.

6. Double-click the Button1 control on the form. The Code window appears.

7. Type three lines of code between the Private Sub and End Sub lines, like so:

```
Private Sub Button1_Click(ByVal sender As System.Object, ByVal e As System.EventArgs)_
Handles Button1.Click
        If OpenFileDialog1.ShowDialog() = DialogResult.OK Then
            MsgBox(OpenFileDialog1.FileName)
        End If
End Sub
```

8. Click the Button control in the Toolbox, mouse over the form, and click the left mouse button to create a second button on the form.

9. Double-click the Button2 control on the form. The Code window appears.

10. Type three lines of code between the Private Sub and End Sub lines, like so:

```
Private Sub Button2_Click(ByVal sender As System.Object, ByVal e As System.EventArgs)_
Handles Button2.Click
        If SaveFileDialog1.ShowDialog() = DialogResult.OK Then
            MsgBox(SaveFileDialog1.FileName)
        End If
End Sub
```

11. Press F5 to display your user interface, then click the Button1 control. An Open dialog box appears because of the BASIC code you typed in step 7.

12. Click a filename and click Open. A message box appears, displaying the drive, directory, and the name of the file you just chose—such as *C:\My Documents\Form1.vb*. Click OK to close the message box.

13. Click the Button2 control on the form. A Save dialog box appears.

14. Click in the File Name text box and type a name, such as **MyTest.doc**, and click Save. A message box appears, displaying the filename you typed. Click OK to close the message box.

NOTE *The Save dialog box won't actually create a file or save anything in it until you write BASIC code to create a file and stuff that file with actual data.*

15. Press ALT-F4 to stop your program, then choose File ▸ Close Project. A Close Project dialog box appears. Click Discard.

Using the Folder Browser Dialog Box

Creating and Using a Folder Browser Dialog Box

Use a Folder Browser dialog box to either let a user choose a folder or drive by clicking the folder or drive name, or create a new folder by clicking a button, as shown in Figure 17-4. (When the user clicks an existing folder or creates a new one, the name of that folder is stored in the Folder Browser dialog box's SelectedPath property.) If the user clicks the Make New Folder button, a new folder is automatically created with a name that the user specifies; no BASIC code is necessary.

When the Folder Browser dialog box appears, it displays the contents of the folder defined by the RootFolder property in the Properties window. By default, the RootFolder property is set to Desktop (as shown in Figure 17-4), but you can set it to any folder you wish, as shown in Figure 17-5.

The Folder Browser dialog box lets the user view only those folders that are stored inside the folder you specify in the RootFolder property. For example, if you specify the My Music folder in the RootFolder property, the user will be able to view only folders stored inside the My Music folder.

Limiting users to the folders they can browse simply keeps them from viewing folders that aren't relevant to the program. For example, if your program helps users edit music files stored in the My Music folder, there's no reason for them to be able to view the contents of a different folder that doesn't (normally) contain any music files.

Figure 17-4: The Browse for Folder dialog box lets users click a drive or folder they want to use, or create a new folder.

Figure 17-5: The RootFolder property defines which folder initially appears in the Folder Browser dialog box.

Hands-on Tutorial: Using a Folder Browser Dialog Box

This tutorial shows you how to retrieve the name of the folder that the user selects in the Folder Browser dialog box.

1. Start a new project, then click OK to display a blank form.
2. Choose View ▸ Toolbox to display the Toolbox, then choose Window ▸ Auto Hide to keep the Toolbox visible.
3. Double-click the FolderBrowserDialog control under the Dialogs category of the Toolbox. The FolderBrowserDialog control appears under your blank form.
4. Click the Button control in the Toolbox, mouse over the center of the form, and click the left mouse button to create a button on the form.
5. Double-click the Button1 control on the form. The Code window appears.
6. Type two lines of code between the `Private Sub` and `End Sub` lines, as shown here:

```
Private Sub Button1_Click(ByVal sender As System.Object, ByVal e As System.EventArgs)_
Handles Button1.Click
        If FolderBrowserDialog1.ShowDialog() = Windows.Forms.DialogResult.OK Then
            MsgBox(FolderBrowserDialog1.SelectedPath)
        End If
End Sub
```

7. Press F5 to display your user interface, then click the Button1 control. A Folder Browser dialog box appears because of the BASIC code you typed in step 6.

8. Click a folder name and click Open. A message box appears, displaying the drive and the name of the folder you just chose. Click OK to close it.

9. Press ALT-F4 to stop your program, then choose File ▶ Close Project. Click Discard.

Using the Font Dialog Box

Creating and Using a Font Dialog Box

The Font dialog box lets users choose a font, font style, and font size, as well as whether to use strikeout or underline effects, as shown in Figure 17-6. Table 17-2 lists the properties in which the Font dialog box stores the user's choices.

NOTE *The Script list box in Figure 17-6 lets users select different language characters such as Arabic or Vietnamese.*

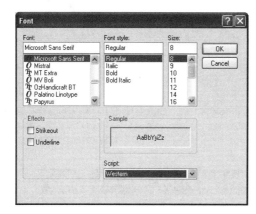

Figure 17-6: The Font dialog box lets users define different appearances for text.

Table 17-2: Properties That Store User Data from the Font Dialog Box

Property	What it does
Font.Name	Contains the name of the font that the user chooses, such as Papyrus or MT Extra. (The default is Microsoft San Serif.)
Font.Bold	If the value is True, the user chose Bold. If the value is False, the user did not choose Bold. (The default is False.)
Font.Italic	If the value is True, the user chose Italic. If the value is False, the user did not choose Italic. (The default is False.)
Font.Size	Contains a numeric value that defines the size of the font, such as 12. (The default is 8.25.)
Font.Strikeout	If the value is True, the user chose Strikeout. If the value is False, the user did not choose Strikeout. (The default is False.)
Font.Underline	If the value is True, the user chose Underline. If the value is False, the user did not choose Underline. (The default is False.)

Hands-on Tutorial: Using the Font Dialog Box

Table 17-2 lists all the properties that store the choices the user can make in a Font dialog box. While you could assign individual Font properties (such as Font.Underline and Font.Size) to define text that appears in another control, it's often easier to assign all the Font properties directly to the another control, such as a text box.

1. Start a new project, then click OK to display a blank form.
2. Choose View ▶ Toolbox to display the Toolbox, then choose Window ▶ Auto Hide to keep it visible.
3. Double-click the FontDialog control under the Dialogs category of the Toolbox. The FontDialog control appears under your blank form.
4. Click the TextBox control in the Toolbox, move the mouse over the form, and click the left mouse button to create a text box on the form.
5. Click the Button control in the Toolbox, mouse over the center of the form, and click the left mouse button to create a button on the form.
6. Double-click the Button1 control on the form. The Code window appears.
7. Type two lines of code, `FontDialog1.ShowDialog()` and `TextBox1.Font = FontDialog1.Font`, between the `Private Sub` and `End Sub` lines, like so:

```
Private Sub Button1_Click(ByVal sender As System.Object, ByVal e As_
System.EventArgs) Handles Button1.Click
    FontDialog1.ShowDialog()
    TextBox1.Font = FontDialog1.Font
End Sub
```

8. Press F5 to display your user interface, then click in the text box and type a word or two, such as **I see you**.
9. Click the Button1 control. A Font dialog box appears because of the `Fontdialog1 .ShowDialog()` command you typed in step 7.
10. Choose a font, font style, and size, and then click OK. Notice that the text in your text box appears in the font, font style, and size you just chose.
11. Press ALT-F4 to stop your program, then choose File ▶ Close Project. Click Discard.

Using the Color Dialog Box

Creating and Using a Color Dialog Box

The Color dialog box lets users choose a color or even create a custom one, as shown in Figure 17-7.

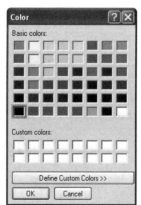

Figure 17-7: The Color dialog box lets users choose from a palette of different colors or create a custom color.

Table 17-3 lists the properties that store data from the user's choice in the Color dialog box.

Table 17-3: Properties That Store User Data from the Color Dialog Box

Property	What it does
Color.B	Contains the numeric value of the amount of blue used in the color that the user chose.
Color.G	Contains the numeric value of the amount of green used in the color that the user chose.
Color.Name	Contains the name of the color chosen (such as red). If the user selected a custom color, its RGB (red, green, blue) value will be stored instead.
Color.R	Contains the numeric value of the amount of red used in the color that the user chose.

Using the properties listed in Table 17-3, you could access individual values from the Red (Color.R), Green (Color.G), or Blue (Color.B) properties, or you could access the entire color name directly from the Color.Name property. But if you need to change the color of another control, it's easier to use BASIC to assign the Color property of the Color dialog box to the Color property of another control, such as a text box, as follows:

```
TextBox1.Color = ColorDialog1.Color
```

This simply changes the Color property of a text box named TextBox1 to the color the user selects from the Color dialog box named ColorDialog1.

Making Your Own Dialog Box

In addition to standard dialog boxes, Visual Basic Express offers two additional dialog boxes that you might find useful: a message box and an input box. A *message box* is designed to display simple messages, warnings, or questions that require the user's response. *Input boxes* let the user enter some data, such as a number or text.

Creating a Message Box with the MsgBox Command

The MsgBox command displays a question to the user and waits for the user to click a button to answer, as shown in Figure 17-8. To create a message box, the MsgBox command uses three items to define its appearance:

```
MsgBox (Prompt, ButtonStyle, Title)
```

Prompt is the text that you want to display inside the message box, *ButtonStyle* is the number and types of buttons that will appear inside the message box, and *Title* is the text that appears in the title bar of the message box.

The following BASIC code created the message box shown in Figure 17-8:

```
MsgBox ("Do you want to increase global warming to boost the economy?", MsgBoxStyle.YesNo,_
"Kyoto Treaty Alert")
```

This example defines the prompt ("Do you want to increase global warming to boost the economy?"), the button style (MsgBoxStyle.YesNo), and title ("Kyoto Treaty Alert").

Title —
Prompt —
Buttons —

Figure 17-8: The MsgBox command displays a simple dialog box.

NOTE   *Both the button style and title are optional. If you don't define a button style, the message box defaults to displaying a single OK button. If you don't define a title, the message box defaults to displaying just the name of your project.*

Button styles define the appearance and number of buttons your dialog box will display. Table 17-4 lists the different button styles you can choose from, with a short explanation and an example of each one.

Table 17-4: Button Styles Used to Define a Dialog Box

Button Style	What it does	Example
MsgBoxStyle.AbortRetryIgnore	Displays three buttons: Abort, Retry, and Ignore.	
MsgBoxStyle.ApplicationModal	Displays a single OK button and a close box.	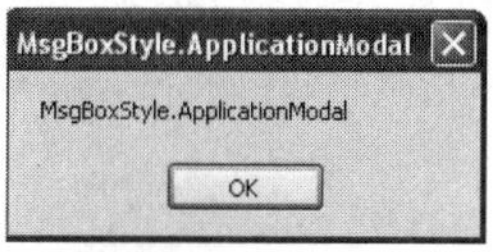
MsgBoxStyle.Critical	Displays a single OK button, a red critical icon, and a close box.	
MsgBoxStyle.DefaultButton1, MsgBoxStyle.DefaultButton2, and MsgBoxStyle.DefaultButton3	Displays a single OK button and a close box.	
MsgBoxStyle.Exclamation	Displays a single OK button, a yellow exclamation point icon, and a close box.	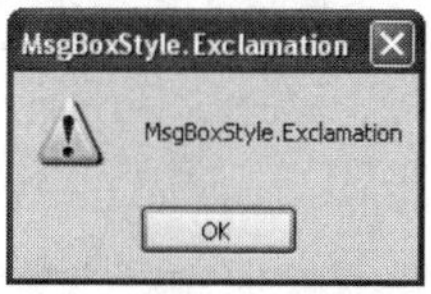
MsgBoxStyle.Information	Displays a single OK button, a white information balloon icon, and a close box.	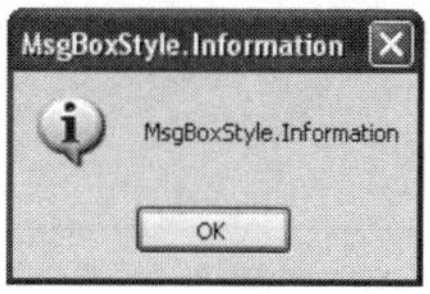

(continued)

Table 17-4: Button Styles Used to Define a Dialog Box (continued)

Button Style	What it does	Example
MsgBoxStyle.MsgBoxHelp	Displays an OK and Help button and a close box.	
MsgBoxStyle.MsgBoxRight	Displays a single OK button and a close box while right-aligning the prompt text.	
MsgBoxStyle.MsgBoxRtlReading	Displays a single OK button and a close box that appears in the upper-left corner of the dialog box.	
MsgBoxStyle.MsgBoxSetForeground	Displays a single OK button and a close box.	
MsgBoxStyle.OKCancel	Displays an OK and Cancel button and a close box.	
MsgBoxStyle.OKOnly	Displays a single OK button and a close box.	
MsgBoxStyle.Question	Displays a single OK button, a question mark balloon icon, and a close box	
MsgBoxStyle.RetryCancel	Displays a Retry button, a Cancel button, and a close box.	
MsgBoxStyle.SystemModal	Displays a single OK button and a close box.	

(continued)

Table 17-4: Button Styles Used to Define a Dialog Box (continued)

Button Style	What it does	Example
MsgBoxStyle.YesNo	Displays Yes and No buttons along with a close box.	
MsgBoxStyle.YesNoCancel	Displays Yes, No, and Cancel buttons along with a close box.	

Hands-on Tutorial: Using the MsgBox Command

Once you've created a message box, you can determine which button the user clicked to make the message box go away. Table 17-5 lists the integer values that the MsgBox command returns, depending on which button the user clicks.

Table 17-5: Values that Define Button Clicks

Constant	Value	Constant	Value
OK	1	Ignore	5
Cancel	2	Yes	6
Abort	3	No	7
Retry	4		

Here's how to do it:

1. Start a new project, then click OK to display a blank form.
2. Choose View ▸ Toolbox to display the Toolbox, then choose Window ▸ Auto Hide to keep it visible.
3. Click the Button control in the Toolbox, mouse over the center of the form, and click the left mouse button to create a button on the form.
4. Double-click the Button1 control on the form. The Code window appears.
5. Type the following three lines between the Private Sub and End Sub lines:

```
Private Sub Button1_Click(ByVal sender As System.Object, ByVal e As System.EventArgs)_
Handles Button1.Click
        Dim I As Integer
        I = MsgBox("Do you want to develop weapons of mass destruction?",_
MsgBoxStyle.YesNoCancel, "PC-Apocalypse")
        MsgBox("This is the button you clicked: " & CStr(I))
End Sub
```

(You'll learn what the Dim I As Integer line means in Chapter 18 and what the CStr(I) command means in Chapter 20.)

6. Press F5 to display your user interface, then click the Button1 control. A message box appears, as shown in Figure 17-9.

7. Click No. A new dialog box appears, as shown in Figure 17-10, which displays the number 7. From Table 17-5, you can see that the number 7 means that the user clicked the No button. By knowing which button the user clicked, your program can then take appropriate action. Click OK to close the dialog box.

8. Press ALT-F4 to stop your program, then choose File ▶ Close Project. Click Discard.

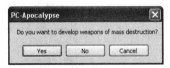

Figure 17-9: The MsgBox command displays a simple message box.

Figure 17-10: The second MsgBox command shows a dialog box displaying the number of the button the user clicked.

Creating a Different Message Box with the MessageBox Command

As an alternative to the MsgBox command discussed so far, Visual Basic Express offers a similar MessageBox command that creates a message box that looks similar to Figure 17-11.

Figure 17-11: A message box created with the MessageBox command

To create this type of message box, use the following BASIC syntax:

```
MessageBox.Show(Text, Caption, Buttons, Icon, DefaultButton)
```

Text contains the word or phrase that you want to appear inside the message box. Caption contains the text that will appear in the title bar of the message box. Buttons defines the number and type of buttons that will be displayed, such as an OK, Cancel, Yes, or Retry button. Icon defines the type of icon, if any, to display inside the message box. DefaultButton defines the button that appears highlighted when the message box first appears.

The following BASIC commands created the message box shown in Figure 17-11:

```
MessageBox.Show("Would you eat insect parts in your food?", "Hot dog question",_
MessageBoxButtons.OKCancel, MessageBoxIcon.Hand, MessageBoxDefaultButton.Button1)
```

While this example of a message box shows an OK and Cancel button, you can choose from six different types and numbers of buttons, as listed in Table 17-6.

Table 17-6: Button Choices for a Message Box

Button Style	What it does
MessageBoxButtons.AbortRetryIgnore	Displays three buttons: Abort, Retry, and Ignore. (The close box appears dimmed.)
MessageBoxButtons.OK	Displays a single OK button and a close box.

(continued)

Table 17-6: Button Choices for a Message Box (continued)

Button Style	What it does
MessageBoxButtons.OKCancel	Displays an OK button, a Cancel button, and a close box.
MessageBoxButtons.RetryCancel	Displays a Retry button, a Cancel button, and a close box.
MessageBoxButtons.YesNo	Displays a Yes button, a No button, and a close box.
MessageBoxButtons.YesNoCancel	Displays a Yes button, a No button, a Cancel button, and a close box.

In addition to displaying text inside a message box, you can also display one of nine different types of icons, as listed in Table 17-7.

Table 17-7: Icons You Can Display in a Message Box

Icon	What it does
MessageBoxIcon.Asterisk	Displays a lowercase *i* inside a balloon.
MessageBoxIcon.Error	Displays a white *X* inside a red circle.
MessageBoxIcon.Exclamation	Displays an exclamation point inside a yellow triangle.
MessageBoxIcon.Hand	Displays a white *X* inside a red circle (identical to the Error icon).
MessageBoxIcon.Information	Displays a lowercase *i* inside a balloon (identical to the Asterisk icon).
MessageBoxIcon.None	Does not display an icon.
MessageBoxIcon.Question	Displays a question mark inside a circle.
MessageBoxIcon.Stop	Displays a white *X* inside a red circle (identical to the Error icon).
MessageBoxIcon.Warning	Displays an exclamation point inside a yellow triangle (identical to the Exclamation icon).

And you can designate a default button that appears highlighted when the message box first appears. Because a message box can only display up to three buttons, you can choose one of three default buttons:

MessageBoxDefaultButton.Button1   Highlights the first button closest to the left edge of the message box.

MessageBoxDefaultButton.Button2   Highlights the second button from the left.

MessageBoxDefaultButton.Button3   Highlights the third button from the left.

Hands-on Tutorial: Using the MessageBox Command

This tutorial shows you how to use the MessageBox command to create a message box and determine which button the user clicked.

1. Start a new project, then click OK to display a blank form.
2. Choose View ▸ Toolbox to display the Toolbox, then choose Window ▸ Auto Hide to keep it visible.
3. Click the Button control in the Toolbox, mouse over the center of the form, and click the left mouse button to create a button on the form.
4. Double-click the Button1 control on the form. The Code window appears.

5. Type the following three lines between the `Private Sub` and `End Sub` lines:

```
Private Sub Button1_Click(ByVal sender As System.Object, ByVal e As System.EventArgs)_
Handles Button1.Click
        Dim Button As String
        Button = MessageBox.Show("Click a button", "Button Test",_
MessageBoxButtons.YesNoCancel)
        MessageBox.Show("This is the button you chose = " & Button)
End Sub
```

6. Press F5 to display your user interface, then click the Button1 control. The message box appears, as shown in Figure 17-12.

7. Click Yes. A dialog box appears (Figure 17-13), which displays the number 6. From Table 17-5, you can see that this means that the user clicked the Yes button.

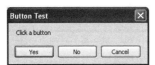

Figure 17-12: The message box created by the `MessageBox` command

Figure 17-13: The dialog box displays the number of the button the user clicked.

8. Click OK to close the dialog box, then press ALT-F4 to stop your program. Choose File ▸ Close Project, then click Discard.

Creating an Input Box

An *input box* displays a prompt, title, and text box where the user can enter data, as shown in Figure 17-14. The BASIC syntax for creating an input box looks like this:

```
InputBox (Prompt, Title, Default answer)
```

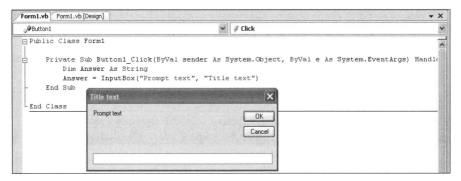

Figure 17-14: An input box allows the user to enter data. In this example, there is no Default answer.

Prompt represents text that appears inside the input box, and *Title* represents text that appears in the title bar. *Default answer* represents data that always appears inside the input box whenever it pops up on the screen. If you don't want to display a default answer, you can just shorten the `InputBox` command like so:

```
InputBox (Prompt, Title)
```

To retrieve a value from an input box, you need to assign a variable, as a string data type, to the InputBox command. For example:

```
Dim Answer As String
Answer = InputBox("Prompt text", "Title text")
```

Hands-on Tutorial: Using an Input Box

Getting Data from an Input Box

This tutorial shows you how to use an input box to retrieve data entered by the user.

1. Start a new project, then click OK to display a blank form.
2. Choose View ▸ Toolbox to display the Toolbox, then choose Window ▸ Auto Hide to keep it visible.
3. Click the Button control in the Toolbox, mouse over the center of the form, and click the left mouse button to create a button on the form.
4. Double-click the Button1 control on the form. The Code window appears.
5. Type the following three lines between the Private Sub and End Sub lines:

```
Private Sub Button1_Click(ByVal sender As System.Object, ByVal e As System.EventArgs)_
Handles Button1.Click
        Dim Answer As String
        Answer = InputBox("Prompt text", "Title text")
        MsgBox(Answer)
End Sub
```

6. Press F5 to display your user interface, then click the Button1 control. An input box appears (see Figure 17-14). Type **I am here** into the box and click OK. A dialog box appears, displaying the text you typed. Click OK to close the dialog box.
7. Choose File ▸ Close Project then click Discard.

KEY FEATURES TO REMEMBER

Visual Basic Express provides built-in dialog boxes and message boxes that you can plug into your programs to provide a consistent user interface. When creating these boxes, you need to know how to display them and how to retrieve the specific choices the user makes in Visual Basic Express includes several standard dialog boxes that you can create and display, such as Print, Open, and Save dialog boxes.

- You can customize most dialog boxes.

- When the user makes a choice from a dialog box, that choice is stored in a property of the dialog box control.

- You can use the MsgBox or MessageBox command to create your own message boxes that you can customize with text, icons, and the number and type of buttons to display, such as an OK or Ignore button.

- An input box lets the user enter data.

- Dynamic Help changes its list of help topics based on what you're doing when you choose help.

PART IV

WRITING BASIC CODE

18

USING VARIABLES AND CONSTANTS

When a program accepts data from the user, it stores that data temporarily in the computer's memory. Because the value of any data can vary each time the program runs, the portion of the computer's memory that stores data temporarily is called a *variable*. Without variables, not only would programs be unable to accept data from the user, but they could work only with fixed values, meaning that the program would do the same thing every time it ran.

To see how useless fixed values can be in a program, examine the following BASIC code that simply multiplies 2 times 2 and displays the result in a dialog box:

```
Dim Total As Integer
Total = 2 * 2
MsgBox (Total)
```

This code's three lines do the following:

Line 1   This line consists of three parts: Dim, Total, and As Integer. The Dim keyword (short for *dimension*) tells the computer to set aside, or dimension, part of its memory to store data. Total is the name of the variable used to identify the data. As Integer tells the computer that the variable can store only integers (whole numbers, like 4 or 89, but not decimal numbers, such as 2.34 or 120.9).

Line 2   This line multiplies 2 times 2 and stores the result in the variable Total.

Line 3   This line tells the computer to run the MsgBox command, which displays a message box on the screen and displays the contents of the Total variable.

This program works, but it's relatively useless because it calculates the same results every time. More useful are programs that can accept different data and manipulate that data in a consistent way, as shown in the following BASIC code:

```
Dim Total, Boxes, ItemsPerBox as Integer
Boxes = InputBox ("How many boxes do you have?")
ItemsPerBox = InputBox ("How many items are in each box?")
Total = Boxes * ItemsPerBox
MsgBox (Total)
```

This example consists of five lines that do the following:

Line 1   The Dim keyword creates three variables called Total, Boxes, and ItemsPerBox, which can all hold integer (whole number) values.

Line 2   This line uses the InputBox command to display an input box to the user that asks "How many boxes do you have?" The number the user enters in the input box is stored in the Boxes variable.

Line 3   This line also uses the InputBox command to display an input box that asks "How many items are in each box?" The number the user enters in the input box is stored in the ItemsPerBox variable.

Line 4   This line multiplies the value stored in the Boxes variable by the value stored in the ItemsPerBox variable. This result is stored in the Total variable.

Line 5   This line runs the MsgBox command, which displays a message box on the screen showing the contents of the Total variable.

Unlike the previous example, which always multiplied 2 times 2, because this example uses variables it can multiply any two numbers that the user enters into the program. Variables simply make programs more versatile and ultimately more useful.

Declaring Variables

Declaring
Variables

Before you can use a variable, you must first create, or *declare*, it. When you declare a variable you:

- Tell the computer which parts of your program have permission to store and retrieve data in a variable
- Tell the computer the name of your variable
- Define the type of information that variable is allowed to hold

You must declare a variable before you can use it. If you don't, Visual Basic Express alerts you by underlining the variable name in your code with a blue squiggly line, as shown in Figure 18-1.

Variable declarations usually appear as one of the first lines in your BASIC code, with the following syntax:

```
ScopeType VariableName As DataType
```

Blue squiggly lines identify undeclared variables

Figure 18-1: Visual Basic Express shows you any undeclared variables in your code.

ScopeType defines which parts of your program can access the variable. The two keywords you can use for *ScopeType* are Dim or Public, as in these examples:

- Dim *VariableName* As *DataType*
- Public *VariableName* As *DataType*

The Dim keyword creates variables that can be modified only within one part of your program. This helps reduce errors, because the fewer parts of your program that can modify a variable, the less likely your program will store the wrong data into a variable by mistake. The Public keyword creates variables that can be modified by all parts of your program. This increases the chance of errors because one part of your program may accidentally modify a variable that another part of your program needs.

VariableName defines the name of the variable, which is often a short, descriptive name that identifies the variable contents, such as FirstName or PhoneNumber.

DataType defines the type of information (known as the *data type*) the variable can hold. By restricting the type of information a variable can hold, you can prevent your program from accidentally storing the wrong data in a variable. For example, if a variable is supposed to hold a number, such as a price, storing a name in that variable will likely cause problems because you can't use a name in a mathematical equation.

Defining a Data Type

The most important part of a variable declaration is the *data type*, which defines the data the variable is allowed to hold. A data type can be either a *number* or *text*. Numbers can be as simple as 7 or 21 or as extreme as −3.095751375 or 266,819,031.764. Text can consist of one or more keyboard characters, including letters (a, B, X, u), symbols ($, *, &, @), and numbers (1, 32, 984.84).

Declaring Variables as a String Data Type

To define a variable to hold only text, you must declare it as a *string* data type, like so:

```
Dim VariableName As String
```

If you store numbers in a variable defined as a string data type, you can't perform any mathematical calculations on those numbers until you convert them from a string to a number data type such as an integer (this is explained in Chapter 20).

Here are some examples of string data type variable declarations:

```
Dim CompanyName As String
Dim SocialSecurityNumber As String
```

To store text into a string variable, you enclose data inside quotation marks, like so:

```
CompanyName = "Seattle Computer"
SocialSecurityNumber = "123-00-9876"
```

Visual Basic treats everything within double quotation marks as a string, whether that information is a letter, a symbol, or a number. If you omit the beginning or ending quotation mark, your program won't work correctly.

Technically, computers can understand only numbers. Computers assign a unique numeric value to every character you might want to display, including letters, symbols, and foreign language characters. To allow computers to share data with one another, all computers assign the same unique numeric values to the same characters, according to a universally accepted method of representing characters known as *Unicode*.

In Visual Basic, a string variable can hold anywhere from zero to 2 billion Unicode characters. Obviously, the more Unicode characters you store, the more memory your variable will need, which is measured in storage units known as *bytes*.

Table 18-1 lists the technical specifications for the string data type, showing how much data you can store in a single String variable and how much storage memory the variable will require.

Table 18-1: Technical Specifications for the String Data Type

Data type	Range of values it can hold	Storage
String	0 to approximately 2 billion Unicode characters	10 bytes + (2 * string length)

For example, to store a string that consists of 25 Unicode characters, the computer would need approximately 10 bytes + (2 * 25), or 60 bytes, of storage.

Declaring Variables as a Whole Number Data Type

In order to declare a variable to hold only numbers, you must decide the following:

- The type of numbers you want to store, whether whole numbers (integers) or decimal numbers
- The minimum and maximum range of numbers you want your variable to hold

To store whole numbers, you can declare a variable to be one of four different data types: *byte, short, integer,* or *long.*

```
Dim Dogs As Byte
Dim NumberofElves As Short
Dim IQLevel As Integer
Dim LiesTold As Long
```

Visual Basic offers four different data types that all hold whole numbers because, as you can see in Table 18-2, each data type can hold a different range of values.

What criteria should you follow when choosing each type? For example, if you want a variable to hold a person's age, you *could* declare it as a long data type, like so:

```
Dim YourAge As Long
```

Table 18-2: Technical Specifications for Whole Number Data Types

Data type	Range of values it can hold	Storage
Byte	0 to 255	1 byte
Short	–32,768 to 32,767	2 bytes
Integer	–2,147,483,648 to 2,147,483,647	4 bytes
Long	–9,223,372,036,854,775,808 to 9,223,372,036,854,775,807	8 bytes

Unfortunately, defining a variable as a long data type means that someone could enter a value of -746,294,543 for her age and your program would happily store it—and possibly crash when faced with such an obviously incorrect age. Because you know a person's age can range from 0 to around 100 (single to triple-digit numerals), you should declare the YourAge variable as a byte data type, because it can store only values from 0 to 255. Figure 18-2 shows what happens if the user enters data outside the acceptable range of values for a specific data type, such as the byte data type.

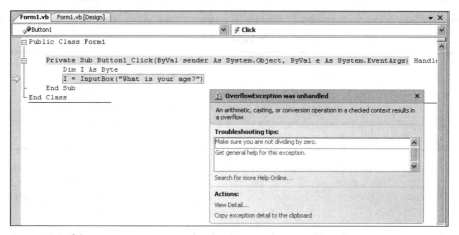

Figure 18-2: If the user tries to store a value that lies outside a variable's data type range, Visual Basic Express displays a warning.

By choosing the correct data type for a variable, you can protect your program from inadvertently accepting invalid information, such as an age of 978 or the number of children in a family as –46.

As an added bonus, the smaller the range of values a data type can hold, the less memory it requires to hold it. Consider the following two variables:

```
Dim Boys As Byte
Dim Girls As Integer
Boys = 14
Girls = 14
```

Although both the Boys and Girls variables hold a value of 14, Boys is a byte data type, which requires only 1 byte of memory to store, while Girls is an integer data type, which requires 4 bytes of memory to store. While the difference of 3 bytes may seem fairly trivial, the choice of a data type that requires the smallest amount of storage space, while still holding the range of values you need, can make your program run slightly faster and use less memory.

Declaring Variables as a Decimal Number Data Type

Whole numbers are convenient to use, but you may need to use decimal numbers to represent other types of data, such as temperatures (98.6), prices (13.95), or percentages (75%). When storing decimal numbers, you can declare a variable as one of three different data types—*single*, *double*, and *decimal*—like so:

```
Dim StarTrekFanatic As Single
Dim Twins As Double
Dim IQofaPolitician As Decimal
```

The single data type gets its name from the fact that the range of values it can store are known as *single-precision values*. As Table 18-3 shows, the highest value a single data type can store is 3.402823E38, which is written in scientific notation (the *E* stands for *exponent*). Using scientific notation, rather than typing a number as 1,409,904,392, you can type the number as 1.409904392E9.

Table 18-3: Technical Specifications for Single, Double, and Decimal Data Types

Decimal number data types	Range of values it can hold	Storage
Single	–3.402823E38 to –1.401298E-45 (negative values) 1.401298E-45 to 3.402823E38 (positive values)	4 bytes
Double	–1.79769313486231E308 to –4.94065645841247E-324 (negative values) 4.94065645841247E-324 to 1.79769313486232E308 (positive values)	8 bytes
Decimal	+/–79,228,162,514,264,337,593,543,950,335 (no decimal point) +/–7.9228162514264337593543950335 (up to 28 decimal places)	12 bytes

The double data type gets its name from the range of values it can store, known as *double-precision values*. The double data type can store an even greater range of extremely small or extremely large decimal numbers, but using twice the storage space as a single data type.

The decimal data type can hold the widest range of extremely small to extremely large decimal numbers, and its greater storage space requirements (12 bytes) reflect the additional memory needed to hold such extreme values.

Assigning Values to Numeric Data Types

To store numbers into either a *decimal* (single, double, decimal) or *whole number* (byte, short, integer, long) data type, you can assign a number directly to the variable, assign a variable to another variable, or assign a mathematical expression to a variable.

To assign a number directly to a variable, enter the number itself, like so:

```
Dim DumbCEOs As Long
Dim PercentageofGreedyCEOS As Double
DumbCEOs = 8452
PercentageofGreedyCEOS = 42.0197
```

You can also assign the value of one variable to another, like so:

```
Dim DeadRats, HotDogs As Integer
DeadRats = 57
HotDogs = DeadRats
```

When assigning the value of one variable to another, each variable must consist of the same data type. In this example, the DeadRats and the HotDogs variables are both integer data types.

If you assign the value of a decimal variable type (such as single) to a whole number data type (such as integer), visual Basic rounds off your numbers. For example, consider the following:

```
Dim Age As Single
Dim FakeAge As Integer
Age = 57.85
FakeAge = Age
```

The last line assigns the value of 57.85 to the FakeAge variable, but because the FakeAge variable can hold only integer values, the FakeAge variable rounds the number to 58 and stores that value instead.

This problem can also occur when assigning values from different decimal data types, such as from a decimal data type to a single data type. Because a single variable type can't hold numbers with as many decimal places as a decimal or double data type can, Visual Basic will round off your numbers, which may skew the accuracy of your data.

Finally, you can also assign a mathematical expression to a variable, like so:

```
Dim StockPrice, Shares, Total As Single
Total = StockPrice * Shares
```

Be careful when mixing different data types in a mathematical expression, because if your mathematical expression calculates values using decimal data types, but you assign the result to a whole number data type, Visual Basic will round off the result to fit it in the whole number data type.

Declaring Variables as a Date

Visual Basic can also create variables that hold dates and times. Table 18-4 shows that the *date* data type can store dates ranging from 0:00:00 (midnight) January 1, 0001, to 11:59:59 PM December 31, 9999.

Table 18-4: Technical Specifications for the Date Data Type

Data type	Range of values it can hold	Storage
Date	0:00:00 (midnight) January 1, 0001, to 11:59:59 PM December 31, 9999	8 bytes

To assign a date to a Date variable, you must do the following:

- Enter the date in the format *MM/DD/YYYY* and the time in the format *hh:mm:ss*
- Enclose the date and/or time between # symbols, like so: #12/3/2006#

When you assign a date to a Date variable, you can omit defining the time, like this:

```
Dim EndoftheWorld As Date
EndoftheWorld = #04/15/2007#
```

When you omit a time, Visual Basic assumes the time to be 0:00:00 (midnight), so this BASIC code stores the date April 15, 2007, into the EndoftheWorld variable along with the time of 0:00:00.

When specifying a time, you can specify either AM or PM, or use military time, like so:

```
Dim EndoftheWorld As Date
EndoftheWorld = #04/15/2007 4:32:07 PM#
```

or

```
Dim EndoftheWorld As Date
EndoftheWorld = #04/15/2007 16:32:07#
```

Declaring Variables as Boolean and Character Values

Visual Basic provides two other data types called *boolean* and *char*. A boolean data type can hold only one of two values: True or False. To assign a value to a boolean data type, you can either assign the True or False value directly to a variable or a *conditional expression* (see Chapter 21) that evaluates to a True or False value, like so:

```
Dim ILoveLinux As Boolean
ILoveLinux = False
ILoveLinux = (34 > 2)
```

The second line stores the value of False into the ILoveLinux variable. However, the next line contains a conditional expression, which evaluates whether 34 is greater than the number 2. Because this is true, it stores the value True into the ILoveLinux variable.

A char data type can hold only a single character, such as the letter *X* or the symbol *&*. To assign a character to a Char variable, surround the character in double quotation marks, like this:

```
Dim Grade As Char
Grade = "A"
```

Table 18-5 shows the range of values the boolean and char data types can hold, along with their memory storage requirements.

Table 18-5: Technical Specifications for the Boolean and Char Data Types

Data type	Range of values it can hold	Storage
Boolean	True or False	2 bytes
Char	A character code from 0 to 65,535	2 bytes

Naming a Variable

A variable name can identify the type of information a variable can hold. For example, to store a name, you could use a variable called Name or one called EP4_8Cje. The only rule when naming a variable is that all variable names must begin with a letter, but the name itself can consist of both uppercase and lowercase letters and characters. For example, BirthRate, Tax_Account_Info_2005, and G73leW31 are all valid variable names.

Generally, you should keep variable names short (because you may have to type them multiple times), but descriptive (so you can figure out exactly what type of information they hold). Be sure to spell variables correctly everywhere you want to use them, because if you misspell a variable name, Visual Basic Express will not be able to identify the misspelled variable and your program may not work correctly.

Defining the Scope of a Variable

The *scope* defines which parts of your program can access a particular variable. A variable can have four types of scope:

Block A small chunk of code within a procedure.

Procedure A miniature program typically designed to perform one specific task. It is usually defined by a first line that begins with `Private Sub` and a last line that ends with `End Sub`. Most variables are defined within the scope of a procedure.

Module A separate file that can contain one or more procedures.

Namespace A group of names that include one or more files that make up an entire Visual Basic project.

To prevent errors, programmers define the scope of variables as narrowly as possible to restrict access to those variables. The fewer parts of your program that can change the contents of a variable, the less likely that a variable may change in an unpredictable way that could mess up the way your program works.

Defining Procedure Scope

The most common way to define the scope of a variable is within a procedure. The other types of scope (block, module, and namespace) are used only when you need to either restrict access to a variable to a small chunk of code (block scope) or open up access to a variable from other parts of your program outside of a single procedure (module and namespace scopes).

To define a variable with a procedure scope, you must use the following syntax as one of the first lines inside a procedure:

```
Dim VariableName As DataType
```

Any BASIC code that appears inside the same procedure as your variable declaration can now store data in and retrieve data from that variable, like so:

```
Private Sub Button1_Click(ByVal sender As System.Object, ByVal e As_
System.EventArgs) Handles Button1.Click
    Dim Total As Integer
    Total = 4
    MsgBox (Total)
End Sub
```

In this example, the `Total` variable can be used by any BASIC code inside this procedure. However, any BASIC code outside this procedure will be unable to use the `Total` variable.

Defining Block Scope

You can also restrict access to a variable within a chunk of BASIC code (known as a *block*). Visual Basic defines a block of code as anything containing a starting and ending statement, such as an If-Then statement, where the start of the block is defined by the If keyword and the end of the block is defined by the End-If statement. For example:

```
If Condition Then ' Starting statement
    Dim Total As Integer
End If    ' Ending statement
```

If you look at the following example, you'll see a variable named NewTotal declared within the block of an If-Then statement. The boldface code is the piece that can access the NewTotal variable. In this case, the block is defined by the beginning and end of an If-Then statement.

```
Private Sub Button1_Click(ByVal sender As System.Object, ByVal e As_
System.EventArgs) Handles Button1.Click
    Dim Total As Integer
    Total = 4
    MsgBox (Total)
    If Total = 4 Then
        Dim NewTotal As Integer
        NewTotal = -97
        MsgBox (NewTotal)
    End If
    Total = NewTotal'This line won't work
    MsgBox (Total)
End Sub
```

The boldface area defines the block where the NewTotal variable can be accessed. The third line from the bottom, Total = NewTotal, won't work, because, since it is outside of the block, the NewTotal variable is undeclared and Visual Basic treats the NewTotal variable as nonexistent and thus raises an error message.

Defining Module Scope

A *module* is a file that can contain multiple procedures. When you declare a variable with *module scope*, any BASIC code stored in the same module can access it. To create a variable with module scope, declare the variable as one of the first lines in a module and outside of any procedures, as in the following:

```
Public Class Form1
    Dim ModuleTotal As Integer

    Private Sub Button1_Click(ByVal sender As System.Object, ByVal e As_
System.EventArgs) Handles Button1.Click
        Dim Total As Integer
        ModuleTotal = 40
        MsgBox(ModuleTotal)
        Total = ModuleTotal / 2
        MsgBox(Total)
    End Sub
End Class
```

Here, ModuleTotal is a variable that can be accessed by any procedure stored in the same module, while the Total variable can be accessed only from within a single procedure. The first MsgBox command displays the value of the ModuleTotal variable, which is declared outside the procedure but assigned a value of 40. The second MsgBox command divides the value of ModuleTotal and displays it in a dialog box (Figure 18-3).

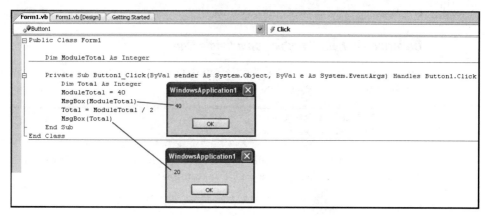

Figure 18-3: A variable declared outside a procedure can be accessed by any procedure stored in that same module.

Defining Namespace Scope

Namespace scope means that every part of your program, even procedures stored in separate files, can access your variable. While this might seem convenient, be careful when you use this type of scope, because it may make it possible for one part of your program to alter a variable that ultimately screws up and crashes your entire program.

To create a variable with namespace scope, declare the variable as one of the first lines in a module and *outside* any procedures using the Public keyword instead of Dim:

```
Module Module1
    Public GlobalVariable As Integer
End Module

Public Class Form1
    Private Sub Button1_Click(ByVal sender As System.Object, ByVal e As_
System.EventArgs) Handles Button1.Click
        Dim Total As Integer
        GlobalVariable = 50
        MsgBox(GlobalVariable)
        Total = GlobalVariable / 2
        MsgBox(Total)
    End Sub
End Class
```

This example shows BASIC code stored in two different files. The first file, Module1, simply declares GlobalVariable as a namespace scope variable accessible by any part of the program. The second file, Form1, assigns a value of 50 to GlobalVariable, displays its value in a message box, and then divides the value of GlobalVariable in half to display this result in a second message box.

Variable Declaration Shortcuts

Using
Variable
Declaration
Shortcuts
and
Constants

Every programming language includes many shortcuts that make it easier for you to write programs. Visual Basic allows you to:

- Declare multiple variables on a single line
- Declare variables with initial values

Declaring Multiple Variables on a Single Line

To declare multiple variables of different data types, you can store each variable declaration on a separate line, like so:

```
Dim Total As Integer
Dim FirstName As String
```

However, the more variables you declare, the messier your code can get if you store each declaration on a separate line. For example:

```
Dim Total As Integer
Dim NumberOfPlayers As Integer
Dim Answer As String
Dim FirstName As String
```

While you can store one variable declaration per line, you can save space by combining multiple variables in a single declaration and separating them with commas:

```
Dim Total, NumberOfPlayers As Integer
Dim Answer, FirstName As String
```

If you declare a variable but don't use it anywhere in your program, Visual Basic Express highlights the unused variable with a green squiggly line, as shown in Figure 18-4.

NOTE *Visual Basic Express highlights undeclared variables with a blue squiggly line. If you declare a variable but don't use it, it highlights those variables with a green squiggly line.*

Green squiggly lines identify unused variables

```
Form1.vb | Module1.vb | Form1.vb [Design] | Getting Started
Button1                                              Click
Public Class Form1
    Private Sub Button1_Click(ByVal sender As System.Object, ByVal e As System.EventArgs) Handles Button1.Click
        Dim Total, Y, Z As Integer
        Dim Unused local variable: 'Total'.
        GlobalVariable = 50
        MsgBox(GlobalVariable)
        Z = GlobalVariable / 2
        MsgBox(Z)
    End Sub
End Class
```

Figure 18-4: Unused variables are highlighted so you can either write code to use them or delete them.

Declaring a Variable and Assigning an Initial Value on a Single Line

Normally, using a variable is a two-step process: First, you declare a variable, then you assign a value to it, like this:

```
Dim LostRecords As Integer
LostRecords = 120
```

As a shortcut, you can declare a variable and assign it a value on one line:

```
Dim LostRecords As Integer = 120
```

This code declares LostRecords as an integer and assigns it a value of 120.

NOTE *To declare a variable and assign it a value, you can declare only one variable at a time.*

Declaring Constants

Unlike variables, *constants* always contain a fixed value. To declare a constant, use the following syntax:

```
Const ConstantName As DataType = ConstantValue
```

ConstantName represents the name of your constant; *DataType* represents the type of data the constant represents, such as an integer or string; and *ConstantValue* represents a fixed value, as shown here:

```
Const MinHeight As Integer = 48
```

The main reason to use a constant is to avoid having to type a specific value into your code, such as:

```
Dim Total, Price As Single
Price = InputBox ("What price did you pay?")
Total = Price * 0.075
```

In this code, the value 0.075 might not make any sense. However, if you use a constant, you can replace a cryptic value with a descriptive name, like so:

```
Dim Total, Price As Single
Const SalesTax As Single = 0.075
Price = InputBox ("What price did you pay?")
Total = Price * SalesTax
```

In this example, you can see that the value 0.075 actually represents a sales tax. Now suppose you write a huge program that uses the value 0.075 in a dozen different places. If the value of sales tax changes from 0.075 to 0.085, you would have to change this value in *each* of a dozen different places. If you forget to do this in just one place, your program might not work correctly. However, if you use constants, you'd need to change this value only once, in the *constant declaration,* and Visual Basic would automatically insert the new value of 0.085 everywhere the SalesTax constant is used.

Using constants offers two advantages:

- Constants replace specific values with descriptive names.
- Constants let you change a specific value in multiple places quickly and easily.

If you want every part of your program to access a constant, you can declare the constant using the Public keyword:

```
Public Const MinHeight As Integer = 48
```

Because constants never change their values, you don't have to worry that any part of your program will accidentally mess up the value of a constant.

Hands-on Tutorial: Declaring Variables and Constants

Variables allow a program to respond to different data types and values. In this tutorial, you'll see how the Code window can help you create variables, how to use constants, and how the scope of different variables works.

1. Load Visual Basic Express, then press CTRL-N to display the New Project dialog box. Click OK to display a blank form.
2. Choose View ▸ Toolbox to display the Toolbox.
3. Click the Button control in the Toolbox, mouse over the center of the form, and click the left mouse button to create a button on the form.
4. Double-click the Button1 control on the form. The Code window appears.
5. Type **Dim MyAge As Integer** between the Private Sub and End Sub lines, like so:

```
Private Sub Button1_Click(ByVal sender As System.Object, ByVal e As_
System.EventArgs) Handles Button1.Click
        Dim MyAge As Integer
End Sub
```

6. The MyAge variable is underlined a green squiggly line, as shown in Figure 18-5.

Green squiggly lines identify unused variables

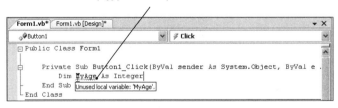

Figure 18-5: Mouse over a variable underlined by a squiggly line to display an explanation of why Visual Basic Express underlined the variable name.

7. Type **MyAge = InputBox ("What is your age?")** between the Private Sub and End Sub lines:

```
Private Sub Button1_Click(ByVal sender As System.Object, ByVal e As_
System.EventArgs) Handles Button1.Click
        Dim MyAge As Integer
    MyAge = InputBox ("What is your age?")
End Sub
```

8. The green squiggly line under the `MyAge` variable disappears because you're now using the `MyAge` variable in your program.

9. Press F5. Your user interface appears.

10. Click the Button1 control. An input box appears.

11. Type **Five** and click OK. The Code window highlights the code displaying the input box and displays an error message to help you identify the problem.

12. Click the close box of this error message window, then choose Debug ▶ Stop Debugging. Your program stops running and displays the Code window again.

NOTE *When testing your program within Visual Basic Express you are* debugging. *When you choose Debug ▶ Stop Debugging, you stop your program from running.*

13. Type three lines, shown here in boldface, between the `Private Sub` and `End Sub` lines, like so:

```
Private Sub Button1_Click(ByVal sender As System.Object, ByVal e As_
System.EventArgs) Handles Button1.Click
        Dim MyAge As Integer
    Const Dog As Integer = 7
    MyAge = InputBox ("What is your age?")
    DogAge = MyAge * Dog
    MsgBox ("Your age in dog years = " & CStr(DogAge))
End Sub
```

14. Notice that the Code window underlines `DogAge` with a blue squiggly line. Mouse over `DogAge` and a window pops up to help you identify the problem: *Name "DogAge" is not declared.*

15. Choose Project ▶ Add Module. An Add New Item dialog box appears.

16. Click Add. A Module1.vb file appears inside the Solution Explorer window and the Code window appears.

17. Type **Public DogAge As Integer** between the `Module` and `End Module` lines to create a variable with namespace scope (which can be accessed by your entire program):

```
Module Module1
        Public DogAge As Integer
End Module
```

18. Click the Form1.vb tab in the Code window (see Figure 18-6). The squiggly line no longer appears under the `DogAge` variable because it has been declared in the Module1.vb file. Even though you can't see the `DogAge` variable declaration in the Form1.vb Code window, you can still use it because it's been declared.

19. Press F5 to display your user interface, then click the Button1 control. An input box appears and asks, *What is your age?*

20. Type **5** and click OK. A dialog box appears and displays *Your age in dog years = 35.* Click OK to close the dialog box.

21. Press ALT-F4 to stop your program and the Close Project dialog box appears. Click Discard.

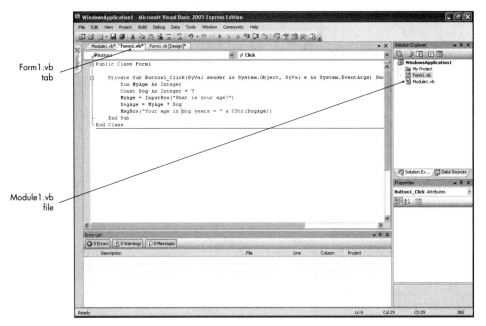

Form1.vb tab

Module1.vb file

Figure 18-6: Click tabs in the Code window to switch between different parts of your program in which you've typed BASIC code.

KEY FEATURES TO REMEMBER

Variables act like temporary storage bins for holding data received from the user or from calculations.

- The value of a variable can change while your program runs.

- Unlike variables, constants represent a fixed value that never changes.

- Both constants and variables should have descriptive names that explain what type of data they hold.

- The scope of a variable defines which parts of your program can access and change the value of a variable. The four scope types are block, procedure, module, and namespace.

- You can declare a variable and assign it a value in a single line.

19

MATHEMATICAL OPERATORS

Once your program receives data from the outside world through its user interface, it needs to manipulate that data as either numbers or text using operators, functions, and methods.

Operators are symbols that manipulate data. Examples include + (addition), * (multiplication), and / (division). *Functions* act like miniature programs that accept data and spit out a specific result. For example, `InStr` and `Trim` search for a string within a string (`InStr`) then remove extra spaces from the string's beginning and end (`Trim`).

Functions are built into Visual Basic. *Methods* are functions that are stored in separate files known as *classes*. Methods work like functions except that you can use a function in your Visual Basic code simply by stating its name, such as `InStr`. On the other hand, to use a method, you must state the class filename and the method you want to use, such as `Math.Sqrt`, where `Sqrt` is the method you want to use and `Math` is the class filename where the `Sqrt` method is stored.

NOTE *Methods and class files are part of* object-oriented programming, *a programming method you'll use to store and organize programs. You'll learn more about object-oriented programming in Chapter 26.*

Using Mathematical Operators

The mathematical operators available in Visual Basic Express are shown in Table 19-1.

Table 19-1: Mathematical Operators Available in the Visual Basic Language

Operator	What it does	Example
^ (Exponentiation)	Raises a number to an exponential power.	2 ^ 4 = 16
- (Negation)	Turns a positive number into a negative number and vice versa.	A = -2
* (Multiplication)	Multiplies two numbers.	3 * 8 = 24
/ (Division)	Divides one number by another.	64 / 32 = 2
\ (Integer division)	Divides a number and returns an integer value, dropping any fractions.	15 \ 6 = 2
mod (Modula division)	Divides a number and returns the remainder.	15 mod 6 = 3
+ (Addition)	Adds two numbers together.	2 + 3 = 5
- (Subtraction)	Subtracts one number from another.	12 - 4 = 8

Mathematical operators work with numeric values such as these:

- *Specific values*, such as 2 and 4.125
- *Variables*, which represent specific values
- *Mathematical expressions*, which evaluate to a single specific value

For example, you can add two numbers like this:

```
Dim Total As Integer
Total = 2 + 4
MsgBox(Total)
```

This code simply displays the number *6* in a message box every time. Calculating specific values produces the same result every time, but most programs use mathematical operators with either variables or mathematical expressions so that data can be manipulated, like this:

```
Dim Total, X, Y As Integer
X = InputBox ("Type a number to add:")
Y = InputBox ("Type a second number to add:")
Total = X + Y
MsgBox(Total)

Or

Dim Total, X As Integer
X = InputBox ("Type a number")
Total = 23 + (X ^ 4)
MsgBox(Total)
```

In this case, the mathematical expression is (X ^ 4) and the two mathematical operators are + (addition) and ^ (exponentiation).

NOTE   *It's helpful (but not necessary) to enclose mathematical expressions in parentheses to make them easier to see and understand. Parentheses also tell Visual Basic the order of operations (as discussed in "Defining Your Own Operator Precedence" on page 250).*

Understanding Operator Precedence

Under-
standing
Operator
Precedence

Adding two variables together, such as X + Y, is pretty straightforward. But what if you want to combine multiple mathematical operators like this: X + Y * 7 ^ Z – 65 + 98?

When calculating a mathematical expression that contains multiple mathematical operators, Visual Basic calculates the mathematical operators with the highest *precedence* first. Here is the order of precedence from highest to lowest:

- Exponentiation (^)
- Negation (-)
- Multiplication and division (*, /)
- Integer division (\)
- Modulus arithmetic (mod)
- Addition and subtraction (+, -)

Because exponentiation always has the highest precedence, the previous example first calculates the exponentiation operator. The original mathematical expression looks like this:

```
X + Y * 7 ^ Z - 65 + 98
```

If we assume that X = 2, Y = 3, and Z = 4, calculating the revised mathematical expression according to precedence looks like this:

```
X + Y * 7 ^ 4 - 65 + 98
```

7 ^ 4 evaluates to 2401 (7 * 7 * 7 * 7), so the new mathematical expression looks like this:

```
X + Y * 2401 - 65 + 98
```

The multiplication operator has the next highest precedence, so Visual Basic calculates it next. Replacing Y with the value 3 gives:

```
X + 3 * 2401 - 65 + 98
```

3 * 2401 is 7203, so the new mathematical expression looks like this:

```
X + 7203 - 65 + 98
```

Both the addition and subtraction have equal precedence, so Visual Basic next evaluates the first operator, moving from left to right. Replacing the variable X with 2 gives this mathematical expression:

```
2 + 7203 - 65 + 98
```

Adding 2 + 7203 creates gives this revised mathematical expression:

```
7205 - 65 + 98
```

Subtracting 65 from 7205 gives this revised mathematical expression:

```
7140 + 98
```

Finally, adding this together gives the final result: 7238

Defining Your Own Operator Precedence

If you string a mathematical expression together with multiple mathematical operators, Visual Basic calculates the entire mathematical expression based on operator precedence. However, you may want to override the usual precedence of operators and force Visual Basic to calculate a mathematical operator of lower precedence first. To do this, you surround the data and a mathematical operator in parentheses.

Let's see how this would look. We'll assume the same values of X = 2, Y = 3, and Z = 4, and force Visual Basic to calculate different mathematical operators by surrounding them with parentheses, like this:

```
X + (Y * 7) ^ Z - 65 + 98
```

This expression would first calculate the value of (Y * 7), which is (3 * 7) or 21:

```
X + 21 ^ Z - 65 + 98
```

Once Visual Basic finishes evaluating all expressions within parentheses, it calculates the rest of the expression based on operator precedence. Therefore, the next calculation is 21 ^ Z. Substituting 4 for the variable Z gives 21 ^ 4, or 194481 (21 * 21* 21 * 21).

Because the addition and subtraction mathematical operators have equal precedence, Visual Basic now evaluates them from left to right.

```
X + 194481 - 65 + 98
```

Replacing the variable X with 2 gives:

```
194483 - 65 + 98
```

Subtracting 65 from 194483 gives this:

```
194418 + 98
```

And finally, we have the result: 194516. As you can see, this value is completely different from the nearly mathematical expression without the parentheses, which was otherwise identical. By changing operator precedence, you can completely change the result of any mathematical expression.

Using Mathematical Methods

Mathematical operators let you create formulas to calculate any type of result. However, it can be tedious and error-prone to re-create common mathematical formulas from scratch using various combinations of mathematical operators. Therefore, Visual Basic includes many mathematical methods stored in a math file called a *class*, which provides different ways to calculate numbers suitable for scientific or technical use. (If you simply want to add or multiply numbers, you can safely ignore this class entirely.)

To use these math methods, you feed in data, have the method perform a specific calculation on that data, and wait for a result. Table 19-2 lists some of the many math methods you can use in Visual Basic.

Table 19-2: Some Mathematical Methods Available in the Visual Basic Language

Method	What it does	Example
Math.Abs	Absolute value	Math.Abs(-89) = 89
Math.Atan	Arc tangent	Math.Atan(0.5) = 0.463647609000806
Math.Cos	Cosine	Math.Cos(0.5) = 0.877582561890373
Math.Exp	Exponential, raises the value of the mathematical constant *e* to a specified power	Math.Exp(1) = 2.71828182845905
Math.Log	Natural logarithm of a number	Math.Log(1.5) = 0.405465108108164
Math.Round	Rounds to the nearest integer	Math.Round (0.5) = 0 Math.Round(0.51) = 1
Math.Sign	Sign, returns 1 or -1	Math.Sign(-89) = -1 Math.Sign(4) = 1
Math.Sin	Sine	Math.Sin(0.5) = 0.479425538604203
Math.Sqrt	Square root	Math.Sqrt(64) = 8

Math functions accept data and return a numeric result. This means that you can assign a variable to a math function or use a math function in place of a variable or fixed value, like so:

```
Dim MyValue As Single
MyValue = Math.Sqrt(100)
MsgBox(Math.Round(MyValue))
```

This example assigns the Math.Sqrt function to the MyValue variable and then displays the value of the Math.Round(MyValue) function in a message box. In this case, the number *10* appears in the message box (10 is the square root of 100).

NOTE *To learn more about the mathematical methods available in the Math class file, search for the phrase* Math Members.

Now, suppose you type the command Math.Sin. This command consists of two parts that tell Visual Basic to use the Sin function stored in the Math class file. If you need to use math functions often, you may find that typing Math in front of each function (such as Math.Abs or Math.Sqrt) can get tiresome. To avoid this, add the following BASIC code to the top of the Code window, as shown in Figure 19-1:

```
Imports System.Math
```

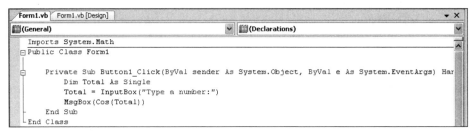

Figure 19-1: The Imports System.Math command must be the first line in the Code window.

This code tells Visual Basic to import the Math class file into the current file. In essence, this means that all the Visual Basic code hidden in the Math class file can be treated as if you had copied it into the current file. As a result, instead of typing math function commands like this:

```
Math.Cos (X)
```

you can drop the Math part of the command and just type the function name, like so:

```
Cos (X)
```

Using Assignment Operators

Assignment operators store a value into a variable. The simplest assignment operator (=) takes a value and assigns it to a variable, like so:

```
X = 28
```

You can also use the assignment operator to add, subtract, multiply, or divide a value to the existing value of a variable:

```
X = X + 109
```

This Visual Basic code says, "Take the value of X, add 109 to it, and store this new result in the variable X, overwriting its previous value."

Consider this example:

```
X = 28
X = X + 109
```

The first line assigns the value 28 to X. The second line adds the number 109 to the value of X, which is currently assigned the value 28. This new value, 28 + 109, or 137, is then assigned to the variable X.

Visual Basic includes a variety of additional operators that can perform the following two functions at once:

- Calculate a result
- Assign the result to a variable

Table 19-3 lists all available assignment operators and their function. With the exception of the equal (=) assignment operator, all of these operators are shortcuts for calculating a result and assigning it to a variable.

Table 19-3: Assignment Operators Available in the Visual Basic Language

Operator	What it does	Example
=	Assigns the value on the right side of the equal sign to an item on the left side of the equal sign.	X = 10.58 X = Math.Sqrt(X)
^=	Raises an item to an exponential power and assigns the value to an item on the left side of the ^= operator.	X ^= Y is equivalent to X = X ^ Y
*=	Multiplies two items and assigns the value to an item on the left side of the *= operator.	X *= Y is equivalent to X = X * Y
/=	Divides two items and assigns the value to an item on the left side of the /= operator.	X /= Y is equivalent to X = X / Y
\=	Integer division of two items and assigns the value to an item on the left side of the \= operator.	X \= Y is equivalent to X = X \ Y
+=	Adds two items and assigns the value to an item on the left side of the += operator.	X += Y is equivalent to X = X + Y
-=	Subtracts two items and assigns the value to an item on the left side of the -= operator.	X -= Y is equivalent to X = X - Y

The assignment operators in Table 19-3 are used to modify the value currently stored in a variable. For example, you could use the following BASIC code to change the value of a variable X:

```
Dim X As Integer
X = 29
X = X + 15
```

Or, you could replace the last line with the += assignment operator, like this:

```
Dim X As Integer
X = 29
X += 15
```

The difference between the lines X = X + 15 and X += 15 is personal; they are functionally the same. Just be aware that using assignment operators such as += or ^= can make your program look cryptic and make it more difficult to understand as a result.

Converting String Data Types to Numeric Data Types

You can use a mathematical operator on variables that represent two different data types, such as an integer and a single data type, but you may lose a certain amount of precision in the number of decimal places that the calculation stores. It's safer to perform mathematical operations on variables that represent *identical* data types, by converting one data type to another, using the *conversion functions* listed in Table 19-4.

Table 19-4: Numeric Conversion Functions

Function	What it does
CByte	Converts a numeric value or string to a byte data type
CDbl	Converts a numeric value or string to a double data type
CDec	Converts a numeric value or string to a decimal data type
CInt	Converts a numeric value or string to an integer data type
CLng	Converts a numeric value or string to a long data type
CShort	Converts a numeric value or string to a short data type
CSng	Converts a numeric value or string to a single data type

When converting one data type to another, Visual Basic may round numbers off during the data type conversion. For example:

```
Dim X As Byte
Dim Y As Single
X = 4
Y = 3.28
MsgBox (X + CByte(Y))
```

In this example, the CByte function converts the number 3.28 into a byte value by rounding 3.28 to 3, because byte data types can only hold whole numbers.

Another problem with numeric data type conversions is that certain data types can only hold a fixed range of numbers. For example, the byte data type can only hold a whole number that falls within the range of 0 to 255. If you exceed the range for a certain data type, your program won't work correctly. For example:

```
Dim X As Byte
Dim Y As Single
X = 4
Y = 259.28
MsgBox (X + CByte(Y))
```

In this example, the CByte function rounds the value of Y from 259.28 to 259. However, byte data types can hold only whole numbers that range from 0 to 2556. Because the value of Y is greater than 255 even after rounding, this code will cause an error.

When converting numbers from one data type to another, remember:

- Numeric data type conversion functions may round numbers, which could affect the accuracy of mathematical calculations.
- Every data type has a specific range of numbers that it can hold. When converting data types, make sure you don't exceed the ranges of a given data type.

Not only can these conversion functions convert one numeric data type to another, but they can also convert a string into a numeric data type.

For example, when the user types a number in a text box or through the InputBox command, that number is stored as a string. Before Visual Basic can perform mathematical operations on a number saved as a string variable, you need to convert that numeric string to a numeric data type.

The following code uses the InputBox command to get a number from the user, and then converts that number from a string to an integer value so it can multiply that number and display the result in a message box.

```
Dim A As String
Dim B As Integer
A = InputBox ("Type a number:")
MsgBox ("This is a string: " & A)
B = CInt(A) * CInt(A)
MsgBox (B)
```

In this example, the ampersand (&) character takes two strings and smashes them together into a single string. (You'll learn more about the ampersand operator in Chapter 20.)

The InputBox command accepts a number from the user and stores it in a string variable named A and displays the string in the MsgBox. For example, if the user types the number 5 into the input box, the program stores the string 5 into the variable A.

NOTE *The numeric data conversion functions can only convert numeric strings into numbers, such as the string "5" into the integer 5. If the user types in the string "five", none of Visual Basic's data conversion functions can convert it into a numeric data type.*

Once the program retrieves the number that the user types into the input box, the CInt function converts the A string variable (5 in this case) into an integer (5), multiplies the two numbers (5 * 5), and uses a second MsgBox command to display the result (25).

Hands-on Tutorial: Playing with Mathematical Methods

Using the Math Class Library

This tutorial shows you how to use three of the functions stored in the Math class file by using both the Imports System.Math code and typing the Math class name in front of each function name you want to use.

1. Start a new Visual Basic Express, then click OK to display a blank form.

2. Choose View ▸ Toolbox to display the Toolbox.

3. Click the Button control in the Toolbox, mouse over the center of the form, and click the left mouse button to create a button on the form.

4. Double-click the Button1 control on the form. The Code window appears.

5. Move the cursor to the left of the top line, Public Class Form1, and press ENTER to create a blank line at the top of the Code window.

6. Type Imports System.Math. Notice as you type that Visual Basic Express displays pop-up menus with lists of possible commands from which to choose, as shown in Figure 19-2.

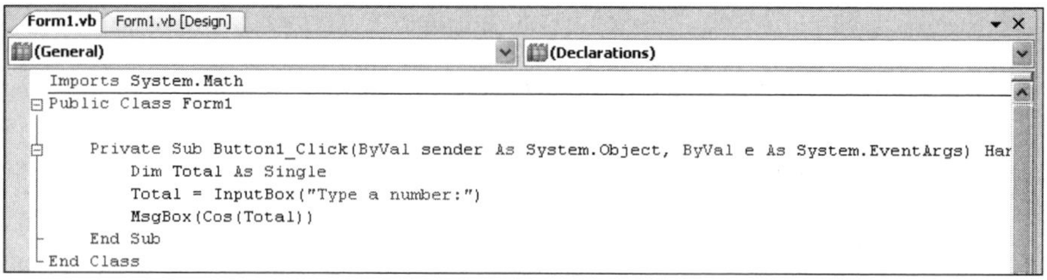

```
Form1.vb   Form1.vb [Design]                                                              ▾ ✕
(General)                              ▾  (Declarations)                                    ▾
    Imports System.Math
  ⊟ Public Class Form1

  ⊟       Private Sub Button1_Click(ByVal sender As System.Object, ByVal e As System.EventArgs) Han
              Dim Total As Single
              Total = InputBox("Type a number:")
              MsgBox(Cos(Total))
          End Sub
   └ End Class
```

Figure 19-2: As you type the Imports System.Math *line, pop-up menus help you choose a command so you don't have to type it yourself.*

7. Type the following boldface code:

```
Imports System.Math
Public Class Form1
    Private Sub Button1_Click(ByVal sender As System.Object, ByVal e As_
System.EventArgs) Handles Button1.Click
        Dim Number, X, Y, Z As Single
        Number = InputBox("Type a number:")
        X = Cos(Number)
        Y = Sin(Number)
        Z = Tan(Number)
        MsgBox("Cosine = " & CStr(X))
        MsgBox("Sine = " & CStr(Y))
        MsgBox("Tangent = " & CStr(Z))
    End Sub
End Class
```

NOTE   *The ampersand (&) operator is used to put two strings together to display in a message box.*

8. Press F5. Your user interface appears.
9. Click the Button1 control. An input box appears.
10. Type **1.2** and click OK. A dialog box appears and displays the Cosine value.
11. Click OK. Another dialog box appears and displays the Sine value.
12. Click OK. A third dialog box appears and displays the Tangent value.
13. Click OK.
14. Press ALT-F4 to stop your program. The Code window appears.
15. Delete the line Imports System.Math. Notice that Visual Basic Express displays a squiggly line under the Cos, Sine, and Tan functions because these functions are no longer valid.

16. Type **Math.** in front of the Cos, Sine, and Tan functions so your code looks like this:

```
Public Class Form1

    Private Sub Button1_Click(ByVal sender As System.Object, ByVal e As_
System.EventArgs) Handles Button1.Click
        Dim Number, X, Y, Z As Single
        Number = InputBox("Type a number:")
        X = Math.Cos(Number)
        Y = Math.Sin(Number)
        Z = Math.Tan(Number)
        MsgBox("Cosine = " & CStr(X))
        MsgBox("Sine = " & CStr(Y))
        MsgBox("Tangent = " & CStr(Z))
    End Sub
End Class
```

Notice that the green squiggly lines under the Cos, Sine, and Tan functions disappear in the Code window.

17. Press F5. Your user interface appears.

18. Repeat steps 9 to 14 and notice that your programs works exactly the same as before, after modifying your code in steps 15 and 16.

19. Choose File ▶ Close Project. A Close Project dialog box appears. Click Discard.

KEY FEATURES TO REMEMBER

Operators, functions, and methods let you tell your program to manipulate data in a useful manner.

- Operators, functions, and methods can work with specific values, variables, or mathematical expressions.

- Functions act like miniature programs that accept data and return a specific result. Methods are miniature programs stored in separate class files.

- The Visual Basic language includes libraries of prewritten functions, but you can create your own functions (which you'll learn about in Chapter 25).

- Visual Basic evaluates operations based on precedence, which means operations are evaluated in a predefined order.

- The Math class contains several methods you can use to calculate mathematical results, such as evaluating logarithms or cosine values.

- Assignment operators can either assign a new value to a variable or modify a variable through multiplication, division, addition, subtraction, or exponentiation.

- Data conversion functions can convert numeric values from one data type to another, such as converting an integer to a single value and vice versa.

20

STRING MANIPULATION

In addition to manipulating numbers, computer programs can also manipulate text, known as *strings*. The Visual Basic language includes operators and functions you can use to manipulate strings in different ways.

As you learned in Chapter 19, operators are symbols that let you combine two or more strings. Functions are miniature programs that accept a string and manipulate it in some way, such as removing extra spaces or searching for specific text within a string.

Concatenating a String

Manipulating
Strings

The simplest string operator is a *concatenation operator* (&), which combines two strings into a single string, like so:

```
Dim First, Last As String
First = "Joe "
Last= "Smith"
First = First & Last
MsgBox(First)
```

Line 1   Declares two String variables called First and Last

Line 2   Assigns the string "Joe " (note the additional space before the closing quotation mark) to the First variable

Line 3   Assigns the string "Smith" to the Last variable

Line 4   Concatenates the strings stored in the First and Last variables and stores the result in the First variable

Line 5   Displays the string stored in the First variable, "Joe Smith", in the message box

NOTE   *Because you need to leave an empty space between strings in order to separate two concatenated strings, you add a space between the word Joe and the closing quotation mark. If you were to omit the space, the & concatenation operator would cram the strings together like this: JoeSmith.*

Concatenating Multiple Strings

To concatenate several strings, you could use the & concatenation operator multiple times, like this:

```
String1 & String2 & String3 & String4 & ... & StringN
```

But this can get clumsy and tedious to write. Instead, Visual Basic offers a shortcut method called String.Concat, which accepts and combines any number of strings. Here's how it looks:

```
String.Concat (String1, String2, String3, String4, ..., StringN)
```

Here's how to use the String.Concat method:

```
Dim First, Last, Middle, Complete As String
First = "Joe "
Middle = "Allen "
Last= "Smith"
Complete = String.Concat (First, Middle, Last)
MsgBox(Complete)
```

Line 1   Declares the string variables First, Last, Middle, and Complete.

Line 2   Assigns the string "Joe " (note the extra space before the closing quotation mark) in the First variable.

Line 3   Assigns the string "Allen " (note the one extra space before the closing quotation mark) in the Middle variable.

Line 4   Assigns the string "Smith" in the Last variable.

Line 5   Uses the String.Concat method to combine all the strings stored in the First, Middle, and Last variables and store the result in the Complete variable.

Line 6   Displays the string stored in the Complete variable in a message box. Because the value of the Complete variable is "Joe Allen Smith", this name appears in the message box.

NOTE   *Add a space between each string so that the String.Concat function won't cram the strings together like this: JoeAllenSmith.*

To concatenate strings that don't already have an extra space, insert extra strings between double quotation marks as shown here. As you can see in this example, one extra space appears between the First and Middle variables and another extra space appears between the Middle and Last variables:

```
Dim First, Last, Middle, Complete As String
First = "Joe"
Middle = "Allen"
Last= "Smith"
Complete = String.Concat (First, " ", Middle, " ", Last)
MsgBox(Complete)
```

Concatenating Multiple Strings Stored in an Array

If you have an *array* of strings, (essentially, a list of items, such as a names or numbers), you can combine all strings stored in the array into a single string using the String.Join function. (You'll learn more about arrays in Chapter 23.)

To use the String.Join function, you define the *name* of the array that contains the strings you want to combine as well as a *separator string*, such as a comma or dash, that will appear between each string in the array. For example:

```
String.Join("Separator", Array)
```

where *Separator* is the character that you want to separate each array element. The character you choose must be enclosed within double quotation marks. For example, to use an asterisk (*) as your separator, type "*". *Array* is the name of the array that contains multiple strings.

For example, consider an array named NurseryArray with the following strings:

```
{"Soldier", "Sailor", "Tinker", "Tailor"}
```

You could combine these strings into a single string using String.Join, like so:

```
NewString = String.Join(" - ", NurseryArray)
```

The value of NewString would then be:

```
"Soldier - Sailor - Tinker - Tailor"
```

Hands-on Tutorial: Concatenating Multiple Strings

The following tutorial shows you how to combine multiple strings from an array, separating each string with a comma:

1. Press CTRL-N to display the New Project dialog box, then click OK to display a blank form. Choose View ▶ Toolbox.
2. Click the Button control in the Toolbox, mouse over the center of the form, and click the left mouse button to create a button on the form.
3. Double-click the Button1 control on the form. The Code window appears.

4. Type the following code between the Private Sub and End Sub lines, like this:

```
Private Sub Button1_Click(ByVal sender As System.Object, ByVal e As_
System.EventArgs) Handles Button1.Click
    Dim StringArray() As String = {"Red", "Blue", "Green"}
    Dim NewString As String
    NewString = String.Join (",", StringArray)
    MsgBox(NewString)
End Sub
```

The first line declares an array and fills it with the strings "Red", "Blue", and "Green". (The curly brackets are Visual Basic's way of organizing a list of data to store in an array, as you'll learn in Chapter 23.)

5. Press F5 to display your user interface, then click the Button1 control. A message box appears, displaying the joined string, NewString, which is "Red,Blue,Green".

6. Press ALT-F4 to stop your program.

7. (Optional) Replace the comma (",") in the String.Join command with any other character, such as the asterisk ("*") or a dash ("-"), and repeat steps 5 and 6.

8. Choose File ▸ Close Project, then click Discard.

Counting Characters in a String

To determine the total number of characters (including spaces between words) in a string, use the Len function:

```
Len (String)
```

For example, the following code counts the total number of characters in a string and displays the result in a message box:

```
Dim First, Last, Middle, Complete As String
First = "Joe "
Middle = " Allen "
Last= " Smith"
Complete = String.Concat (First, Middle, Last)
MsgBox(Len(Complete))
```

In this example, both the First and Middle string variables ("Joe " and "Allen ", respectively) contain one extra space at the end. When the String.Concat method combines the values of the First, Middle, and Last string variables, the total number of characters is 15 (13 characters plus two spaces).

Trimming Strings

Sometimes a string may have a bunch of extra spaces at the beginning or end, like so:

```
"    This string has extra spaces in the beginning. "
"This string has extra spaces at the end.            "
```

Visual Basic offers three functions to help you trim extra spaces from a string:

LTrim Removes extra spaces from the beginning of a string (*leading spaces*)

RTrim Removes extra spaces from the end of a string (*trailing spaces*)

Trim Removes extra spaces from both the beginning and end of a string

To use these functions, specify the string that you want to trim:

```
LTrim (string)
```

The `Trim` function is equivalent to running both the `LTrim` and `RTrim` functions on the same string, as follows:

```
RTrim(LTrim(string))
```

The following code shows how the `LTrim` and `RTrim` functions can strip away spaces from a string:

```
Dim Cats As String
Cats = "    This cat is bothering me.      "
MsgBox(Len(Cats))
Cats = LTrim(Cats)
MsgBox(Len(Cats))
Cats = RTrim(Cats)
MsgBox(Len(Cats))
```

In this BASIC code, the first `MsgBox` command displays the number *34* in a message box, which tells us that the original string, `Cats`, consists of 34 characters. Once the `LTrim` function strips away leading spaces, the second `MsgBox` command runs and displays the number *30* in a message box. Once the `RTrim` function runs and strips away all trailing spaces, a third `MsgBox` command displays the number *25* to show that the trimmed string now consists of only 25 characters.

Of course, strings may not always have extra spaces. Sometimes a string may have other types of characters that you want to remove, such as the asterisks here:

```
"******password"******"
```

To help you trim repetitive characters other than spaces from a string, Visual Basic offers three methods:

String.TrimStart   Removes extra characters from the beginning of a string

String.TrimEnd   Removes extra characters from the end of a string

String.Trim   Removes extra characters from both the beginning and end of a string

To use any of these methods, use the following syntax:

```
StringName.MethodName(Character)
```

where *StringName* is the variable containing the string you want to trim, *MethodName* is one of three methods (`TrimStart`, `TrimEnd`, or `Trim`), and *Character* is the character you want to remove.

For example, to remove the & character from the beginning of a string called `string1`, you could use the following BASIC code:

```
Dim string1 As String
string1 = "&&&&&&b"
MsgBox(string1)
string1 = string1.TrimStart("&")
MsgBox(string1)
```

In this example, the first `MsgBox` command displays the original `string1` as `"&&&&&&b"`. The second `MsgBox` command displays the trimmed string `"b"`.

Removing Characters from a String

You can also remove a group of characters (whether repetitive or not) buried inside of a string, using the `String.Remove` method. Here's the syntax:

```
StringName.Remove(StartIndex, NumberToRemove)
```

In this example, `StringName` is the name of the string that you want to edit; `StartIndex` is the position in the string where you want to start removing characters (0 is the first character of a string, 1 is the second, and so on); and `NumberToRemove` is the total number of characters you want to remove.

For example, to remove eight characters from a string, beginning with the fifth character (with an index value of 4), you could use the following BASIC code:

```
Dim string1 As String
string1 = "I sleep outside"
MsgBox(string1)
string1 = string1.Remove(4, 8)
MsgBox(string1)
```

In this example, the first `MsgBox` command displays the string "I sleep outside", and the `string1.Remove(4, 8)` command removes eight characters beginning with the fourth index position, as shown in Table 20-1.

Table 20-1: How the Value of string1 Changes with the string1.Remove Command

Value of string1	Step
"I sleep outside"	string1 = "I sleep outside"
"I sl ide"	string1.Remove(4,8) removes eight characters starting with the fourth index position
"I slide"	string1.Remove(4,8) condenses the string to its final form

Once the `string1.Remove(4, 8)` command runs, the second `MsgBox` command displays the edited string, "I slide".

NOTE *The fifth character has an index value of 4 because the first character of a string has an index value of 0, the second character has an index value of 1, and so on.*

Padding a String

Padding a string with extra characters is the opposite of *trimming* a string. To pad the *beginning* of a string with characters, use the `String.PadLeft` method, like so:

```
StringName.PadLeft(StringLength, "Character")
```

where `StringName` is the name of the string you want to pad, `StringLength` is the total length of your string after you pad it with characters, and `Character` is the character (enclosed within double quotation marks) that you want to use to pad your string.

For example, if your string's original length consists of 10 characters and you want to pad it with an extra three characters, the value of `StringLength` should be 13 (the sum of 10 + 3).

To pad the end of a string, use the `String.PadRight` method, like so:

```
StringName.PadRight(StringLength, "Character")
```

Unlike the `String.PadLeft` method, the `String.PadRight` method adds characters to the *end* of a string.

The following BASIC code pads a string with the $ character and stores the padded string in a different string variable:

```
Dim OldString, NewString As String
OldString = "Bo the Cat"
NewString = OldString.PadLeft(15, "$")
MsgBox(OldString)
MsgBox(NewString)
```

The value of `OldString` remains "Bo the Cat", but the value of `NewString` becomes "$$$$$Bo the Cat", because of the `PadLeft` command. Because the original string "Bo the Cat" consists of 10 characters, by specifying 15 in the `PadLeft` method we add five extra $ characters to the string.

Searching Strings

A string can be as short as one character or as long as a novel. If you have a particularly large string, you may want to search for other strings, such as names, buried within the it. Visual Basic provides several ways to search strings by *position* or string *content*.

You can use one of two nearly identical commands to accomplish this task. One command maintains compatibility with older versions of Visual Basic while the other provides compatibility with the latest version of Microsoft's other programming languages, including C# and Visual C++. The biggest difference between the commands is that the older one defines the first character of a string as position (or index) 1, the second character as position 2, and so on. Because these commands assume the first character of a string starts at position 1, these commands are considered *one-based*.

The newer commands define the first character of a string as position (or index) 0, the second character at position 1, and so on. Because these commands assume the first character of a string starts at position 0, they are considered *zero-based*.

Table 20-2 lists the different commands available for searching strings and identifies which commands are one-based and which are zero-based.

Table 20-2: String Searching Commands

String searching command	One- or zero-based
StringName.Chars	Zero-based
String.IndexOf	Zero-based
String.LastIndexOf	Zero-based
InStr	One-based

Retrieving Single Characters with the Chars Property

Every string has a `Chars` property that lets you retrieve individual characters based on their *position* in a string. To use the `Chars` property, specify the string name to search for and the position in the string to retrieve a character. The syntax looks like this:

```
StringName.Chars(Index)
```

where *StringName* is the name of the string to search for and *Index* is the numeric location in the string.

For example, to retrieve the first character of a string, the value of *Index* would be 0; to retrieve the second character of a string, the value of *Index* would be 1; and so on.

The following BASIC code displays the letter *c* (the first letter in the word *computers*) in a message box:

```
Dim Alphabet As String
Alphabet = "Will computers ever be bug-free?"
MsgBox(Alphabet.Chars(5))
```

Searching for the Position of a Specific Character

If you want to find a specific character within a string, you can find its index position with the String.IndexOf or String.LastIndexOf method. The String.IndexOf method finds the *first* character in a string and the String.LastIndexOf method finds the *last* character in a string. To use either method, define the string name and the character you want to find using the following syntax:

```
StringName.IndexOf("Character")
StringName.LastIndexOf("Character")
```

where *StringName* is the string to search and *Character* is the specific character you want to find within the string.

```
Dim Alphabet As String
Alphabet = "Will computers ever be bug-free?"
MsgBox(Alphabet.IndexOf("e"))
MsgBox(Alphabet.LastIndexOf("e"))
```

In this code, the first MsgBox command (IndexOf) displays the number *11*, which represents the position of the first e in the string, which is the *e* in the word *computers*. The second MsgBox command (LastIndexOf) displays the number *30*, which represents the position of the last e in the string, which is the last *e* in the word *bug-free*.

Searching for the Position of a String Within Another String

Both the String.IndexOf and String.LastIndexOf methods let you search a string for the position of a specific character. To search a string for the position of another string, use the InStr function, with the following syntax:

```
InStr(StringToSearch, StringToFind)
```

where *StringToSearch* is the string that you want to examine, and *StringToFind* is the string you want to find.

If *StringToFind* does not appear inside *StringToSearch*, the InStr function returns 0. If it does appear inside *StringToSearch*, the InStr function returns a *number* that represents where it is in the searched string.

The Instr function is a one-based command; that is, when it searches for a string, it considers the first character of a string to be in *position 1*.

NOTE *Other Visual Basic string manipulation functions are zero-based commands; that is, they consider the first character of a string to be in* position 0 *(zero).*

For example, the following BASIC code displays the number *3* in a message box, because the beginning of the string "ace" starts at the third position inside the string "Peace through war."

```
Dim Target, FindMe As String
Target = "Peace through war."
FindMe = "ace"
MsgBox(InStr(Target, FindMe))
```

Hands-on Tutorial: Searching Strings

This tutorial demonstrates how the various string searching commands work in Visual Basic. You'll create a simple program that lets you enter a string and then search for different characters.

1. Press CTRL-N to display the New Project dialog box, then click OK. A blank form appears.
2. Choose View ▸ Toolbox to display the Toolbox, then choose Window ▸ Auto Hide to keep the Toolbox visible.
3. Click the TextBox control in the Toolbox, move the mouse pointer near the top of the form, and click the left mouse button to create a text box on the form.
4. Click the Button control in the Toolbox, mouse over the center of the form, and click the left mouse button to create a button on the form.
5. Double-click the Button1 control on the form. The Code window appears.
6. Type the following bolded code lines between the Private Sub and End Sub lines so that the code reads as follows:

```
Private Sub Button1_Click(ByVal sender As System.Object, ByVal e As_
System.EventArgs) Handles Button1.Click
        Dim string1 As String
        string1 = TextBox1.Text
        MsgBox("The third character is = " & string1.Chars(2))
        MsgBox("The first letter e is at = " & string1.IndexOf("e"))
        MsgBox("The last letter e is at = " & string1.LastIndexOf("e"))
        MsgBox("The word 'the' is at = " & InStr(string1, "the"))
End Sub
```

Line 1   Declares a variable called string1, which can hold string data.

Line 2   Stores the contents of TextBox1's Text property in the string1 variable.

Line 3   Uses the Char property to retrieve the third character in the string stored in the string1 variable, and displays the result in a message box using the MsgBox command.

Line 4   Uses the IndexOf method to find the first occurrence of the letter *e* in the string1 variable, then displays the numeric position in a message box using the MsgBox command.

Line 5   Uses the LastIndexOf method to find the last occurrence of the letter *e* in the string1 variable then displays the numeric position in a message box using the MsgBox command.

Line 6 Uses the `InStr` function to search for the position of the word *the* inside the `string1` variable, then displays the position in a message box using the `MsgBox` command.

7. Press F5 to display your user interface, then click in the text box and type **Theater of the Mind**.

8. Click the Button1 control. A message box appears and displays *The third character is = e*. This message box gets its data from the `string1.Chars(2)` command.

9. Click OK. A second message box appears and displays, *The first letter e is at = 2*. This message box gets its data from the `string1.IndexOf("e")` command.

10. Click OK. A third message box appears and displays, *The last letter e is at = 13*. This message box gets its data from the `string1.LastIndexOf("e")` command.

11. Click OK. A fourth message box appears and displays, *The word "the" is at = 12*. This message box gets its data from the `InStr(string1, "the")` command.

12. Click OK to make this fourth message box disappear.

13. Press ALT-F4 to stop your program, choose File ▸ Close Project, then click Discard.

Comparing Strings

Use the `StrComp` function to compare two strings to see if they're equal. Two strings are equal if they're exactly identical, including the same uppercase and lowercase letters. To use the `StrComp` function, give it the two strings you want to compare, using this syntax:

```
StrComp(String1, String2)
```

If the two strings are equal, the `StrComp` function returns a value of 0. The `StrComp` function returns a value of -1 if, sorted alphabetically, `String1` would appear first *before* `String2`. The `StrComp` function returns a value of 1 if, sorted alphabetically, `String1` would appear *after* `String2`.

Uppercase characters sort before lowercase characters. For example, in the following code, the `MsgBox` command would display -1 in the message box, which means Visual Basic would sort `String1` ("B") before `String2` ("b"):

```
Dim string1, string2 As String
string1 = "B"
string2 = "b"
MsgBox(StrComp(string1, string2))
```

If you were to replace `string1` and `string2` with the following values, the `MsgBox` command in the BASIC code would display a value of *1* in the message box, because Visual Basic would sort `string1` ("Build a better mousetrap.") after `string2` ("Build").

```
Dim string1, string2 As String
string1 = "Build a better mousetrap."
string2 = "Build"
MsgBox(StrComp(string1, string2))
```

Although both strings contain the word *Build*, because `string1` contains additional characters, Visual Basic sorts it after the shorter "Build" string stored in the `string2` variable.

String.Compare

As an alternative to using the StrComp function, which is built into the Visual Basic language, you can also use the following syntax, which is a method stored in the String class library:

```
String.Compare(String1, String2, IgnoreCase)
```

where *String1* is the first string to compare and *String2* is the second string to compare.

IgnoreCase is a True or False value. If this value is True, the String.Compare method ignores uppercase and lowercase letters between *String1* and *String2*. If this value is False, the String.Compare command considers uppercase and lowercase characters to be entirely different.

Like the StrComp function, the String.Compare method returns a 0 if two strings are equal, a -1 if *String1* would be sorted before *String2*, and a 1 if *String1* would be sorted after *String2*. The main difference between the two methods is that String.Compare lets you specify a True or False value to represent *IgnoreCase*.

As an example, the following BASIC code would cause the MsgBox command to display a value of -1:

```
Dim string1, string2 As String
String1 = "b"
String2 = "B"
MsgBox(String.Compare(string1, string2, False))
```

This String.Compare method tells Visual Basic to compare *String1* and *String2* without ignoring the case of each string. If you were to change the String.Compare method to use True, thus ignoring case:

```
Dim string1, string2 As String
String1 = "b"
String2 = "B"
MsgBox(String.Compare(string1, string2, True))
```

the MsgBox command would display a value of 0 instead.

Comparing Strings with the Like Operator

The Like operator compares a pattern to a string and returns a True value if the pattern matches the string, or a False value if the pattern does not match. The syntax for the Like operator is:

```
String1 Like Pattern
```

where *String1* is the string to search for and *Pattern* is what you want to find inside *String1*.

Matching Strings

At the simplest level, a pattern can be a string itself, like so:

```
Dim FirstString, SecondString as String
Dim Flag as Boolean
FirstString = "Ignorance is Strength."
```

```
SecondString = FirstString
Flag = FirstString Like SecondString
MsgBox(Flag)
```

In this listing:

Line 1 Declares two string variables named `FirstString` and `SecondString`.

Line 2 Declares a boolean variable called `Flag`. (Boolean variables can hold a value of True or False only, as explained in Chapter 18.)

Line 3 Stores the string `"Ignorance is Strength."` into the `FirstString` variable.

Line 4 Copies the contents of the `FirstString` variable and stores it in the `SecondString` variable.

Line 5 Uses the `Like` operator to compare the values of the `FirstString` variable to the `SecondString` variable. Because both strings are equal, the value of True is stored in the `Flag` variable.

Line 6 Displays True in a message box because the two string variables, `FirstString` and `SecondString`, contain identical strings.

If the `Like` operator compares two strings that contain even a slight variation (for example, one string has an uppercase letter while the other has a lowercase letter, or one has a period at the end and the other does not), the `Like` operator will return a False value. For example, the following BASIC code displays False in a message box because the `FirstString` variable contains a period at the end but the `SecondString` variable does not:

```
Dim FirstString, SecondString as string
Dim Flag as Boolean
FirstString = "Ignorance is Strength."
SecondString = "Ignorance is Strength"
Flag = FirstString Like SecondString
MsgBox(Flag)
```

Pattern Matching with the Single-Character Wildcard

The `Like` operator can also compare one string to a *pattern*, where a pattern consists of characters and *wildcards* that can represent one or more additional characters.

For example, say you want to know whether a certain string begins with the letter *s* and ends with the letter *t* and contains exactly one character in between. While you could check every three-character string that begins with s and ends with t, such as `"sat"` and `"sit"`, it's much easier to use a single-character wildcard (?) instead.

The following BASIC code shows how to use the ? wildcard to search for a three-character string that begins with s and ends with t:

```
Dim FirstString, SecondString as string
Dim Flag as Boolean
FirstString = "sat"
SecondString = "s?t"
Flag = FirstString Like SecondString
MsgBox(Flag)
```

In this example, the `Like` operator compares the `"sat"` string with the `"s?t"` pattern, finds that the letter *a* matches the single-character wildcard (?), and thus concludes that the `"sat"` string is like the `"s?t"` pattern.

You can use the ? wildcard multiple times to match multiple characters. For example, the pattern "s??t" would match the strings "soot" and "silt" because the two ? wildcards represent two characters between the s and the t. But the "s??t" pattern would not match "sit" or "shoot", because "sit" has only one character between the s and the t and "shoot" has three characters between the s and the t.

Pattern Matching with the Multiple-Character Wildcard

The ? wildcard matches any single character. However, if you want to match any three characters in a string, you would need to use a pattern like "s???t". This pattern would match the string "shoot" but not the string "silt" because "silt" has only two characters between the s and the t, while the pattern "s???t" requires exactly three characters.

Since it can be cumbersome to use multiple ? wildcards, you can use the * wildcard instead, which can represent zero or more characters. Thus, the pattern "s*t" would match the strings "sit", "shoot", and even "st", as shown in the following BASIC code:

```
Dim FirstString, SecondString as string
Dim Flag as Boolean
FirstString = "st"
SecondString = "s*t"
Flag = FirstString Like SecondString
MsgBox(Flag)
```

In this example, the Like operator compares the "st" string with the "s*t" string, finds zero characters between the s and the t, and returns a True value. If the value of FirstString were "shoot", then the pattern "s*t" would still return True because the * wildcard would match the three characters hoo sandwiched between the s and the t in the "s*t" pattern.

Pattern Matching with the Single Numeric-Character Wildcard

The # wildcard works like the ? wildcard except that it only matches any number, not any other characters. For example, a pattern like "9##" would match the string "911" but not the string "96", because "96" has only one character following the 9. Here's the BASIC code:

```
Dim FirstString, SecondString as string
Dim Flag as Boolean
FirstString = "96"
SecondString = "9##"
Flag = FirstString Like SecondString
MsgBox(Flag)
```

In this example, the Like operator compares the "96" string with the "9##" string, finds that the "96" string does not contain exactly two numbers following the 9, and thus returns a value of False.

Pattern Matching with Lists

Wildcards can match zero or more characters, but what if you want to know whether a particular character falls within a *range* of characters or numbers? To do this, you can see if a single character in a string falls within a *list* that contains a range of characters defined within square brackets. For example, to determine whether a character is a letter, you could use the pattern "[A-Z, a-z]", as follows:

```
Dim FirstString, SecondString as string
Dim Flag as Boolean
FirstString = "A"
SecondString = "[A-Z, a-z]"
Flag = FirstString Like SecondString
MsgBox(Flag)
```

The "[A-Z, a-z]" pattern, stored in the SecondString variable, looks to see whether a single character falls within the range of A–Z or a–z. In this example, the letter *A* falls within the range of A–Z, so the MsgBox command displays True in a message box. To see whether a character falls only within the range of all uppercase letters, such as A–Z, you could simplify the pattern and use "[A-Z]" instead.

You can also use lists to see whether a character falls within a *numeric* range. For example:

```
Dim FirstString, SecondString as string
Dim Flag as Boolean
FirstString = "8"
SecondString = "[0-9]"
Flag = FirstString Like SecondString
MsgBox(Flag)
```

In this example, the MsgBox command displays *True* in a message box because the string "8" falls within the range of the list "[0-9]".

Lists can also determine whether a character does *not* fall within a specific range. For example, to see if a certain character is anything *but* an uppercase letter, you could do the following:

```
Dim FirstString, SecondString as string
Dim Flag as Boolean
FirstString = "a"
SecondString = "[!A-Z]"
Flag = FirstString Like SecondString
MsgBox(Flag)
```

This MsgBox command would display *True* in a message box, meaning that the string "a" did not fall within the range of A–Z. The exclamation point (!) in the [!A-Z] list tells Visual Basic to determine whether a character does *not* fall within the range of A–Z.

Lists check only a *single* character. If you had a string "AA", the following would return a False value:

```
"AA" Like "[A-Z]"
```

The "AA" string consists of two characters, but the pattern list "[A-Z]" only checks for a single character. To see if both characters are uppercase letters, you would use the pattern "[A-Z][A-Z]".

For maximum flexibility, combine wildcards with lists and specific characters in a pattern, as shown in Table 20-3.

Table 20-3: Examples of Patterns and the Strings They Match

Pattern	Matches these strings
`"Sam?I???"`	`"Sam I am"`
	`"Sam Iztu"`
`"Free*"`	`"Freedom is slavery."`
	`"Free"`
	`"Freedom88jndklu3"`
`"###-####"`	`"123-4567"`
	`"039-7156"`
`?b*`	`"absolute"`
	`"oboe"`
	`"AbE"`
`[A-Z]?E*"`	`"ABE"`
	`"ZCEFGH"`
	`"YgEkldjfie"`
`[!A-Z]##"`	`"987"`
	`"&56"`
	`"q21"`

Hands-on Tutorial: Comparing Strings

Pattern matching can be a powerful way to compare two strings, but it can be confusing. This tutorial gives you practice in typing different patterns to see how they work.

1. Start a new project, then click OK to display a blank form.
2. Choose View ▸ Toolbox to display the Toolbox, then choose Window ▸ Auto Hide to keep the Toolbox visible.
3. Click the TextBox control in the Toolbox, move the mouse pointer near the top of the form, and click the left mouse button to create a text box on the form.
4. Click the TextBox control again in the Toolbox, mouse over the center of the form, and click the left mouse button to create a second text box on the form.
5. Click the Button control in the Toolbox, mouse over the center of the form, and click the left mouse button to create a button on the form.
6. Double-click the Button1 control on the form. The Code window appears.
7. Type `MsgBox(TextBox1.Text Like TextBox2.Text)` between the `Private Sub` and `End Sub` lines so the code looks as follows:

```
Private Sub Button1_Click(ByVal sender As System.Object, ByVal e As_
System.EventArgs) Handles Button1.Click
      MsgBox(TextBox1.Text Like TextBox2.Text)
End Sub
```

8. Press F5 to display your user interface, then click in the top text box and type **Linux**.

9. Click in the second text box and type **[A-Z]i??x**.

10. Click the Button1 control. A message box appears and displays *True*, which tells you that the pattern you typed in the second text box matches the string you typed in the top text box. Click OK.

11. Repeat steps 7 through 9, substituting the patterns and strings from Table 20-2, such as "Free*" and "Freedom is slavery." Make sure you type the complete string in the top text box and the pattern in the second text box, or Visual Basic will treat the pattern literally and try to match an asterisk with another asterisk, a question mark with another question mark, and so on.

12. Press ALT-F4 to stop your program, then choose File ▶ Close Project. Click Discard.

Replacing Strings

Visual Basic's string-replacing commands are one-based, meaning that they consider the first character of a string to be at position or index 1. They are shown in Table 20-4.

Table 20-4: String Replacing Commands

String replacing command	One- or zero-based
Mid	One-based
Replace	One-based

The Mid function lets you replace part of a string with another string, using this syntax:

```
Mid (String, Position, CharactersToReplace) = ReplacementString
```

where *String* is the string that contains the characters that you want to replace and *Position* is the location in the string where you want to start replacing characters. The first character is position 1, the second is position 2, and so on. (Remember that some Visual Basic string functions treat the first character of a string as position 0 while others, such as the Mid function, treat the first character as position 1.)

CharactersToReplace defines the numbers of characters you want to overwrite in the original string and *ReplacementString* is the string you want to insert into another string. The value of *CharactersToReplace* must *equal* the number of characters in *ReplacementString*. If its value is *less than* the number of characters in *ReplacementString*, the Mid function will use only part of the *ReplacementString*. If the value of *CharactersToReplace* is *more than* the number of characters in *ReplacementString*, the Mid function will use the entire *ReplacementString*.

The following BASIC code shows how the Mid function can replace part of a string:

```
Dim FirstString as string
FirstString = "We always need more wars to have peace."
MsgBox(FirstString)
Mid(FirstString, 11, 4) = "want"
MsgBox(FirstString)
```

The first MsgBox command displays, "We always need more wars to have peace." Before the second MsgBox command runs, the Mid function overwrites the characters in the FirstString variable from the 11th, 12th, 13th, and 14th positions, replacing the string "need" with the string "want" so the second MsgBox command displays, *We always want more wars to have peace.*

The Mid function can replace strings based on an index position within the string, but what if you want to search for certain characters embedded in a string and replace them with other characters (much like the search and replace feature in a word processor)? To do this, use the Replace function, which looks like this:

```
Replace (String, SearchString, ReplacementString)
```

where *String* is the string that contains the characters that you want to replace, *SearchString* is the specific string that you want to find, and *ReplacementString* is the string to replace *SearchString*.

Here's how you would search for the string "cat" and replace it with the string "dog":

```
Dim FirstString, SecondString as string
FirstString = "I own a cat."
MsgBox(FirstString)
SecondString = Replace (FirstString, "cat", "dog")
MsgBox(SecondString)
```

The first MsgBox command displays the string *I own a cat.* in a message box. Once the Replace function replaces the string "cat" with "dog", the second MsgBox command displays *I own a dog.* in a message box.

Normally, the Replace function starts searching for a string from the *beginning* (position 1), but you can specify a different position with the following syntax:

```
Replace (String, SearchString, ReplacementString, Start)
```

where *Start* is an integer that represents the position in a string. To begin searching from the second character in a string, use 2 for the value of *Start*.

Finally, the Replace function normally searches and replaces a string once and then stops. To search and replace a string multiple times, use this syntax:

```
Replace (String, SearchString, ReplacementString, Start, Count)
```

where *Count* is an integer that represents how many times you want to search and replace a string. For example, to search and replace six strings, use the value 6 for *Count*.

Here's how to search and replace multiple strings:

```
Dim A, B As String
A = "Under capitalism, people exploit people."
MsgBox (A)
B = Replace (A, "capitalism", "communism")
B = Replace (B, "people", "comrades", 1, 2)
MsgBox (B)
```

In this example, the first MsgBox command displays the string *Under capitalism, people exploit people.* The first Replace function replaces capitalism with communism and the second Replace function replaces people twice with comrades (the number 1 tells Replace to start at the beginning of the string defined by variable B, while the number 2 specifies to replace the string twice). The result is that the second MsgBox command displays, *Under communism, comrades exploit comrades.*

Extracting Strings

Visual Basic's string extracting commands are zero-based, as shown in Table 20-5.

Table 20-5: String Extracting Commands

String extracting command	One or zero-based
`Strings.Left`	One-based
`Strings.Right`	One-based
`Strings.Mid`	One-based
`Strings.Substring`	Zero-based

You can *extract* or remove part of a string from a larger string by using one of these methods:

`Strings.Left`   Extracts characters from the left or start of a string

`Strings.Right`   Extracts characters from the right or end of a string

`Strings.Mid`   Extracts characters from the middle of a string

The `Left` function syntax looks like this:

```
Strings.Left (String, Length)
```

where `String` is the string from which you want to remove characters and `Length` is the number of characters you want to remove, starting from the left or beginning of `String`.

The syntax for the `Right` function looks exactly the same, except that `Right` extracts characters from the right, or end, of a string:

```
Strings.Right (String, Length)
```

To extract characters from the *middle* of a string, use the `Mid` function, which looks like this:

```
Strings.Mid (String, Start, Length)
```

where `String` is the string from which you want to remove characters and `Start` defines the position at which to start extracting characters from a string. For example, to start extracting the second character, the value of `Start` would be 2.

`Length` is the number of characters you want to remove starting from the left or beginning of `String`. If you don't define a value for `Length`, the `Mid` function extracts characters from the position defined by `Start` all the way to the end of the string.

```
Dim Original, A, B, C As String
Original = "Who cares how you vote if you don't know who counts them?"
A = Strings.Left(Original, 3)
B = Strings.Right(Original, 5)
C = Strings.Mid(Original, 5, 18)
MsgBox(A)
MsgBox(B)
MsgBox(C)
```

The first `MsgBox` command displays the string *Who* in a message box, because it contains the three-character string extracted from the left of the original string. The second `MsgBox` command displays the string *them?* which is the last five characters extracted from the original string. The third `MsgBox` command displays the string *cares how you vote* because the word *cares* starts in the fifth position of the original string and the `Strings.Mid` method extracts eighteen characters to create the string "cares how you vote".

The `SubString` method is an alternative to the `Strings.Mid` method:

```
StringName.SubString (Start, Length)
```

where *StringName* is the name of the string from which you want to extract characters and *Start* is the index position where you want to start extracting characters. (The first character in a string is index value 0, the second is index value 1, and so on.) *Length* is the number of characters you want to extract.

Here's how to use the `SubString` method to extract characters from the middle of a string:

```
Dim Original, A As String
Original = "Who cares how you vote if you don't know who counts them?"
A = Original.SubString(4, 18)
MsgBox(A)
```

In this example, the `MsgBox` command displays *cares how you vote* in a message box.

NOTE *When using the `SubString` method, the first position in a string is index 0, the second character is 1, the third character is 2, and so on. Thus, the index value of 4 means the fifth character in the `Original` string, which is the position of the letter c in the "cares how you vote" string that the `SubString` method extracts.*

Hands-on Tutorial: Extracting Strings

This tutorial shows you how to use the `Len` function to count the length of a string, the `Strings.Left` function to extract a new string from an existing one, and the NumericUp-Down control to give your program a range of different values.

1. Start a new project in Visual Basic Express, then click OK to display a blank form.
2. Choose View ▸ Toolbox to display the Toolbox, then choose Window ▸ Auto Hide to keep the Toolbox visible.
3. Click the Label control in the Toolbox, move the mouse pointer near the top of the form, and click the left mouse button to create a label control.
4. Click the TextBox control in the Toolbox, mouse over the center of the form, and click the left mouse button to create a text box on the form under the label control.
5. Click the NumericUpDown control in the Toolbox, move the mouse pointer near the bottom of the form, and click the left mouse button to create a NumericUpDown control on the form. (See Chapter 15 for more on this control.) Your user interface should look like Figure 20-1.

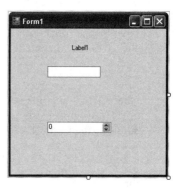

Figure 20-1: A label control, a text box control, and a NumericUpDown control on a form

6. Double-click the NumericUpDown1 control on the form. The Code window appears.

7. Type two lines between the `Private Sub` and `End Sub` lines so that the code appears as follows:

```
Private Sub NumericUpDown1_ValueChanged(ByVal sender As System.Object,_
ByVal e As System.EventArgs) Handles NumericUpDown1.ValueChanged
        NumericUpDown1.Maximum = Len(TextBox1.Text)
        Label1.Text = Strings.Left(TextBox1.Text, NumericUpDown1.Value)
End Sub
```

The first line uses the `Len` function to count the number of characters in the `Text` property of the text box named TextBox1. Next, it uses this value to define the maximum number (the `Maximum` property) that the NumericUpDown control can display. The second line uses the `Strings.Left` method to remove characters from the `Text` property of the text box named TextBox1. The number of characters to remove is defined by the current number (the `Value` property) displayed in the NumericUpDown control. For example, if the current number in the `Value` property of the NumericUpDown control is 4, the `Strings.Left` method extracts four characters from the string stored in the `Text` property of TextBox1 and stores the result in the `Text` property of the label named Label1.

8. Press F5 to display your user interface, then click in the text box and type any message, such as **I want a Mac.**

9. Click the up arrow in the NumericUpDown control. Notice that each time you click the up arrow, the label control displays another character from the string you typed in the text box.

10. Click the up arrow in the NumericUpDown control until the string in the label control appears identical to the string that you typed in the text box in step 8.

11. Click the down arrow on the NumericUpDown control. Notice that each time you click the down arrow, another character disappears from the right of the string displayed in the label control.

12. Press ALT-F4 to stop your program, then choose File ▸ Close Project. Click Discard.

Converting Strings

Your program's user interface can display strings in a text box or a message box to present information on the screen. However, if you need to display data stored in a numeric data type, such as integer or double, you'll need to convert that number into a string first using the `CStr` function, which looks like this:

```
CStr (Data)
```

where `Data` is any non-string data type such as a single, boolean, or date.

Here's how to convert different data types so you can concatenate them into a single string to display in a message box:

```
Dim Message As String = "Is it "
Dim Flag as Boolean = True
Dim TaxRate As Single = 7.75
Message = Message & CStr(Flag) & CStr(TaxRate)
MsgBox(Message)
```

Line 1 Creates a string variable called `Message`, which stores the string `"Is it "`, including the one extra space at the end.

Line 2 Creates a boolean variable called `Flag` and sets its value to True.

Line 3 Creates a `Single` variable called `TaxRate` and sets its value to `7.75`.

Line 4 Concatenates the string stored in the `Message` variable with the values stored in the `Flag` and `TaxRate` variables. Because neither the `Flag` nor `TaxRate` variables are string data types, the fourth line uses two `CStr` functions to convert the `Flag` variable and the `TaxRate` variable into a string. Then the `MsgBox` command displays the final concatenated string, *Is it True7.75*, in a message box. Notice that the value of `Flag` and `TaxRate` get smashed together (*True7.75*), because the code doesn't insert an extra space between the converted string `Flag` (`CStr(Flag)`) and the converted string `TaxRate` (`CStr(TaxRate)`).

Reversing Strings

Visual Basic Express includes a rather odd function called `StrReverse`, which does nothing more than reverse a string so the last character becomes the first and vice versa. It looks like this:

```
StrReverse (String)
```

The following BASIC code shows how the `StrReverse` function reverses a string:

```
Dim Original As String = "Good-bye cruel world"
MsgBox(StrReverse(Original))
```

The `MsgBox` command displays the nonsensical string *dlrow leurc ,eyb-dooG* in a message box.

KEY FEATURES TO REMEMBER

Visual Basic Express provides multiple ways to manipulate strings by adding, removing, or searching for specific characters.

- The concatenate operator (&) and the `String.Concat` method can smash two strings together. When concatenating strings, be sure to insert a blank space between each string to separate phrases or words, unless you want to smash the strings together.

- The `LTrim`, `RTrim`, and `Trim` functions and `String.TrimStart`, `String.TrimEnd`, and `String.Trim` methods can remove repetitive characters (such as empty spaces) from a string.

- Some Visual Basic string functions consider the first character of a string to be at position 0 (called zero-based), while others consider the first character of a string to be at position 1 (called one-based).

- The `String.Remove` method can remove any type of characters from the middle of a string.

- The `StrComp` function and the `String.Compare` method let you compare two strings to determine which string is "greater" or "less" than another string based on the order Visual Basic would sort them alphabetically.

- The `Like` operator lets you compare a string to a pattern, which can consist of either another string, single and multiple character wildcards, or lists.

- The `Mid` and the `Replace` functions can overwrite characters in a string.

- The `Strings.Left`, `Strings.Mid`, and `Strings.Right` methods let you extract characters from a string.

21

DECISION-MAKING STATEMENTS

A program is nothing more than a series of instructions. A simple program might consist of a list of instructions to be followed, one at a time, in the same order every time, without accepting user input. Such a program might be handy but it would have only limited uses. For greater flexibility, programs should accept user input and respond to the user input accordingly.

For example, a video game that confronted you with the same obstacles every time would be boring. To make that game more interesting its programmers need to have it interact with the player and respond differently depending on how the game is being played. For example, it might show different monsters or different corridors to explore depending on how quickly the player moved through the game or how many secret keys had been found. You get the idea.

Programs need to make decisions based on user input in order to make them more powerful and flexible. Your program should examine certain data and respond, just as in real life we take an umbrella (usually) when it's raining, or we take the bus if the car won't run.

In the context of computer programming, decision-making involves:

Conditional expressions   The outside information (user input) that your program evaluates

Control structures   The choice of different instructions to follow based on the conditional expression

Understanding Conditional Expressions

Under-
standing
Conditional
Expressions

A *conditional expression* compares two items, then returns a True or False value. In real life, a conditional expression might determine whether it's raining or whether the car won't run. All conditional expressions boil down to a True or False answer.

When programming, a simple conditional expression might look like:

```
4 > 90
```

This conditional expression asks, "Is the number 4 greater than the number 90?" Because the answer is no, the answer to this conditional expression is always False.

But the real power of conditional expressions comes when you use variables, such as:

```
Variable > 90
```

The value of this conditional expression depends entirely on the value of `Variable`. If the value of `Variable` is greater than 90, the expression returns a True value. If the value of `Variable` is equal to or less than 90, the expression returns a value of False.

To compare the values of two variables, do the following:

```
Variable1 > Variable2
```

This conditional expression will return a True or False value depending on the values of both `Variable1` and `Variable2`.

For even greater flexibility, compare a value to a mathematical expression, like so:

```
Variable1 > (Variable2 * 45) - Variable3
```

This conditional expression will return either a True or False value depending on the values stored in `Variable1`, `Variable2`, and `Variable3`.

How Comparison Operators Work

You can compare two values using six different *comparison operators*, as shown in Table 21-1.

Table 21-1: Comparison Operators Available in Visual Basic

Comparison operator	What it means
=	Equal
<>	Not equal
<	Less than
<=	Less than or equal to
>	Greater than
>=	Greater than or equal to

Comparing Characters and Strings

Comparison operators compare two values. A value can be *fixed* value (such as 35.4), a *variable* (which represents a number or text), or even a mathematical expression (such as X + 98.6).

Comparing numbers is straightforward enough, but comparing characters can be a bit more confusing. When Visual Basic Express compares characters, it compares the *ASCII (American Standard Code for Information Interchange)* code that represents each character. ASCII codes allow computers to represent specific characters with numbers, such as ASCII code 66, which represents the capital letter *B*. ASCII codes also contain codes to represent Western characters such as letters with accents ($\hat{o}$).

NOTE   *To view an ASCII chart, choose Help ▸ Search from the Visual Basic Express menu and type **ASCII Character codes** in the Search text box.*

Table 21-2 lists examples of valid conditional expressions and whether they represent a True or False value.

Table 21-2: Valid Conditional Expressions and Their Values

Conditional expression	Value
3 = 35.4	False
"a" = "a"	True
94 <> 94	False
"Hello" <> "Good-bye"	True
100 < 0.49	False
"A" < "X"	True
15 <= 1.24	False
15 <= 15	True
"A" > "Z"	False
"Z" > "A"	True
107 >= 948	False
948 >= 107	True

When evaluating a conditional expression like the following:

```
"A" < "a"
```

Visual Basic first converts each character into its ASCII code equivalent. In this example, "A" translates into the ASCII code 65 and "a" translates into the ASCII code 97. Replacing the characters with their ASCII code equivalent turns the conditional expression into:

```
65 < 97
```

This conditional expression evaluates to True.

When a conditional expression compares *strings* of characters, Visual Basic Express converts each character into its ASCII code equivalent until it finds a difference, like so:

```
"abcz" < "abc6"
```

In this case, the ASCII values for the first three characters in each string, abc, are equal on both sides of the expression. However, because the ASCII code for z is 122 and for 6 is 54, the value of this conditional expression is False.

When you compare strings of different lengths, Visual Basic first compares the ASCII codes of each character. If the characters in the shorter string are identical to the characters in the longer string, Visual Basic considers the longer string "greater" than the shorter one. For example:

```
"ABCDEFG" > "ABCD"
```

Because the first four characters in both strings are identical, the ABCDEFG string is considered "greater" than the ABCD string, and this conditional expression evaluates to True.

Combining Conditional Expressions

Besides comparing one conditional expression to another, you can also compare multiple conditional expressions using something called *logical operators*.

The six different kinds of logical operators include And, Or, Xor, Not, AndAlso, and OrElse. By combining conditional expressions with logical operators, you can make your program consider more complicated situations than simply a single condition.

Logical operators combine two True or False values (such as two conditional expressions) and return a single True or False value. For example, in real life, you might combine conditional expressions in this way: "If it's raining outside AND the car won't run, then we stay home," or "If the cat is hungry OR the dog has to go out, then we get out of bed."

Using the And Logical Operator

The And logical operator evaluates two conditional expressions and returns a True value only if both expressions also return a True value. (Table 21-3 shows all possible values for the And operator.)

For example, consider this statement: "If it's raining AND the car won't run, then we stay home." If it's true that it's raining but false that the car won't run (that is, it will run), then you don't have to stay home. Likewise, if the car won't run but it's not raining, then you don't have to stay home either. Only if it's raining (True) and the car won't run (True) is the conclusion true, and we stay home.

Table 21-3: Truth Table for the And Operator

Conditional expression 1	Conditional expression 2	Result
True	True	True
True	False	False
False	True	False
False	False	False

Consider the And logical operator in the following:

```
(4 > 56) And ("Cat" = "Cat")
```

The conditional expression (4 > 56) evaluates to False and the conditional expression ("Cat" = "Cat") evaluates to True, so this expression can be rewritten as:

```
False And True
```

In Table 21-3, you see that when And compares a False and True value, the result is False. So the two conditional expressions with the And operator (4 > 56) And ("Cat" = "Cat") returns a False value.

This raises one problem with the And operator, which is that it always evaluates two conditional expressions before determining whether to return a True or False value. For example:

```
(3 > 902) And (X > 100)
```

In this example, (3 > 902) always evaluates to False, so no matter what the value of the X variable is, the two expressions will always return a False value. Even so, your program will still spend time evaluating the (X > 100) conditional expression, which wastes time.

To make your programs run more quickly, substitute the And operator with AndAlso. Unlike the And operator, if AndAlso determines that the first expression is False, it won't bother to evaluate the second expression and will simply return a False value. Table 21-4 shows how AndAlso works.

Table 21-4: Truth Table for the AndAlso Operator

Conditional expression 1	Conditional expression 2	Result
True	True	True
True	False	False
False	(never evaluated)	False

You can replace the And operator with AndAlso, like so:

```
(3 > 902) AndAlso (X > 100)
```

The results will be the same, but your program will run slightly faster. While this may not seem like a big deal in a single line of code, when your code consists of several hundred or several thousand lines, replacing And with AndAlso can offer improve performance significantly.

Using the Or Logical Operator

The Or logical operator evaluates two conditional expressions and returns a False value only if both expressions also return a False value. For example, consider the expression: "If the cat is hungry OR the dog has to go out, then we get out of bed." In this case, if the cat is hungry (True), you have to get out of bed. If the dog has to go out (True), you still have to get out of bed, and if the cat is hungry and the dog has to go out, you also have to get out of bed. The only way you can stay in bed is if the cat is not hungry (False) and the dog does not have to go out (False). Table 21-5 lists all possible values for the Or operator.

Table 21-5: Truth Table for the Or Operator

Conditional expression 1	Conditional expression 2	Result
True	True	True
True	False	True
False	True	True
False	False	False

Consider the Or logical operator in the following:

```
(4 > 56) Or ("Cat" = "Cat")
```

The expression (4 > 56) evaluates to False and ("Cat" = "Cat") evaluates to True, so this expression can be rewritten as:

```
False Or True
```

In Table 21-5 you can see that when the Or operator compares a False and True value, the result is True. Thus, this example returns a True value.

As with the AndAlso operator, you can speed up your program by substituting OrElse for the Or operator. Unlike the Or operator, when OrElse determines that the first conditional expression is True, it won't evaluate the second conditional expression and will simply return a True value. Table 21-6 shows how the OrElse operator works.

Table 21-6: Truth Table for the OrElse Operator

Conditional expression 1	Conditional expression 2	Result
True	(never evaluated)	True
False	True	True
False	False	False

Using the Xor Logical Operator

Xor returns a False value if both conditional expressions evaluate the same: either both True or both False. If one expression evaluates to True and another to False, Xor returns a True value. Table 21-7 lists all possible values for the Xor operator.

Table 21-7: Truth Table for the Xor Operator

Conditional expression 1	Conditional expression 2	Result
True	True	False
True	False	True
False	True	True
False	False	False

Consider the Xor logical operator in the following:

```
(4 > 56) Xor ("Cat" = "Cat")
```

The conditional expression (4 > 56) evaluates to False and ("Cat" = "Cat") evaluates to True, so this expression can be rewritten as:

```
False Xor True
```

In Table 21-7, you can see that when Xor compares a False and True value, the result is True. So the two conditional expressions with the Xor operator, (4 > 56) Xor ("Cat" = "Cat"), returns a True value.

Using the Not Logical Operator

Unlike the other logical operators, Not accepts only one conditional expression and returns its opposite value. For example, the following conditional expression evaluates to False:

```
(34 <> 34)
```

Not simply converts a False value to True and a True value to False:

```
Not (34 <> 34)
```

In this example, (34 <> 34) is False, but because Not converts a False value to True, Not (34 <> 34) ultimately evaluates to True.

Using an If-Then Statement

Under-
standing
Decision
Structures

Conditional expressions help a program evaluate input and decide what to do next. Once a program makes that decision, it needs to choose an instruction or a group of instructions to run.

To provide your program with a choice of instructions, you use a *control structure* (sometimes also called a *branching structure*, because it acts like a fork in a path to provide your program with choices).

A control structure consists of two parts:

- An evaluation of a conditional expression
- One or more groups of instructions to follow based on the value of the conditional expression

The simplest control structure is If-Then. An *If-Then structure* evaluates a conditional expression; if it evaluates to True, the If-Then statement runs one line of BASIC code, as shown in the following syntax:

```
If (conditional expression) Then instruction
```

For example:

```
If (MoronTotal >= 250) Then MsgBox ("You win!")
```

If the value of the MoronTotal variable is 250 or higher, then the conditional expression evaluates to True and the If-Then statement runs the MsgBox command to display

You win! on the screen. If the value of the MoronTotal variable is 249 or lower, then the conditional expression evaluates to False and the MsgBox command does not run.

You can combine conditional expressions in an If-Then statement using logical operators such as And, Or, Xor, AndAlso, and OrElse, as shown in the following example:

```
If (MoronTotal >= 250) And (IQ < 100) Then MsgBox ("You win!")
```

If we use a value of 300 for MoronTotal and 50 for IQ, the above command evaluates the first conditional expression (MoronTotal >= 250) as True and the second conditional expression (IQ < 100) as True. Thus, the entire command evaluates to:

```
If True And True Then MsgBox ("You win!")
```

Next, Visual Basic evaluates the True And True conditional expression, which evaluates to True. Finally, it examines the entire BASIC command, which now looks like this:

```
If True Then MsgBox ("You win!")
```

and the MsgBox command displays a message box that says *You win!*

One problem with the simple If-Then statement is that it can run only one BASIC command if its conditional expression evaluates to True. If you need to run two or more BASIC commands, you have to use a slightly different If-Then statement like this:

```
If (conditional expression) Then
     Instruction1
     Instruction2
End If
```

For example, this If-Then statement can run multiple commands:

```
If SalesTax < 0.075 Then
     MsgBox ("This is the first command that runs")
     MsgBox ("And this is the second!")
End If
```

In this example, the conditional expression is SalesTax < 0.075. If the value of the SalesTax variable is less than 0.075, the If-Then statement runs the two MsgBox commands. If the value of the SalesTax variable is equal or greater than 0.075, the If-Then statement ignores the two MsgBox commands.

Using an If-Then-Else Statement

The ordinary If-Then statement runs a set of instructions only if a certain condition is True. But what if you want to run one set of instructions if a certain condition is True, but a second set of instructions if that same condition is False? You could write two separate If-Then statements:

```
If Amount > 45 Then
          MsgBox ("True")
End If
If Amount <= 45 Then
```

```
        MsgBox ("False")
End If
```

or you could use the *If-Then-Else* statement, which simplifies things:

```
If (Conditional expression) Then
        Instructions1
Else
        Instructions2
End If
```

The If-Then-Else statement says that if a certain condition is True, follow one set of instructions, but if that condition is False, follow a different set of instructions. Replacing the two previous If-Then statements with a single If-Then-Else statement would give us this:

```
If Amount > 45 Then
        MsgBox ("True")
Else
        MsgBox ("False")
End If
```

Unlike a single If-Then statement that only runs a set of instructions if a certain condition is True, If-Then-Else contains two sets of instructions and always runs one set of instructions.

To create an If-Then-Else statement in the Code window:

1. In the Code window, right-click where you want to create an If-Then-Else statement, then click Insert Snippet in the pop menu that appears. Another pop-up menu appears.
2. Double-click Visual Basic Language. Another pop-up menu appears.
3. Double-click Evaluate An If…Else Statement. Visual Basic Express inserts a generic If-Then-Else statement that you can customize, as shown in Figure 21-1.

NOTE *It can be convenient to use code snippets to create an If-Then-Else statement, but once you're more familiar with using Visual Basic, you may prefer to type the whole thing yourself rather than use the clumsy code snippet pop-up menus.*

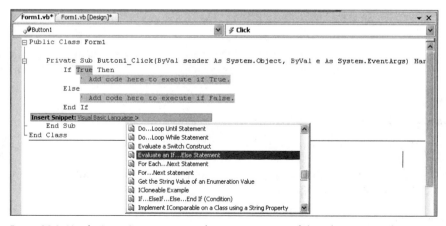

Figure 21-1: Use the Insert Snippet command to create a generic If-Then-Else statement that you can modify.

Using an If-Then-ElseIf Structure

If you need to compare similar conditional expressions, you may need to use *multiple* If-Then structures, like so:

```
If StockPrice > 45 Then
        MsgBox ("Sell")
End If
If (StockPrice <= 45) And (StockPrice > 25) Then
        MsgBox ("Hold")
End If
If (StockPrice <= 25) And (StockPrice > 1) Then
        MsgBox ("Buy")
End If
```

Because each of these If-Then structures compares similar conditions (the value of the variable StockPrice), you could condense this code by using the If-Then-ElseIf structure, like so:

```
If StockPrice > 45 Then
        MsgBox ("Sell")
ElseIf StockPrice > 25 Then
        MsgBox ("Hold")
ElseIf StockPrice > 1 Then
        MsgBox ("Buy")
End If
```

The If-Then-ElseIf structure can contain multiple sets of instructions, but there's still no guarantee that any of those instructions will ever run. For example, in the above listing, none of the MsgBox commands will run if the value of the StockPrice variable is less than 1.

To guarantee that at least one set of instructions will run, add an Else statement at the end of your If-Then-ElseIf structure, like so:

```
If StockPrice > 45 Then
        MsgBox ("Sell")
ElseIf StockPrice > 25 Then
        MsgBox ("Hold")
Else
        MsgBox ("Buy")
End If
```

In this example, if the value of the StockPrice variable is 46 or greater, the MsgBox ("Sell") command will run; if it is between 45 and 26, the MsgBox ("Hold") command will run; and if it is 24 or lower, the MsgBox ("Buy") command will run.

Using a Select-Case Structure

If you need to compare a variable to multiple values, the If-Then-ElseIf structure can be somewhat clumsy and difficult to understand. As an alternative, you can use a *Select-Case statement*, which compares a variable to different values to determine which set of instructions to follow. For example:

```
Select Case Variable
    Case Value1
```

```
        Instructions1
    Case Value2
        Instructions2
End Select
```

If the value of Variable is equal to Value1, the program follows Instructions1. If the value of Variable is equal to Value2, the program follows Instructions2. Here's a working example:

```
Select Case StockPrice
    Case 45
        MsgBox ("The stock price is 45")
    Case 30
        MsgBox ("The stock price is 30")
End Select
```

If the value of StockPrice is 45, a message box displays *The stock price is 45*; if the value of StockPrice is 30, a message box displays *The stock price is 30*; and if the value of StockPrice is any other value, such as 31 or 46, then the Select-Case statement does nothing.

The above Select-Case statement is equivalent to:

```
If StockPrice = 45 Then
        MsgBox ("The stock price is 45")
ElseIf StockPrice = 30 Then
        MsgBox ("The stock price is 30")
End If
```

NOTE *There is no functional difference between the If-Then-ElseIf statement and the Select-Case statement. Most programmers prefer the Select-Case statement because it can be easier to read and understand.*

Selecting from a Range of Values

Comparing a variable to an exact value can be limiting, especially if you need to compare multiple values, like so:

```
Select Case StockPrice
    Case 59
        MsgBox ("Sell")
    Case 47
        MsgBox ("Sell")
    Case 30
        MsgBox ("Buy")
    Case 31
        MsgBox ("Buy")
    Case 32
        MsgBox ("Buy")
End Select
```

Rather than list each value separately, you can compare a variable to a range of values by doing one of the following:

- Explicitly stating all values (such as X, Y, Z)
- Defining a range of values (such as A to Z)

The following example shows both methods:

```
Select Case StockPrice
    Case 45, 47, 59
        MsgBox ("The stock price is 45, 47, or 59")
    Case 30 To 39
        MsgBox ("The stock price is between 30 and 39")
End Select
```

The first Case statement explicitly lists all values (45, 47, 59) the variable must equal before running the MsgBox command to display the message *The stock price is 45, 47, or 59*. If the value of StockPrice does not match these values (46 or 58, for example), the Select-Case statement won't run any instructions. The second Case statement lists a range of values. If the value of the StockPrice variable lies between 30 and 39, the message box will display *The stock price is between 30 and 39*.

Using Comparison Operators

Rather than explicitly listing all values that a variable must equal or a range of values that a variable must lie between, you can also use *comparison operators*:

=	<>	>	>=	<	<=

To use a Select-Case statement with a comparison operator, you need to modify the Case statement as follows:

```
Case Is (comparison operator) Value
```

For example, to see if a variable is greater than or equal to a certain value, you could use the following:

```
Select Case StockPrice
    Case Is > 45
        MsgBox ("Sell")
    Case Is >= 25
        MsgBox ("Hold")
    Case Is > 0
        MsgBox ("Buy")
    End Select
```

In this example, if the value of the StockPrice variable is 46 or greater, the MsgBox ("Sell") command runs; if the value is between 45 and 25, the MsgBox ("Hold") command runs; and if the value is between 24 and 1, the MsgBox ("Buy") command runs.

Hands-on Tutorial: Playing with Conditional Expressions

This tutorial shows how to use the Select-Case statement to specify different instructions to be run, depending on the value of outside data. You'll learn how to enter two different numbers, choose a comparison operator, and have the program tell you whether the two numbers you entered are equal or not equal to, less than or greater than, less than or equal, or greater than or equal to each other.

1. Start a new project in Visual Basic Express, then click OK. A blank form appears.
2. Choose View ▶ Toolbox to display the Toolbox, then choose Window ▶ Auto Hide to keep the Toolbox visible.
3. Click the TextBox control in the Toolbox, move the mouse near the top of the form, and click the left mouse button to create a text box near the top of the form.
4. Click the ComboBox control in the Toolbox, move the mouse under the text box you just created, and click the left mouse button to create a combo box.
5. Click the TextBox control in the Toolbox, move the mouse pointer underneath the combo box you just created, and click the left mouse button to create a text box.
6. Click the Label control in the Toolbox, mouse over the form underneath the second text box you created, and click the left mouse button.
7. Click the Button control in the Toolbox, mouse over the bottom of the form, and click the left mouse button to create a button on the form. Your user interface should look like Figure 21-2.
8. Click the combo box control and press F4 to open the Properties window, then click the Items property. An ellipsis button appears.
9. Click the ellipsis button to display the String Collection Editor dialog box.
10. Type the operators =, >, >=, <, <=, and <> on separate lines in the String Collection Editor dialog box, as shown in Figure 21-3, then click OK to close the dialog box.

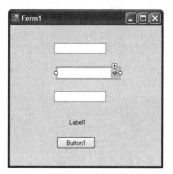

Figure 21-2: Two text boxes, a combo box, a label, and a button on a form.

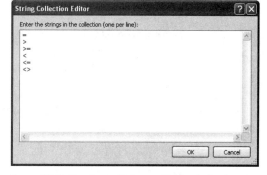

Figure 21-3: The String Collection Editor dialog box lets you define the items that appear inside of a combo box.

11. Double-click the Button1 control on the form to open the Code window.
12. Type the following lines between the Private Sub and End Sub lines so the Button1_Click event procedure in the Code window looks like this:

```
Private Sub Button1_Click(ByVal sender As System.Object, ByVal e As System.EventArgs)_
Handles Button1.Click
        Dim x, y As Single
        Dim Test As Boolean
        x = CSng(TextBox1.Text)
        y = CSng(TextBox2.Text)
        Select Case ComboBox1.Text
            Case "="
                Test = (x = y)
```

```
            Case ">"
                Test = (x > y)
            Case ">="
                Test = (x >= y)
            Case "<"
                Test = (x < y)
            Case "<="
                Test = (x <= y)
            Case "<>"
                Test = (x <> y)
        End Select
        Label1.Text = Test
End Sub
```

When the user types a number into either of the text boxes on your form, those numbers are stored as a string. The CSng command, near the top of the Button1_Click event procedure, converts that string into a single data type.

13. Press F5 to display your user interface, then click the top text box control and type any number, such as **23.5**.

14. Click the second text box and type another number, such as **948**.

15. Click in the combo box and choose a comparison operator, such as <> or <=.

16. Click the Button1 control. The Label1 control displays the word *True* or *False*.

17. Repeat steps 13 (you don't have to press F5 again in step 13) to 15, typing different numbers into the two text boxes on your form. Notice that the Label1 control displays a True or False value when you type different numbers in the two text boxes and click different comparison operators in the combo box.

18. Press ALT-F4 to stop your program, then choose File ▶ Close Project. Click Discard.

KEY FEATURES TO REMEMBER

Decision-making involves using a variation of the If-Then statement or using the Select-Case statement, which run a set of instructions only if a certain condition becomes true.

- To make decisions, your program needs to use conditional expressions, which typically compare a variable to a fixed value.

- Conditional expressions always evaluate to either a True or a False value.

- Logical operators combine two conditional expressions to determine a new True or False value.

- The AndAlso and OrElse logical operators can replace the And and Or operators to make your program run more efficiently.

- The If-Then statement runs one set of instructions only if a certain condition is True.

- The If-Then-Else statement runs one set of instructions if a certain condition is True and another set of instructions if a certain condition is False.

- The If-Then-ElseIf statement may not run any set of instructions unless it includes a final Else statement.

- The Select-Case statement is a more convenient way to store multiple instructions than the If-Then-ElseIf statement.

- A Select-Case statement can either check whether a variable equals one or more values, falls within a range of values, or is greater than or less than a value.

22

REPEATING CODE
WITH LOOPS

Understanding
Loops

Suppose you want to count from 1 to 10. The following
BASIC code would work:

```
MsgBox (1)
MsgBox (2)
MsgBox (3)
MsgBox (4)
MsgBox (5)
MsgBox (6)
MsgBox (7)
MsgBox (8)
MsgBox (9)
MsgBox (10)
```

but it's cumbersome because it repeats itself with only minor changes (displaying a different number in the MsgBox command). And imagine what this would
look like if you wanted to count from 1 to 5,000. You'd have to write the MsgBox
command 5,000 separate times!

To save time, programmers invented the *loop*, which lets you run one or more lines of code multiple times. For example, instead of typing the MsgBox command 10 times as we did in the previous example, you could use a loop, like this:

```
For Count As Integer = 1 To 10
    MsgBox(Count)
Next
```

In addition to making code more efficient and saving you a considerable amount of typing, loops offer another advantage. For example, suppose you want to run the MsgBox command 5,000 times. Using a loop, you would simply modify a single line of code, replacing the value of 10 with 5000. The loop would then run the MsgBox command 5,000 times:

```
For Count As Integer = 1 To 5000
    MsgBox(Count)
Next
```

As you can see, loops can provide two advantages:

- They are shorter and easier to write than typing the same command multiple times.
- They can be easily modified to change the number of times they repeat a command.

Using a For-Next Loop

One of Visual Basic's simplest loops is the *For-Next* loop, which repeats one or more BASIC commands a fixed number of times, whether that's 10 or 5,000 times. A typical For-Next loop looks like this:

```
For VariableCounter As Integer = LowerRange To_ UpperRange
    Instructions
Next
```

You need to define only these four parts in a For-Next loop:

VariableCounter This variable name can be anything you want.

LowerRange An integer value, where LowerRange is less than UpperRange. The usual value of LowerRange is 1, but you can specify a different number to do something like count by employee ID numbers that range from 1,000 to 2,500.

UpperRange An integer value, where UpperRange is greater than LowerRange.

Instructions This contains one or more BASIC commands that you want to run multiple times, as long as the value of VariableCounter lies between the values of LowerRange and UpperRange.

To create a For-Next loop, follow these steps:

1. Right-click in the Code window where you want to insert the For-Next loop. A pop-up menu appears.
2. Click Insert Snippet. Another pop-up menu appears.
3. Double-click Visual Basic Language. Another pop-up menu appears.
4. Double-click For...Next Statement. Visual Basic Express creates a generic For-Next loop for you to modify, as shown in Figure 22-1.

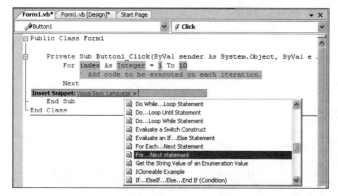

Figure 22-1: Creating a For-Next loop using the Insert Snippet command.

Counting by Different Step Increments

A For-Next loop normally counts by *step increments* of 1, beginning with the LowerRange value and progressing to the UpperRange value. To count by a different increment, such as by 2s or by 5s, add the Step keyword to a For-Next loop, like so:

```
For Variable As Integer = LowerRange To UpperRange Step Increment
    Instructions
Next
```

Increment is any integer value, including negative numbers. If you enter a decimal value, such as 2.43, you must declare the For-Next loop variable as a Decimal (rather than an Integer) data type. If you declare the For-Next loop variable as an integer but type a decimal number for the Increment value, Visual Basic rounds the decimal number to its nearest whole number value, so 2.43 would be rounded down to 2.

The following example counts by 2s:

```
For Counter As Integer = 1 To 10 Step 2
    MsgBox (Counter)
Next
```

This BASIC code is equivalent to:

```
MsgBox (1)
MsgBox (3)
MsgBox (5)
MsgBox (7)
MsgBox (9)
```

This For-Next loop tells the computer to repeat the loop as long as the value of the Counter variable lies between 1 and 10. When the value of Counter reaches 9, the MsgBox command runs one last time before the Counter variable increases by 2 from 9 to 11. Because 11 is beyond the range 1 to 10, the For-Next loop stops running at that point.

If the value of Increment is a negative number, the LowerRange and the UpperRange values of the For-Next loop must be reversed. For example, in the following listing, LowerRange equals 10 and UpperRange equals 1:

```
For Counter As Integer = 10 To 1 Step -3
    MsgBox (Counter)
Next
```

This BASIC code is equivalent to this:

```
MsgBox (10)
MsgBox (7)
MsgBox (4)
MsgBox (1)
```

Skipping an Iteration

The For-Next loop usually runs a fixed number of times, say 10 or 25 times. However, you can also make the loop "skip," so that instead of running exactly 10 times, it runs four times in a row, skips the fifth time, and runs the remaining five times in a row.

For example, you might use a For-Next loop to retrieve 10 names and addresses from a database and print a form letter. However, if one address is outside your country, you might want to skip it and print only form letters destined for domestic addresses.

To make a For-Next loop skip, use the Continue For statement along with a control structure, such as an If-Then statement (see Chapter 21):

```
For Counter As Integer = 1 To 10
    If Counter = 5 Then Continue For
    MsgBox (Counter)
Next
```

In this example, the Continue For statement immediately increments the Counter variable without running any instructions inside the For-Next loop. The listing above is equivalent to this BASIC code:

```
MsgBox (1)
MsgBox (2)
MsgBox (3)
MsgBox (4)' Notice that the number 5
MsgBox (6)' never appears.
MsgBox (7)
MsgBox (8)
MsgBox (9)
MsgBox (10)
```

Exiting a Loop

A For-Next loop typically runs a fixed number of times, but you may occasionally want to exit out of a For-Next loop prematurely. For example, say you create a video poker game that uses a For-Next loop to deal five cards to each player. What if someone is playing your video poker game and his boss approaches? Without a way out of a For-Next loop, your video poker game would keep dealing until all five cards were dealt, at which point the player would be chewed out by his boss. It would be better to allow the player to press the ESC key, to exit the For-Next loop, stop dealing cards, and, even better, display a fake spreadsheet on the screen instead.

To exit from a For-Next loop prematurely, you need to use the Exit For statement along with a control structure, like so:

```
For Counter As Integer = 1 To 10
    If Counter = 5 Then Exit For
```

```
        MsgBox (Counter)
   Next
```

This BASIC code will run until the value of the Counter variable is 5, at which point the For-Next loop will stop. This is equivalent to:

```
MsgBox (1)
MsgBox (2)
MsgBox (3)
MsgBox (4)
```

Hands-on Tutorial: Playing with For-Next Loops

In this tutorial, you'll create a program that lets the user enter a number to define how many times the For-Next loop should repeat itself. To keep the user from typing an invalid number (such as a negative number) or a number higher than 10 (which would make the For-Next loop repeat too often), the For-Next loop uses the Exit For command to exit out of the loop.

1. Start a new Visual Basic project, then click OK to display a blank form.
2. Choose View ▸ Toolbox to display the Toolbox, then choose Window ▸ Auto Hide to keep it visible at all times.
3. Click the TextBox control in the Toolbox, move the mouse pointer near the top of the form, and click the left mouse button to create a text box.
4. Click the Button control in the Toolbox, mouse over the center of the form, and click the left mouse button to create a button on the form.
5. Double-click the Button1 control on the form. The Code window appears.
6. Type the following between the Private Sub and End Sub lines so the Code window looks like this:

```
Private Sub Button1_Click(ByVal sender As System.Object, _ByVal e As_
System.EventArgs) Handles Button1.Click
        Dim Upper As Integer
        Upper = CInt(TextBox1.Text)
        For index As Integer = 1 To Upper
            If (Upper > 10) Or (Upper < 1) Then Exit For
            MsgBox(index)
        Next
        MsgBox("Loop all done.")
        TextBox1.Text = ""
End Sub
```

When the user types a number into the Text property of the TextBox1 control, that number is stored as a string. The CInt (short for Convert to Integer) command converts the value of the Text property (a string) into an integer.

The last line in the event procedure places an empty string in the Text property of the TextBox1 control. This clears the text box so the user can type something else into it without having to delete any previously entered number.

7. Press F5. Your user interface appears.
8. Click the text box control and type **3**.

9. Click the Button1 control. A dialog box appears, displaying the number *1*.

10. Click OK. Another dialog box appears and displays the number *2*.

11. Click OK. A third dialog box appears and displays the number *3*.

12. Click OK. A fourth dialog box appears and displays the message *Loop all done*. Click OK to close the dialog box.

13. Click in the text box and type **210**.

14. Click the Button1 control. A dialog box displays *Loop all done*. Because the value 210 is greater than the value 10, the Exit For command runs, which prevents the MsgBox command from running and displaying any more numbers. Click OK to close the dialog box.

15. Press ALT-F4 to stop your program, choose File ▶ Close Project, then click Discard.

Loops That Run Zero or More Times

A For-Next loop always runs a fixed number of times, but sometimes you may not know exactly how many times your loop should run. Instead of counting a fixed number of times, you can repeat instructions until a certain condition becomes True or False, using one of two different types of loops to do so:

- Do-While loop
- Do-Until loop

A *Do-While* loop runs while a certain condition remains True. It looks like this:

```
Do While (conditional expression)
    Instructions
    Instructions to change conditional expression
Loop
```

This BASIC code tells Visual Basic to keep looping while a certain condition remains True. If that condition is never True, the loop won't run at all.

But perhaps the most important part of a Do-While loop is that it must contain instructions that can alter the conditional expression and make it eventually return a False value. This ensures that the Do-While loop will not become an *endless loop* that keeps running but never exits. An endless loop makes your program appear to freeze while running, and will refuse all attempts by the user to regain control by moving the mouse or typing keyboard commands.

Here's an example of a Do-While loop that counts from 1 to 10:

```
Dim Counter As Integer
Counter = 1
Do While Counter <= 10
    MsgBox (Counter)
    Counter = Counter + 1
Loop
```

The first two lines initialize the Counter variable, which determines how many times the loop repeats itself. The Do While Counter <= 10 line tells the loop to keep repeating itself as long as the value of the Counter variable is less than or equal to 10. The MsgBox command displays the value of Counter in a message box. Perhaps the most important line is Counter = Counter + 1, which alters the Counter variable to change the conditional expression that the Do-While loop depends on. If you omit the `Counter = Counter + 1` line, the value of the `Counter` variable never changes; thus, the Do-While loop's conditional expression never changes, and the loop runs endlessly.

The Do-Until loop is similar to the Do-While loop. It looks like this:

```
Do Until (conditional expression)
    Instructions
    Instructions to change conditional expression
Loop
```

Unlike the Do-While loop, which repeats while a certain condition *is* True, the Do-Until loop repeats until a certain condition *becomes* True (which is equivalent to looping while a certain condition remains False). For example, to count from 1 to 10 using a Do-Until loop, you could use the following:

```
Dim Counter As Integer
Counter = 1
Do Until Counter > 10
    MsgBox (Counter)
    Counter = Counter + 1
Loop
```

In this case, the conditional expression is `Counter > 10`, which remains False until the value of `Counter` equals 11. As soon as `Counter` equals 11, the Do-Until loop stops.

Before either the Do-While and Do-Until loop run, they check the value of a conditional expression. If the conditional expression is initially False (for a Do-While loop) or True (for a Do-Until loop), the loop won't run at all.

To create a generic Do-While or Do-Until loop that will run zero or more times, follow these steps:

1.   Right-click in the Code window where you want to create a Do-While or Do-Until loop. A pop-up menu appears.
2.   Double-click Visual Basic Language. A pop-up menu appears.
3.   Click either Do Until...Loop Statement or Do While...Loop Statement as shown in Figure 22-2. Visual Basic Express creates a generic Do-While or Do-Until loop.

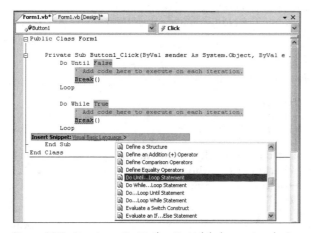

Figure 22-2: Creating a Do-Until or Do-While loop using the Insert Snippet command.

In the example BASIC code in Figure 22-2, the `Insert Snippet` command creates a generic loop that includes the `Break()` command. The `Break()` command automatically exits from your loop and is placed in the generic code as a reminder that you must add a line that alters the conditional expression somehow so your loop will eventually stop running. If you don't replace the `Break()` command with a control structure, the `Break()` command will always exit out of your loop without waiting for the loop's conditional expression to change values.

Loops That Run at Least Once

Depending on the conditions that you've set, it is possible that Do-Until or Do-While loop will not run any instructions. To create a loop that will always run its instructions at least once, you'll have to use two loop variations that check to see whether a certain condition is True after the loop has run at least once.

For example, you might use a loop to display a window that asks the user for a password. You always want your program to ask for a password at least once, and to keep asking for a password until the user types in a valid one.

The *Do Loop While* is a loop that always runs at least once. It looks like this:

```
Do
    Instructions
    Instructions to change conditional expression
Loop While (conditional expression)
```

To count from 1 to 10, you could use the following:

```
Dim Counter As Integer
Counter = 1
Do
    MsgBox (Counter)
    Counter = Counter + 1
Loop While Counter <= 10
```

Notice that this loop runs once before checking its conditional expression, `Counter <= 10`. If for some reason this conditional expression were False, the loop would still run once and then stop.

Another way to write the above BASIC code is to replace the `While` keyword with the `Until` keyword and change the conditional expression from `Counter <= 10` to `Counter > 10`, like so:

```
Dim Counter As Integer
Counter = 1
Do
    MsgBox (Counter)
    Counter = Counter + 1
Loop Until Counter > 10
```

Like the previous Do Loop While statement, this *Do Loop Until* statement also runs at least once before checking its conditional expression (`Counter > 10`).

To create a generic Do Loop While or Do Loop Until statement that runs at least once, follow these steps:

1. Right-click in the Code window where you want to create a Do Loop While or Do Loop Until statement. A pop-up menu appears.

2. Double-click Visual Basic Language. A pop-up menu appears.

3. Click either Do...Loop Until Statement or Do...Loop While Statement. Visual Basic Express creates a generic Do Loop While or Do Loop Until statement.

Exiting from a Do-While/Do-Until Loop Prematurely

A Do-While loop keeps repeating while a certain condition *remains* True and the Do-Until loop keeps repeating until a certain condition *becomes* True. However, you can also exit out of a loop prematurely.

For example, you could use a Do-While loop to keep displaying a login screen until the user types in a valid user ID number or until the user presses the ESC key (which exits out of the Do-While loop prematurely). To do this, you need to insert a control structure somewhere inside your Do-While/Do-Until loop and use the Exit Do statement, like so:

```
Dim Counter As Integer
Counter = 1
Do
     If Counter = 5 Then Exit Do
     MsgBox (Counter)
     Counter = Counter + 1
Loop Until Counter > 10
```

This BASIC code counts up to 4, at which point the conditional expression, Counter = 5, becomes True. This condition causes the Exit Do statement to run, which exits out of the loop and stops the loop from continuing to run the MsgBox command.

Hands-on Tutorial: Playing with Do-While Loops

Here's how to use a Do-While loop to count and display its value through a progress bar.

1. Start a new Visual Basic project, then click OK to display a blank form.

2. Choose View ▸ Toolbox to display the Toolbox, then choose Window ▸ Auto Hide to keep the Toolbox visible.

3. Click the ProgressBar control in the Toolbox, move the mouse pointer to the center of the form, and click the left mouse button to create a progress bar.

4. Click the Button control in the Toolbox, mouse over the bottom of the form, and click the left mouse button to create a button on the form.

5. Double-click the Button1 control. The Code window appears.

6. Type the following between the Private Sub and End Sub lines so the Button1_Click event procedure looks like this:

```
Private Sub Button1_Click(ByVal sender As System.Object, ByVal e As_
System.EventArgs) Handles Button1.Click
   Dim Total As Integer
        Const BigMax As Integer = 1000000
        Total = 0
        ProgressBar1.Maximum = BigMax
        Do While Total < BigMax
            ProgressBar1.Value = Total
            Total = Total + 1
```

```
            Loop
            MsgBox("All done!")
    End Sub
```

7. Press F5 to display your user interface.

8. Click the Button1 control. The progress bar slowly fills up with green bars because the Do-While loop that you typed in step 6 keeps increasing the value in the progress bar. When the progress bar completely fills up, a dialog box appears and displays the message *All done!* Click OK to close the dialog box.

9. Press ALT-F4 to stop your program. The Code window appears.

10. Choose File ▸ Close Project. A Close Project dialog box appears. Click Discard.

Comparing
Loops

KEY FEATURES TO REMEMBER

Loops allow you to replace multiple, identical commands with a single generic command. Visual Basic Express provides several types of loops that can repeat BASIC code.

- A For-Next loop runs a fixed number of times.

- By adding the Increment keyword, you can make a For-Next loop count backward or count by increments other than 1.

- The Continue For statement lets you skip a loop iteration.

- The Exit For statement lets you exit out of a For-Next loop prematurely. The Exit Do statement lets you exit out of a Do-While or Do-Until loop prematurely.

- A Do-While or Do-Until loop can run zero or more times because it checks a conditional expression before starting the loop.

- A Do Loop While and a Do Loop Until statement always run at least once because they check a conditional expression after running the loop once.

- An endless loop occurs when the condition to terminate the loop never changes from inside the loop.

23

DATA STRUCTURES: STRUCTURES, ARRAYS, AND COLLECTIONS

As you saw in Chapter 18, at the simplest level, Visual Basic can store data in variables. However, variables can hold only one item at a time, so if you want to store a list of related variables, such as names, you must create a different variable for each name you want to store. For example, to store 1,000 names, you would have to create 1,000 different variables. Obviously, this can be impractical.

To avoid this problem, Visual Basic lets you store data in a *data structure*. A data structure acts like a super variable that can store multiple items in a single location. There are three common types of data structures in Visual Basic:

- Structures
- Arrays
- Collections

Using a Structure

From what we know so far, if you wanted to store a person's name, age, and salary, you would have to create three separate variables, like so:

```
Dim Name As String
Dim Age As Integer
Dim Salary As Single
```

Unfortunately, trying to keep track of several separate variables isn't as easy as keeping track of a single variable. To solve this problem, Visual Basic offers a data structure, known simply as a *structure,* that acts like a single variable but which can store multiple data of different types. The syntax used to create a structure looks like this:

```
Structure StructureName
        VariableDeclarations
End Structure
```

StructureName is a descriptive name for the data the structure contains. *VariableDeclarations* are one or more variable declarations that look like this:

```
Public VariableName As DataType
```

The BASIC code to create a single structure that can hold three different variables (Name, Age, and Salary) might look like this:

```
Structure Employees
        Public Name As String
        Public Age As Integer
        Public Salary As Single
End Structure
```

Employees is the *structure name.* It includes the three variables, Name, Age, and Salary, which are known as the *properties* of the Employees structure. Each property is defined with the Public keyword to allow other parts of your program to store and retrieve data stored in these properties.

Declaring and Defining a Structure

Before you can use a structure, you must first define it outside of any procedures, as shown here:

```
Public Class Form1
    Structure Employees
        Public Name As String
        Public Age As Integer
        Public Salary As Single
    End Structure
End Class
```

This code creates a structure named Employees, which is stored in the Form1 file. The Public Class Form1 and End Class lines define the start and end of the Form1 file, which contains BASIC code.

NOTE   *In technical terms, every form file you create is considered an object or a class, hence the keywords* Public Class; *a term used in object-oriented programming, as explained in Chapter 26.*

Once you've defined a structure, the next step is to declare a variable as the structure type. In the following example, the structure is declared within the `Button1_Click` event procedure, shown in boldface code:

```
Public Class Form1
    Structure Employees
        Public Name As String
        Public Age As Integer
        Public Salary As Single
    End Structure
    Private Sub Button1_Click(ByVal sender As System.Object, ByVal e As System.EventArgs)_
Handles Button1.Click
        Dim TestMe As Employees
    End Sub
End Class
```

In this example, the structure `Employees` is defined outside the `Button1_Click` event procedure. Inside the event procedure, the `TestMe` variable is declared as the `Employees` structure data type. This means that the `TestMe` variable can actually hold the name, age, and salary data, as defined by the original structure declaration.

Once you define a structure and then declare a variable to hold data defined by it, you can start storing and retrieving data inside that structure.

Storing and Retrieving Data in a Structure

When you store a value into an *ordinary variable*, one that can hold numbers or strings, you can use code like this:

```
Dim Name As String
Dim Age As Integer
Name = "Bo the Cat"
Age = 13
```

However, to store data inside a variable that *represents a structure*, you must define both the variable name and the property name where you want to store the data, like so:

```
VariableName.PropertyName = Value
```

For example, to store the number 13 into the `Age` property of the `TestMe` variable, you could use the following:

```
Dim TestMe As Employees
TestMe.Age = 13
```

To retrieve data from a structure, you need to specify the variable name and the property that contains the data you want. For example:

```
Dim EmployeeAge As Integer
EmployeeAge = TestMe.Age
```

Structures are rarely used by themselves, and creating a single variable to represent a structure is like storing information on a single index card. For greater flexibility, you should create a list of structures (index cards), using *arrays* or *collections*.

Using an Array

An *array* acts like a variable that can store multiple items in a list. This list can contain zero or several thousand items. All items stored in an array must consist of the same data type.

A typical array declaration looks like this:

```
Dim ArrayName(Size) As DataType
```

where *ArrayName* is any name you want to give to your array. This is usually something descriptive, such as NameArray or List_Of_People_I_Hate; *Size* is the size of the array, which defines how many items or elements the array can hold; *DataType* is the type of data you want the array to hold, such as integer, string, or single.

What makes an array particularly useful is its ability to store multiple items in a single variable. If, for example, you were to create a variable called NextHit to hold a string, that variable can hold only one string at a time. But if you were to create a variable called HitList as an array, that array could hold multiple strings, as shown in Figure 23-1.

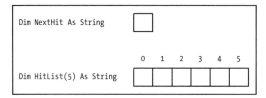

Figure 23-1: An array acts like a variable that can hold multiple items.

When you specify the size of an array, the array's first element is always numbered 0, so (5) specifies an array that can actually hold six items, numbered 0 to 5. In Figure 23-1, the HitList array consists of the name HitList of size (5). As String limits the array to string data types only.

Storing and Retrieving Data from an Array

Once you've created an array, you can store data in its elements. To store data inside an array, you must specify:

- The array name
- The numeric position (known as the *array index*) where you want to store the data

The first array element is at index number 0, the second is at index number 1, the third is at index number 2, and so on (see Figure 23-1). To store data in an array, you specify the array name and the index number, like this:

```
ArrayName(Index) = Value
```

For example, to store the string "George" in the HitList array at index 3, you would use the following BASIC code:

```
HitList(3) = "George"
```

To retrieve data from an array, you assign a variable to an array name and give its index number, like so:

```
Variable = ArrayName(Index)
```

For example, to retrieve the value of the string stored in the HitList array at index 3, do this:

```
NextHit = HitList(3)
```

Defining the Size of an Array

The size of an array defines how many items (known as *elements*) the array can hold. To define an array size, specify a number, like this:

```
Dim ArrayName(10) As DataType
```

NOTE   *Remember that the size of an array is always one element greater than the number you specify, because the first element in an array is at index number 0. Defining an array with a size of 10 actually creates an array that consists of 11 elements, numbered 0 through 10.*

One problem with defining an array size is that you may not know ahead of time how many items your program needs to store. If you specify an array that's too large, your program wastes the computer's memory. If you specify a size that's too small, your program may fill up the array and have no more room to hold anything else unless you start erasing previously stored data.

To solve this problem, create a *dynamic array*, which lets you change the size of your array while your program runs. That way, you can shrink your array to save memory and later expand it to hold more data when your program needs it.

To create a dynamic array, omit the array size when you declare an array, like this:

```
Dim ArrayName() As DataType
```

However, before you can store any data in a dynamic array, you must resize a dynamic array before you can store data in it.

Resizing an Array

When you create an array, whether a dynamic array or one of fixed size, you can resize that array at any time, as often as you like, by using the ReDim keyword, like this:

```
Dim ArrayName() As Integer
ReDim ArrayName(10)
```

In this listing, the first line creates a dynamic array; the second line uses the ReDim keyword to resize the array to contain 11 (numbered 0 to 10) elements.

You can also use the ReDim keyword to resize an array whose size had been previously defined, like this:

```
Dim ArrayName(5) As Integer
ReDim ArrayName(10)
```

In this example, the first line creates an array consisting of 6 (0 to 5) elements; the second line resizes the array to consist of 11 (0 to 10) elements.

Resizing an array can make your program more flexible. For example, you might use an array to store the names and phone numbers of important business contacts, but as you add and delete names, you can resize your array to grow and shrink.

When you resize an array, Visual Basic clears out any data stored in the array so that you can make the array larger or smaller. If you want to preserve any data currently stored in your array, you must add the Preserve keyword, like so:

```
Dim ArrayName(5) As Integer
ArrayName(3) = 90
MsgBox(ArrayName(3))
ReDim Preserve ArrayName(10)
MsgBox(ArrayName(3))
```

In this example, the first MsgBox command displays the number *90* in a message box. The ReDim and Preserve keywords expand the array, initially containing 6 elements, to hold 11 (0 to 10) elements, but it keeps the number 90 stored in the array element 3. Therefore, when the second MsgBox command runs, it also displays the number *90* in a message box.

What if you use the ReDim Preserve keywords to retain data already stored in an array and you shrink the array? Consider the following:

```
Dim MyArray(10) As Integer
MyArray(2) = 7
MyArray(10) = 9
ReDim Preserve MyArray(2)
```

In this example, the array elements 2 and 10 contain data, but when the ReDim Preserve MyArray(2) command resizes the array, Visual Basic Express discards the data stored in the 11th element (the number 9). When shrinking an array, while preserving its contents, you can accidentally discard data that you might need later, as shown in Figure 23-2.

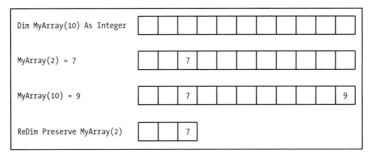

Figure 23-2: If you preserve an array's contents but shrink an array's size, you risk losing previously stored data in that array.

Initializing an Array

When first created, an array contains absolutely nothing until you begin storing data into each of its elements. However, if you create a dynamic array, you can store initial values into that array when you first create the dynamic array by using the following syntax:

```
Dim ArrayName() As DataType = {Value1, Value2,...,ValueN}
```

NOTE *The curly brackets define the start and end of a list of values to store in an array.*

For example, to create a dynamic array that holds integers with 45, 102, and 390 as the first three numbers stored in that array, you could use the following BASIC code:

```
Dim ArrayName() As Integer = {45, 102, 390}
```

You can only create and initialize dynamic arrays on the same line. If you define the size of an array, you must declare the array on one line and then store values into each element individually on another line, like this:

```
Dim ArrayName(2) As Integer
ArrayName(0) = 45
ArrayName(1) = 102
ArrayName(2) = 390
```

Creating Multidimensional Arrays

The simplest array stores data in a list. In programming terms, a list is considered to be one-dimensional because it stores data one item after another in a straight line. Rather than store data in a list (one dimension), you can also store data in a grid that consists of rows and columns. Because a grid can store data both horizontally (in rows) or vertically (in columns), a grid is considered to be two-dimensional.

When you define the size of an array, you're defining both how many items the array can hold and its *dimensions*. When you define a single number for the size of an array, you're creating a *one-dimensional* array, which acts like a list. For example:

```
Dim MyArray(12) As Integer
```

Unlike a one-dimensional array that stores items in a list, a *two-dimensional array* stores items in a grid consisting of rows and columns. A two-dimensional array might be useful for representing a grid on which to play a game, display the dates of a calendar, or a map of cubicles in an office with the names of each person in each cubicle. Figure 23-3 shows an array that defines two sizes and thus two dimensions.

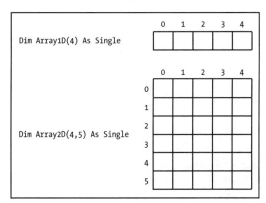

Figure 23-3: The two-dimensional array, at the bottom of the figure, stores data in rows and columns.

To create multidimensional arrays, you specify a size for each dimension. In the example in Figure 23-3, the size of the first dimension of Array2D is 4 and the size of the second dimension is 5. This array can hold data in a grid consisting of five columns and six rows.

You can even create arrays with three, four, five, or twelve dimensions, but the more dimensions you add to an array, the more complex it becomes, and the more difficult it can be to understand how to store and retrieve data from it. As a result, most programmers stick with one- or two-dimensional arrays because it can be difficult to work with and visualize a multidimensional array.

To store data in a multidimensional array, you must specify the array name and the exact position where you want to store the data. For example, if you wanted to store the number 25 in the second column and the fourth row of a two-dimensional array, you could do this:

```
Dim Array2D(12,5) As Integer
Array(2,4) = 25
```

Just as you can change the size of a one-dimensional array using the ReDim keyword, so can you change the size of a multidimensional array. However, you can only change the size of the last dimension of a multidimensional array, like so:

```
Dim Array2D(12,5) As Integer
ReDim Array2D(12,2)
ReDim Array2D(12,36)
```

In this example, the first dimension is fixed at a size of 12, but the second dimension can change from its initial size of 5 to any other size. Here we've changed it to 2 and then 36.

You can create multidimensional, dynamic arrays by not specifying an initial size when you create the array. To create a dynamic, two-dimensional array, do something like this:

```
Dim Array2D(,) As Integer
```

If you want to store initial values into a multidimensional array, you need to define the same number of initial items for each dimension. Here we define exactly three items for each dimension:

```
Dim Array2D(,) As Integer = {{1,3,5},{2,4,6}}
```

This BASIC code creates a two-dimensional array filled with the data we've specified, as shown here:

1	3	5
2	4	6

When initializing a multidimensional array, Visual Basic fills the first dimension of the array with data, then fills the next dimension, and so on. In the preceding example, the first set of data, {1, 3, 5}, is stored in the first row of the two-dimensional array, and the second set of data, {2, 4, 6}, is stored in the next row.

Manipulating Arrays

Once you've created and stored data in an array, Visual Basic provides several built-in commands for counting, searching, and clearing the data in your arrays.

Finding the Size of an Array

Arrays can change in size as your program runs. You can always find out the array's current size to determine how many elements it holds by using the UBound function, like so:

```
UBound(ArrayName)
```

where *ArrayName* is the name of the array you want to examine.

For example, if you created an array, you could use the UBound function to determine its size or bounds, like so:

```
Dim BigArray(100) As Integer
MsgBox(UBound(BigArray))
ReDim BigArray(55)
MsgBox(UBound(BigArray))
```

In this listing, the first MsgBox command displays *100* in a message box. Then, once the ReDim command resizes BigArray to its new size of 55, the second MsgBox command displays *55* in a message box.

NOTE   *Remember that the number of elements in an array is always the size of the array plus one (1) because every array counts from an initial array element numbered zero (0) up to its current size.*

If you have a multidimensional array, you can use the UBound function and specify which dimension you want to examine, like this:

```
UBound(ArrayName,Dimension)
```

where *ArrayName* is the name of the array you want to examine and Dimension is the dimension of the array you want to examine.

If you created a two-dimensional array, you could use the UBound function to determine the size or bounds of both dimensions, like so:

```
Dim BigArray(100, 57) As Integer
MsgBox(UBound(BigArray, 1))
MsgBox(UBound(BigArray, 2))
```

In this example:

Line 1   Defines a two-dimensional array, where the size of the first dimension is 100 and the size of the second dimension is 57.

Line 2   Defines the UBound function to examine the size of the first (1) dimension, which causes the MsgBox command to display *100*.

Line 3   Defines the UBound function to examine the size of the second (2) dimension, which causes the MsgBox command to display *57*.

Clearing an Array

Many video games display the list of the top 10 scores, which your program could store as an array. However, to give users the chance to clear out all the high scores, you would need to empty out the array that contains this information. While you could empty each array element one at a time, it's faster to clear out the whole array at once.

To empty all or part of a one-dimensional array, use the Clear command with this syntax:

```
Array.Clear (ArrayName,Index,Length)
```

where *ArrayName* is the variable that represents your entire array, *Index* is a number that identifies the first element you want to clear, and *Length* is the number of elements you want to clear.

The following BASIC code creates an array with three numbers and then uses the Clear command to empty it:

```
Dim BigArray() As Integer = {12, 34, 56}
MsgBox(BigArray(0))
Array.Clear (BigArray, 0, UBound(BigArray))
MsgBox(BigArray(0))
```

In this example:

Line 1   Creates an array called BigArray that holds three numbers: 12, 34, and 56.

Line 2   Runs the MsgBox command to display the number stored in the first array element (0), which displays the number *12* in a message box.

Line 3   Runs the Clear command to clear all values stored in the array.

Line 4   Runs the MsgBox command a second time to show that the first array element is now empty and contains a zero (0).

This example uses the UBound function to determine the size of the array, which also tells you the index value of the last element in the array. Thus, the command Array.Clear (BigArray, 0, UBound(BigArray)) tells the computer to clear an array named BigArray, starting from the first element (0) and ending with the last element (UBound(BigArray)).

To clear out only part of an array, you can specify an element other than 0. For example, if your array contains six elements but you want to clear only the third, fourth, and fifth elements, you could use the following:

```
Dim TestArray() As Integer = {12, 34, 56, 78, 90, 115}
Array.Clear (TestArray, 2, 4)
```

This is equivalent to:

```
TestArray(0) = 12
TestArray(1) = 34
TestArray(2) = 0
TestArray(3) = 0
TestArray(4) = 0
TestArray(5) = 0
```

(Remember that the first element of an array is always numbered 0, so the array elements numbered 2 through 4 actually refer to the third, fourth, and fifth array elements.)

Once the Array.Clear command runs, the contents of TestArray look like this:

```
{12, 34, 0, 0, 0, 0}
```

Sorting a One-Dimensional Array

Once you've filled a one-dimensional array with data, you can sort the data in ascending (a-to-z and A-to-Z, or 0-to-9) order. To sort an entire array in ascending order, use the Array.Sort command, like so:

```
Array.Sort (ArrayName)
```

The following BASIC code shows how to sort an entire array:

```
Dim SortedArray() As Integer = {5, 4, 9, 1, 0, 8}
Dim I As Integer
Array.Sort (SortedArray)
For I = 0 To 5
  MsgBox(SortedArray(I))
Next
```

Once the `Array.Sort (SortedArray)` command completes, the array looks like this:

```
{0, 1, 4, 5, 8, 9}
```

To sort only part of an array, use this syntax:

```
Array.Sort (ArrayName,Index,Length)
```

where *Index* is the array element to start sorting and *Length* is the number of array elements to sort.

For example, to sort the second, third, and fourth array elements (the numbers 4, 9, and 1 stored in the following `SortedArray` example), you could use the following:

```
Dim SortedArray() As Integer = {5, 4, 9, 1, 0, 8}
Dim I As Integer
Array.Sort (SortedArray, 1, 3)
For I = 0 To 5
  MsgBox(SortedArray(I))
Next
```

Once the `Array.Sort (SortedArray, 1, 3)` command completes, the array looks like this:

```
{5, 1, 4, 9, 0, 8}
```

When sorting strings, Visual Basic sorts lowercase characters before uppercase ones. For example, if you were to sort an array of strings (`{"B", "s", "S", "N", "n", "b"}`) in ascending order, like this:

```
Dim SortedArray() As String = {"B", "s", "S", "N", "n", "b"}
Dim I As Integer
Array.Sort (SortedArray)
For I = 0 To 5
  MsgBox(SortedArray(I))
Next
```

the sorted array would look like this:

```
{"b", "B", "n", "N", "s", "S"}
```

Searching a One-Dimensional Array

To search for data stored in a one-dimensional array, you can use the `IndexOf` command, which returns the array index (the numeric position in the array) where the data is found. If the data isn't found in the array, the `IndexOf` command returns -1. The `IndexOf` command uses the following syntax:

```
Array.IndexOf (ArrayName,Value)
```

where *ArrayName* is the name of the one-dimensional array to search and *Value* is the data you want to find in the array.

The following BASIC code searches an array for the number 90, which appears in the array index of 4.

```
Dim MyList() As Integer = {9, 1, 8, 4, 90, 12}
MsgBox(Array.IndexOf(MyList, 90))
```

The IndexOf command searches an array beginning with the first data, which is stored in the array index numbered 0. If you search for data that appears in two or more places in an array, the IndexOf command will find only the data stored in the index closest to the beginning of the array. For example, if you have the number 90 stored in the array indexes of 2 and 4, the IndexOf command would return only a value of 2, as shown in the following BASIC code:

```
Dim MyList() As Integer = {9, 1, 90, 4, 90, 12}
MsgBox(Array.IndexOf(MyList, 90))
```

If you don't want the IndexOf command to begin searching from the first array element (0), indicate a specific start position with this syntax:

```
Array.IndexOf (ArrayName,Value, Start)
```

where Start is the index number to begin searching from, other than 0.

In the following code, the IndexOf command returns a value of 4, because it begins searching the array from the fourth array element (index 4).

```
Dim MyList() As Integer = {9, 1, 90, 4, 90, 12}
MsgBox(Array.IndexOf(MyList, 90, 4))
```

When searching only part of an array, you can specify both the index to begin searching from, and how many array elements you want to search for. For example:

```
Array.IndexOf (ArrayName,Value,Start,Count)
```

where *Count* is the number of array elements to search, beginning with the index position defined by Start.

To begin searching from index position 3, but to search for only two array elements, you could use the following:

```
Dim MyList() As Integer = {9, 1, 90, 4, 90, 12}
MsgBox(Array.IndexOf(MyList, 90, 3, 2))
```

In this example, the IndexOf command begins searching at index 3 (which contains the number 4), and searches two array elements (index positions 3 and 4), which appear in the boldface portion of the array list. Thus, the MsgBox command displays the number *4* because the number 90 is stored in the fourth element of the array.

You can also use the LastIndexOf command to search from the *end* of an array. The LastIndexOf command uses the same syntax as the IndexOf command. As the following code shows, the LastIndexOf command will find the number 90 in index position 4 while the IndexOf command will find the number 90 in index position 2:

```
Dim MyList() As Integer = {9, 1, 90, 4, 90, 12}
MsgBox(Array.IndexOf(MyList, 90))
MsgBox(Array.LastIndexOf(MyList, 90))
```

An array can be useful for storing a list of items, while a structure can be useful for keeping related data together. Combine a structure with an array and you can store a list of related data in the much the same way that you might store names, addresses, and phone numbers on an index card and store a bunch of index cards in a file. This tutorial shows you how to create an array that can create a list of structures for storing names, addresses, and phone numbers.

1. Start a new Visual Basic Express project, then click OK to display a blank form.
2. Choose View ▸ Toolbox to display the Toolbox.
3. Click the Button control in the Toolbox, mouse over the form, and click the left mouse button to create a button on the form.
4. Double-click the Button1 control on the form. The Code window appears.
5. Type the boldface code shown next, just underneath the Public Class line and above the Private Sub line:

```
Public Class Form1
    Structure Names
        Public Name As String
        Public Address As String
    End Structure
    Private Sub Button1_Click(ByVal sender As System.Object, ByVal e As_
System.EventArgs) Handles Button1.Click
    End Sub
End Class
```

The boldface code defines a structure called Names, which contains two properties, Name and Address, both of which are String variables.

6. Type the boldface code shown next in between the Private Sub and End Sub lines, as follows:

```
Public Class Form1
    Structure Names
        Public Name As String
        Public Address As String
    End Structure
    Private Sub Button1_Click(ByVal sender As System.Object, ByVal e As_
System.EventArgs) Handles Button1.Click
        Dim MyContacts(1) As Names
        Dim I As Integer
        Dim TotalString As String
        For I = 0 To 1
            MyContacts(I).Name = InputBox("Type a name")
            MyContacts(I).Address = InputBox("Type an address")
        Next
        For I = 0 To 1
            TotalString = MyContacts(I).Name & vbCr & vbLf & MyContacts(I).Address
            MsgBox(TotalString)
        Next
    End Sub
End Class
```

In this listing:

Line 1   Creates an array that can hold two (0 to 1) structures as defined by the Names structure definition you wrote in step 5 (see Figure 23-4).

Line 2   Creates a variable named I, which can hold integer values.

Line 3   Creates a String variable called TotalString.

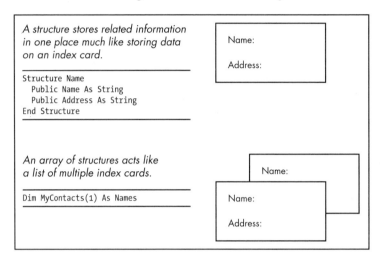

Figure 23-4: An array of structures acts like a simple database on index cards.

Lines 4 and 7   Define the start and end of a For-Next loop.

Line 5   (Trapped inside the For-Next loop.) This line displays an input box that asks the user to type a name. The name the user types is stored in the Name property of the first element of the MyContacts array.

Line 6   Displays an input box that asks the user to type an address. The address the user types is stored in the Address property of the first element of the MyContacts array.

Lines 8 and 11   Define the start and end of a second For-Next loop.

Line 9   Takes the name stored in the Name and Address of a structure and stores its contents in the TotalString variable. To avoid smashing the Name and Address strings together, the line adds the vbCr (carriage return) and vbLf (line feed) characters so that the text stored in the Address property will appear directly below the text stored in the Name property.

Line 10   Uses the MsgBox command to display the contents of the TotalString variable.

7. Press F5. Your user interface appears.

8. Click the Button1 control. An input box appears, asking you to type a name.

9. Type **Joe Smith** and click OK. This name will be stored in the first structure (element number 0) in the MyContacts array. Another input box appears, asking you for an address.

10. Type **99 Penny Lane** and click OK. This address will be stored in the first structure (element number 0) of the MyContacts array. Another input box appears, asking you to type a second name.

11. Type **Mary Jane** and click OK. This name will be stored in the second structure (element number 1) in the MyContacts array. Another input box appears, asking you for an address.

12. Type **101 Abbey Road** and click OK. This address will be stored in the second structure (element number 1) of the MyContacts array. A message box appears, displaying *Joe Smith* with the address *99 Penny Lane* directly underneath, as shown in Figure 23-5.

Figure 23-5: The MsgBox command displays the contents of each structure in a message box.

13. Click OK. A second message box appears that displays the contents of the second structure (*Mary Jane* and *101 Abbey Road*) of the MyContacts array. Click OK to close the dialog box.

14. Press ALT-F4 to stop your program. A Close Project dialog box appears. Click Discard.

Using a Collection

A collection acts like an array but it has several major differences:

- Collections can hold different data types, such as integers and strings. Arrays can hold only one data type, such as integers.
- Collections can insert new data between existing elements while arrays cannot.
- Collections can identify the location of data by either an index number or a key that the programmer defines. Arrays can identify the location of data only with an index number.
- The first element of an array is numbered index 0. The first element (member) of a collection is numbered index 1.
- A collection consists of a single list of data. An array can consist of multiple dimensions of lists.

Understanding Collections

The Parts of a Collection

A collection consists of:

- One or more *members*. A member acts like a box that holds data.
- An *index number* that identifies each member. The first member in a collection always has an index value of 1, the second element has an index of 2, and so on.
- An optional *key* to identify each member. A key is a unique descriptive string that can identify each chunk of data stored in a collection. By defining keys, you can search for data much more easily in a collection.

To create a collection, declare a name for your collection using the following syntax:

```
Dim CollectionName As New Collection
```

where CollectionName is the name of a variable used to represent your collection.

NOTE *Unlike an array, when you declare a collection, you don't have to specify a size or data type.*

Storing Data in a Collection

When you initially create a collection, it has zero members. To add members to a collection, you need to store data in that collection. You can add any type of data to your collection using the following syntax:

```
CollectionName.Add(Data)
```

where *CollectionName* is the name of the collection and *Data* is the information you want to store in the collection.

Collections store data chronologically, so the first item added to a collection is stored as the first member of a collection (index 1), the second item added is stored as the second member (index 2), and so on.

The following code creates a collection and stores three items in it:

```
Dim LoserList As New Collection
LoserList.Add("McPherson")
LoserList.Add("Lee")
LoserList.Add(489)
```

After this BASIC code runs, the LoserList collection stores the following data:

```
{"McPherson", "Lee", 489}
```

NOTE *Until you retrieve data from a collection and display it on screen or print it out, you won't be able to see the collection's contents.*

Normally, each time you add an item to a collection, Visual Basic stores the new item at the end of the collection. However, you can specify whether you want an added item to appear before or after an existing item in a collection. This can be handy if you're storing names in a collection and want to keep the data in alphabetical order.

To store data *before* an existing member in a collection, use the following syntax:

```
CollectionName.Add(Data, , Before)
```

where *Before* is the index of a member in the collection before which you want to insert the new data in the collection. The empty space between the two commas is meant to let you assign a key to each item you add to a collection. You'll learn more about keys in the section "Searching for Data in a Collection" on page 321.

For example, suppose you had a collection named LoserList, as follows:

```
{"McPherson", "Lee", 489}
```

If you wanted to insert new data ("Reese") before the second (2) member of the collection ("Lee"), you could use the following:

```
LoserList.Add("Reese", ,2)
```

The collection now looks like this:

```
{"McPherson", "Reese", "Lee", 489}
```

You can also store data *after* a member in a collection by using the following syntax:

```
CollectionName.Add(Data, , ,After)
```

where *After* is the index of a member in the collection after which you want to insert the new item in the collection. The first blank space between the two commas is meant for assigning a key to the data you're adding to the collection. The second blank space between the two commas is where you would type an index number to specify a *Before* value. Because you can't specify both a Before and After index number, the space for the Before number is left blank.

For example, suppose you had a collection named LoserList, as follows:

```
{"McPherson", "Reese", "Lee", 489}
```

If you wanted to insert new data ("Swanson") after the first member (index number 1) of the collection, you could use the following:

```
LoserList.Add("Swanson", , ,1)
```

This will make the collection look like this:

```
{"McPherson", "Swanson", "Reese", "Lee", 489}
```

Searching for Data in a Collection

When you store data in a collection, you may eventually want to locate a specific chunk of data, but you might not know its exact position. While you could search through a collection one item at a time, it's much easier to find data if you store that data in a collection using a key, which is just any unique string. To add data to a collection along with a unique key, use the following syntax:

```
CollectionName.Add (Data, key)
```

The following code creates a collection and stores three items in it along with their keys:

```
Dim LoserList As New Collection
LoserList.Add("McPherson", "0")
LoserList.Add("Lee", "666")
LoserList.Add(489, "Junk")
```

Once you've stored data in a collection with a key, you can retrieve it by using the following syntax:

```
Variable = CollectionName.Item(key)
```

The following code creates a collection named LoserList, fills it with three items, assigns a key to each item, uses a key to retrieve an item from the collection, and then displays that retrieved item in a message box:

```
Dim LoserList As New Collection
Dim Name As String
LoserList.Add("McPherson", "0")
LoserList.Add("Lee", "666")
LoserList.Add("Reese", "SWM")
Name = LoserList.Item("666")
MsgBox(Name)
```

This example retrieves the item identified by the "666" key, which happens to be the string "Lee".

You can also use the Item command to retrieve an item from a collection based on its index number. For example, to find the second member in a collection, you could use the following:

```
CollectionName.Item(2)
```

NOTE   *The one problem with retrieving data using the index number is that as you add or remove items from a collection, the index numbers of all items in a collection can change. For that reason, it's better to search for data using its key.*

Removing Data from a Collection

Just as you can add items to a collection, you can also remove them. Removing an item from a collection doesn't leave any empty gaps, because the collection automatically moves all other items in the collection to fill in any gaps, as shown in Figure 23-6.

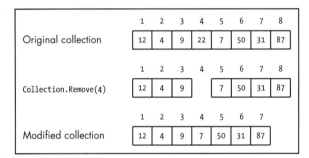

Figure 23-6: When you remove items from a collection, the collection automatically moves all remaining data to fill in the gap, which can change the index number of each member.

To remove an item from a collection, use the following:

```
CollectionName.Remove(Index)
```

where *CollectionName* is the name of the collection and *Index* is an integer that represents the item you want to remove. For example, to remove the fourth item in the collection, you would use the following:

```
CollectionName.Remove(4)
```

As an alternative to specifying an index position, you can also specify a key. The following BASIC code stores three items, with keys, in a collection:

```
Dim LoserList As New Collection
LoserList.Add("McPherson", "0")
LoserList.Add("Lee", "666")
LoserList.Add("Reese", "SWM")
```

This creates a collection that looks like this:

```
{"McPherson", "Lee", "Reese"}
```

To remove "Lee" from the collection, you would use this command:

```
LoserList.Remove("666")
```

This command removes the item associated with the key "666", which is the name "Lee". So now the collection looks like this:

```
{"McPherson", "Reese"}
```

Counting All the Members in a Collection

Because you can keep adding and removing items from a collection, you might want to know the total number of items in a collection at any given time. To count the total members of a collection, use the Count command with the following syntax:

```
CollectionName.Count
```

where *CollectionName* is the name of the collection you want to count.

The following code creates a collection, stores four items in it, and then runs the MsgBox command to display the total number of items stored in the collection (a total of four):

```
Dim Dogs As New Collection
Dogs.Add("Pepper")
Dogs.Add("Tippy")
Dogs.Add("Buster")
Dogs.Add("Taffy")
MsgBox(Dogs.Count)
```

Using the For Each Next Loop

Using the For Each Next Loop

We know that both arrays and collections can vary in size as your program runs. So what if you want to access every single item in an array or collection, one at a time? Use a *For Each Next* loop, which looks like this:

```
For Each Element In Group
    Instructions
Next
```

where *Element* is a variable that represents the same data type that's stored in the array or collection that you're searching and *Group* is a variable that represents the array or collection you want to search.

For example, to search an array, you could use the following code:

```
Dim ArrayName(5) As String
Dim ArrayItem As String
ArrayName(0) = "Bo"
ArrayName(1) = "Scraps"
ArrayName(2) = "Tasha"
ArrayName(3) = "Nuit"
ArrayName(4) = "Buster"
ArrayName(5) = "Spots"
```

```
For Each ArrayItem In ArrayName
        MsgBox (ArrayItem)
Next
```

In this example:

Line 1   Defines an array called ArrayName, which consists of six elements (numbered 0 to 5), which can hold string data.

Line 2   Defines a variable called ArrayItem as a string data type.

Lines 3 to 8   Assign various strings to each element in ArrayName.

Lines 9 and 11   Define the start and end of the For Each Next loop. This loop tells the computer to go through the entire array, one element at a time, and run the tenth line, which uses the MsgBox command to display each string stored in the array. Because the array contains six elements, the For Each Next loop runs the MsgBox command six times.

To search a collection, you could use the following BASIC code:

```
Dim Cats As New Collection
Dim Animal As Object
Cats.Add("Bo")
Cats.Add("Scraps")
Cats.Add("Tasha")
Cats.Add("Nuit")
Cats.Add("Buster")
Cats.Add("Spots")
For Each Animal In Cats
        MsgBox (Animal)
Next
```

In this example:

Line 1   Creates a collection named Cats.

Line 2   Creates a variable called Animal and defines it as an object data type. An object data type lets you store different types of values such as integers and text. All collections are automatically defined as storing object data types.

Lines 3 through 8   Store different strings in the Cats collection.

Lines 9 and 11   Define the start and end of the For Each Next loop. This loop tells the computer that for each member in the Cats collection, run the tenth line, which uses the MsgBox command to display each member of the collection.

The best thing about using a For Each Next loop is that you never have to worry about how many items you have stored in your array or collection, because the For Each Next loop will step through each item in the array or collection until it reaches the end.

Hands-on Tutorial: Playing with Collections

This tutorial has you create a collection, store different types of data in it, and then use a For Each Next loop to display its entire contents.

1.   Start a new project, then click OK to display a blank form.

2.   Choose View ▸ Toolbox to display the Toolbox, then choose Window ▸ Auto Hide to keep the Toolbox visible.

3. Click the TextBox control in the Toolbox, move the mouse pointer near the top of the form, and click the left mouse button to create a text box.

4. Click the ComboBox control in the Toolbox, move the mouse pointer underneath the text box on the form, and click the left mouse button to create a combo box underneath the text box.

5. Click the Label control in the Toolbox, move the mouse pointer underneath the combo box on the form, and click the left mouse button to create a label.

6. Click the Button control in the Toolbox, move the mouse pointer near the bottom of the form, and click the left mouse button to create a button on the form. Your user interface should look like Figure 23-7.

7. Click the combo box control and press F4 to open the Properties window.

8. Click the Items property in the Properties window. An ellipsis button appears. Click the ellipsis button and a String Collection Editor dialog box appears.

Figure 23-7: A user interface with a text box, combo box, label, and button control on a form

9. Type **Beginning** and press ENTER, then type **End** and click OK.

10. Double-click the Button1 control on the form. The Code window appears.

11. Type the boldface code shown between the Public Class line and the Private Sub line, as follows:

```
Public Class Form1
    Dim Cats As New Collection
    Dim Animal As Object
    Private Sub Button1_Click(ByVal sender As System.Object, ByVal e As_
System.EventArgs) Handles Button1.Click

    End Sub
End Class
```

The first line of boldface code creates a collection named Cats. The second line declares a variable named Animal, which can hold object data types, the same data types that all collections always use. Object data types can hold anything from strings and integers to decimal numbers and Boolean values.

12. Type the boldface code shown between the Private Sub and End Sub lines, as follows:

```
Public Class Form1
    Dim Cats As New Collection
    Dim Animal As Object
    Private Sub Button1_Click(ByVal sender As System.Object, ByVal e As_
System.EventArgs) Handles Button1.Click
        Select Case ComboBox1.Text
            Case "Beginning"
                Cats.Add(TextBox1.Text, , 1)
            Case Else
```

```
                Cats.Add(TextBox1.Text)
        End Select
        Label1.Text = ""
        For Each Animal In Cats
            Label1.Text = Label1.Text & " " & Animal
        Next
    End Sub
End Class
```

Line 1   Defines the start of a Select Case statement and retrieves the data stored in the Text property of the ComboBox1 control. The entire Select Case statement consists of lines 1 through 6.

Line 2   Compares the string "Beginning" to the string stored in the Text property of the ComboBox1 control, retrieved by the first line.

Line 3   If the value of the ComboBox1's Text property exactly matches the "Beginning" string, the third line runs, which inserts the data stored in the Text property of the TextBox1 control, at the beginning of the Cats collection. (Note that the Cats.Add (TextBox1.Text, , 1) command leaves a blank space in between TextBox1.Text and the number 1. Normally, this space would be used to define a key to identify the data added to the Cats collection, but a key is not needed for this example.)

Line 4   Tells the Select Case statement to run the instruction on the fifth line if the value of the Text property in TextBox1 does not exactly equal the "Beginning" string.

Line 6   Marks the end of the Select Case statement.

Line 7   Clears the Text property of the Label1 control by setting the Text property to an empty string.

Lines 8 and 10   Mark the start and end of a For Each Next loop that steps through each item in the Cats collection, runs the ninth line which yanks out each member of the Cats collection, stores it in the Animal variable, and displays it in the Label1 control's Text property.

13. Click in the Class Name list box and click (Form1 Events).

14. Click in the Method Name list box and choose Load. The Code window displays a blank Form1_Load event procedure.

15. Type the boldface code shown between the Private Sub and the End Sub lines of the Form1_Load event procedure, as shown here:

```
Public Class Form1
    Dim Cats As New Collection
    Dim Animal As Object
    Private Sub Button1_Click(ByVal sender As System.Object, ByVal e As_
System.EventArgs) Handles Button1.Click
        Select Case ComboBox1.Text
            Case "Beginning"
                Cats.Add(TextBox1.Text, , 1)
            Case Else
                Cats.Add(TextBox1.Text)
```

```
            End Select
            Label1.Text = ""
            For Each Animal In Cats
                Label1.Text = Label1.Text & " " & Animal
            Next
    End Sub
    Private Sub Form1_Load(ByVal sender As System.Object, ByVal e As_
System.EventArgs) Handles MyBase.Load
        Cats.Add("Bo")
        Cats.Add("Scraps")
        Cats.Add("Tasha")
    End Sub
End Class
```

The three boldface lines add the strings "Bo", "Scraps", and "Tasha" to the Cats collection.

16. Press F5. Your user interface appears.

17. Click the Button1 control. The Label1 control displays the current contents of the Cats collection, which is the "Bo Scraps Tasha" string.

18. Click in the text box and type **Joe**, then click the downward-pointing arrow in the combo box and click Beginning.

19. Click the Button1 control. Notice that the Label1 control now shows the revised contents of the Cats collection with the name *Joe* at the front of the list.

20. Click in the text box and type **Sally**, then click in the combo box and click End.

21. Click the Button1 control. Notice that the Label1 control now displays *Sally* as the last item in the Cats collection.

22. Press ALT-F4 to stop your program. A Close Project dialog box appears. Click Discard.

KEY FEATURES TO REMEMBER

Data structures act like variables that can combine related information in a single location.

- A structure can store multiple variables within a single variable. These multiple variables are called properties.

- An array must contain identical data types. The first element of an array is numbered zero (0), the second is numbered one (1), and so on.

- Visual Basic provides built-in commands for sorting, searching, and clearing a one-dimensional array.

- A collection can contain different data types. The first member of a collection is numbered one (1), the second is numbered two (2), and so on.

- Visual Basic provides built-in commands for sorting, searching, and removing members from a collection.

- A For Each Next loop can access each item stored in an array or collection.

24

ADVANCED DATA STRUCTURES: QUEUES, STACKS, AND HASH TABLES

To provide greater flexibility in storing information, Visual Basic includes three data structures called *queues, stacks,* and *hash tables,* which, as with arrays and collections, do nothing more than store data in a list. However, they offer different ways to search, store, and remove data, which can make them more useful than arrays or collections, depending on what you want your program to do.

Using a Queue

Understanding Queues

A *queue* always adds data to the end of a list but removes data from the front of the list. A queue takes its name from the way it stores and removes data, which mimics the way people wait in line: the first person in line is the first one to leave. Because of the way a queue adds and removes data, queues are sometimes called a *First In, First Out (FIFO)* data structure.

A queue can be useful for creating an inventory program in which you want to remove the oldest stored item first. If you were to use a different data structure, such as a collection, to remove an item, old items could be left sitting idly by or rotting away in your inventory, which would waste your company's resources.

Figure 24-1 shows a queue in three different stages. The top stage shows the number 61 being added to an existing queue already full of data. The middle stage shows how the existing queue has grown by one additional item, in this case the number 61. The bottom stage shows that the only way to remove an item from a queue is from the front of the queue, which is the opposite end from where new data is added.

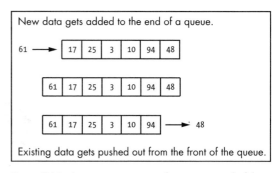

Figure 24-1: A queue stores new data at one end of the list and removes old data from the other end.

To create a queue, you need to declare a variable as a queue, like so:

```
Dim VariableName As New Queue
```

When you create a queue, it contains no data, so the first step to using a queue is to stuff it with data. Like a collection, a queue can store different types of data, such as string, integers, and boolean values.

Adding Data to a Queue with the Enqueue Method

When you add data to a queue, the data is stored at the end of the queue. Each time you add data to a queue, the queue gets longer and longer. To add data to a queue, use the Enqueue method, which looks like this:

```
QueueName.Enqueue (Data)
```

where *QueueName* is the name of the queue and *Data* is the data you want to store in a queue.

The following code creates a queue and stores three items in it: a number, a string, and a boolean True value, as shown in Figure 24-2:

```
Dim MyQueue As New Queue
MyQueue.Enqueue (29)
MyQueue.Enqueue ("Cat")
MyQueue.Enqueue (True)
```

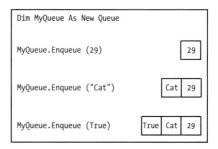

Figure 24-2: The Enqueue method stores data in a queue, putting the first stored item at the front of the list and adding new items to the back of the list.

Checking the Contents of a Queue

As you fill a queue with data, you may lose track of what data is actually stored in it. To search the queue for specific data, use the Contains method, which returns a True or False value, like so:

```
QueueName.Contains (Data)
```

where *QueueName* is the name of the queue and *Data* is the data you want to find in the queue.

The following code stores three items in a queue and then searches to determine whether the queue contains the string "Cat". Because the queue contains "Cat", the MsgBox command displays *True* in a message box.

```
Dim MyQueue As New Queue
MyQueue.Enqueue (29)
MyQueue.Enqueue ("Cat")
MyQueue.Enqueue (True)
MsgBox(MyQueue.Contains("Cat"))
```

When you search for data in a queue, you must search for the exact data. For example, if a queue contains the string "Cat" (uppercase C) but you search for the string cat (lowercase c), the Contains method will return False because "Cat" is not exactly identical to the string "cat".

If you want to know only the data currently stored at the front of the queue, use the Peek method, like so:

```
Dim MyQueue As New Queue
MyQueue.Enqueue (29)
MyQueue.Enqueue ("Cat")
MyQueue.Enqueue (True)
MsgBox(MyQueue.Peek)
```

In this example, the number 29 is stored at the front of the queue because it was the first item placed in the queue. Therefore, the Peek method returns the number *29* and displays that in a message box.

NOTE *The Peek method doesn't remove any data from the queue. It simply returns the value of the next chunk of data that you can remove from the queue.*

Counting the Contents of a Queue

The number of items that a queue can hold may vary as your program stores and removes data from the queue. To determine the current number of items stored in a queue, use the Count method, like so:

```
QueueName.Count
```

where *QueueName* is the name of the queue.

The following BASIC code adds three items to a queue, runs the Count method, and displays the number *3* in a message box after counting three items in the queue:

```
Dim MyQueue As New Queue
MyQueue.Enqueue (29)
MyQueue.Enqueue ("Cat")
MyQueue.Enqueue (True)
MsgBox(MyQueue.Count)
```

Removing Data from a Queue

You can remove data only from the front of the queue, which means that the oldest item you stored in the queue will also be the next item you can remove. To remove an item from a queue, use the Dequeue method, like so:

```
QueueName.Dequeue
```

where *QueueName* is the name of the queue.

When you use the Dequeue method, you physically remove the first item from the queue, as shown in Figure 24-3.

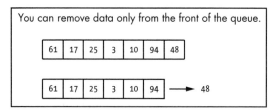

You can remove data only from the front of the queue.

| 61 | 17 | 25 | 3 | 10 | 94 | 48 |

| 61 | 17 | 25 | 3 | 10 | 94 | → 48

Figure 24-3: The Dequeue method removes the first item from the front of the queue, shortening the length of the queue by one item.

The following BASIC code adds three items to a queue, then uses Dequeue to remove the first item. In this case, the first item is the number *29*, so the MsgBox command displays *29* in a message box:

```
Dim MyQueue As New Queue
Dim MyData As Object
MyQueue.Enqueue (29)
MyQueue.Enqueue ("Cat")
MyQueue.Enqueue (True)
MyData = MyQueue.Dequeue
MsgBox(MyData)
```

Because a queue stores data as object data types, when you want to retrieve data from a queue, you must always store it in a variable that represents an object data type. In the preceding code, the MyData variable represents an object data type.

As an alternative to removing data from a queue one item at a time, you can empty a queue completely by using the Clear method, like so:

```
QueueName.Clear()
```

where *QueueName* is the name of the queue.

The following code adds three items to a queue, displays the total number of items (*3*), empties the queue, and then runs the Count method to count the total number of items stored in the queue, which is zero:

```
Dim MyQueue As New Queue
MyQueue.Enqueue (29)
MyQueue.Enqueue ("Cat")
MyQueue.Enqueue (True)
MsgBox(MyQueue.Count)
MyQueue.Clear()
MsgBox(MyQueue.Count)
```

In this example, the first MsgBox command displays a *3* in a message box. Next, the Clear method runs and empties the queue before the second MsgBox command displays a *0* in a message box to let you know the queue is really empty.

When you remove data from a queue using the Dequeue method, you can store the removed data in a variable, but when you empty a queue using the Clear method, you lose all the emptied data. To save the entire contents of a queue before emptying it, copy the data to an array first.

Copying Data from a Queue to an Array

As an alternative to removing data from a queue one item at a time using the Dequeue method, you can copy all the data from a queue and place it in an array. When you copy data from an array, the contents of your queue is unchanged.

Because a queue can vary in size, you first need to create a queue and a dynamic array that stores object data types. Then, after filling the queue with data, you can use the ToArray method to assign the contents of the queue to that array, as follows:

```
Dim QueueName As New Queue
Dim ArrayName() As Object
QueueName.Enqueue(Data)
ArrayName = QueueName.ToArray()
```

where QueueName is the name of your queue, ArrayName is the name of the dynamic array that holds object data types, and Data is the data, such as a number or string, that you want to store in your queue.

When you copy data from a queue to an array, the first item in the queue is stored at index 0 of the array, the second item is stored in index 1 of the array, and so on.

The following code stores four items in a queue, copies them into an array, and then uses a For-Next loop to display each item in the array. Because arrays begin counting at index position 0, the For-Next loop has to start counting at 0 and stop counting at the total number of items in the queue minus one, which is 3.

```
Dim cat As New Queue
Dim MyArray() As Object
Dim J As Integer
cat.Enqueue("Bo")
cat.Enqueue(False)
cat.Enqueue(75.4)
cat.Enqueue("Nuit")
MyArray = cat.ToArray()
For J = 0 To (cat.Count- 1)
    MsgBox(MyArray(J))
Next
```

An alternative to copying data from a queue to an array is to use the CopyTo method. Unlike the ToArray method, which always stores the first item of the queue in the first position (index 0) of an array, the CopyTo method lets you store data from the queue starting in any index position of the array, like so:

```
QueueName.CopyTo(ArrayName, Index)
```

where QueueName is the name of your queue, ArrayName is the name of the dynamic array that holds object data types, and Index is the index position where you want to start storing data in the array. If the value of Index is 0, the first item in the queue is stored at index position 0 of the array, the second item is stored in index position 1 of the array, and so on.

Before you can copy data from a queue to an array, you must resize your array with the ReDim keyword, as shown here:

```
Dim cat As New Queue
Dim MyArray() As Object
Dim I As Integer
```

```
cat.Enqueue("Bo")
cat.Enqueue(False)
cat.Enqueue(75.4)
cat.Enqueue("Nuit")
ReDim MyArray(6)
cat.CopyTo(MyArray, 2)
For I = 0 To 6
    MsgBox(MyArray(I))
Next
```

This example resizes the dynamic array (MyArray) to hold seven elements (0 through 6) and then uses the CopyTo method to copy the data from the queue into the array, starting at index position 2, which is the third position in the array. When the For-Next loop runs, it first displays two blank message boxes (because the initial two elements of MyArray are empty) and then displays the data copied from the queue.

Using a Stack

Understanding Stacks

A *stack* is a data structure that mimics a stack of plates stored in a cafeteria. The last item stored in the stack is also the first item removed from the stack, often known as a *Last In, First Out (LIFO)* data structure, as shown in Figure 24-4.

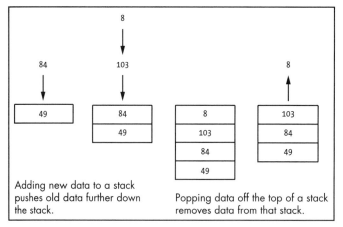

Figure 24-4: A stack pushes new data on top of old data and pops off data to remove it from the top of the stack.

To create a stack, you need to declare a variable as a stack, like so:

```
Dim VariableName As New Stack
```

When you create a stack, it contains no data, so the first step is to *push* data on to the top of the stack. To remove data from a stack, you *pop* it off the top.

Like a queue, a stack can store different types of data, such as string, integers, and boolean values. Stacks are often used to store data temporarily. For example, calculator programs use stacks to store different numbers and mathematical operators (plus sign, division sign, and so on) that the user chooses. Each time the user types a number, the program stores that number on the stack. When the user types a mathematical operator such as the plus sign (+), that is also stored on the stack. As soon as the user types another number, the program pops the mathematical operator off the stack along with the previously stored number on the stack and calculates a final result.

Pushing Data

To store data on a stack, use the `Push` method, like so:

```
StackName.Push(Data)
```

where *StackName* is the name of the stack where you want to add new data and *Data* is the data you want to push on top of the stack.

The following code shows how to push three items on to a stack, as shown in Figure 24-5:

```
Dim cat As New Stack
cat.Push("Bo")
cat.Push(False)
cat.Push(304)
```

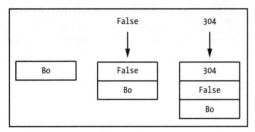

Figure 24-5: The string Bo is the first item pushed on a stack and will be the last item that can be removed from the stack.

Checking the Contents of a Stack

Once you've stored data on a stack, you can use the `Peek` method to see the last data stored on top of the stack. The `Peek` method doesn't remove the data from the stack; it just returns the value of that data.

To use the `Peek` method, use the following syntax:

```
StackName.Peek
```

The following BASIC code pushes two items onto a stack and then runs the `MsgBox` command to display data in a message box:

```
Dim idiots As New Stack
idiots.Push("Pauly")
idiots.Push("Bobby")
MsgBox(idiots.Peek)
```

This example pushes the string "Pauly" onto the stack and then shoves another string, "Bobby", right on top of it. When the `Peek` method runs, it returns the value of the last item stored on the stack, which is the string "Bobby", then the `MsgBox` command displays *Bobby* in a message box.

The `Peek` method is handy for letting you check on the value of the last item stored on top of a stack, but if you want to search for data that may be stored somewhere else in a stack, you'll have to use the `Contains` method, which uses this syntax:

```
StackName.Contains(Data)
```

where *StackName* is the name of the stack that you want to search and *Data* is the data you want to find inside the stack.

The Contains method returns a True or False value. If you search and find data exactly matching any data stored in a stack, the Contains method returns a True value; otherwise, it returns a False value.

The following code pushes three items onto a stack and then searches for an item:

```
Dim wmd As New Stack
wmd.Push("Smallpox")
wmd.Push("Uranium")
wmd.Push("Nerve gas")
MsgBox(wmd.Contains("Uranium"))
```

In this example, the Contains method searches for the string "Uranium" in the stack named wmd. Because the string "Uranium" is already stored in the stack, the Contains method returns a True value and the MsgBox command displays *True* in a message box.

If you search for "uranium" (lowercase u) in a stack but the stack contains only the string "Uranium", (uppercase U), the Contains method will return a False value because the strings are not exactly identical.

NOTE   *The Contains method tells you only whether certain data is stored in a stack; it won't tell you where in the stack that data may be stored.*

Counting the Contents of a Stack

A stack can grow and shrink as you push data in and pop data off it. To count the number of items stored in a stack, use the Count method, like so:

```
StackName.Count
```

The following code pushes three items onto a stack and then uses the Count method to count the total number of items in the stack (3).

```
Dim wmd As New Stack
wmd.Push("Smallpox")
wmd.Push("Uranium")
wmd.Push("Nerve gas")
MsgBox(wmd.Count)
```

In this example, the Count method returns a value of 3, so the MsgBox command displays *3* in a message box.

Popping Data from a Stack

To remove data from a stack, use the Pop method, which removes the last item stored on the stack. If you want to save the contents of the popped data, you need to store the popped data into a variable declared to hold object data types, such as the following:

```
Dim VariableName As Object
VariableName = StackName.Pop
```

The following code pushes three items onto a stack and then uses the Pop method to remove the last item pushed onto the stack.

```
Dim axis As New Stack
axis.Push("North Korea")
axis.Push("Iraq")
axis.Push("IRS")
MsgBox(axis.Pop)
```

In this example, the Pop method pops off the last item stored, which is IRS, so the MsgBox command displays *IRS* in a message box.

To clear out all data stored in a stack (without saving any of it), you can use the Clear method, like so:

```
StackName.Clear
```

The following code pushes three items onto a stack, uses the Count method to display *3* in a message box, uses the Clear method to remove all data from the stack, and then uses the Count method again to display *0* in a message box, showing you that the stack is now empty:

```
Dim axis As New Stack
axis.Push("North Korea")
axis.Push("Iraq")
axis.Push("IRS")
MsgBox(axis.Count)
axis.Clear
MsgBox(axis.Count)
```

Copying Data from a Queue to an Array

Popping data off a stack one item at a time can be tedious, so you can also copy the entire contents of a stack to an array using either the ToArray or CopyTo methods.

To use the ToArray method, you first create a dynamic array that stores object data types, then you use the ToArray method to assign the contents of the stack to that array, as follows:

```
Dim StackName As New Stack
Dim ArrayName() As Object
StackName.Push(Data)
ArrayName = StackName.ToArray()
```

where *StackName* is the name of your stack; *ArrayName* is the name of your dynamic array that holds object data types; and *Data* is the data, such as a number or string, that you want to store in your stack.

When you copy data from a stack to an array, Visual Basic pops the top item off the stack (the last item stored on the stack) and stores it in the first position of the array (index position 0). It then pops the next item off the stack and stores it in index position 1 of the array, and so on.

The following code stores three items on a stack, copies them into an array, and then uses a For-Next loop to display each item in the array. Because arrays begin counting at index position 0, the For-Next loop has to start counting at 0 and stop counting at the total number of items in the stack minus one, which is 2.

```
Dim axis As New Stack
Dim MyArray() As Object
```

```
Dim I As Integer
axis.Push("North Korea")
axis.Push("Iraq")
axis.Push("IRS")
MyArray = axis.ToArray()
For I = 0 To axis.Count - 1
    MsgBox(MyArray(I))
Next
```

This example runs the `MsgBox` command three times. The first time the `MsgBox` command displays *IRS*, the second time it displays *Iraq*, and the third and last time it displays *North Korea* in a message box.

Another way to copy data from a stack to an array is to use the `CopyTo` method. Unlike the `ToArray` method, which always stores the first item of the queue in the first position (index 0) of an array, the `CopyTo` method lets you store data from the stack starting with any index position of the array:

```
StackName.CopyTo(ArrayName, Index)
```

where *StackName* is the name of your stack, *ArrayName* is the name of your dynamic array that holds object data types, and *Index* is the index position where you want to start storing data in the array. If the *Index* value is 0, the first item popped off the stack is stored at index position 0 of the array, the second item is stored in index position 1, and so on.

Before you can copy data from a stack to an array, you must resize your array using the `ReDim` keyword, as the following code demonstrates:

```
Dim axis As New Stack
Dim MyArray() As Object
Dim I As Integer
axis.Push("North Korea")
axis.Push("Iraq")
axis.Push("IRS")
ReDim MyArray(5)
axis.CopyTo(MyArray, 1)
For I = 0 To 5
    MsgBox(MyArray(I))
Next
```

This example resizes the dynamic array (`MyArray`) to hold six elements (0 through 5) and then uses the `CopyTo` method to pop data, one at a time, from the stack into the array, starting at index position 1, which is the second position in the array. When the For-Next loop runs, it first displays one blank message box (because the initial element of the `MyArray` is empty at index position 0), and then displays the data copied from the stack.

Using a Hash Table

Under-
standing
Hash Tables

A *hash table* acts like a list that stores data along with a unique *key* that can identify that data, as shown in Figure 24-6. The data associated with a key can be as simple as a single number or string or as complicated as a stack, a structure, or a two-dimensional array. These keys will help you to identify and find that data later on, no matter where it is in the hash table.

NOTE   *Every key stored in a hash table must be unique; you cannot use the same key twice, or your program won't work.*

Keys act like shortcuts to help you find data. For example, you could have a key named CEO and the data associated with it could be a structure that stores the name, address, and phone number of the company's current CEO. To find the CEO's phone number, you could look up the key CEO and that person's name would pop up. Without keys, you would have to search for the specific data you want to find. If you can search for the correct key, you'll always be able to find the CEO's private information.

Keys	Data
"VB"	"Visual Basic"
666	"Politicians"
"BAK"	"Backup"
"RB"	80394
"DLL"	"Dynamic Link Library"
2006	"Year of the Dog"
"OS 9"	"Buggy OS"

Figure 24-6: A hash table stores data in a list where each chunk of data is associated with a unique key.

To create a hash table, declare a variable Hashtable, like so:

```
Dim VariableName As New Hashtable
```

Hash tables are initially empty, so you need to store data in them. This data can be any data type, such as a mix of integer and single data types.

Adding Data to a Hash Table

When you add data to a hash table, you need to add the actual data plus the unique key that you want to associate with that data. Both the key and the data you want to add to the hash table can be any data type, such as a number or a string.

To add data to a hash table, use the Add method, like so:

```
HashtableName.Add(Key, Data)
```

where *HashtableName* is the name of the hash table where you want to add data, *Key* is the unique value used to identify the data you want to add, and *Value* is the actual data to add to the hash table.

The following code adds two items to a hash table:

```
Dim ColdHash as New Hashtable
ColdHash.Add(1, "Potatoes")
ColdHash.Add("y", "Meat")
```

While this example adds two items to a hash table, nothing will appear to happen because you can't actually see anything being added to the hash table.

Retrieving Data from a Hash Table

Once you've stored keys and data in a hash table, you can use the key to retrieve the data later. When you retrieve data using a key, you simply copy the data from the hash table into a variable; you don't physically remove the data from the hash table itself.

To retrieve data from a hash table, use the Item method, like so:

```
HashtableName.Item(Key)
```

where *HashtableName* is the name of the hash table where you want to retrieve data and *Key* is the unique item associated with the data stored in the hash table.

For example, the following code adds two items to a hash table, searches for the data associated with the y key, and displays that data in a message box:

```
Dim ColdHash as New Hashtable
ColdHash.Add(1, "Potatoes")
ColdHash.Add("y", "Meat")
MsgBox(ColdHash.Item("y"))
```

In this example, the hash table contains two items (`Meat` and `Potatoes`) and the `Item` method retrieves the data associated with the y key, which happens to be the `Meat` string. As a result, the `MsgBox` command displays the item associated with the y key, *Meat*, in a message box.

Copying Values from a Hash Table to an Array

The `Item` method can retrieve data from a hash table one item at a time. If you want to retrieve all the data stored in a hash table, you can use the `CopyTo` method to copy everything out of a hash table and into a one-dimensional array.

To use the `CopyTo` method, you need to use the index position where you want to start copying data from the hash table into the array, like so:

```
HashtableName.CopyTo(ArrayName, Index)
```

where *HashtableName* is the name of your hash table, *ArrayName* is the name of your dynamic array that holds DictionaryEntry data types, and *Index* is the index position where you want to start storing data in the array. (If this value is 0, the first item from the hash table is stored at index position 0 of the array, the second item is stored in index position 1 of the array, and so on.)

A DictionaryEntry data type stores both a key and its associated value. While a data type can usually hold only a single item, a DictionaryEntry data type is specially designed to work with hash tables to hold two items: a key (either a string or a number) and any associated data (a string, a number, a collection, an array, a queue, and so on).

Before you can copy data from a hash to an array, you must resize your array using the ReDim keyword, as the following code demonstrates:

```
Dim ColdHash As New Hashtable
Dim BreakfastArray() As DictionaryEntry
Dim stuff As DictionaryEntry
ColdHash.Add(1, "Potatoes")
ColdHash.Add("y", "Meat")
ReDim BreakfastArray(ColdHash.Count - 1)
ColdHash.CopyTo(BreakfastArray, 0)
For Each stuff In BreakfastArray
MsgBox(stuff.Key & "    " & stuff.Value)
Next
```

This example creates a dynamic array that can hold DictionaryEntry data types and a variable that can also hold DictionaryEntry data types. After adding the string `Potatoes` to the hash table and the string `Meat` after that, the program next resizes the `BreakfastArray` variable to hold the number of items in the hash table minus one.

The CopyTo method copies all the data out of the hash table and stores it in the BreakfastArray, starting at index position 0, the first position of the array. Next, the For Each loop starts at the beginning of the hash table and displays its contents, which includes both the key and the data.

The For Each loop starts at the beginning of the array and displays each key/data pair in a message box. The first message box displays *y   Meat* and the second message box displays *1   Potatoes.*

Counting Data in a Hash Table

Because a hash table can grow and shrink depending on the amount of data stored in it at any given time, use the Count method to count the number of items currently stored in a hash table, with this syntax:

```
HashtableName.Count
```

where *HashtableName* is the name of the hash table that contains the data you want to count.

The following code adds two items to a hash table and then uses the Count method to count the number of items stored in the hash table:

```
Dim ColdHash as New Hashtable
ColdHash.Add(1, "Potatoes")
ColdHash.Add("y", "Meat")
MsgBox(ColdHash.Count)
```

After adding two items to the hash table, the Count method returns a value of 2, which the MsgBox command displays in a message box.

Checking Whether Keys or Data Are Stored in a Hash Table

Once you've added data to a hash table, you can check to see whether the hash table contains a certain key or chunk of data, using the ContainsKey or ContainsValue methods. Both methods return a True or False value.

The ContainsKey method works like this:

```
HashtableName.ContainsKey(Key)
```

where *HashtableName* is the name of the hash table that contains the data you want to count and *Key* is the key you want to look for in the hash table.

The ContainsValue method works like this:

```
HashtableName.ContainsValue(Value)
```

where *HashtableName* is the name of the hash table that contains the data you want to count and *Value* is the data you want to look for in the hash table.

NOTE *Neither the ContainsKey nor ContainsValue method alters or removes the data from the hash table.*

The following code adds two items to a hash table and then uses the `ContainsKey` and `ContainsValue` methods to determine whether the hash table contains a specific key or value:

```
Dim ColdHash as New Hashtable
ColdHash.Add(1, "Potatoes")
ColdHash.Add("y", "Meat")
MsgBox(ColdHash.ContainsKey(1))
MsgBox(ColdHash.ContainsValue("MSG"))
```

In this example, the first `MsgBox` command displays a True value because the `ContainsKey` method finds the key 1 in the hash table. However, the second `MsgBox` command displays a False value because the `ContainsValue` method searches for `MSG` stored in the hash table. Because `MSG` isn't stored in the hash table, the `ContainsValue` method returns a False value.

Removing Data from a Hash Table

Just as you can add data to a hash table, you can also remove data, either by removing items one at a time or by clearing out the entire hash table all at once. To wipe out all the data in a hash table, use the `Clear` method:

```
HashtableName.Clear()
```

where *HashtableName* is the name of the hash table that contains the data you want to count.

The following code adds two items to a hash table and then uses the `Count` method to count all items in the hash table and display the total in a message box using the `MsgBox` command. The first `MsgBox` command displays 2. Then the `Clear` method runs and empties the hash table before the second `MsgBox` command runs and displays 0.

```
Dim ColdHash as New Hashtable
ColdHash.Add(1, "Potatoes")
ColdHash.Add("y", "Meat")
MsgBox(ColdHash.Count)
ColdHash.Clear()
MsgBox(ColdHash.Count)
```

Rather than clear out an entire hash table, you can use the `Remove` method to selectively remove individual items from a hash table by deleting the data associated with a specific key, like so:

```
HashtableName.Remove(Key)
```

where *HashtableName* is the name of the hash table that contains the data you want to count and *Key* is the key associated with the data you want to remove.

The following code adds two items to a hash table and then removes the data associated with the y key:

```
Dim ColdHash as New Hashtable
ColdHash.Add(1, "Potatoes")
ColdHash.Add("y", "Meat")
MsgBox(ColdHash.Count)
```

```
ColdHash.Remove("y")
MsgBox(ColdHash.Count)
```

This example uses the Count method to display the number of items in the hash table (in this case, *2*), then it removes the data associated with the y key, which happens to be the "Meat" string. Next, the Count method counts the total number of items in the hash table and displays that in a message box, which is now *1*.

Hands-on Tutorial: Playing with Queues, Stacks, and Hash Tables

This tutorial stores identical data in a queue, stack, and hash table so you can see how different data structures store identical information.

1. Start a new project, then click OK to display a blank form.
2. Choose View ▶ Toolbox to display the Toolbox.
3. Click the Button control in the Toolbox, mouse over the form, and click the left mouse button to create a button on the form.
4. Double-click the Button1 control on the form. The Code window appears.
5. Type the following between the Private Sub and End Sub lines so the Button1_Click event procedure in the Code window looks like this:

```
Private Sub Button1_Click(ByVal sender As System.Object, ByVal e As System.EventArgs)_
Handles Button1.Click
        Dim MyQueue As New Queue
        Dim MyStack As New Stack
        Dim MyHashTable As New Hashtable
        Const Data1 As Integer = 29
        Const Data2 As String = "Joe Smith"
        Const Data3 As Single = 39.05
        MyQueue.Enqueue(Data1)
        MyQueue.Enqueue(Data2)
        MyQueue.Enqueue(Data3)

        MyStack.Push(Data1)
        MyStack.Push(Data2)
        MyStack.Push(Data3)

        MyHashTable.Add(1, Data1)
        MyHashTable.Add(2, Data2)
        MyHashTable.Add(3, Data3)

        MsgBox(MyQueue.Peek)
        MsgBox(MyStack.Peek)
        MsgBox(MyHashTable.Item (2))
End Sub
```

- The first three lines (which start with the Dim keyword) create a queue, a stack, and a hash table, respectively. The fourth through sixth lines, which start with the Const keyword, which defines a variable with a fixed or constant value, create three constant values: an integer (29), a string, ("Joe Smith"), and a single-precision number (39.05).

- The next three lines add the constant values (29, "Joe Smith", and 39.05) to the queue data structure using the Enqueue method.

- The next three lines add the constant values (29, "Joe Smith", and 39.05) to the stack data structure using the Push method.

- The next three lines add the constant values (29, "Joe Smith", and 39.05) to the hash table using the Add method. In addition, each item is assigned a key so the first item gets a key of 1, the second gets a key of 2, and the third gets a key of 3.

- The last three lines use the MsgBox command to show you the contents of one item in each data structure. The first MsgBox command uses the Peek method to show you the next item that you can remove from the queue, which is the number *29*, the first item stored in the queue.

- The second MsgBox command uses the Peek method to show the next item that you can pop off the stack, which is the number *39.05*, the last item added to the stack.

- The third MsgBox command uses the Item method to retrieve the item identified by the 2 key value, which happens to be the *Joe Smith* string added to the hash table.

6. Press F5. Your user interface appears.

7. Click the Button1 control. The first MsgBox command displays a message box with the number *29*.

8. Click OK. The second MsgBox command displays a message box with the number *39.05*. Notice that the last item added to a stack is the first item you can remove from a stack, which is the exact opposite of adding and removing data to a queue.

9. Click OK. The third MsgBox command displays a message box with the string *Joe Smith* in it. Click OK.

10. Press ALT-F4 to stop your program, then choose File ▶ Close Project. A Close Project dialog box appears. Click Discard.

KEY FEATURES TO REMEMBER

Queues, stacks, and hash tables are just fancier ways to store data than an array or a collection. All three types of data structures can store object data types, which means you can mix different types of data in these data structures.

- A queue is known as a FIFO (First In, First Out) data structure because the first item stored in the queue is also the first item retrieved from the queue.

- A stack is known as a LIFO (Last In, First Out) data structure because the first item stored on the stack is the last item retrieved.

- Adding data to a stack is known as pushing data on the stack. Removing data from a stack is known as popping data from the stack.

- A hash table stores data along with a unique key that identifies that specific chunk of data.

25

CREATING PROCEDURES
AND FUNCTIONS

While you can create an entire program made up of a long series of instructions, doing so would be like trying to write an entire novel as a single sentence that's 300 pages long. That might make for an interesting novel, but it wouldn't make for a practical program.

Rather than force you to write one huge program, Visual Basic lets you divide a single program into separate parts called *subprograms* or *procedures*. Procedures are mini-programs that typically perform one specific task, such as retrieving data from the user interface or calculating a mathematical formula. Think of procedures as building blocks that you can create one at a time and paste together to form a much larger and more complicated program. Visual Basic lets you create three types of procedures:

- Event procedures
- General procedures
- Functions

Event procedures, which we examined in Chapter 11, are part of your program's user interface. They run in response to the user's actions, such as clicking a button or typing text into a text box. Event procedures typically contain BASIC code that sends or retrieves data to or from the user interface.

General procedures typically contain one or more instructions that calculate a result using the data retrieved from the user interface. A general procedure often contains instructions that the computer needs to follow multiple times. Rather than type these instructions in multiple locations, as shown in Figure 25-1, you can type them in a single location, store them in a general procedure, and give the procedure a unique name, as shown in Figure 25-2. When you want to run these same instructions in another part of your program, you can simply call the procedure by name. This call tells the computer which group of instructions you want to run next.

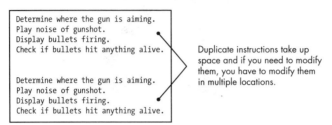

Figure 25-1: Without procedures, you would have to type commonly used sets of instructions in multiple places.

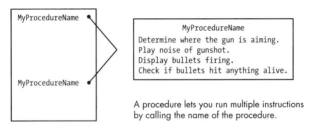

Figure 25-2: Procedures replace identical sets of instructions. You can use them to run, or call, a set of instructions by name, instead of typing the same instructions in multiple times in your program.

A *function* acts like a more specialized procedure which is designed to perform a single calculation. While a procedure can run without accepting any data, functions always accept data and return a single result. In Figure 25-2, the procedure MyProcedureName accomplishes the overall task of shooting a gun in a video game. A function, on the other hand, might be used to calculate the trajectory of a cartoon bullet on the screen by feeding the program the angle of the gun and the type of bullets being fired.

Visual Basic comes with an entire library of mathematical functions stored in a file or class called Math. The Math.Sqrt function is a typical function in the Math class. It accepts a single number and returns the square root of that number. Like procedures, functions are useful for storing frequently used instructions in a single location.

Creating a General Procedure

Creating Event and General Procedures

A general procedure can help you break a large program into a few smaller procedures and also isolate frequently used instructions in a single location. In this way, if you need to modify those instructions, you can change them all in one place, whereas had you typed identical instructions in six different locations in your program, you would have had to modify the same instruction in all six places.

The syntax for creating a procedure looks like this:

```
Sub ProcedureName
    Instructions
End Sub
```

where *ProcedureName* is a unique, descriptive name for your procedure and *Instructions* are one or more lines of BASIC code.

Storing Procedures in Form and Module Files

You can store general procedures in either *form files* or *module files.* Form files contain user interface controls, such as buttons, and event procedures to make your user interface controls work. Module files contain only general procedures.

If you want to write a procedure that can be used by any part of your program, you must store it in a module file. If your procedure will be used only by event procedures and other general procedures stored in a form file, you can store the procedure in either a form file or a module file.

For example, say you have a form file that displays a window asking users to enter a password. The moment the user types in a password and clicks an Enter button, that button's event procedure retrieves the password that the user typed. You could then have a general procedure match that password to a list of valid passwords.

By dividing the task of retrieving a password from the screen (an event procedure) and verifying whether the password is valid (a general procedure), you divide a task into parts. Thus, if one part of your program doesn't work, you can more easily isolate the problem. If your program isn't correctly letting people enter a valid password, you can check the event procedure to see whether it's retrieving the password accurately. If that's not the problem, you can next check the general procedure that verifies the password.

As a general rule, *it's better to use form files to store only event procedures and module files to store all your general procedures.* That way, if your program doesn't work, you can isolate the problem either to your event procedures stored in a form file or your general procedures stored in a module file. If you store general procedures in both form and module files, and one of your general procedures doesn't work, you'll have to search through both form files and module files to find the malfunctioning procedure rather than simply searching your module files.

Creating a General Procedure in a Form File

When you create a general procedure in a form file, only procedures (both general and event procedures) stored in that same form file can use your general procedure. To create a general procedure in a form file:

1. Open the Code window for the form file in which you want to save your general procedure by clicking the Code Window tab of a form file.
2. Move the cursor *outside* of any other procedures. To make it easy to find a list of all general procedures used in a file, many programmers store all general procedures at the top of every form file. Figure 25-3 shows two examples of general procedures stored before and after an event procedure.

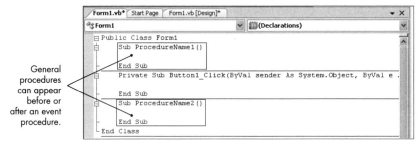

General
procedures
can appear
before or
after an event
procedure.

Figure 25-3: A form file can contain both event and general procedures.

3. Type **Sub** followed by the name of your procedure, then press ENTER. Visual Basic automatically indents your code and completes your general procedure so that it looks like the following, where *ProcedureName* is the name you typed for your procedure:

```
Sub ProcedureName

End Sub
```

4. Move the cursor between the Sub and End Sub lines and type one or more lines of BASIC code.

Creating a General Procedure in a Module File

When you create a general procedure in a *form file*, that procedure can be used only within that form file. To create a procedure that any part of your program can use, store a general procedure in a *module file*.

Unlike a form file that contains both the user interface and BASIC code (event procedures) to make the user interface work, module files contain only BASIC code. Module files help prevent you from having to cram too much BASIC code into a form file.

To create a module file, follow these steps:

1. Choose Project ▶ Add Module. An Add New Item dialog box appears.

2. Type a name for your module file in the Name text box and click Add. By default, Visual Basic gives your module a generic name such as Module1.vb, then displays the code window for your newly created module file, with code that looks like this:

```
Module Module1

End Module
```

where *Module1* is the name you gave your module in step 2.

3. Type **Sub** and your procedure name between the Module and End Module lines and press ENTER. Visual Basic creates an empty procedure that looks like this, where *ProcedureName* is any name you choose for your procedure (see Figure 25-4):

```
Sub ProcedureName

End Sub
```

Figure 25-4: A module file can contain only general procedures.

If you designate a procedure as Private, the procedure can be used only by other procedures stored within the same module file. A Private procedure looks like this:

```
Private Sub ProcedureName

End Sub
```

4. Type one or more lines of BASIC code between the Sub and the End Sub lines. Unless you specifically designate your procedure as Private, your procedure can be used by any other procedure in your program, even ones stored in separate module or form files.

Hands-on Tutorial: Creating a Procedure in a Module File

This tutorial shows you how to create a general procedure called ExplodingWindow in a module file. The ExplodingWindow procedure is called from the Button1_Click event procedure. This event procedure is stored in a separate form file, so when the user clicks the button named Button1, the instructions stored in the ExplodingWindow procedure run.

1. Start a new Visual Basic project, then click OK. A blank form appears.
2. Choose View ▶ Toolbox to display the Toolbox.
3. Click the Button control in the Toolbox, mouse over the form, and click the left mouse button to create a button.
4. Double-click the Button1 control on the form. The Code window appears.
5. Type ExplodingWindow() between the Private Sub and End Sub lines, like so:

```
Private Sub Button1_Click(ByVal sender As System.Object, ByVal e As System.EventArgs)_
Handles Button1.Click
        ExplodingWindow()
End Sub
```

The ExplodingWindow() command *calls* the ExplodingWindow procedure and tells it to run all of its instructions.

1. Choose Project ▶ Add Module. An Add New Item dialog box appears and displays the default name *Module1.vb* in the Name text box.
2. Click Add. The Code window appears, displaying an empty module file.
3. Type the following lines into the module file so it looks like this:

```
Module Module1
    Sub ExplodingWindow()
        Dim I As Integer
        Form1.Text = "Exploding window"
        For I = 1 To 150
```

```
                Form1.Size = New Size(I + I, I * 2)
          Next
      End Sub
End Module
```

Line 1   Creates an integer variable named I.

Line 2   Stores the string "Exploding window" into the Text property of the form named Form1.

Lines 3 and 5   Define a For-Next loop that repeats 150 times.

Line 4   Inside the For-Next loop, changes the Size property of the form in increasing increments to make the window appear to "grow" or "explode" on the screen.

4.   Press F5. Your user interface appears.

5.   Click the Button1 control. Notice that each time you click the Button1 control, the window appears to grow or explode on the screen.

6.   Press ALT-F4 to stop your program, then choose File ▶ Close Project. A Close Project dialog box appears. Click Discard.

Passing Parameters to Procedures

Passing
Parameters

A procedure contains a set of instructions for the program to follow the same way every time. For greater flexibility, procedures can also accept data, so the program can vary its behavior. When a program calls a procedure and gives it additional data, it's *passing a parameter.*

To create a procedure that can accept passed parameters, you must create a *parameter list* that defines the following:

• The number of items the procedure accepts

• The data types of each item that the procedure accepts

For example, if you want a procedure to accept a string, your entire procedure and parameter list might look like this:

```
Sub MyProcedure (ByVal MyText As String)

End Sub
```

This parameter list says that the procedure can accept a string (As String), which is stored in the variable MyText. The keyword ByVal is short for *By Value,* which you'll learn more about in the section "Modifying Data in a Procedure" on page 351.

NOTE   *When you type a parameter list for a procedure, you can type the name of your variable and Visual Basic Express will add the ByVal keyword in front of it automatically.*

Once you've defined a parameter list for your procedure, you can call that procedure and feed it data that matches the parameter list.

In the preceding example, the procedure expects a string, so you could call that procedure by name, followed by either a string or a string variable inside parentheses, like so:

```
MyProcedure ("This is a string")
```

or

```
Dim GetText As String
GetText = "This is a string."
MyProcedure (GetText)
```

When you call a procedure and give it data, you must exactly match the number of items the parameter list expects and the proper data types. For example, the following lines won't work:

```
MyProcedure (45.25)
MyProcedure ("Hello," 45.25)
```

The first example won't work because the MyProcedure parameter list expects a string, not a number like 45.25. The second example won't work either, because the MyProcedure parameter list expects one item—a string—and not a string and a number.

Adding Multiple Items to a Parameter List

A parameter list can accept as many different items as you want. All you have to do is define each parameter using the following syntax:

```
ByVal VariableName As DataType
```

where *VariableName* is the name of each parameter and *DataType* is the data type for each parameter.

To define multiple parameters, insert a comma between each parameter definition. For example, if you want a parameter list to accept a string and an integer, your parameter list might look like this:

```
(ByVal Msg As String, ByVal MyNumber As Integer)
```

You can add as many parameters as you want, but the more parameters you add, the messier your entire parameter list will look.

Modifying Data in a Procedure

The more parts of your program there are that can modify data, the greater the chance that your program will modify data by mistake, causing it to run incorrectly. When procedures run, they normally do not change any data used by any other part of your program.

Despite the potential for errors, you may still want a procedure to modify data. Normally, when you pass a procedure data, you do so by *value*, which is identified with the ByVal keyword. Parameters passed by value cannot be changed by the procedure. To pass a procedure data that the procedure *can* change, you must pass a parameter by *reference*, identified by the ByRef keyword, like so:

```
Sub MyProcedure (ByRef MyText As String)

End Sub
```

Here, the ByRef keyword tells the procedure that any modifications it makes will be sent back to the part of the program that originally called the procedure and passed it data.

The following code shows how a procedure can accept data by reference, alter it, and send it back to the part of the program that originally sent the data to the procedure:

```
Sub ChangeText(ByRef NewData As String)
        NewData = Replace(NewData, "war", "peace")
End Sub

Private Sub Button1_Click(ByVal sender As System.Object, ByVal e As System.EventArgs)_
Handles Button1.Click
        Dim Message As String
        Message = "I love war."
        MsgBox(Message)
        ChangeText(Message)
        MsgBox(Message)
End Sub
```

In this example, the Button1_Click event procedure creates a Message string variable that stores the string "I love war." The first MsgBox command displays the string "I love war." in a message box. Next, the Button1_Click event procedure calls the ChangeText procedure and passes it the data stored in the Message variable.

The ChangeText procedure stores the contents of the Message variable in the NewData variable, runs the Replace method to replace the string "war" with the string "peace". Then it returns the modified string back to the Button1_Click event procedure, which runs the second MsgBox command, displaying the altered string in the Message variable, *I love peace*.

You can have a combination of ByVal and ByRef variables in your parameter list, like so:

```
Sub ChangeText(ByRef NewData As String, ByVal Num As Integer)
```

Hands-on Tutorial: Passing Parameters to a Procedure

In this tutorial, you'll create a general procedure in a form file and pass a string parameter to the procedure.

1. Start a new Visual Basic project, then click OK. A blank form appears.
2. Choose View ▸ Toolbox to display the Toolbox.
3. Click the Button control in the Toolbox, mouse over the form, and click the left mouse button to create a button.
4. Double-click the Button1 control on the form. The Code window appears.
5. Type ExplodingWindow("This text appears in the title bar.") between the Private Sub and End Sub lines, like so:

```
Private Sub Button1_Click(ByVal sender As System.Object, ByVal e As System.EventArgs)_
Handles Button1.Click
        ExplodingWindow("This text appears in the title bar.")
End Sub
```

The ExplodingWindow command *calls* the ExplodingWindow procedure and passes it the string "This text appears in the title bar."

6. Move the cursor to the line directly above the Private Sub line of the Button1_Click event procedure and add the following lines, so the code now looks like this:

```
Public Class Form1
    Sub ExplodingWindow(ByVal OutsideMsg As String)
```

```
            Dim I As Integer
            Me.Text = OutsideMsg
            For I = 1 To 150
                Me.Size = New Size(I + I, I * 2)
            Next
        End Sub

    Private Sub Button1_Click(ByVal sender As System.Object, ByVal e As_
    System.EventArgs) Handles Button1.Click
            ExplodingWindow("This text appears in the title bar.")
        End Sub
End Class
```

In this listing:

Line 1   Defines the procedure name and its parameter list, which accepts a string (As String) and stores it in the OutsideMsg variable.

Line 2   Creates an integer variable named I.

Line 3   Takes the string stored in the OutsideMsg variable and stores it in the Text property of the form named Form1. Because this code is stored in the Form1 form file, Visual Basic won't let you type a command like: Form1.Text = OutsideMsg. Instead, you have to replace Form1 with the Me keyword so the command looks like: Me.Text = OutsideMsg. The Me keyword helps clarify when your BASIC code is modifying the same form file that it's stored in and when it's modifying a different form file, which you can identify by name such as Form2 or MyPassWordForm.

Lines 4 and 6   Define a For-Next loop that runs 150 times.

Line 5   Changes the Size property of the form in increasing increments to make the window appear to grow or explode on the screen. Instead of typing Form1.Size, you replace Form1 with the Me keyword, so the command looks like: Me.Size.

7.   Press F5. Your user interface appears.

8.   Click the Button1 control. The Button1_Click event procedure calls the ExplodingWindow procedure and passes the string "This text appears in the title bar." Notice that each time you click the Button1 control, the window grows.

9.   Press ALT-F4 to stop your program, then choose File ▶ Close Project. A Close Project dialog box appears. Click Discard.

Creating a Function

Creating
Functions

A function accepts data and returns a value. To create a function, you need to define the function name, the type of data it represents (such as an integer or boolean data type), and the value you want the function to represent, like so:

```
Function FunctionName (Parameter list) As DataType
    Instructions
    Return Value
End Sub
```

where *FunctionName* is the name of your function; *Parameter list* is the list of variables and data types that your function accepts; *Instructions* are one or more lines of BASIC code that manipulate the data from your parameter list; *Value* is the final value that the function calculates; and *DataType* is the type of data the function name represents, such as Integer.

The following code shows how to create a function that accepts an integer, calculates the square of that integer (multiplies that integer by itself).

It returns the result:

```
Function Square(ByVal X As Integer) As Integer
      Return X * X
End Sub

Private Sub Button1_Click(ByVal sender As System.Object, ByVal e As System.EventArgs)_
Handles Button1.Click
    MsgBox (Square(8))
End Sub
```

This example defines a function called `Square`, which accepts an integer value that it stores in variable `X`. Within the `Button1_Click` event procedure, the `MsgBox` command calls the `Square` function and sends it the number 8. The `Square` function stores the value of 8 into `X`, multiples the value of `X` by itself (8 * 8), and returns the answer 64, which appears in the message box created by the `MsgBox` command.

Because a function returns a single value, you can use a function either in place of a value, such as `MsgBox(Square(8))`, or you can assign a variable to a function like so:

```
Dim I As Integer
I = FunctionName(Data)
```

where `FunctionName` is the name of your function and `Data` is the data your program sends to the function.

If we were to rewrite the preceding example it might look like this:

```
Private Sub Button1_Click(ByVal sender As System.Object, ByVal e As System.EventArgs)_
Handles Button1.Click
    Dim I As Integer
    I = Square(8)
      MsgBox (I)
End Sub
```

Both of these methods are equivalent. Some programmers prefer the first method, which treats a function like a variable, while others prefer to first store the value of any function into a descriptive variable name. The second method requires more code but it can be easier to understand.

KEY FEATURES TO REMEMBER

Procedures are miniature programs that contain a set of instructions that often run multiple times. Procedures allow you to break a large program into several smaller ones and to store frequently used instructions in a single location.

- Any general procedures stored in a form file can only be used by other procedures in that same form file.

- Any general procedures stored in a module file can be used by any other part of your program. If you type the word `Private` in front of a general procedure, that procedure can be used only by other procedures stored in that same module file.

- A parameter list defines how many items and the data types a procedure can accept.

- A procedure can modify data if you use the `ByRef` keyword in its parameter list.

- A function represents a single value. When you define a function, you have to define a parameter list, the data type you want the function name to represent, the specific value that you want the function name to represent, and the data type you want the function name to return.

26

UNDERSTANDING OBJECT-ORIENTED PROGRAMMING

The larger the program, the more complicated it can be, and the more difficult it can be to write. It takes time and effort to get a program to work the way you want it to, and once you get it to work, you eventually need to update it or fix problems. If the program is particularly large, fixing all of its parts can seem like a never-ending job.

While people have been writing computer programs for decades, they still haven't gotten much better at writing large programs that work the first time, or that are easy to fix and modify. To make this process a little easier and help programmers create large programs that are easier to modify, computer scientists developed *object-oriented programming*, also known as *OOP*.

Object-oriented programming lets programmers physically divide a large program into smaller parts, based on three core ideas:

- Encapsulation
- Inheritance
- Polymorphism

Understanding Encapsulation

The concepts underlying object-oriented programming are based on dividing a large problem into smaller ones, solving the smaller ones, and then combining the solutions to these smaller problems to create a large program that works.

With traditional programming, you can divide a large program into smaller procedures, but two problems remain. First, while dividing a large program into smaller procedures can make writing a program easier, you must take care that two different procedures don't modify the same data by mistake. This problem can occur especially often when two or more people work on different parts of the same program.

Second, programs typically store *data* in one part of a program (as a variable or inside a data structure) but store the *procedures* that manipulate that data in a different part of a program. As a result, modifying a program to fix or update the way the program works means finding all the places where your program stores data *and* all the places where it changes that data. In a small program, this can be as troublesome as trying to find your car keys in your apartment. But in a large program, this can be as frustrating as trying to find your car keys somewhere inside a 50-story apartment building.

Encapsulation solves both problems by storing data, and the procedures that alter that data, in a single location known as an *object* (see Figure 26-1). Encapsulation hides data from other parts of a program and stores related data in a single location. By hiding data in this manner, encapsulation ensures that no other part of your program can accidentally modify the data incorrectly.

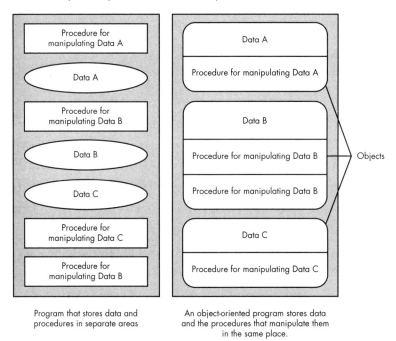

Figure 26-1: Object-oriented programming lets you store data and procedures to manipulate that data in a single location.

Of course, encapsulation doesn't guarantee that the object's own procedures, called *methods*, won't accidentally modify its own data incorrectly. But if your program messes up its own data, you can isolate the problem to any of the methods stored in that object, because that object's methods are the only ones that can manipulate that data.

Encapsulation makes programming easier by protecting data from being changed by other parts of a program and by organizing data and the methods that manipulate it in a single location.

Understanding Inheritance

To make the job of programming faster, programmers often copy part of one program for use in another part of the same program. When a programmer copies and pastes code, two or more identical copies of the same code exist (see Figure 26-2), which also means that if there's a mistake in the copied code, the programmer must correct that same code in every copy scattered throughout the program.

Object-oriented programming solves the problem of copying and reusing code with *inheritance*. With inheritance, one copy of code is trapped inside an object. To reuse the code, you create a new object that inherits the code contained in the first object without physically copying the code.

For example, although Object 2 in Figure 26-3 appears to contain only Code D, Object 2 actually inherits all the code from Object 1 so Object 2 physically contains Code D but can also run Code A, Code B, and Code C—all of which are stored in Object 1.

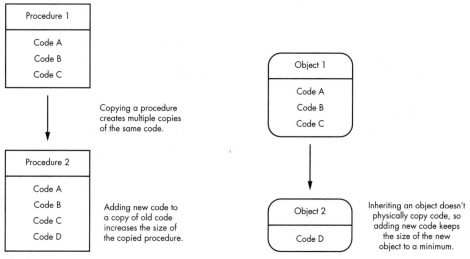

Figure 26-2: Copying code to reuse it means putting identical copies in multiple places, increasing the problems of updating that code.

Figure 26-3: An object can inherit code from another object without actually copying the code.

By using inheritance, you can fix or update the code contained in only one object, and automatically fix or update code contained elsewhere in your program. Inheritance makes programming easier by letting you reuse code without making your program larger and by letting you fix or update code in a single location.

Understanding Polymorphism

Every object organizes code into *methods* (procedures) and gives each method a unique name. When one object inherits code from another object, it inherits the code and the method (procedure) names that manipulate that object's data or properties. For example, if an object has a method named Move, inheriting code from it would create a second object that also has a method named Move with the exact same code inside.

But what if one object represents a monster in a video game and a second object represents an airplane? You'd still want both objects to have a Move method to move the object on the screen, but the code inside each Move method would need to be different, since an airplane object moves differently than a monster object.

To solve this problem, OOP offers a feature called polymorphism. *Polymorphism* means that an object can inherit a method name from another object, but it can substitute new code inside the inherited method name, as shown in Figure 26-4.

When you replace existing code in a method with new code that uses that same method name, you are *overloading* or *overriding*. Overriding old methods with new code is the main idea behind polymorphism. In traditional programming, you can't give two procedures or variables identical names, but in OOP, different objects can share the same method names.

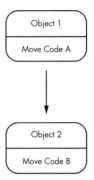

Polymorphism lets an object inherit just a method name and fill it up with new code.

Figure 26-4: Polymorphism lets an object inherit method names from another object but lets you add new code inside it.

Polymorphism makes programming easier by letting you use the same descriptive method name among multiple objects, even if each object's methods contain completely different code.

OOP offers several advantages over traditional programming techniques as shown in Table 26-1.

Table 26-1: Differences Between OOP and Traditional Programming

Task	Object-oriented programming	Traditional programming
Dividing a large program into parts	Organizes data and the procedures that manipulate that data in a single location known as an object.	Data may be stored in one part of a program while the procedures that manipulate them could be stored in a different part of a program, thus making it difficult to know exactly which procedures can alter data and where those procedures might be.
Modifying a program	Objects act like self-contained, isolated building blocks. Changing the way an object works won't accidentally change the way the rest of a program works.	Changing one part of a program might accidentally affect the way another part of a program works.
Reusing code	Objects can be copied and altered without modifying the existing code, thereby eliminating the chance of accidentally affecting other parts of the program.	Code can be copied and reused but may require modifications that could accidentally alter how the rest of the program works.

Problems with Object-Oriented Programming

Of course, OOP isn't a magic solution that lets you write programs faster and that always work correctly. OOP simply provides guidelines that encourage programmers to write well-organized programs, just as traffic laws encourage people to drive cautiously to reduce the risk of crashing. You can still write a sloppy, error-ridden program using OOP (and many people do), but OOP can reduce the chances of doing so.

Perhaps the biggest drawback to OOP is that it's complex, both from the computer and the programmer's points of view. Object-oriented programming requires more memory to run, and learning OOP techniques is much more difficult than learning traditional programming techniques. Because object-oriented programs can be more confusing to understand, they can also be more difficult to modify or reuse, which kind of defeats the theoretical advantages of OOP in the first place.

Can OOP make programming easier and faster? Theoretically, yes. Can OOP make programming more difficult and slower? As many programmers have found out when trying to apply OOP in practical use, the answer is also yes.

Object-oriented programming is a tool, and like any tool it can be used properly or poorly. Object-oriented programming is just another way to write programs regardless of the programming language you ultimately choose to use.

Designing Objects

Objects in a program are meant to mimic items in the real world. For example, if you were writing a video game, one object could represent a monster on the screen, another object could represent a gun that the player controls, and a third object could represent a car.

By developing objects that correspond to the real world, you can create programs that are easier to understand. An object that represents a monster in a video game is much easier to understand than one represented in a traditional program using data structures that store a bunch of numbers and a dozen different procedures that manipulate those numbers.

Every object consists of *data* (called *properties*) and *procedures* (called *methods*) for manipulating that data. Table 26-2 shows examples of different properties and methods for a variety of objects.

Table 26-2: Types of Properties and Methods Used by Objects

Object	Properties	Methods
A monster object in a video game	*X and Y coordinates* define the monster's position on the screen.	*Move* moves the monster on the screen by changing the value of the X and Y coordinates.
	Damage points define how much damage the monster can take before dying.	*Attack* makes the monster attack another object.
	Temper defines whether the monster is friendly, an enemy, or neutral.	*Defend* makes the monster defend against an attack from another object.
	Size defines the monster's physical size as it appears in relation to other objects in the video game.	*Die* removes the monster from the screen.
A printer object in a word processor	*Orientation* defines the printing layout— either Landscape or Portrait.	*Print* tells the printer object to start printing.
	Page size defines the size of the paper to use for printing.	*Stop* tells the printer object to stop printing.
	Copies defines the number of copies to print.	*Pause* tells the printer object to pause printing.

(continued)

Table 26-2: Types of Properties and Methods Used by Objects (continued)

Object	Properties	Methods
A scanner object in an antivirus program	*Disks* defines the number of disk drives to check	*Scan* tells the scanner object to start searching for problems.
	Problems defines the number of potential problems found.	*Stop* tells the scanner object to stop scanning.
	LastUpdate contains the date of the last update to the antivirus program.	*Pause* tells the scanner to stop scanning temporarily.
		Update tells the scanner object to update its database of problems to look for.

NOTE *Although Table 26-2 lists several sample properties and methods for different types of objects, no one-to-one relationship exists between the number of properties and the number of methods that an object can have.*

The way you divide your program into objects, and the type of properties and methods you give each object, are completely arbitrary. There is no "right" way to divide a program into objects or to assign different properties and methods to objects. The right way is the way that makes programming easier for you and anyone else who helps you to write and maintain your program. As a result, the true value of OOP often boils down to the programmer's individual skill. The more you use OOP, the better you'll be at designing objects and learning from your mistakes.

Once you understand the theory behind OOP and the advantages it offers, the next step is to learn how to create object-oriented programs in a particular programming language such as Visual Basic.

Working with Objects in Visual Basic

Under-
standing
How
Objects
Work

As you know, every user interface in Visual Basic consists of objects, such as buttons, check boxes, and pull-down menus. These objects have properties that define their size, color, or appearance, and methods (event procedures) that make them do something.

Creating an object in Visual Basic involves three steps:

1. Create a class file.
2. Write BASIC code inside the class file to define the properties and methods of your object.
3. Declare an object within your actual program (either in a form or module file).

Creating a Class File

A class file simply holds the code needed to define all the data (properties) and procedures (methods) to manipulate that data. You'll need to create one class file for every object you want to create in your program. To create a class file:

1. Choose Project ▶ Add Class. An Add New Item dialog box appears.

2. Type a name for your class file in the Name text box and click Add. Visual Basic displays the Code window for your class file and an empty class file like this:

```
Public Class ClassName

End Class
```

where *ClassName* is the name of the class file that you typed in step 2.

If you have already created a class file and want to modify its contents:

1. Open the Code window for a class file by right-clicking the class filename in the Solution Explorer window and, when a pop-up menu appears, clicking View Code.
2. Click the Code window tab of a class file, then make your changes.

Writing Code in a Class File

Once you've created a class file, you can write code inside it to define a class. A class acts like a blueprint that describes an object. A small program may require only one class file, but a large program might need a dozen or more class files. Every class consists of three parts:

Variables   Stores data temporarily when manipulating data. You'll need at least one variable for each property.

Properties   Contains variables that hold data to share with other parts of your program.

Methods   Include procedures that manipulate any data stored in its properties.

All three parts work together. Each property requires a variable, and each method copies data from a property and stores it in a variable to be manipulated in some way.

Creating Properties

A property definition within a class looks like this:

```
Public Property PropertyName() As PropertyDataType

End Property
```

where *PropertyName* is the name of the property, which can be any name that describes or identifies the property's purpose. The Public keyword lets other parts of your program access your object's property, and *PropertyDataType* is the type of data the property holds, such as integer, string, or double, which can hold a whole number, text, or a decimal number such as 32.456, respectively.

For example, to have your object store a string, you could define a string property called TextDisplay like this:

```
Public Property TextDisplay() As String

End Property
```

To store a string in the TextDisplay property, use code like this:

```
ObjectName.TextDisplay = "Hello, world!"
```

To retrieve the contents from the object's TextDisplay property, you could use code like this:

```
Dim Message As String
Message = ObjectName.TextDisplay
```

An object's properties simply act like variables that contain data that other parts of your program can either retrieve or store data within.

Defining Variables for Each Property

Once you've chosen a name for your property (such as TextDisplay) and defined the type of data it can hold (such as a string or integer), you need to write code to allow that property to store an actual value. But first you must declare a variable outside of your property definition, which represents the same data type as your property. This variable will temporarily store values to retrieve from the property and place modified values back into that property. This *variable declaration* looks like this:

```
Private PropertyVariable1 As PropertyDataType
Public Property PropertyName() As PropertyDataType

End Property
```

where *PropertyVariable1* is the name of your variable, which can be anything useful or convenient. The Private keyword hides this variable from the rest of your program. *PropertyDataType* is the type of data the variable holds, such as integer, string, or double, which must be the same data type used by the property with which you want the variable to work.

Each variable declaration you create is used only within the object itself and is not shared or accessible by any other part of your program. While an object's property holds data, your object doesn't physically manipulate the data stored in its properties. Instead, an object stores data in a property and then copies that data into a variable. The object then manipulates the data stored in the variable and copies the newly calculated result back into the object's property.

Properties are meant to share data with the rest of your program. Variables are meant to copy data out of a property temporarily, perform some calculation on it, and then copy the new result back into the object's property. For example, if you created a property called TextDisplay that holds a string data type, you would need to create an accompanying variable that also holds a string data type, like so:

```
Private Temp As String
    Public Property TextDisplay() As String

    End Property
```

Once you've defined a variable for your property, you need to write additional code to copy the data from the property into the variable you just defined.

Retrieving Data from a Property

To retrieve a value from a property and store it in a variable, use the `Set` and `End Set` commands, like so:

```
Private PropertyVariable1 As PropertyDataType
Public Property PropertyName() As PropertyDataType
    Set(ByVal value As PropertyDataType)
        PropertyVariable1 = value
    End Set
End Property
```

The `Set(ByVal value As PropertyDataType)` command retrieves the data stored in the object's property. The `PropertyVariable1 = value` line copies the data from the object's property and stores it in the `PropertyVariable1` temporary variable. The `End Set` line simply marks the end of the BASIC code that retrieves data from the object's property. At this point, the object stores identical data in both `PropertyName` and `PropertyVariable1`.

The Set-End Set block needs to contain only a single line of code that copies the data from the object's property into a temporary variable. For example, if you created a property called `TextDisplay` that holds a string data type, you would need to create a Set-End Set block to copy the data from the `TextDisplay` property into the `Temp` variable, like so:

```
Private Temp As String
    Public Property TextDisplay() As String
        Set(ByVal value As String)
            Temp = value
        End Set
    End Property
```

Storing New Data into a Property

Once you've written a Set-End Set block to retrieve data from a property, you also need to write additional code to store new data back into a property. To do so, create a Get-End Get block of code like this:

```
Private PropertyVariable1 As PropertyDataType
Public Property PropertyName() As PropertyDataType
    Get
        Return PropertyVariable1
    End Get
    Set(ByVal value As Integer)
        PropertyVariable1 = value
    End Set
End Property
```

The Get-End Get block needs only one line of code, which uses the `Return` keyword that copies the contents of the `PropertyVariable1` back into the `PropertyName`. For example, if you created a property called `TextDisplay` that holds a string data type, you would need to create an accompanying variable that also holds a string data type, like so:

```
Private Temp As String
    Public Property TextDisplay() As String
        Get
```

```
        Return Temp
    End Get
    Set(ByVal value As String)
        Temp = value
    End Set
End Property
```

Every property needs both a Get-End Get and Set-End Set block that retrieves data from an object's property and stuffs data back into the property. Once you've defined an object's property, you still need to write code that actually manipulates or uses the data stored in its properties.

Writing Methods to Change Data

A method can either change the data stored in an object's property or use the data in some way, such as displaying it on the screen. To write a method, you create a general procedure inside your class file, like so:

```
Public Sub MethodName()
    Instructions
End Sub
```

where *MethodName* is the name of your method, which should describe what the method does, such as Move to move the object or Color to color the object. The Public keyword lets other parts of your program *call* your method and tell your object to do something. *Instructions* contains one or more lines of code that uses or changes the value of a variable that has already retrieved a value from a property.

A simple object definition might look like the following, stored in a class file:

```
Public Class ClassName
    Dim PropertyVariable1 As PropertyDataType

    Property PropertyName() As PropertyDataType
        Get
            Return PropertyVariable1
        End Get
        Set(ByVal value As PropertyDataType)
            PropertyVariable1 = value
        End Set
    End Property

    Sub MethodName()
        Instructions
    End Sub
End Class
```

As you can see, a class consists of three parts:

Variables A variable copies data from a property, lets an object's methods manipulate the value stored in that variable, and then assigns this modified value back into the property. You need to declare at least one variable for each property you define.

Properties Each property can hold one chunk of data, such as a string or integer. Each property consists of a Get-End Get block to retrieve a value from its property and a Set-End Set block that stores a modified value back into that property. There is no fixed number of properties an object can hold.

Methods Methods contain code to change, alter, and manipulate data retrieved from an object's properties. There is no fixed number of methods an object can hold.

Declaring an Object

Once you've defined a class in a class file, the final step is to create an object based on that class. You can create an object in a form or module file (but not in a class file) with this syntax:

```
Dim ObjectName As New ClassName
```

ObjectName is the name of your object. This name should describe what the object represents, such as Car or Scanner. *ClassName* is the name of the class file that contains the class you want to create.

Hands-on Tutorial: Creating and Using Objects

In this tutorial, you'll create a simple object with a single property and two methods, and then actually use that object in a program.

1. Start a new Visual Basic project, then click OK. A blank form appears.
2. Choose Project ▶ Add Class. An Add New Item dialog box appears.
3. Click Add. The Code window appears, displaying a blank class file.
4. Right-click between the Public Class and End Class lines. A pop-up menu appears.
5. Click Insert Snippet. Another pop-up menu appears.
6. Double-click Visual Basic Language. Another pop-up menu appears.
7. Scroll down this list and double-click Define A Property. Visual Basic Express creates generic BASIC code for defining a property:

```
Public Class Class1
    ' Declare the variable the property uses.
    Private XValue As Integer

    Public Property X() As Integer
        Get
            Return XValue
        End Get
        Set(ByVal value As Integer)
            XValue = value
        End Set
    End Property
End Class
```

This code defines a property called X and a private variable called XValue, both of which can hold integer data types.

8. Move the cursor to the Private XValue As Integer line and replace Integer with String so the entire line looks like: Private XValue As String. Notice that Visual Basic Express automatically replaces Integer with String throughout your class file.
9. Click in front of the last line, End Class, and press ENTER.

10. Type the following two methods:

```
Public Sub Reverse()
        XValue = StrReverse(XValue)
End Sub

Public Sub Display()
        MsgBox(XValue)
End Sub
```

The first method, named Reverse, takes the current value of the XValue variable and reverses the string using the StrReverse function (see Chapter 20 for more on this function). The second method, Display, takes the string stored in the XValue variable and displays it in a message box using the MsgBox command. (Notice that methods never use properties directly; they use only the variable associated with a particular property.)

11. Click the Form1.vb [Design] tab near the top of the Code window. A blank form appears.

12. Choose View ▶ Toolbox to display the Toolbox.

13. Click the Button control in the Toolbox, mouse over the form, and click the left mouse button to create a button.

14. Double-click the Button1 control on the form. The Code window appears.

15. Type the following in between the Private Sub and End Sub lines:

```
Private Sub Button1_Click(ByVal sender As System.Object, ByVal e As System.EventArgs)_
Handles Button1.Click
        Dim TextObject As New Class1
        TextObject.X = "Bo the Cat"
        TextObject.Display()
        TextObject.Reverse()
        TextObject.Display()
End Sub
```

In this listing:

Line 1 Defines an object called TextObject, based on the definition stored in the Class1 class file.

Line 2 Assigns the string "Bo the Cat" into the X property of TextObject.

Line 3 Runs the TextObject's Display method.

Line 4 Runs the TextObject's Reverse method.

Line 5 Runs the TextObject's Display method again.

16. Press F5. Your user interface appears.

17. Click the Button1 control. A message box appears and displays *Bo the Cat* on the screen. This message box appears because of the first TextObject.Display() command you typed in step 15.

18. Click OK. A second message box appears, displaying the text *taC eht oB* on the screen. The TextObject.Reverse() command reversed the string stored in the TextObject.X property and the second TextObject.Display() command displays the message box with the reversed string. (Notice that your Button1_Click event procedure never sees

or accesses the way the TextObject stores data or manipulates it.) Click OK to close the second message box.

19. Press ALT-F4 to stop your program, then choose File ▶ Close Project. A Close Project dialog box appears. Click Discard.

Working with Inheritance

When you want to reuse code stored in another object, you need to use inheritance. To inherit code from another object, you need to use the Inherits keyword as the first line in another class file, such as:

```
Public Class NewClassName
    Inherits ExistingClassName
End Class
```

where NewClassName is the name of a new class file and ExistingClassName is the name of an existing class file that contains the code you want to copy.

As you can see, inheriting code is much simpler than copying and pasting code from one class to another. Too, any changes made to the first class file automatically change the code in the inherited class file.

Hands-on Tutorial: Inheriting from Objects

This tutorial shows you how to create a simple class and inherit its code for use in a second class.

1. Start a new Visual Basic Express project, then click Windows Application and click OK. A blank form appears.
2. Choose Project ▶ Add Class. An Add New Item dialog box appears.
3. Click Add. The Code window appears, displaying a blank class file.
4. Right-click between Public Class and End Class lines. A pop-up menu appears.
5. Click Insert Snippet. Another pop-up menu appears.
6. Double-click Visual Basic Language. Another pop-up menu appears.
7. Scroll down this list and double-click Define A Property. Visual Basic Express creates generic BASIC code for defining a property.
8. Move the cursor after the End Property line and press ENTER. Type in a method named Increase so the entire code looks like this:

```
Public Class Class1
    ' Declare the variable the property uses.
    Private XValue As Integer

    Public Property X() As Integer
        Get
            Return XValue
        End Get
        Set(ByVal value As Integer)
            XValue = value
        End Set
```

```
        End Property

        Public Sub Increase()
      XValue = XValue * 3
        End Sub
End Class
```

The `Public Sub Increase()` line defines a method named `Increase`. It contains a single line of BASIC code that multiplies the value of `XValue` by 3.

9. Choose Project ▶ Add Class. An Add New Item dialog box appears.

10. Click Add. The Code window appears and displays an empty class named Class2.

11. Type `Inherits Class1` between the `Public Class` and `End Class` lines. This essentially copies all the code you created in step 8 and stores it in your new Class2 file. Your code should look like the following:

```
Public Class Class2
    Inherits Class1
End Class
```

12. Move the cursor to the end of the `Inherits Class1` line, press ENTER, and right-click the mouse. A pop-up menu appears.

13. Choose Insert Snippet. Another pop-up menu appears.

14. Double-click Visual Basic Language. Another pop-up menu appears.

15. Double-click Define A Property. Visual Basic Express creates generic code for defining a property.

16. Click in the `Private XValue As Integer` line and change the *X* to a *Y* so the line reads `Private YValue As Integer`. Visual Basic Express automatically changes the *X* to a *Y* throughout the class file, so your entire class file should look like this:

```
Public Class Class2
    Inherits Class1
    ' Declare the variable the property uses.
    Private YValue As Integer

    Public Property Y() As Integer
        Get
            Return YValue
        End Get
        Set(ByVal value As Integer)
            YValue = value
        End Set
    End Property
End Class
```

17. Click the Form1.vb [Design] tab near the top of the Code window. A blank form appears.

18. Choose View ▶ Toolbox to display the Toolbox.

19. Click the Button control in the Toolbox, mouse over the form, and click the left mouse button to create a button.

20. Double-click the Button1 control on the form. The Code window appears.

21. Type the following between the Private Sub and End Sub lines:

```
Private Sub Button1_Click(ByVal sender As System.Object, ByVal e As System.EventArgs)_
Handles Button1.Click
        Dim ObjectOne As New Class1
        Dim ObjectTwo As New Class2
        ObjectOne.X = 23
        ObjectTwo.X = 8
        ObjectTwo.Y = 6
        MsgBox(ObjectOne.X)
        MsgBox(ObjectTwo.X)
        ObjectOne.Increase()
        ObjectTwo.Increase()
        MsgBox(ObjectOne.X)
        MsgBox(ObjectTwo.X)
End Sub
```

In this listing:

Line 1 Defines an object called ObjectOne, based on the definition stored in the Class1 class file. ObjectOne contains a property called X and a method called Increase.

Line 2 Defines an object called ObjectTwo, based on the definition stored in the Class2 class file. ObjectTwo contains a property called X and a method called Increase, both of which it inherits from the Class1 file. ObjectTwo also contains a Y property, which is explicitly defined in the Class2 file.

Line 3 Stores the value 23 into the X property of ObjectOne.

Line 4 Stores the value 8 in the X property of ObjectTwo.

Line 5 Stores the value 6 to the Y property of ObjectTwo.

Line 6 Uses the MsgBox command to display a message box that displays the contents of ObjectOne's X property, which is *23*.

Line 7 Uses the MsgBox command to display a message box that displays the contents of ObjectTwo's X property, which is *8*.

Line 8 Runs the Increase method on the X property of ObjectOne.

Line 9 Runs the Increase method on the X property of ObjectTwo.

Line 10 Runs the MsgBox command again to display the contents of the X property of ObjectOne.

Line 11 Runs the MsgBox command to display the contents of the X property of ObjectTwo.

22. Press F5. Your user interface appears.
23. Click the Button1 control. A message box appears and displays *23*, which is the value of ObjectOne's X property.
24. Click OK. A second message box appears, displaying *8*, which is the value of ObjectTwo's X property.
25. Click OK. A third message box appears, displaying *69*, which is the new value of ObjectOne's X property that the ObjectOne.Increase() line has modified.
26. Click OK. A fourth message box appears, displaying *24*, which is the new value of ObjectTwo's X property that the ObjectTwo.Increase() line has modified.
27. Click OK to make the second message box go away.

28. Press ALT-F4 to stop your program, then choose File ▸ Save All. A Save Project dialog box appears.

29. Type ObjectExample and click Save.

Working with Polymorphism

Polymorphism lets you change an inherited method while retaining the method's original name. As a result, polymorphism prevents you from having to create different method names for different objects. When an object inherits another object's method names but changes the BASIC code inside of a method, it is *overloading* or *overriding* a method.

To use polymorphism, you need to:

- Create an object and define one or more properties and methods using the Overridable keyword. Any property or method not defined with the Overridable keyword cannot be overridden by another object.

- Create a new object that inherits properties and methods from another object and identify all overridden properties or methods with the Overrides keyword.

To define which properties and methods in an object can later be overridden by other objects, you need to include the Public keyword with the Overridable keyword, like so:

```
Public Class Class1
    Public x As Integer

    Public Property xspot() As Integer
        Get
            Return x
        End Get
        Set(ByVal value As Integer)
            x = value
        End Set
    End Property

    Public Overridable Sub Change()
        x = x - 5
    End Sub
End Class
```

In this example, the Class1 file specifies that the Change method can be overridden, but the xspot property cannot be overridden because the xspot property is not defined with the Overridable keyword.

The following code creates a second class file named Class2, which inherits code from Class1. To override an overridable defined property or method, use the Overrides keyword with the Public keyword, like so:

```
Public Class Class2
    Inherits Class1
    Private y As Integer
    Public Property yspot() As Integer
        Get
            Return y
        End Get
        Set(ByVal value As Integer)
```

```
            y = value
        End Set
    End Property
    Public Overrides Sub Change()
        x = x - 5
        y = y + 5
    End Sub
End Class
```

To test out the inherited Class2 file, you could use the following code in a button's event procedure:

```
Dim test As New Class2
test.xspot = 11
test.yspot = 20
test.Change()
MsgBox(test.xspot)
MsgBox(test.yspot)
```

In this listing:

Line 1 Defines test as a new object based on the Class2 file, which inherits code from the Class1 file.

Line 2 Stores the value 11 into the xspot property of the test object. The xspot property was originally defined in the Class1 file but inherited in the Class2 file.

Line 3 Stores the value 20 in the yspot property of the test object. The yspot property is defined in the Class2 file.

Line 4 Runs the Change method. Although there are two Change methods, one stored in the Class1 file and the other stored in the Class2 file, the test object is based on the Class2 file. So the Change method that runs is the one defined in the Class2 file. In this case, the Change method subtracts 5 from the value stored in the xspot property and adds 5 to the value stored in the yspot property.

Line 5 Runs the MsgBox command to display the value of the xspot property of the test object. In this case, it's 11 – 5, or 6.

Line 6 Runs the MsgBox command to display the value of the yspot property of the test object. In this case, it's 20 + 5, or 25.

Hands-on Tutorial: Playing with Polymorphism

This tutorial builds on the last tutorial program where you created a class file that inherited properties and methods from another class file. If you haven't followed "Hands-on Tutorial: Inheriting from Objects" on page 367, go back and do so now.

In this tutorial, you'll modify the class files you used in the inheritance tutorial to override both a property and a method.

1. Load Visual Basic Express.

2. Choose File ▸ Recent Projects and click the ObjectExample project that you created in the previous tutorial.

3. Right-click the Class1 file in the Solution Explorer window and choose View Code. The Code window appears.

4. Replace the `Public Sub` lines with `Public Overridable Sub`, so your code looks like this:

```
Public Class Class1
    ' Declare the variable the property uses.
    Public XValue As Integer

    Public Property X() As Integer
        Get
            Return XValue
        End Get
        Set(ByVal value As Integer)
            XValue = value
        End Set
    End Property

    Public Overridable Sub Increase()
  XValue = XValue * 3
    End Sub
End Class
```

The `Public Overridable` keywords allow any other class files to inherit the `Increase` method name but change the Visual Basic code stored in the `Increase` method.

5. Right-click the Class2 file in the Solution Explorer window and choose View Code. The Code window appears and displays the Class2 file.

6. Type the boldfaced code so that the Code window looks like this:

```
Public Class Class2
    Inherits Class1
    ' Declare the variable the property uses.
    Private YValue As Integer

    Public Property Y() As Integer
        Get
            Return YValue
        End Get
        Set(ByVal value As Integer)
            YValue = value
        End Set
    End Property

    Public Overrides Sub Increase()
        XValue = XValue + YValue
    End Sub
End Class
```

Notice that the original Increase method (in the Class1 file) simply multiplied the XValue variable by 3. However, this new Increase method uses the Public Overrides keywords to redefine the Increase method to add the YValue variable to the XValue variable instead.

7. Press F5. Your user interface appears.

8. Click the Button1 control on the form. A message box appears, displaying the number *23*, which is the original value stored in ObjectOne's X property.

9. Click OK. A second message box appears, displaying the number *8*, which is the original value of ObjectTwo's X property.

10. Click OK. A third message box appears, displaying the number *69*, which is the newly calculated result from the Increase method stored in the Class1 file.

11. Click OK. A fourth message box appears, displaying the number *14*, which is the calculation of the new Increase method stored in the Class2 file, which adds the value of XValue (8) to the value of YValue (6).

12. Click OK to make the message box go away.

13. Press ALT-F4 to stop the program, then choose File ▶ Save All to save the changes you made.

KEY FEATURES TO REMEMBER

Object-oriented programming provides guidelines for organizing your program into independent parts known as objects. The three main features of object-oriented programming are encapsulation, inheritance, and polymorphism.

- Encapsulation lumps data and procedures that manipulate that data in a single location.

- Inheritance allows you to copy code from one object and use it in another without physically making duplicate copies of that code.

- Polymorphism lets you inherit a method name but substitute its original code with new code.

- A class file is where you can write BASIC code to define the properties and methods of an object.

- Every property definition in a class file needs an accompanying variable declared in that same class file.

- Properties contain data. Methods contain procedures for manipulating that data.

- To create an object, you need to declare a variable as a class.

- To override a method, you must declare a method with the Public Overridable keywords. Then you must create a new method, with the same name, using the Public Overrides keywords.

27

COMMENTS, ERROR HANDLING, AND DEBUGGING

No program ever works 100 percent correctly. When a company like Microsoft develops a product, free *beta versions* are sent to people who test the program to see how well it works—or doesn't work. When enough people report identical problems, the programmers sift through the code to find what might be wrong. Any problem that keeps a program from working 100 percent correctly is known as a *bug*, and the process of identifying and fixing these problems is known as *debugging*.

Every new program contains bugs. Programmers try to eliminate bugs in three ways:

- By writing simple, easy-to-understand code that can be read and fixed by any competent programmer
- By writing code that traps errors so that when bugs do occur, they don't stop the program from working
- By exhaustively running a program and examining its behavior to root out bugs and wipe them out

Identifying Bugs

Bugs are nothing more than mistakes in a program. Some mistakes can be relatively harmless, such as a window not displaying the colors intended. Other bugs, called *showstoppers*, are more drastic and can keep a program from working at all. Generally, you'll find three types of bugs in a program:

- Syntax errors
- Logic errors
- Run-time errors

Identifying Syntax Errors

Syntax errors occur when the programmer mistypes a language command, such as spelling a variable one way, and then spelling it differently the second time it is used. When Visual Basic Express finds a syntax error, it highlights it with a squiggly line and displays a brief description of the problem when you mouse over the line (see Figure 27-1).

Visual Basic Express highlights errors in your code

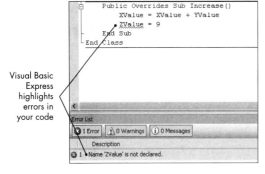

Figure 27-1: Visual Basic Express highlights syntax errors so you can fix them.

In addition to spelling errors, syntax errors can also be caused by typing in the wrong number of parameters for a procedure. For example, the Math.Sqrt function expects a single number, like so:

```
Dim I As Single
I = Math.Sqrt(90)
```

However, if you gave the Math.Sqrt function too many parameters, the result would be a syntax error. In the following example, the Math.Sqrt function doesn't know what to do with three numbers when it's expecting only one number. The result is a syntax error.

```
Dim I As Single
I = Math.Sqrt(90, 4.5, 210)
```

Visual Basic Express won't let you run a program until you fix all the syntax errors identified in it.

Identifying Logic Errors

Syntax errors are fairly easy to root out and destroy, but *logic errors* are more difficult to find and fix. Logic errors occur when you write your code correctly, but your code doesn't work exactly the way it should.

For example, the following BASIC code stuffs four integers into an array and then uses the MsgBox command to display the contents of the array, one item at a time. While this code works, there's a problem: the For-Next loop starts counting at 1, so the first element it displays with the MsgBox command is the second element of the array, not the first one. (Remember that the first element in an array is located at index position 0, not 1.)

```
Dim MyArray() As Integer = {23, 45, 908, 2}
    Dim I As Integer
    For I = 1 To 4
        MsgBox(MyArray(I))
    Next
```

Logic errors can be extremely difficult to find and correct because you have to search for flaws in your own thought process. Visual Basic will happily run a program riddled with logic errors, and none of those errors may be apparent until the user does something that triggers a logic error that stops your program from working correctly.

Identifying Run-Time Errors

Run-time errors can also be tough bugs to find and correct. Your code may work perfectly and your logic may be impeccable, but run-time errors can still occur when your program receives unexpected data from the outside world—such as user input. Such unexpected data can cause your program to crash or behave erratically.

The following code asks the user to enter his or her age, multiplies the age by 7, and then displays the age in dog years. This code works correctly every time—except if the user types in a negative number. Although the code still works, it returns a nonsensical number, because nobody we know of can have an age that's a negative number.

```
Dim I, J As Integer
I = InputBox("How old are you?")
J = I * 7
MsgBox("In dog years, you would be " & CStr(J) & " years old.")
```

Run-time errors occur when your code makes assumptions that the real world doesn't understand. For example, if someone enters his age as a negative number, a run-time error would result.

Because you can't know what type of data someone might try to give your program, you may never be able to foresee and correct all possible problems ahead of time. This is why a program can sometimes work perfectly for years, and then suddenly start messing up when it receives unexpected data.

As with logic errors, finding run-time errors involves examining any incorrect assumptions you made about what type of data your program will receive both now and in the future.

Clarifying Your Code

Nobody purposely writes a bug into a program because they want their program to work. Because you can never guarantee that you'll never write a flawed program (logic error) or write a program that expects the outside world to behave a certain way all the time (run-time error), the best you can do is to write programs that are easy to understand and fix. The basic rules for doing so are simple.

Keep Programs Short

The shorter and smaller the program, the easier it can be to understand. When tackling a large program, divide the program into smaller, easier to understand chunks. As a general rule, if a chunk of code, such as a procedure or an object's method, can't be viewed easily on one or two screens, it's probably too long.

Write Simple Code

Trying to read and understand how a three-line program works will always be easier than trying to read and understand how a 300-line program works. However, sometimes shorter isn't always better, because it's possible to use language shortcuts that take up less space but which can be much more difficult to understand. Visual Basic, like every programming language, offers shortcuts that can be easier to write but confusing to understand.

For example, consider the cryptic IIf function in the last line of the following BASIC code:

```
Dim Number As Integer
Number = InputBox("Type a number from 1 to 10.")
MsgBox(IIf(Number < 5, "Less than five.", "Equal or greater than five."))
```

Can you guess what this code does? The IIf function is a shortcut for the If-Then-Else statement. So although the IIf function can make your program shorter, it's not as easy to read and understand as the following, which is slightly longer but equivalent to the code above:

```
Dim Number As Integer
Number = InputBox("Type a number from 1 to 10.")
If Number < 5 Then
    MsgBox("Less than five.")
Else
    MsgBox("Equal or greater than five.")
End If
```

Use Descriptive Names for Variables

Visual Basic doesn't care what names you give your variables. As far as Visual Basic is concerned, the following are both perfectly good variable declarations:

```
Dim Age As Integer
Dim Xc893Goo_p As Integer
```

The first step to naming variables is to give them short but descriptive names that identify the type of data they contain. An Age variable most likely contains a number that represents how old somebody may be, but a Xc893Goo_p variable gives no clue as to what type of data it may contain. Also, keep in mind that the longer a variable name, the more likely you will misspell it.

Adding Comments

Writing small chunks of easy-to-understand code and using descriptive variable names can help you (or another programmer) understand how your code works so you (or they) will know how to fix or update it later. Still, none of this can be as helpful as having written *comments* embedded in a program. Comments explain to anyone reading your program just how a chunk of code works, what type of data it expects, how it calculates a new result, and what type of data it spits out for another part of the program to use.

Comments are text that's included in a program, marked in such a way that the computer knows to ignore them. To create a comment in Visual Basic, you use either the REM keyword or the single quote symbol (') in front of any text that you want the computer to ignore, like so:

```
REM This program written by John Smith
' This code written by an outsourced programmer
```

The computer ignores anything that appears to the right of either the REM keyword or the single quote symbol.

NOTE *To help you identify comments in your code, Visual Basic Express displays them in green text.*

A comment can take up an entire line or only part of a line, as shown here:

```
REM This program calculates the state sales tax
REM Program written on April 1, 2006 by Joe Smith
REM Last updated on December 3, 2006 by Amy Jackson

Dim Total, TaxRate As Single

' Total retrieved from the TextBox1.Text
' TaxRate retrieved from the TextBox2.Text

Total = Total * TaxRate ' Fix code in case Total < 0
MsgBox (Total)
```

To increase readability, you may want to insert blank lines between comments and actual code. Although the preceding code looks large because of the extra spaces and comments, the computer ignores all extra lines and comments and treats the code as though it looked like this:

```
Dim Total, TaxRate As Single
Total = Total * TaxRate
MsgBox (Total)
```

Because comments can make one or more lines of code invisible to the computer, you can also use comments to hide code temporarily that you suspect may be causing an error or bug in your program. For example, consider the following code:

```
Dim x, a, b, c As Single
x = (-b + Math.Sqrt((b ^ 2) - (4 * a * c))) / (2 * a))
MsgBox (x)
```

If you wanted to see how your program would run without the second line in this listing, you could erase it, but then you'd have to type it back in if you wanted to use it again. Instead of erasing a line, you can comment it out, which essentially tells the computer to ignore it:

```
Dim x, a, b, c As Single
' x = (-b + Math.Sqrt((b ^ 2) - (4 * a * c))) / (2 * a))
MsgBox (x)
```

The single quote symbol in front of the second line turns the entire second line into a comment. The computer would then treat the code as though it looked like this:

```
Dim x, a, b, c As Single

MsgBox (x)
```

By removing the single quote symbol, you can convert a comment back into working code without having to retype anything.

Adding REM or the single quote symbol can be handy to hide one or more lines of code temporarily, but if you want to comment out multiple lines, adding and erasing the REM or single quote symbol in front of each line can be tedious. As a shortcut, Visual Basic Express lets you highlight multiples lines of code and automatically comment and uncomment out the entire highlighted code.

To comment out multiple lines of code, follow these steps:

1. Highlight one or more lines of code.
2. Click the Comment Out The Selected Lines icon on the Standard toolbar.

Visual Basic Express automatically inserts the single quote symbol in front of your highlighted lines, turning every highlighted line into a comment, as shown in Figure 27-2. This technique, however, works only if the multiple lines of code are sequential.

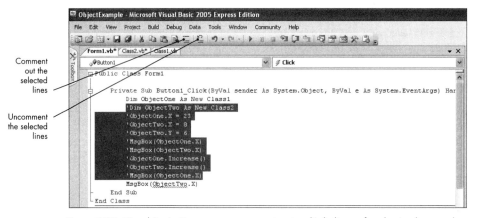

Figure 27-2: Visual Basic Express can comment out multiple lines of code simultaneously.

To uncomment out multiple lines of code:

1. Highlight one or more lines of comments in your code.
2. Click the Uncomment The Selected Lines icon on the Standard toolbar (see Figure 27-2). Visual Basic Express automatically removes the single quote symbol in front of the highlighted lines.

Although comments don't affect your program's behavior, they serve three important functions:

Summary If you put comments in front of a chunk of code, you can describe your assumptions, list the names of previous programmers who wrote or modified the code, and show where the code expects to receive data and where it expects to send out data.

Explanation Comments can provide detailed explanations about how chunks of code work when their purpose or behavior isn't obvious at first glance.

Testing Comments can temporarily remove one or more lines of code from your program without physically erasing them. By doing this, you can determine whether removing certain lines of code changes the behavior of your program, to help you fix any bugs.

Trapping Errors

Using the
Try-Catch
Statement

Comments, small and simple programs, and descriptive variable names can all help you write code that's easier to understand. However, because you can never eliminate the possibility of bugs creeping into your programs, no matter how careful you may be, it's best to plan and prepare for them. One problem with bugs is that they often occur in one part of a program but wind up affecting an entirely different part of the program, which makes tracking down the cause that much more troublesome.

To isolate or trap bugs in the part of your program where they occur, Visual Basic offers a Try-Catch statement that looks like this:

```
Try
    Instructions to run
Catch ex As Exception
    Instructions to handle error
End Try
```

where `Instructions to run` contains the code you want to run, `ex` is a special variable that identifies the exact error that occurred, and `Instructions to handle error` contains instructions to deal with errors that may occur.

When your program runs, it always runs the code directly underneath the `Try` keyword. The code sandwiched between the `Catch` and `End Try` keywords runs only if an error occurs.

By using the Try-Catch-End Try statements in every procedure or method in your program, your program can notify you of run-time errors and pinpoint exactly where they occur in your program.

NOTE *The Try-Catch-End Try statement is great for catching run-time errors, but it won't help you to find logic errors. The reason is that logic errors occur when the code works correctly from the computer's point of view, but doesn't do what you wanted it to do because of your own mistakes.*

Hands-on Tutorial: Catching Errors with the Try-Catch Statement

Normally, if your program encounters an error, it may crash or stubbornly attempt to run anyway but wind up not working correctly. If you use the Try-Catch statement, your program will not crash but can run BASIC code specifically designed to handle the error. In this tutorial, you'll see how the Try-Catch statement can display an error message to help you identify a problem that might normally crash your program.

1. Start a new Visual Basic project, then click OK. A blank form appears.

2. Choose View ▶ Toolbox. The Toolbox appears.

3. Click the Button control, mouse over the form, and click the left mouse button to create a button control on your form.

4. Double-click this button control. The Code window appears.

5. Type the following code so the entire event procedure looks like this:

```
Private Sub Button1_Click(ByVal sender As System.Object, ByVal e As System.EventArgs)_
Handles Button1.Click
    Dim x, y As Byte
    x = 20
    y = 40
    Try
        x = x - y
        MsgBox(x)
    Catch ex As Exception
        MsgBox(ex.ToString)
    End Try
End Sub
```

6. Press F11 to run the Step Into command. This lets you examine how your program works, line by line, as explained in the section "Debugging Your Program" on page 383. Your user interface appears.

7. Click the Button1 control. The Code window highlights the `Private Sub` line.

8. Press F11. The Code window highlights the `x = 20` line.

9. Press F11. The Code window highlights the `y = 40` line.

10. Press F11. The Code window highlights the `Try` line.

11. Press F11. The Code window highlights the `x = x - y` line. This assigns the value of `20 - 40`, or `-20`, to the value of x. Because `-20` lies outside the byte data range (byte data types can hold only values from 0 to 255), this causes an error.

12. Press F11. Because `-20` lies outside the byte data range, Visual Basic immediately skips over the `MsgBox(x)` command and jumps straight to the `Catch ex As Exception` line, where you can trap errors.

13. Press F11. The Code window highlights the `MsgBox(ex.ToString)` line.

14. Press F11. The `MsgBox(ex.ToString)` command runs and displays a message box on screen that tells you exactly what error occurred, as shown in Figure 27-3. The error message displayed in Figure 27-3 gives the line number where the error occurred (line 8) and displays a brief description of the problems ("Arithmetic operation resulted in an overflow.") The `MsgBox (ex.ToString)` command is just an example of what you could insert in the Try-Catch-End Try statement to notify you of errors. Because displaying an error message won't help an ordinary user of your program, you may want to insert different code that gracefully allows your program to recover from the error, such as ignoring the error or using a default value, rather than displaying an error message that the user can't do anything about anyway.

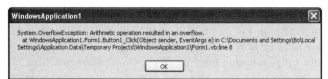

Figure 27-3: By inserting a MsgBox command in a Try-Catch-End Try statement, you can see the exact cause of an error in your code.

15. Click OK to close the message box. The Code window highlights the End Try line.
16. Choose Debug ▶ Stop Debugging to stop debugging.
17. Choose File ▶ Save All. A Save Project dialog box appears.
18. Type **TryCatch** and click Save.

Debugging Your Program

Debugging
a Program

Your first line of defense against bugs is to write short and easy-to-understand code. Your second line of defense is to use the Try-Catch-End Try statement to trap bugs. As a third line of defense, you can examine your code while your program is running to see exactly what your program is doing, line by line. This process is known as *debugging*.

By watching your program run line by line, you can immediately spot the line that's causing the error. Once you know where in your program an error is occurring, and how it's happening, you can (hopefully) rewrite your program to fix the problem.

NOTE   *Sometimes a solution to a problem can be worse than the original problem. Programmers have been known to fix one bug, only to create an even bigger problem by mistake. If this happens, you'll just have to debug your revised program over again, line by line.*

Stepping Line by Line

Stepping means that Visual Basic highlights each line of code as it runs so that you can see what happens next. To *step* through a program, use the Step Into command to begin running your program by clicking the Step Into icon on the standard toolbar.

Your program's user interface will appear as normal, but the moment you cause a command to run by clicking a button or choosing a pull-down menu, the Code window will pop up and Visual Basic will highlight the first line of code that's running, as shown in Figure 27-4.

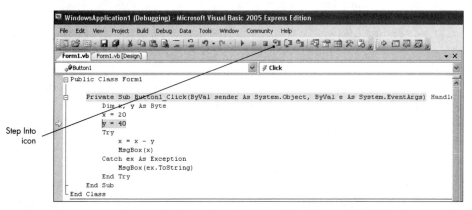

Figure 27-4: When you step through a program, Visual Basic Express highlights the currently running line.

While you're stepping through your code line by line, another part of your program's user interface may appear, such as a dialog box. When this happens, you'll have to choose an option from the user interface (click a button, pull-down menu, or whatever) before you can see the next line of code currently running.

Watching Your Variables

Stepping through a program line by line can show you which line of code your program runs next, which can be handy for seeing which chunk of code runs in an If-Then or Select-Case statement. While seeing which line of code runs next can help you determine how your program works, you may also want to know how each line of code may be changing the data stored in your program's variables. The moment you see which variable may be storing incorrect data, you'll also know which line of code is responsible for doing this.

Examining the contents of your variables as your program runs is known as *watching*. To *watch* the value of a variable, follow these steps:

1. Click the Step Into icon on the standard toolbar.
2. Highlight the variable that you want to examine.
3. Choose Debug ▸ QuickWatch. The QuickWatch dialog box appears, as shown in Figure 27-5.
4. Click Add Watch. Visual Basic Express displays the chosen variable in a Watch window at the bottom of the screen. (If you don't click the Add Watch button, you can watch your variables change only as long as the QuickWatch dialog box remains on screen. To take a quick peek at a variable, use the QuickWatch dialog box; to track how a variable changes over a longer period of time, it's probably more convenient to add variables to the Watch window at the bottom of the screen.)

Figure 27-5: The QuickWatch dialog box lets you select a variable to watch or give a variable a different value.

5. Click Close to close the QuickWatch dialog box.
6. Choose the Step Into command. As soon as a line of code changes the value of the variable you chose in step 2, you can see its new value, as shown in Figure 27-6.

If you no longer want to watch a variable, you can remove it from the Watch window by following these steps:

1. Right-click the variable you want to remove in the Watch window. A pop-up menu appears.
2. Click Delete Watch or Clear All (to clear all the variables displayed in the Watch window), as shown in Figure 27-7.

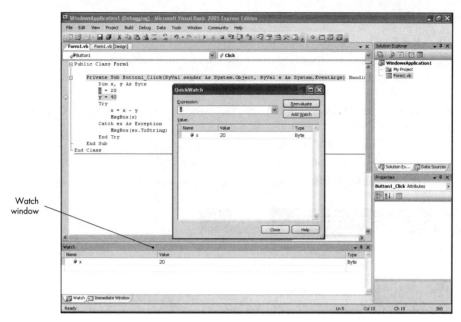

Watch
window

Figure 27-6: The Watch window shows the current values and data types of your program's variables.

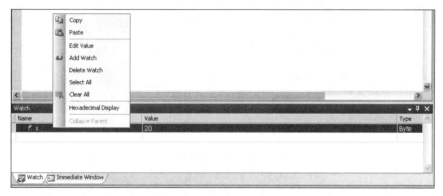

Figure 27-7: Right-clicking a variable in the Watch window displays a pop-up menu of additional options.

Changing the Values of Your Variables

Stepping through a program line by line and watching how your variables change can help you identify which lines of code may be storing or manipulating data incorrectly. For greater flexibility, you can also change a variable's value while your program is running. This allows you to see how your program works when using different values. By changing values of variables, such as seeing how your program handles a variable that's a negative or an extremely large number, you can identify other possible bugs in your program.

To change the value of a variable while your program is running:

1. Click the Step Into icon.
2. Choose Debug ▶ QuickWatch to open the QuickWatch dialog box.
3. Click in the Value column of the variable you want to change and type a new value for your variable.
4. Click Reevaluate. The Watch window at the bottom of the screen displays the new value for your variable.
5. Click Close. The QuickWatch dialog box disappears.
6. Choose the Step Into command to see how the new value of your variable affects the way your program works.

Hands-on Tutorial: Watching a Variable

In this tutorial, you'll learn how to watch a variable to see how it changes as your program runs.

1. Start a new Visual Basic project, then click OK. A blank form appears.
2. Choose View ▶ Toolbox. The Toolbox appears.
3. Click the Button control, mouse over the form, and click the left mouse button to create a button control on your form.
4. Double-click the button control. The Code window appears.
5. Type the following code so the entire event procedure looks like this:

```
Private Sub Button1_Click(ByVal sender As System.Object, ByVal e As System.EventArgs)_
Handles Button1.Click
    Dim x, y As Integer
    For x = 1 to 10
      y = x * x
    Next
End Sub
```

6. Press F11 to run the Step Into command, which lets you examine how your program works line by line. Your user interface appears.
7. Click the Button1 control. The Code window highlights the `Private Sub` line.
8. Press F11. The Code window highlights the `For x = 1 to 10` line.
9. Choose Debug ▶ QuickWatch or press CTRL-ALT-Q. The QuickWatch dialog box appears.
10. Type **x** and click Add Watch. The Watch window displays the x variable at the bottom of the screen.
11. Click Close. The QuickWatch dialog box disappears.
12. Press F11. The Code window highlights the `y = x * x` line. This assigns the value of `1 * 1`, or `1`, to the value of the y variable. (Notice that the Watch window at the bottom of the screen displays the value `1` next to the x variable.)
13. Press F11. The Code window highlights the `Next` line.
14. Press F11. The Code window highlights the `y = x * x` line again. Notice that the value of the x variable in the Watch window is now `2`.
15. Press F11. The Code window highlights the `Next` line.

16. Choose Debug ▸ QuickWatch to display the QuickWatch window.

17. Type **y** in the Expression text box and click the Reevaluate button. Notice that the QuickWatch dialog box displays the y variable and its current value, which is 4.

18. Click Close to close the QuickWatch dialog box.

19. Choose Debug ▸ Stop Debugging then File ▸ Close Project. A Close Project dialog box appears. Click Discard.

Stepping Over and Stepping Out of Procedures

One problem with the Step Into command is the very fact that it forces you to step through your entire program, line by line. Because most programs consist of procedures (or methods, which are simply procedures stored inside objects), each time your program runs another procedure, the Step Into command jumps to highlight every line stored in that procedure.

While this can be handy for debugging procedures, it can be tedious if you're certain that the bug doesn't reside in a particular procedure. So rather than force you to step through each procedure line by line, Visual Basic Express offers two additional commands:

- Step Over (F10)
- Step Out (SHIFT-F11)

The Step Over command works like the Step Into command, except that it skips, or *steps over*, any procedures. So instead of highlighting code stored in every procedure, the Step Over command treats a procedure call as a single line of code and steps over to the next command that immediately follows the procedure call, as shown in Figure 27-8.

The Step Into command forces you to step through every line of code in a procedure. While this can be helpful for tracking down bugs, you may step through half the code in a procedure before realizing that the bug isn't hiding inside that procedure. So rather than keep using the Step Into command to step through the rest of the code in that procedure, you can use the Step Out command instead.

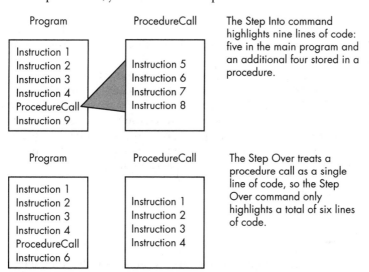

Figure 27-8: The Step Over command lets you examine every line in your program except for those lines of code stored in procedures.

The Step Out command runs all the lines of code in a procedure, without forcing you to highlight them one at a time. Then it highlights the original line of code that called the procedure. You can use Step Into to examine code in a procedure and then use Step Out to skip, or step out, of the procedure when you no longer want to examine the remaining lines of code in that procedure.

For example, the top image in Figure 27-9 shows how Step Into forces you to view every line of code stored in both the main program and a procedure. The Step Into command highlights four lines of code in the main program and then calls a procedure. Once inside the procedure, the Step Into command runs an additional four lines of code before returning to the main program and running one additional line of code. By using Step Into, Visual Basic Express forces you to view nine lines of code plus one procedure call.

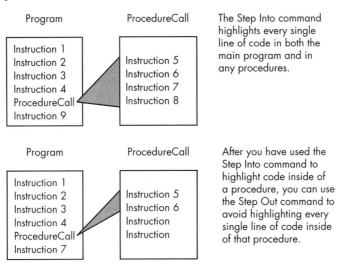

Figure 27-9: The Step Out command lets you stop examining code in a procedure.

The bottom image in Figure 27-9 shows what happens if you use both the Step Into and the Step Out commands. First, the Step Into command highlights four lines of code in the main program and then calls a procedure. Once inside the procedure, Step Into highlights two additional lines of code.

Rather than use Step Into to highlight the remaining two lines of code in the procedure, you can use Step Out to step out of the procedure and highlight the original procedure call. Although Visual Basic will still run the remaining lines of code in the procedure, the Step Out command won't force you to highlight them one at a time.

Once you have stepped out from a procedure, you can return to using Step Into to highlight the remaining line of code. By using both Step Into and Step Out, you can reduce the number of lines of code you need to examine.

NOTE   *The Step Out command is used only once you have already used the Step Into command to highlight code stored in a procedure.*

Using Breakpoints

One problem with the Step Into and Step Over commands is that they always highlight the first line that runs in your program and force you to step through your entire program, line by line. So if you want to examine how the end of your program works, the

Step Into and Step Over commands always force you to start from the beginning of your program and continue until you reach the end.

There's no point stepping code that you don't want to examine, so Visual Basic Express offers *breakpoints*, which let you highlight any line of code in your program. You can run your program and effectively skip examining all code up until the breakpoint. Once your program hits the breakpoint, you can start using the Step Into, Step Over, and Step Out commands to step through the rest of your program.

By using breakpoints, you can selectively examine chunks of code in your program. To set a breakpoint, follow these steps:

1. Open the Code window where you want to begin examining your code line by line, then move the cursor to the line where you want to start your examination.

2. Choose Debug ▶ Toggle Breakpoint. Visual Basic Express highlights the chosen line, as shown in Figure 27-10.

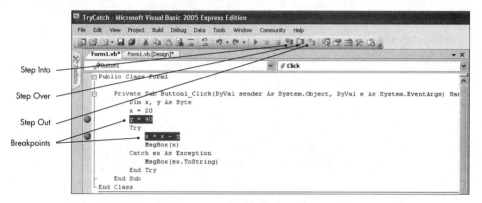

Figure 27-10: Visual Basic Express highlights breakpoints within your code.

3. Run your program by choosing Debug ▶ Start. Visual Basic Express runs all your code until it reaches a breakpoint.

4. Choose the Step Into, Step Over, or Step Out command to start stepping through your code beginning with your breakpoint.

You can place multiple breakpoints throughout your program. To jump to the next breakpoint, choose Debug ▶ Start. To remove a breakpoint, mouse over the breakpoint you want to remove and press F9.

Rather than remove a breakpoint completely, you can disable it temporarily. To do so:

1. Right-click the breakpoint you want to disable. A pop-up menu appears.

2. Choose Breakpoint ▶ Disable Breakpoint as shown in Figure 27-11. The next time you run your program, Visual Basic Express should ignore the disabled breakpoint.

To enable a breakpoint, follow these two steps, but choose Enable Breakpoint instead, from the pop-up menu.

As an alternative to setting breakpoints and removing or disabling them later, you can use your cursor to set a temporary breakpoint; Visual Basic will jump from the current highlighted line of code to the line of code on which the cursor sits. Thus, you can examine a different chunk of code without having to set and remove a breakpoint.

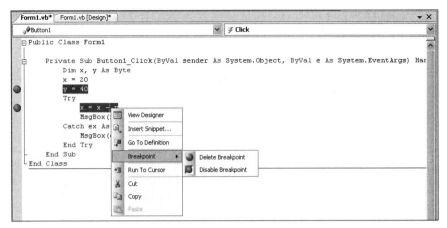

Figure 27-11: Right-click a breakpoint to disable it temporarily.

To use the cursor as a temporary breakpoint:

1. Choose the Step Into (F11) or Step Over (F10) command until Visual Basic highlights one line of code in your program.

2. Right-click the line of code where you want to begin examining your code line by line. A pop-up menu appears.

3. Choose Run To Cursor. Visual Basic runs all the code between the currently highlighted line of code and the line where the cursor currently sits. You can now use Step Into, Step Over, and Step Out to step through the rest of your program.

Stop Debugging

When debugging your program, you could step through it line by line until you reach the end. However, you're more likely to step through a chunk of code, find the error, fix it, and then stop debugging. To stop debugging, click the Stop Debugging icon on the standard toolbar.

Hands-on Tutorial: Debugging a Program

In this tutorial, you'll see how to step through a program line by line and change the value of a variable. To follow this tutorial, you'll need to open the Visual Basic project that you created in the "Hands-on Tutorial: Catching Errors with the Try-Catch Statement" on page 381. If you haven't created and saved the project described in that tutorial, you should do so before continuing.

1. Load Visual Basic Express.

2. Choose File ▸ Recent Projects and click the TryCatch project that you created in the earlier tutorial.

3. Right-click the Form1 file in the Solution Explorer window and choose View Code. The Code window appears.

4. Move the cursor to the end of the Public Class Form1 line and press ENTER.

5. Type the following general procedure:

```
Sub Calculate(ByRef a As Byte, ByVal b As Byte)
        a = a - b
End Sub
```

Line 1 Creates a general procedure called Calculate, which accepts two parameters called a and b, both of which hold byte data types. The a parameter is defined with the ByRef keyword, which means that whatever the value of a becomes, that value will be passed to the rest of the program. The b parameter is defined with the ByVal keyword, which means that no matter what the value of b becomes, that value can be used only within the Calculate procedure.

Line 2 Subtracts the value of b from the value of a and stores this new result back into the a parameter.

6. Replace the line x = x - y with **Calculate(x, y)** so the entire Code window looks like this:

```
Public Class Form1
    Sub Calculate(ByRef a As Byte, ByVal b As Byte)
        a = a - b
    End Sub

    Private Sub Button1_Click(ByVal sender As System.Object, ByVal e As_
System.EventArgs) Handles Button1.Click
        Dim x, y As Byte
        x = 20
        y = 40
        Try
            Calculate(x, y)
            MsgBox(x)
        Catch ex As Exception
            MsgBox(ex.ToString)
        End Try
    End Sub
End Class
```

The Calculate(x, y) line calls the Calculate procedure and passes it two parameters (x and y).

7. Move the cursor to the Try line and press F9 (Enable Breakpoint).

8. Press F5. Your user interface appears.

9. Click the Button1 control on the form. The Code window appears, highlighting the Try line where you placed the breakpoint.

10. Highlight the y variable and choose Debug ▶ Quick Watch (or press CTRL-ALT-Q). The Quick Watch window appears and displays *40* in the Value column.

11. Click in the Value column and type **15**.

12. Click Reevaluate and then click Close.

13. Press F11 (Step Into). The Code window highlights the Calculate(x, y) line.

14. Press F11. The Code window jumps to highlight the Sub Calculate line.

15. Click the Step Out icon on the Standard toolbar (or choose Debug ▸ Step Out). The Code window highlights the Calculate(x, y) line again. When you Step Out of a procedure, Visual Basic Express runs all code stored in that procedure but doesn't force you to step through it line by line.

16. Press F5. This tells Visual Basic Express to run all the code in the rest of your program without stepping through line by line anymore. A message box appears, displaying the number 5. This number is the result of subtracting the value of y (15) from the value of x (20). If you didn't change the value of the y variable in step 11 from 40 to 15, the value of the x variable would have been 20 – 40, or -20, which lies outside the range of acceptable values for a byte data type (0 to 255), and that would have caused an error. Click OK to close the message box.

17. Press ALT-F4 to stop the program then choose File ▸ Save All to save your changes.

KEY FEATURES TO REMEMBER

Every program will have errors or bugs. As a programmer, your goal is to reduce the chance of including errors, trap errors so they won't crash your program, and hunt down errors one by one in your program.

- Bugs can be caused by misspellings (syntax errors), incorrect code that actually works but doesn't do what the programmer really wants it to do (logic errors), or unexpected entered data (run-time errors).
- Short programs, simple commands, and descriptive variable names can help make your programs easier to read and understand.
- Comments let you embed explanations directly into your code or temporarily hide code from the computer.
- The Try-Catch-End Try statement lets you write code to identify and handle any errors that occur.
- Stepping lets you examine which lines of code your program runs at any given time.
- The Step Into command highlights every singe line of code in your program.
- The Step Over command lets you skip over code stored in a procedure.
- The Step Out command lets you stop examining lines of code in a procedure.
- Watching how your variables change in value can help you determine how each line of code may be storing or manipulating data incorrectly.
- Breakpoints help you step through isolated parts of your program where you think an error may be occurring.

PART V

ENHANCING YOUR VISUAL
BASIC PROGRAMS

28

CONNECTING TO FILES AND DATABASES

Because most programs save and retrieve information stored in files, your program needs to know how to store data in a file and then retrieve it. Visual Basic can store and retrieve data in two types of files:

- Text files
- Database files

Text files contain only characters. While text files are the simplest files to use, they can be cumbersome for storing and retrieving data because text files store data *sequentially*. That means if you want to find data stored in the middle or at the end of a text file, you must scroll through the file from start to finish until you find what you want. As a result, text files are suitable for storing small amounts of data but clumsy for storing large amounts.

Database files let you store data in discrete chunks that you can retrieve and remove quickly by jumping right to the data you want. Database files are like CD-ROMs, because they can access the specific information you want quickly, even if it's buried within a large amount of data.

Using Text Files

Text files (also called *ASCII* files, for *American Standard Code for Information Interchange*) are the simplest files to create and use. The major advantage of storing data in a text file is that most programs running on any computer (from an IBM mainframe computer to an obsolete Apple II computer) can read information stored in a text file.

Creating and Storing Data in a Text File

Visual Basic can create a text file and store data in it at the same time. To create a text file, you use the `WriteAllText` command (which is part of the `My.Computer.FileSystem` class), like so:

```
My.Computer.FileSystem.WriteAllText (File, Text, Append)
```

where `File` is the drive, directory, and filename that you want to create. Any directories you specify must already exist or this command will cause an error. `Text` is the text you want to store in the text file. `Append` is a True or False value; if set to True, then the `Text` data is added to the end of any existing text stored in the text file. If set to False, the `Text` data overwrites any data currently stored in the text file, essentially wiping out any old data in the text file.

For example, to create a text file in the C:\My Stuff directory and store the string "I like Linux" inside it, you could use this command:

```
My.Computer.FileSystem.WriteAllText ("C:\My Stuff", "I like Linux", False)
```

This command would create a text file named My Stuff that contains the string "I like Linux".

To add or append information to a text file that already contains data, you need to specify the text file to append, the new text you want to add, and a True value in the *Append* part of the `WriteAllText` command, like so:

```
My.Computer.FileSystem.WriteAllText ("C:\My Stuff", "I like Macs too", True)
```

For example, if the My Stuff text file already contains the string "I like Linux", the above BASIC command would add the string "I like Macs too", and the entire text file would contain this:

```
I like LinuxI like Macs too
```

Because you might not want the `WriteAllText` command to smash your text together, you should insert a *carriage return* (represented by the Visual Basic constant vbCr) and a *line feed* (represented by the Visual Basic constant vbLf) at the end of each string. A carriage return moves the cursor back to the front of the line and a line feed advances the text one line. (Both carriage returns and line feeds recall the old days when computers used to print data on printers that resembled old-fashioned typewriters.)

So instead of storing a single line of text in a text file, you can include a carriage return and a line feed to break up the lines, like so:

```
My.Computer.FileSystem.WriteAllText ("C:\My Stuff", "I like Linux" & vbCr & vbLf, False)
My.Computer.FileSystem.WriteAllText ("C:\My Stuff", "I like Macs too" & vbCr & vbLf, True)
```

As an alternative to using vbCr & vbLf, Visual Basic provides another constant that combines both the carriage return and line feed characters into a single constant, called vbCrLf. For example, you could type the previous two Visual Basic commands like so:

```
My.Computer.FileSystem.WriteAllText ("C:\My Stuff", "I like Linux" & vbCrLf, False)
My.Computer.FileSystem.WriteAllText ("C:\My Stuff", "I like Macs too" & vbCrLf, True)
```

The first WriteAllText command stores the string "I like Linux" and uses the & operator to add a carriage return and line feed in the My Stuff text file. (If the My Stuff file already exists, this command erases any text already in it and fills it with I like Linux instead.)

The second WriteAllText command adds the text I like Macs too plus a carriage return and a line feed. After this second WriteAllText command runs, the contents of the My Stuff text file look like this:

```
I like Linux
I like Macs too
```

Reading Data from a Text File

Once you've stored data in a text file, you can retrieve it using the ReadAllText command (which is part of the My.Computer.FileSystem class), like so:

```
My.Computer.FileSystem.ReadAllText (File)
```

where File is the drive, directory, and text filename that contains the text you want to retrieve.

The ReadAllText command returns the contents of a text file as a string data type. For example, to store the contents of a text file named test.txt into a String variable named FileContents, you could use this code:

```
Dim FileContents As String
FileContents = My.Computer.FileSystem.ReadAllText("C:\test.txt")
```

Hands-on Tutorial: Reading and Writing Text Files

This tutorial shows you how to store text in a text file and then retrieve it.

1. Start a new Visual Basic project, then click OK. A blank form appears.
2. Choose View ▸ Toolbox. The Toolbox appears. Choose Window ▸ Auto Hide to keep the Toolbox visible.
3. Click the TextBox control in the Toolbox, move the mouse near the top of the form, and click the left mouse button to create a text box.
4. Click the Label control in the Toolbox, move the mouse under the text box on the form, and click the left mouse button to create a label directly under the text box you created in step 3.
5. Click the Button control in the Toolbox, move the mouse near the bottom of the form, and click the left mouse button to create a button control on your form.
6. Click the Button control in the Toolbox, move the mouse to the right of the button control you created in step 5, and click the left mouse button. Your user interface should now look like Figure 28-1.

Figure 28-1: A user interface with a text box, label, and two buttons.

7. Type the following to make the entire event procedure look like this:

```
Private Sub Button1_Click(ByVal sender As System.Object, ByVal e As System.EventArgs)_
Handles Button1.Click
        Dim Reverse As String
        Reverse = StrReverse(TextBox1.Text)
        My.Computer.FileSystem.WriteAllText("c:\mystuff", "I like Linux" & vbCr &_
vbLf, False)
        My.Computer.FileSystem.WriteAllText("c:\mystuff", Reverse & vbCr & vbLf,_
True)
End Sub
```

Line 1   Creates a String variable called Reverse.

Line 2   Takes the string stored in the Text property of the TextBox1 control and uses the StrReverse function (discussed in Chapter 20) to reverse the string. This reversed string gets stored in the Reverse variable.

Line 3   Creates a text file called mystuff and stores it in the C:\ directory. Then it stores the string "I like Linux" in the file, followed by the carriage return (vbCr) and line feed (vbLf) characters.

Line 4   Appends the string stored in the Reverse string variable to the end of the mystuff text file, followed by the carriage return and line feed characters.

8. Click in the Class Name list box in the Code window and choose Button2.

9. Click in the Method Name list box in the Code window and choose Click. The Code window displays an empty Button2_Click event procedure.

10. Type the following code so the entire Button2_Click event procedure looks like this:

```
Private Sub Button2_Click(ByVal sender As Object, ByVal e As System.EventArgs)_
Handles Button2.Click
        Label1.Text = My.Computer.FileSystem.ReadAllText("c:\mystuff")
End Sub
```

This line of code reads all the text stored in the mystuff text file and stores it in the Text property of the Label1 control on the form.

11. Press F5. Your user interface appears.

12. Click in the text box and type **I like Macs too**.

13. Click the Button1 control. Nothing appears to happen because the Button1 event procedure creates the mystuff text file and stores the string "I like Linux" and the string "I like Macs too", which you typed in the text box in step 12.

14. Click the Button2 control. The label control displays:

```
I like Linux
oot scaM ekil I
```

15. Press ALT-F4 to stop your program, then choose File ▶ Close Project. A Close Project dialog box appears. Click Discard. (You may want to delete the mystuff text file stored in the C:\ directory later.)

Using Database Files

Database files are useful for storing chunks of related information, such as a person's name, address, rank, and serial number. Database files are faster than text files for retrieving information, and can be shared with popular database programs such as Microsoft Access. This means you can write a Visual Basic program that stores data in a file and someone else can analyze it later using a database program to create reports or charts based on that data.

NOTE *The first CD that comes with this book includes a sample Access database file that you can practice using with Visual Basic (SampleDatabase.mdb in Sample Programs\Chapter 28). After copying this file to your hard disk, the file may be Read-Only, which means you won't be able to modify its contents. If so, right-click the file to display pop-up menu, click Properties, then remove the Read-only check mark that appears in the Attributes group near the bottom of the Properties window.*

Understanding Database Files

Database files contain organized information. The smallest chunk of information a database file can hold is called a *field*. A field is any single piece of data, such as a name, address, or phone number.

A single field of information, such as someone's name or address, is fairly useless by itself, so databases often combine multiple fields, such as the name, address, and phone number of a person. A group of related fields is called a *record*. A business card is a simple example of a record, because it contains related fields for a person, including a name field, a company field, an address field, a phone number field, and so on.

A collection of records is called a *table*. While a database file could contain just one table, it's more common for a database file to contain multiple tables. For example, a database file designed to contain business information might contain one table that lists customers, another that lists suppliers, and a third that lists potential sales prospects.

Linking Database Files to a Visual Basic Project

To link a database file to a Visual Basic project, you need to define the following:

A database source This physically links a database file to a Visual Basic project using the BindingSource control from the Toolbox's Data category. More than one source can provide data to your Visual Basic project.

A data set This identifies a specific table to use inside a database file, because a database file may contain multiple tables. Visual Basic Express automatically creates a data set control when you define the DataSource property of a BindingSource control.

A data adapter This takes care of physically sending and retrieving information to a database file (identified by the DataSource property of a BindingSource control) and a database table (identified by the `DataMember` property of a control). Visual Basic Express automatically creates a data adapter control when you define the `DataMember` property of a control such as the BindingSource control.

NOTE *Visual Basic can retrieve data from other sources, such as the Internet or a web service, but this chapter focuses exclusively on using information stored in database files.*

Connecting a Database File to a Visual Basic Project

Connecting a Database to a Visual Basic Project

Visual Basic can use two types of database files: Microsoft Access and SQL Server database files (*SQL* stands for *Structured Query Language*). To use data stored in a database file, you must first add the database file to the Database Explorer window, then add it to a Visual Basic project. To do so:

1. Choose Tools ▶ Connect To Database. A Choose Data Source dialog box appears, as shown in Figure 28-2.

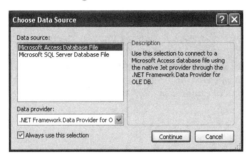

Figure 28-2: The Choose Data Source dialog box lets you choose the type of database file to use.

2. Click either Microsoft Access Database File or Microsoft SQL Server Database File and then click Continue. The Add Connection dialog box appears, as shown in Figure 28-3.
3. Click the Browse button. A Select File dialog box appears.
4. Click the database file you want to use and click Open. The Add Connection dialog box appears again.

NOTE *If you don't have a database file available, you can use the sample database file on this book's first CD named SampleDatabase.mdb in Sample Programs\Chapter 28.*

5. Click OK. Visual Basic Express displays your chosen file in the Database Explorer window, shown in Figure 28-4, which appears at the left of the screen. (The appearance of the Database Explorer window may vary, depending on the structure of the database file you use.)

Defining a Data Source and Creating a Data Set Control

Binding a Database File to a Visual Basic Project

Once you've added a database file to the Data Explorer window, you still need to add (or in Visual Basic terms, *bind*) it to a specific Visual Basic project. To bind a database file to a Visual Basic project:

1. Choose Window ▶ Toolbox to view the Toolbox.
2. Double-click the BindingSource control under the Data category of the Toolbox. Visual Basic displays the BindingSource control on the bottom of the screen.

Figure 28-3: The Add Connection dialog box lets you choose a specific database file to include in your Visual Basic program.

Figure 28-4: The Database Explorer window lists all the available database files you can add to your Visual Basic project.

3. Press F4 to open the Properties window, and click the DataSource property under the Data category. A downward-pointing arrow appears.

4. Click the downward-pointing arrow. A pop-up window appears, as shown in Figure 28-5.

5. Click Add Project Data Source. A Data Source Configuration Wizard dialog box appears, as shown in Figure 28-6. The three choices for the source of data are Database (a database file), Web Service (another computer on a network or Internet), and Object (a non-database file).

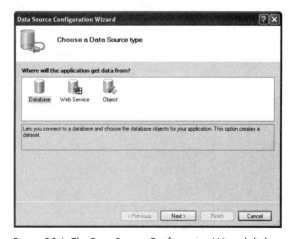

Figure 28-6: The Data Source Configuration Wizard dialog box lets you choose the source of your data.

Figure 28-5: The DataSource property lets you choose a database file stored in the Database Explorer window.

6. Click the Database icon and click Next. Another Data Source Configuration Wizard dialog box appears, as shown in Figure 28-7.

Figure 28-7: This Data Source Configuration Wizard dialog box lets you choose a specific database file previously stored in the Database Explorer window.

7. Click in the list box, click the database file you want to use, and click Next. A Local Database File dialog box appears and asks if you want to add the database file to your Visual Basic project.

8. Click Yes. Another Data Source Configuration Wizard dialog box appears and asks if you want to store a connection string. A *connection string* stores information about how to connect your Visual Basic project to a database file.

9. Click Next. Another Data Source Configuration Wizard dialog box appears, listing all the types of information you can display within your Visual Basic project, such as Tables or Views, as shown in Figure 28-8.

Figure 28-8: This Data Source Configuration Wizard dialog box lets you choose specific database information to include, such as Tables.

10. Click in the check box next to the type of information you want to include in your Visual Basic project, and then click Finish. The Solution Explorer window displays your database file and connection string, as shown in Figure 28-9. Visual Basic Express also creates a data set control that appears under your form.

Creating a Data Adapter Control

Once you've added a BindingSource control to your form and defined its DataSource property to link it to a database file, you need to define the BindingSource control's DataMember property to choose a particular database table to use within that database file. To define a database table, which will automatically create a data adapter control, follow these steps:

1. Click the BindingSource control under your form.
2. Press F4 to open the Properties window and click the DataMember property under the Data category of the Properties window. A downward-pointing arrow appears.
3. Click the downward-pointing arrow. A pop-up window appears, listing all database tables you selected in step 9 of the section "Defining a Data Source and Creating a Data Set Control" (see page 400), as shown in Figure 28-10.
4. Click a database table. Visual Basic Express automatically creates a dataset control next to the BindingSource control under your Visual Basic form.

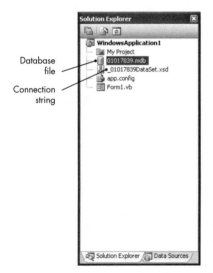

Database file

Connection string

Figure 28-9: The Solution Explorer window lists all the database files currently accessible by your Visual Basic project.

Figure 28-10: The DataMember property lets you define the type of data you want to use in your Visual Basic project.

Viewing Data in a Visual Basic Project

Once you've defined both the DataSource and DataMember properties of a BindingSource control, you can view the actual database information through many different user interface controls, such as text boxes, labels, list boxes, or a special grid for displaying database information called the *DataGridView* control.

Viewing Data with the DataGridView Control

Displaying Information in a Data- GridView Control

The DataGridView control displays database information in a grid, in rows and columns. The biggest advantage to using the DataGridView control is that it lets you see multiple records and fields at once. To use the DataGridView control, follow these steps:

1. Add a database file to the Database Explorer window, as explained in the section "Connecting a Database File to a Visual Basic Project" on page 400.

2. Add the database file to your Visual Basic project, as explained in the section "Defining a Data Source and Creating a Data Set Control" on page 400.

3. Double-click the DataGridView control under the Data category in the Toolbox. The DataGridView control appears on your form and displays a DataGridView Tasks window, as shown in Figure 28-11.

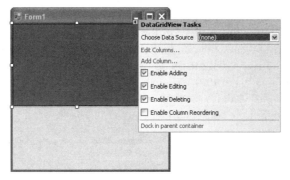

Figure 28-11: The DataGridView Tasks window lets you choose
a source for your data.

4. Click the Choose Data Source list box. A pop-up window appears. Click a name, such as BindingSource1. Choose the name of the binding source control you created in the section "Defining a Data Source and Creating a Data Set Control" on page 400.

5. At this point, you can press F5 to run your program and see your chosen data appear in the DataGridView, as shown in Figure 28-12.

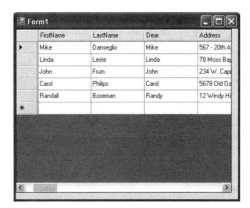

Figure 28-12: The DataGridView control displays
data in rows and columns.

Viewing Data with the BindingNavigator Control

Displaying
Information
with the
Binding-
Navigator
Control

One problem with the DataGridView control is that you may not want to view all the data in rows and columns. As an alternative, you can use the BindingNavigator control along with other controls, such as text boxes, labels, or list boxes, to display part of a database file at a time. So while the DataGridView control can overwhelm you with dozens of names, addresses, and phone numbers of people stored in a database, the BindingNavigator and another control such as a text box or label can display a single field (such as a name or address) at a time.

To use the BindingNavigator control:

1. Add a BindingSource control to your form, as explained in the section "Connecting a Database File to a Visual Basic Project" on page 400.

2. Double-click the Binding-Navigator control under the Data category of the Toolbox. A BindingNavigator control appears at the top of your form, as shown in Figure 28-13.

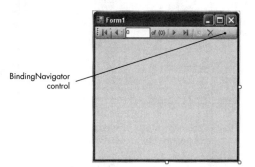

BindingNavigator
control

3. Press F4 to open the Properties window and click the Binding-Source property. A downward-pointing arrow appears.

4. Click the downward-pointing arrow. A pop-up menu appears, listing all the BindingSource control names you've added to your form.

Figure 28-13: The BindingNavigator control provides icons that let you scroll through the information stored in a database.

5. Add another control to your form, such as a text box or label, with a DataBindings property. If you want the user to edit information in a database, use a text box control. If you want to display data without letting the user modify it, use a control like a label or list box.

6. Press F4 to open the Properties window of the control you created in step 5, and double-click the DataBindings property under the Data category of the Properties window. The DataBindings property expands to display a Text property.

7. Click the Text property. A downward-pointing arrow appears.

8. Click the downward-pointing arrow. A pop-up window appears, listing different data sources you can choose.

9. Click the plus sign that appears to the left of the BindingSource control you want to use. A list of specific information stored in a database file appears, as shown in Figure 28-14.

10. Click the type of information, such as First Name or Address, that you want to appear in the control you created in step 5.

11. At this point, you can press F5 to run your program and click the arrows in the BindingNavigator control to view the data in the control you chose in step 5, as shown in Figure 28-15.

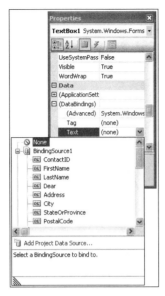

Figure 28-14: Any control with a DataBindings property can display information form a database.

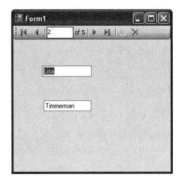

Figure 28-15: The BindingNavigator control works with a label or text box to display data.

Saving Data to a Database

Although the DataGridView control and a text box control (in combination with the BindingNavigator control) let you view and edit any data displayed, any changes you make to the database won't be saved until you write Visual Basic code to save the changes.

You can use the following two commands to update a database:

EndEdit   Tells the computer to stop letting the user edit any displayed data on your user interface, such as text displayed in a text box or a DataGridView control.

Update   Tells the computer to save all changes made to the database.

The syntax for the EndEdit command is:

```
FormName.BindingSourceControlName.EndEdit()
```

FormName is the name of the form that contains the BindingSource control, such as Form2. If the BindingSource control is on the same form that contains the EndEdit Visual Basic command, you must substitute the Me keyword for *FormName*. The Me keyword identifies when code modifies the form on which that code has been stored. *Binding-SourceControlName* is the name of the BindingSource control that you must first create to allow your Visual Basic program to access a database file. By default, Visual Basic names this control something generic, like BindingSource1, but you can change this name to anything you want.

The syntax for the Update command is a bit more complicated:

```
FormName.DataMemberControlName.Update(Me.DataSetName.TableName)
```

where *FormName* is the name of the form that contains the BindingSource control, such as Form2. If the BindingSource control is on the same form that contains the Update Visual Basic command, you must substitute the Me keyword for *FormName*. *DataMemberControlName* is the name of the data control that Visual Basic automatically creates when you define a BindingSource control's DataMember property. *DataSetName* is the name that Visual Basic automatically creates when you define a BindingSource control to bind a database file to your Visual basic project. *TableName* is the name of the information you want to display in on your user interface, such as Contacts or Members.

To save any changes made to a database file, use the EndEdit and the Update commands, as demonstrated in the following tutorials.

Hands-on Tutorial: Using the DataGridView Control

This tutorial lets you modify data stored in a Microsoft Access file using the DataGridView control. To follow this tutorial, insert the first CD that's bundled with this book.

1. Insert the CD into your drive and copy the SampleDatabase.mdb file from the Sample Programs\Chapter 28 directory.
2. Load Visual Basic Express.
3. Choose Tools ▶ Connect To Database. A Choose Data Source dialog box appears.
4. Click Microsoft Access Database File and click Continue.
5. Click Browse. A Select Microsoft Access Database File dialog box appears. Open the SampleDatabase.mdb file on your machine.
6. Click the SampleDatabase file and click Open. The Add Connection dialog box appears.
7. Click OK. Visual Basic Express stores your chosen database in the Database Explorer Window.
8. Press CTRL-N. A New Project dialog box appears. Click OK. A blank form appears.
9. Double-click the BindingSource control under the Data category of the Toolbox. The BindingControl appears under your form.
10. Press F4 to open the Properties window and click the DataSource property. A downward-pointing arrow appears.
11. Click the downward-pointing arrow. A pop-up window appears.
12. Click Add Project Data Source. A Data Source Configuration Wizard dialog box appears.
13. Click the Database icon and then click Next. Another Data Source Configuration Wizard dialog box appears and displays the SampleDatabase database file you selected in step 6.
14. Click Next. A Local database file dialog box appears.
15. Click Yes. Another Data Source Configuration Wizard dialog box appears and displays a connection string for your database file.
16. Click Next. Another Data Source Configuration Wizard dialog box appears and displays check boxes in front of different data you can view, such as Tables and Views.
17. Click the Tables check box and click Finish. Notice that Visual Basic Express automatically creates a SampleDatabaseDataSet control next to the BindingSource1 control at the bottom of the screen, as shown in Figure 28-16. (The SampleDatabaseDataSet is the name of your dataset; you'll need this information when you write code to update our database file.)

Figure 28-16: As soon as you bind a database to a Visual Basic project, Visual Basic Express automatically creates a dataset control, which links your program to a database file.

18. Click in the DataMember property in the Properties window. A downward-pointing arrow appears.

19. Click the downward-pointing arrow. A pop-up window appears and lists the different types of data you can use, such as Calls or Contacts.

20. Click Contacts. Notice that Visual Basic Express automatically creates a Contacts-TableAdapter control near the bottom of the screen, as shown in Figure 28-17. The ContactsTableAdapter control simply retrieves data from the Contacts table of the database file.

Figure 28-17: The ContactsTableAdapter control defines the specific information you've linked to your Visual Basic project.

21. Double-click the DataGridView control under the Data category of the Toolbox. A DataGridView control appears on your form along with a DataGridView Tasks window.

22. Click the Choose Data Source list box in the DataGridView Tasks window. A pop-up window appears.

23. Click BindingSource1.

24. Click the Button control in the Toolbox, mouse over the form, and click the left mouse button to create a button on your form that appears under your DataGrid-View control.

25. Double-click the Button1 control. The Code window appears. Notice that the Code window already includes a Form1_Load event procedure as shown here:

```
Public Class Form1

    Private Sub Form1_Load(ByVal sender As System.Object, ByVal e As_
System.EventArgs) Handles MyBase.Load
        'TODO: This line of code loads data into the 'SampleDatabaseDataSet.Contacts'
table. You can move, or remove it, as needed.
        Me.ContactsTableAdapter.Fill(Me.SampleDatabaseDataSet.Contacts)
    End Sub

    Private Sub Button1_Click(ByVal sender As System.Object, ByVal e As_
System.EventArgs) Handles Button1.Click

    End Sub
End Class
```

NOTE   *MyBase.Load tells the Form1 form to load information from a database. The MyBase.Load code is generated automatically.*

26. Type the following two lines of BASIC code between the `Private Sub` and `End Sub`
    lines of the `Button1_Click` event procedure:

```
Public Class Form1

    Private Sub Form1_Load(ByVal sender As System.Object, ByVal e As_
System.EventArgs) Handles MyBase.Load
        'TODO: This line of code loads data into the 'SampleDatabaseDataSet.Contacts'
table. You can move, or remove it, as needed.
        Me.ContactsTableAdapter.Fill(Me.SampleDatabaseDataSet.Contacts)

    End Sub

    Private Sub Button1_Click(ByVal sender As System.Object, ByVal e As_
System.EventArgs) Handles Button1.Click
        Me.BindingSource1.EndEdit()
        Me.ContactsTableAdapter.Update(Me.SampleDatabaseDataSet.Contacts)
    End Sub
End Class
```

27. Press F5. Your user interface appears.
    Notice that all the data from your data-
    base file appears in the DataGridView,
    as shown in Figure 28-18. Scroll up and
    down and side to side and to see more
    of the data stored in the DataGridView.

28. Click in the FirstName column of row 1
    (which displays the name *Mike*) and
    type **Susan**. At this point, if you quit
    your program, the name *Susan* won't
    be saved in the database file.

*Figure 28-18: The DataGridView displays
all your data in rows and columns.*

29. Click the Button1 control which runs
    the two Visual Basic commands that
    tell the computer to save your changes
    to the database file.

30. Press ALT-F4 to stop your program from running.

31. Press F5 again. Notice that now the DataGridView control displays the name *Susan*
    in the first row.

32. Press ALT-F4 to stop your program from running. Choose File ▶ Close Project.
    A Close Project dialog box appears. Click Discard.

Hands-on Tutorial: Using the BindingNavigator Control

This tutorial lets you modify data stored in a Microsoft Access file using the Binding-
Navigator control and a text box. To follow this tutorial, insert the first CD that came
with this book. Copy the sample database file from the CD to your hard disk so you
can modify it.

1. Copy the SampleDatabase.mdb file from the Sample Programs\Chapter 28
   directory on the CD, then load Visual Basic Express.

2. Choose Tools ▶ Connect To Database. A Choose Data Source dialog box appears.

3. Click Microsoft Access Database File and click Continue.

4. Click Browse. A Select Microsoft Access Database File dialog box appears.

5. Switch to the drive and directory where you copied the SampleDatabase.mdb file from the CD.

6. Click the SampleDatabase file and click Open. The Add Connection dialog box appears.

7. Click OK. Visual Basic Express stores your chosen database in the Database Explorer Window.

8. Press CTRL-N. A New Project dialog box appears. Click OK. A blank form appears.

9. Double-click the BindingSource control under the Data category of the Toolbox. The BindingControl appears under your form.

10. Press F4 to open the Properties window and click the DataSource property. A downward-pointing arrow appears. Click the downward-pointing arrow. A pop-up window appears.

11. Click Add Project Data Source. A Data Source Configuration Wizard dialog box appears.

12. Click the Database icon and click Next. Another Data Source Configuration Wizard dialog box appears and displays the SampleDatabase database file you selected in step 6.

13. Click Next. A Local database file dialog box appears.

14. Click Yes. Another Data Source Configuration Wizard dialog box appears and displays a connection string for your database file.

15. Click Next. A Data Source Configuration Wizard dialog box appears and displays check boxes in front of different data you can view, such as Tables and Views.

16. Click in the Tables check box and click Finish. Notice that Visual Basic Express automatically creates a SampleDatabaseDataSet control next to the BindingSource control at the bottom of the screen (see Figure 28-16). The SampleDatabaseData-Set is the name of your dataset; you'll need to know this name when you write code to update our database file.

17. Click in the DataMember property in the Properties window. A downward-pointing arrow appears. Click the downward-pointing arrow and a pop-up window appears and lists the different type of data you can use, such as Calls or Contacts.

18. Click Contacts. Notice that Visual Basic Express automatically creates a Contacts-TableAdapter control near the bottom of the screen (see Figure 28-17).

19. Double-click the BindingNavigator control under the Data category of the Tool-box. A BindingNavigator control appears at the top of your form, as shown in Figure 28-19.

20. Press F4 to open the Properties window and click the BindingSource property. A downward-pointing arrow appears.

21. Click the downward-pointing arrow. A pop-up window appears and lists all the binding sources available.

22. Click BindingSource1.

23. Click a text box control in the Toolbox, mouse over the form, and click the left mouse button to create a text box control on the form.

24. Press F4 to open the Properties window and click the plus sign that appears to the left of the DataBindings property under the Data category. The DataBindings property expands and displays three additional properties: Advanced, Tag, and Text.

25. Click in the Text property. A downward-pointing arrow appears. Click the downward-pointing arrow and a pop-up window appears.

26. Click the plus sign to the left of BindingSource1. A list of different types of data appears, such as FirstName and Address, as shown in Figure 28-20.

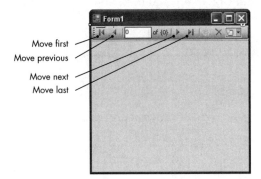

Figure 28-19: The BindingNavigator control provides icons for scrolling through a database, one record at a time.

Figure 28-20: The Text property lets you choose the type of data you want to display inside the text box control.

27. Click FirstName.

28. Click the Button control in the Toolbox, mouse over the form, and click the left mouse button to create a button on your form.

29. Double-click the Button1 control. The Code window appears.

30. Type the following two lines of Visual Basic code between the `Private Sub` and `End Sub` lines of the `Button1_Click` event procedure, as shown:

```
Public Class Form1

    Private Sub Form1_Load(ByVal sender As System.Object, ByVal e As_
System.EventArgs) Handles MyBase.Load
        'TODO: This line of code loads data into the 'SampleDatabaseDataSet.Contacts'
table. You can move, or remove it, as needed.
        Me.ContactsTableAdapter.Fill(Me.SampleDatabaseDataSet.Contacts)

    End Sub

    Private Sub Button1_Click(ByVal sender As System.Object, ByVal e As_
System.EventArgs) Handles Button1.Click
        Me.BindingSource1.EndEdit()
        Me.ContactsTableAdapter.Update(Me.SampleDatabaseDataSet.Contacts)
    End Sub
End Class
```

31. Press F5. Your user interface appears. Notice that the text box displays the first name of the first record of the database file.

32. Click the Move Next/Move Previous and Move First/Move Last buttons on the BindingNavigator control. Notice that each time you view another record, a different name appears.

33. Click the Move Last icon on the BindingNavigator control. The name *Richard* appears.

34. Click in the text box, delete *Richard*, and type **George**. At this point, your data isn't saved yet in the database file.

35. Click the Button1 control. This button runs the two BASIC commands that tell the computer to save your changes to the database file.

36. Press ALT-F4 to stop your program.

37. Press F5, then click the Move Last icon on the BindingNavigator control. Notice that the name *George* now appears in the text box.

38. Press ALT-F4 to stop your program. Choose File ▶ Close Project. A Close Project dialog box appears. Click Discard.

KEY FEATURES TO REMEMBER

Visual Basic lets you create directories and subdirectories along with files, where you can store data. You can store data in a text file or a database file.

- The WriteAllText command lets you create a file and store text in it. To make text appear on separate lines, you may need to insert a carriage return (vbCr) and a line feed (vbLf) character at the end of each line. You can either use the vbCr and vbLf characters together or use the single combination carriage return/line feed constant, vbCrLf.

- The WriteAllText command can either wipe out all text in a file or append text to the existing contents of a file. The ReadAllText command stores the entire contents of a text file as a single string.

- A database file consists of multiple tables. A table consists of multiple records. A record consists of multiple fields, and a field consists of a single chunk of data such as a name, address, or phone number.

- The BindingSource control lets you link a database file to a Visual Basic project.

- You can view the contents of a database file through the DataGridView control or through another control, such as a text box, in combination with the BindingNavigator control.

- The EndEdit and Update commands let you save any changes you made to a database file.

29

PRINTING DATA FROM YOUR PROGRAM

Although printing seems like a simple task from a user's point of view, from a programmer's point of view, printing can involve plenty of messy technical details. To shield you from the technical complexities of communicating directly with a printer, Visual Basic provides a special PrintDocument control that acts as a middleman between your program and the printer. Your program sends data to the PrintDocument control and this control sends data to your printer. All you need to do is specify the type of data you want to print and where you want to print it on the page. The PrintDocument control ensures that your data will print correctly no matter what type of printer you are using.

Preparing Your Program to Print

Preparing Your
Program to Print

To give your Visual Basic project the ability to print you need to:

- Add the `Imports System.Drawing.Printing` line at the top of the Code window. This command allows your program to access the different printing variables and commands that Microsoft has provided for you in a special Printing class file.

- Add the PrintDocument control to your form. This control takes care of sending data to your printer.

To add the `Imports System.Drawing.Printing` line in the Code window of a form, follow these steps:

1. Click a form file displayed in the Solution Explorer window.
2. Choose View ▸ Code. The Code window appears.
3. Move the cursor to the front of the `Public Class` line and press ENTER. This creates a blank line at the top of the Code window.
4. Move the cursor to the new, blank line at the top of the Code window and type **Imports System.Drawing.Printing**. Notice that as you type, Visual Basic Express displays a pop-up menu displaying a list of valid commands, as shown in Figure 29-1.

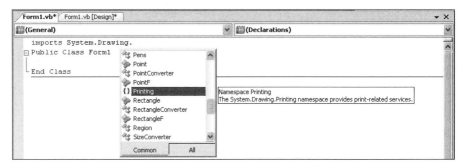

Figure 29-1: Visual Basic Express helps guide you in adding a command.

To add the PrintDocument control to your form:

1. Click a form file displayed in the Solution Explorer window.
2. Choose View ▸ Designer. The user interface of your chosen form file appears.
3. Choose View ▸ Toolbox. The Toolbox appears.
4. Double-click the PrintDocument control under the Printing category of the Toolbox. The PrintDocument control appears under your form.

Writing BASIC Code to Print Data

Writing BASIC Code to Print Data

To make your Visual Basic program print data, you must write BASIC code. The first command you need to use is this:

```
PrintDocumentControlName.Print()
```

PrintDocumentControlName is the name of the PrintDocument control you added to the form, such as PrintDocument1.

This BASIC code tells the PrintDocument control to start printing. Of course, the PrintDocument control has no idea what to print, where to print your data on the page, or even which font or color you want to use. To tell the PrintDocument control exactly what to print and how to print it, you must add code inside the PrintDocument control's PrintPage event procedure. The PrintPage event procedure runs automatically whenever your program tells the PrintDocument control to start printing.

To create a `PrintPage` event procedure for the PrintDocument control:

1. In the Solution Explorer window, click the form file that contains a PrintDocument control on it and shows the `Imports System.Drawing.Printing` line stored at the top of its Code window.

2. Click the Class Name list box at the top of the Code window and choose the name of your PrintDocument control, such as PrintDocument1.

3. Click the Method Name list box and choose PrintPage. The Code window creates an empty `PrintPage` event procedure for the PrintDocument control, as shown next. At this point, the event procedure won't print anything until you write BASIC code to tell the `PrintPage` event procedure exactly what to print.

```
Private Sub PrintDocument1_PrintPage(ByVal sender As Object, ByVal e As_
System.Drawing.Printing.PrintPageEventArgs) Handles PrintDocument1.PrintPage

End Sub
```

The `PrintPage` event procedure uses an object called e, which relies on the built-in classes (`System.Drawing.Printing.PrintPageEventArgs`) that Visual Basic provides for printing data.

Printing Text

The data most commonly printed is text. To print text, use the `DrawString` method, like so:

```
e.Graphics.DrawString(Text, Font, Color, X, Y)
```

where *Text* is the string you want to print; *Font* specifies two items: the font name and the font size, such as Arial and 16; *Color* is the color in which to print your text, such as `Brushes.Black` or `Brushes.Red`; and *X* is the X coordinate where you want the text to appear on the page. The X coordinate measures the distance, in pixels, from the left margin of a page. (A pixel is one of many thousands of tiny dots that form images on screen and on a printed page.)

Y is the Y coordinate where you want the text to appear on the page. It measures the distance, in pixels, from the top margin of a page.

NOTE *Page margins depend on the page margin settings defined by the PageSetUpDialog control described later in this chapter in the section "Using the PageSetupDialog Control" on page 422. Otherwise, the page margin settings are set to zero (0), which prints at the physical edge of the page.*

The following code would print the string "Hello, world!" using the Microsoft Sans Serif font, at a font size of 24, in black, at an X coordinate of 1 and a Y coordinate of 155:

```
Dim font As New Font("Microsoft Sans Serif", 24)
e.Graphics.DrawString("Hello, world!", font, Brushes.Black, 1, 155)
```

In this listing:

Line 1 Defines the font (Microsoft Sans Serif) and the font size to use (24) and stores this information in an object called font.

Line 2 Uses the `DrawString` method to print the string using the `Brushes.Black` color and the X, Y coordinates of 1, 155. To define a color, you can enter the color's numeric value. Because this is cumbersome, Visual Basic provides the Brushes class, which lists predefined colors for printing. To use these colors, you define the Brushes class followed by the specific color you want to use. After you type the Brushes class followed by a period, Visual Basic displays a pop-up menu of 145 different colors to choose from so you can experiment with the color you like best, as shown in Figure 29-2.

Figure 29-2: When you need to define a color to use for printing, Visual Basic displays a pop-up menu that lists all available colors.

Printing Graphic Files

In addition to printing text, you can also print graphics files, such as GIFs or JPEGs. To print a graphic, use the DrawImage method, like so:

```
e.Graphics.DrawImage(Image.FromFile(Filename, X1, Y1, X2, Y2))
```

where *Filename* is the graphic file image you want to print; *X1* defines the X coordinate of the upper-left corner of the graphic image; *Y1* defines the Y coordinate of the upper-left corner of the graphic image; *X2* defines the X coordinate of the bottom-right corner of the graphic image; and *Y2* defines the Y coordinate of the bottom-right corner of the graphic image.

NOTE   *Depending on the differences between the X1 and X2 or Y1 and Y2 coordinates, the graphical image may print out stretched out or squashed.*

The following BASIC code would print a GIF file called linux.gif:

```
e.Graphics.DrawImage(Image.FromFile("C:\BookFiles\linux.gif"), 24, 25, 40, 45)
```

The upper-left corner of the graphical image would appear at the X and Y coordinates 24, 25, while the bottom-right corner of the graphic image would appear at the X and Y coordinates 40, 45.

Printing Lines

You can print straight lines using the DrawLine method, like so:

```
e.Graphics.DrawLine(Color, X1, Y1, X2, Y2)
```

Here, *X1* defines the X coordinate of the upper-left point of the line; *Y1* defines the Y coordinate of the upper-left point of the line; *X2* defines the X coordinate of the bottom-right point of the line; and *Y2* defines the Y coordinate of the bottom-right point of the line.

Color is the color of the line to draw, such as Pens.Black or Pens.Blue. To choose a line color, you can enter its numeric value, or use the Pens class, which contains a list of predefined colors. To use a predefined color, specify the Pens class followed by a period, then choose one of the 145 colors from a pop-up menu.

The following code would print a straight red line starting at the X and Y coordinate 0, 0 and ending at the X and Y coordinate 120, 10:

```
e.Graphics.DrawLine(Pens.Red, 0, 0, 120, 10)
```

Hands-on Tutorial: Printing Text

In this tutorial, you'll create a simple program that lets you type some words and then see your words printed on paper. You'll need to have a printer hooked to your computer in order to follow this tutorial.

1. Start a new Visual Basic project, then click OK. A blank form appears.
2. Choose View ▸ Toolbox to display the Toolbox, then choose Window ▸ Auto Hide to keep it visible at all times.
3. Double-click the PrintDocument control under the Printing category of the Toolbox. The PrintDocument control appears under your form.
4. Click the TextBox control in the Toolbox, mouse over the form, and click the left mouse button to draw a text box on the form.
5. Click the Button control in the Toolbox, move the mouse pointer under the text box control on the form, and click the left mouse button to draw a button control on the form.
6. Double-click the Button1 control on the form. The Code window appears.
7. Move the cursor to the front of the Public Class line and press ENTER to create an empty line at the top of the Code window.
8. Move the cursor to the empty line you just created and type **Imports System.Drawing .Printing** so the entire Code window looks like this:

```
Imports System.Drawing.Printing
Public Class Form1

End Class
```

9. Type **PrintDocument1.Print()** between the Private Sub and End Sub lines of the Button1_Click event procedure as follows:

```
    Private Sub Button1_Click(ByVal sender As System.Object, ByVal e As_
System.EventArgs) Handles Button1.Click
        PrintDocument1.Print()
    End Sub
```

10. Click in the Class Name list box in the Code window and choose PrintDocument1.
11. Click in the Method Name list box of the Code window and choose PrintPage. This creates an empty PrintPage event procedure.
12. Type the following in the PrintPage event procedure:

```
    Private Sub PrintDocument1_PrintPage(ByVal sender As Object, ByVal e As_
System.Drawing.Printing.PrintPageEventArgs) Handles PrintDocument1.PrintPage
        Const LeftEdge = 315
```

```
        Const RightEdge = 515
        Const TopEdge = 495
        Const BottomEdge = 535
        Dim font As New Font("Microsoft Sans Serif", 18)
        For I As Integer = 1 To 5
            e.Graphics.DrawString(TextBox1.Text, font, Brushes.Black, 90 * I, 30 * I)
        Next
        e.Graphics.DrawString("Printing all done!", font, Brushes.Black, 320, 500)
        e.Graphics.DrawLine(Pens.Black, LeftEdge, TopEdge, RightEdge, TopEdge)
        e.Graphics.DrawLine(Pens.Black, LeftEdge, BottomEdge, RightEdge, BottomEdge)
        e.Graphics.DrawLine(Pens.Black, LeftEdge, TopEdge, LeftEdge, BottomEdge)
        e.Graphics.DrawLine(Pens.Black, RightEdge, TopEdge, RightEdge, BottomEdge)
    End Sub
```

Lines 1–4   Use the Const keyword to define four values that will later be used as the X and Y coordinates to draw four lines which will create a box in the middle of the page, using four different DrawLine methods.

Line 5   Defines the name of the font and a font size to store in a font object name.

Lines 6 and 8   Create a For-Next loop that repeats five times.

Line 7   Prints the text, stored in the Text property of TextBox1, using the DrawText method. Each time the For-Next loop runs, another line of text appears on the page, slightly below and to the right of the previous line.

Line 9   Uses the DrawText method to print *Printing all done!* in the middle of the page.

Lines 10–13   Draw a line around the *Printing all done!* text using four different DrawLine methods.

13. Press F5. Your user interface appears. Make sure your printer is turned on and connected to your computer.

14. Click in the text box and type **My program works!**

15. Click the Button1 control. A single sheet of paper should come out of your printer, with *My program works!* printed five times, the text *Printing all done!* printed in the middle of the page, with a box around the *Printing all done!* text.

16. Press ALT-F4 to stop your program. Choose File ▸ Save All. A Save Project dialog box appears. Type **PrintingExample** and click Save.

Using the PrintDialog Control

Displaying a Print Dialog Box

If you don't want to enter all of the code from the previous tutorial to print data, you can have your program display a Print dialog box to make it easy for users to choose which printer to use, as shown in Figure 29-3.

To display a Print dialog box with your program, you need to add the PrintDialog control to your form and write some code. To add a PrintDialog control to your form, follow these steps:

1. Click a form file displayed in the Solution Explorer window that already contains a PrintDocument control.

2. Choose View ▸ Designer, then choose View ▸ Toolbox.

3. Double-click the PrintDialog control under the Printing category in the Toolbox. The PrintDialog control appears under your form.

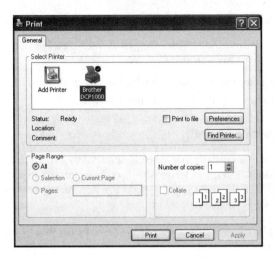

Figure 29-3: You can create and display a typical Print dialog box in your programs.

4. Now write BASIC code to display the Print dialog box:

```
PrintDialogBoxName.ShowDialog()
```

where *PrintDialogBoxName* is the name of your PrintDialog control, such as PrintDialog1.

To give the Print dialog box the ability to start printing something, you need to add two additional commands:

```
PrintDialogBoxName.Document = PrintDocumentControlName
If PrintDialogBoxName.ShowDialog = DialogResult.OK Then
    PrintDocumentControlName.Print()
End If
```

In this listing:

Line 1   Tells the PrintDialog control which PrintDocument control to use, such as PrintDocument1. Because more than one PrintDocument control could be stored on a form, you must always specify which one you want to use.

Lines 2 and 4   Defines an If-Then statement that displays the Print dialog box on the screen using the ShowDialog method described in Chapter 17, and then checks to see whether the user clicked the OK button (identified by DialogResult.OK). If the user clicked OK in the Print dialog box, the If-Then statement tells the PrintDocument control to begin printing.

If you modify the PrintingExample project you created in the tutorial section "Printing Text" on page 415, you could rewrite the Button1_Click event procedure as follows, so that a Print dialog box appears when the user clicks the Button1 control:

```
Private Sub Button1_Click(ByVal sender As System.Object, ByVal e As System.EventArgs)_
Handles Button1.Click
    PrintDialogBoxName.Document = PrintDocumentControlName
    If PrintDialogBoxName.ShowDialog = DialogResult.OK Then
        PrintDocumentControlName.Print()
    End If
End Sub
```

Displaying a Print Preview

Many people prefer viewing their data before they print it using a feature known as *print preview*. You can display a print preview in two ways:

- In a separate window using the PrintPreviewDialog control
- Inside the current form using the PrintPreview control

Using the PrintPreviewDialog Control

Using the
Print
Preview
Control

To use the PrintPreviewDialog control, you must first add it to a form that already has a PrintDocument control on it. Then you write BASIC code to tell the PrintPreviewDialog control what to display and then to display the Print Preview dialog box on the screen. To add a PrintPreviewDialog control to a form:

1. Click a form file displayed in the Solution Explorer window that already contains a PrintDocument control.
2. Choose View ▸ Designer.
3. Choose View ▸ Toolbox to display the Toolbox.
4. Double-click the PrintPreviewDialog control, which appears under the Printing category of the Toolbox. A PrintPreviewDialog control appears under your form.

Once you've added a PrintPreviewDialog control to a form, you need to write two lines of code to make the control work. The first command tells the PrintPreviewDialog control what to print, as defined by the PrintDocument control:

```
PrintPreviewDialogControlName.Document = PrintDocumentControlName
```

NOTE *You must have defined a* PrintPage *event procedure for your* PrintDocument *control, because the* PrintPage *event procedure tells the* PrintDocument *what to print using the* DrawString *and* DrawLines *methods.*

Once you've defined the PrintPreviewDialog control to a PrintDocument control, the next line of code you need to write displays the Print Preview window:

```
PrintPreviewDialogControlName.ShowDialog()
```

This command displays a Print Preview window (see Figure 29-4).

Zoom

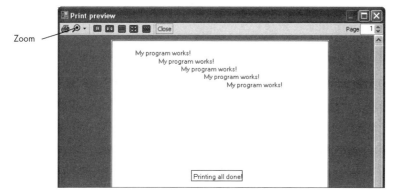

Figure 29-4: The Print Preview window displays your data in a separate window.

Using the PrintPreview Control

The PrintPreview control appears directly on a form and displays the preview of your document. Unlike the PrintPreviewDialog control, PrintPreview doesn't have built-in icons for zooming in and out. To modify the magnification of anything displayed in the PrintPreview control, you must either modify its Zoom property in the Properties window or use code to modify the Zoom property while your program is running, like so:

```
PrintPreviewControlName.Zoom = Value
```

For example, to display a document in the PrintPreview control at 50 percent zoom magnification, you could use the following:

```
PrintPreviewControl1.Zoom = 0.5
```

To use the PrintPreview control, you must add it to a form that contains a PrintDocument control, as shown in Figure 29-5. Then you assign the Document property of the PrintPreview control to a PrintDocument control either through the Properties window or with BASIC code, like so:

```
PrintPreviewControlName.Document = PrintDocumentControlName
```

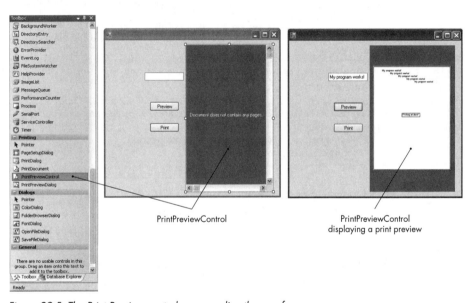

Figure 29-5: The Print Preview control appears directly on a form.

Hands-on Tutorial: Displaying a Print Preview

This tutorial uses the PrintingExample program from the tutorial section "Printing Text" on page 415. If you haven't created that project yet, you should do so now.

1. Load Visual Basic Express.
2. Choose File ▸ Recent Projects ▸ PrintingExample. The PrintingExample project appears.

3. Click the Form1.vb file in the Solution Explorer window and then choose View ▶ Designer. Your user interface appears.

4. Click the Button1 control and press F4 to open the Properties window.

5. Click the Text property and type **Print**.

6. Choose View ▶ Toolbox to display the Toolbox, then choose Window ▶ Auto Hide to keep it visible.

7. Click the Button control, mouse over the form, and click the left mouse button to create a new button control on the form.

8. Click this new button on your form and press F4 to open the Properties window.

9. Click the Text property and type **Preview**. You may want to move the buttons on your form so your user interface looks like Figure 29-6.

10. Double-click the PrintPreviewDialog control under the Printing category of the Toolbox. A PrintPreviewDialog control appears.

11. Double-click the Preview button control. The Code window appears and creates an empty `Button2_Click` event procedure.

Figure 29-6: A user interface with a text box and two buttons displaying the text Print and Preview.

12. Type the following between the `Private Sub` and `End Sub` lines of the `Button2_Click` event procedure:

```
    Private Sub Button2_Click(ByVal sender As System.Object, ByVal e As_
System.EventArgs) Handles Button2.Click
        PrintPreviewDialog1.Document = PrintDocument1
        PrintPreviewDialog1.ShowDialog()
    End Sub
```

13. Press F5. Your user interface appears.

14. Click in the text box and type **My program works!**

15. Click the Preview button control. A Print Preview window appears (see Figure 29-4).

16. Click Close to close the Print Preview window.

17. Press ALT-F4 to stop your program. Choose File ▶ Save All. A Save Project dialog box appears. Click Save.

Using the PageSetupDialog Control

Displaying a Page Setup Dialog Box

The PageSetupDialog control lets the user define a paper size, margins, and paper orientation from a Page Setup dialog box, as shown in Figure 29-7. To use it, you add the control to a form that already contains a PrintDocument control, then write code to tell the PageSetupDialog control which PrintDocument control to use, as well as relay the page setting information of that PrintDocument control.

To add a PageSetupDialog control to a form, follow these steps:

1. Click a form file displayed in the Solution Explorer window that already contains a PrintDocument control.
2. Choose View ▸ Designer, then choose View ▸ Toolbox to display the Toolbox.
3. Double-click the PageSetupDialog control, which appears under the Printing category of the Toolbox. A PageSetupDialog control appears under your form.

Once you've added a PageSetupDialog control, you need to define the PrintDocument control you wish to use as well as the page settings. To define which PrintDocument control to use, use this syntax:

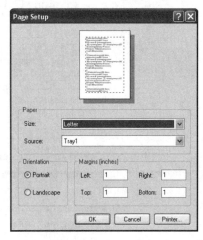

Figure 29-7: A Page Setup dialog box with various options

```
PageSetupDialogControlName.Document = PrintDocumentControlName
```

Next, you display the Page Setup dialog box:

```
If PageSetupDialogControlName.ShowDialog = DialogResult.OK Then
    PrintDocumentControlName.DefaultPageSettings =
PageSetupDialogControlName.PageSettings
    End If
```

The ShowDialog method displays the Page Setup dialog box. If the user clicks the OK button, any changes that she made are stored in the PrintDocument's DefaultPageSettings property.

Hands-on Tutorial: Displaying a Page Setup Dialog Box

This tutorial uses the PrintingExample program you modified in the tutorial section "Printing Text" on page 415. If you haven't created that Visual Basic project yet, you should do so now.

1. Load Visual Basic Express.
2. Choose File ▸ Recent Projects ▸ PrintingExample. The PrintingExample project appears.
3. Click the Form1.vb file in the Solution Explorer window, and then choose View ▸ Designer. Your user interface appears.
4. Choose View ▸ Toolbox to display the Toolbox.
5. Click the Button control in the Toolbox, mouse over the form, and click the left mouse button to create a button on the form.
6. Press F4 to open the Properties window, click the Text property, and type **Setup**. You may want to move the buttons on your form so your user interface looks similar to Figure 29-8.
7. Double-click the Setup button control. The Code window appears and creates an empty Button3_Click event procedure.

8. Type the following between the `Private Sub` and `End Sub` lines of the `Button3_Click` event procedure:

```
    Private Sub Button3_Click(ByVal sender As System.Object, ByVal e As_
System.EventArgs) Handles Button3.Click
        PageSetupDialog1.Document = PrintDocument1
  If pageSetupDialog1.ShowDialog = DialogResult.OK Then
    PrintDocument1.DefaultPageSettings = PageSetupDialog1.PageSettings
  End If
    End Sub
```

9. Press F5. Your user interface appears.

10. Click in the text box and type **My program works!**

11. Click the Setup button control. A Page Setup dialog box appears (see Figure 29-7).

12. Click the Landscape radio button in the Orientation group. Notice that the Page Setup dialog box displays the changed page orientation.

13. Click in the Size list box and choose 3 × 5. Notice how the Page Setup dialog box displays your page shrunken to fit a 3 × 5 index card.

14. Click OK to make the Page Setup dialog box disappear.

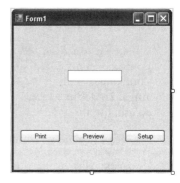

Figure 29-8: A user interface with a text box and three buttons displaying the text Print, Preview, and Setup.

15. Click the Preview button on the form. The Print Preview window appears. Click Close in the Print Preview window to make it go away.

16. Press ALT-F4 to stop your program. Choose File ▶ Save All. A Save Project dialog box appears. You can save your project if you like.

KEY FEATURES TO REMEMBER

To give a Visual Basic project the ability to print data, you must add a PrintDocument control to your form and add the `Imports System.Drawing.Printing` line to your BASIC code. Once you've done this, you need to write BASIC code to define what to print and how to print it.

- Your program won't print anything until you write BASIC code inside a PrintDocument's `PrintPage` event procedure. The `PrintPage` procedure runs whenever you use the `PrintDocumentName.Print()` command, where `PrintDocumentName` is the name of your PrintDocument control, such as PrintDocument1.

- The `DrawString` method prints text. The `DrawImage` method prints graphics files. The `DrawLine` method prints lines.

- The PrintDialog control displays a Print dialog box so the user can choose a printer to use.

- The PrintPreviewDialog control displays a separate Print Preview window. The PrintPreview control lets you display a print preview directly inside an existing form.

- The PageSetupDialog control displays a dialog box for defining paper size, margins, and paper orientation.

30

ADDING THE FINISHING
TOUCHES TO YOUR PROGRAM

You can make your programs more interesting to use by
having them play sounds, display graphics, and display
web pages downloaded from the Internet. Rather than
embed sounds, graphics, or web pages directly into your
program, however, you can store them as *external files* in a special folder so you
can find them again. Then, once you've written your program, tested it, and
added sound and graphics to make it visually and audibly appealing, the final
step is to compile it into a file that you can distribute to others.

This chapter will show you how to add the finishing touches to a Visual Basic
program and make it ready for distribution to the public.

Playing Sounds

You can make your program more interesting by adding sounds. At the simplest
level, you can use the Beep command to sound a simple beep from the computer's
speaker, like so:

```
Private Sub Button1_Click(ByVal sender As System.Object, ByVal e As_
System.EventArgs) Handles Button1.Click
```

```
        Beep
End Sub
```

This event procedure runs the Beep command each time the user clicks the Button1 control. The Beep command is most often used to notify the user when incorrect data is entered or an unavailable control is clicked.

For greater flexibility, you can also play Pulse Code Modulation (PCM) WAV files, one of many audio file formats used for storing sounds such as songs or speech. (Other types of WAV files actually compress audio files, but are not compatible with PCM WAV files. If you load a WAV file and it doesn't work in Visual Basic, chances are good that it's stored in one of many non-PCM WAV file formats.) By playing PCM WAV files, your program can provide background music, spoken messages, or any number of more sophisticated sounds.

Unlike the more popular MP3 files, PCM WAV files gobble up huge amounts of disk space, but without any loss in audio quality. In comparison, MP3 files use compression that reduces the file size, at a slight loss in audio quality. No matter; Visual Basic will only play PCM WAV files, which you can create from audio CDs using a CD ripping program such as Nero (www.nero.com) or Easy Media Creator (www.roxio.com).

NOTE   *When ripping audio files from a CD, make sure you own the copyrights to the audio files or you have the permission of the copyright owner; otherwise, you could be violating copyright laws.*

To play a PCM WAV file, use the Play command with this syntax:

```
My.Computer.Audio.Play(WAVfilename, PlayMode)
```

where *WAVfilename* is the drive, directory, and PCM WAV file you want to play. *PlayMode* determines how the PCM WAV file plays. The three options are Background, Background-Loop, and WaitToComplete. Table 30-1 explains how the different play modes work.

Table 30-1: How Play Modes Play a PCM WAV File

PlayMode	What it does
AudioPlayMode.Background	Plays the WAV file once and then runs the rest of the BASIC code in your program while the WAV file continues to play.
AudioPlayMode.BackgroundLoop	Keeps playing the WAV file over and over until your program either stops or runs the My.Computer.Audio.Stop() command.
AudioPlayMode.WaitToComplete	Plays the WAV file once and temporarily stops running more lines of code in your program. Once the WAV file stops playing, the rest of your code starts running.

For example, to play a PCM WAV file called Hello.wav, stored in the E:\Music\ Sounds drive and directory, you could use this command:

```
My.Computer.Audio.Play("E:\Music\Sounds\Hello.wav", AudioPlayMode.Background)
```

NOTE   *You must specify the .wav file extension or else Visual Basic won't know the exact WAV file you want to play.*

Displaying Pictures

In addition to displaying text in labels and text boxes, Visual Basic lets you display graphical images inside a *PictureBox* control. To add a PictureBox control and display a graphics file inside it, perform the following steps.

1. Double-click the PictureBox control in the Toolbox. A PictureBox control appears on the form, which you may want to move or resize.

2. Click the Tasks button in the upper-right corner of the PictureBox control. A PictureBox Tasks pop-up appears, as shown in Figure 30-1.

3. Click Choose Image. A Select Resource dialog box appears, as shown in Figure 30-2.

4. Click Import. An Open dialog box appears.

5. Click the graphics file you want to use and click Open. You may have to switch drives and folders to find the file you want to use. Your chosen image appears in the Select Resource dialog box.

6. Click OK. Your chosen image appears in the PictureBox control.

7. Click in the Size Mode list box and choose an option such as Zoom or Stretch. Figure 30-3 shows how the different size modes affect the way your image appears. The Size Mode property defines how an image appears inside a PictureBox control.

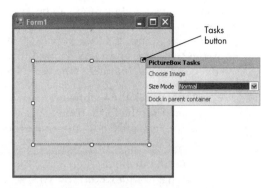

Figure 30-1: The PictureBox Tasks pop-up gives you quick access to defining the graphics file to use and defining how to display it.

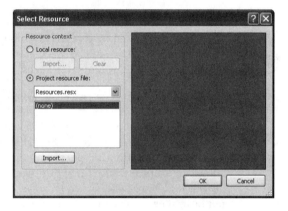

Figure 30-2: The Select Resource dialog box lets you choose an image to display inside a PictureBox control.

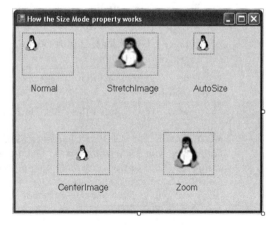

Figure 30-3: The Size Mode property defines how an image appears inside a PictureBox control.

Viewing Web Pages

Displaying text and pictures can be nice, but including web pages can be much more useful, colorful, and interesting. To view web pages, Visual Basic Express includes a *WebBrowser* control that can display HTML (HyperText Markup Language) files stored on the computer or directly access Internet sites—provided, of course, the computer is connected to the Internet at the time. To use the WebBrowser control, follow these steps:

1. Double-click the WebBrowser control in the Toolbox. A WebBrowser control appears on the form. If there are no other controls on the form, the WebBrowser control expands to fill the entire form.
2. Press F4 to open the Properties window and click in the URL property.
3. Enter the drive, directory, and filename of an HTML file to display (such as **C:\ Web pages\index.htm**), or type the address of an Internet website (such as **http:// www.nostarch.com**). Now whenever your program runs, the WebBrowser control will display either your HTML file or a web page from the Internet site you specified.

Using Resources

Storing
Data as
Resources

Many programs need to access and use separate data, such as data for displaying graphics files or playing PCM WAV audio files. While you could specify the exact location of each file you need, such as:

```
My.Computer.Audio.Play("E:\Music\Hello.wav", AudioPlayMode.Background)
```

what if you want to use dozens of different files? In that case, you'd have to type out the drive, directory, and filename of every single file.

Rather than identify specific file names in your code, you can use *resources*, which allow you to store all the files your program needs in a single location called a *resources folder*. Then, in your BASIC code, you specify the resource you want to use only by name, not by its specific filename, drive, or directory location. Resources provide a single, convenient location for storing external files that your program needs.

Visual Basic Express can store four types of resources:

Strings Text, such as single words or short phrases which would appear in the Text property of controls, such as a Label or TextBox.

Images Graphics useful for displaying visual information on a form, such as in a PictureBox control.

Icons A tiny graphical image meant to appear in controls, such as the ToolStrip control.

Audio WAV sound files used with the My.Computer.Audio.Play command.

NOTE *Many programmers use resources to create separate text files for different languages. Rather than type text directly into the Text property of a control, such as a text box or a label, they assign the Text property of a control to a resource file. By replacing an English language resource file with a Spanish or French resource file, they can create multi-language versions of their programs easily, without having to modify their code.*

Storing Short Strings in the Resources Folder

If you need to store only single words or short phrases, you can type your strings directly into the *Resources editor*. When you do, you give your string a unique name and (optionally) a comment that explains its purpose. To type one or more strings into the Resources editor, follow these steps:

1. Load a Visual Basic project.
2. Choose Project ▶ *ProjectName* Properties. (The name of your project will appear in the menu.) A Properties window appears.
3. Click the Resources tab on the left side of the screen. The Resources editor appears.
4. Click the downward-pointing arrow on the Add Resource button. A pull-down menu appears, as shown in Figure 30-4.

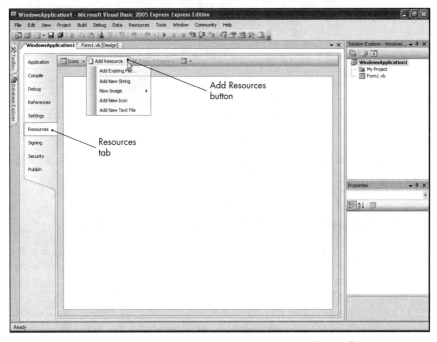

Figure 30-4: The Resources editor lets you add and edit a variety of types of data to use in your Visual Basic projects.

5. Click Add New String. The Resources editor displays rows and columns for storing your strings under the column headings *Name, Value,* and *Comment,* as shown in Figure 30-5.
6. Click in the Name column and type a descriptive name for your string. This will be the name that your code will use to represent the string you store in the Value column.
7. Click in the Value column and type the actual string you want to use in your program. (Although the Value column can hold a large amount of text, it's usually best to store only short strings that you can easily view and edit within the width of the column.)

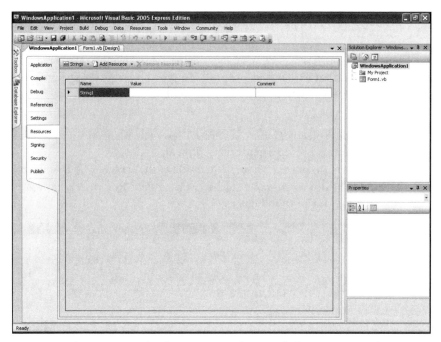

Figure 30-5: The Resources editor lets you type and view multiple strings in a grid.

8. (Optional) Click in the Comment column and type a descriptive comment that explains the purpose of this string.

9. Repeat steps 6 through 8 for each additional string you want to store.

Creating and Storing a Text File in the Resources Folder

If your program needs to store strings of text longer than a single sentence, you may want to store that text in a separate text file instead. You can create a text file using the Notepad program included with Windows, or in any word processor (so you can use its spell-checker). Then save the document in the plain text file format. Once you've stored a large amount of text in a text file, you can store that file in the Resources editor, as explained later in the section "Adding an Existing File to the Resources Folder" on page 432.

As an alternative to using a separate program, Visual Basic Express lets you create and store text in a file directly within the Resources editor by following these steps:

1. Load a Visual Basic project.

2. Choose Project ▶ *ProjectName* Properties. (The name of your project will appear in the menu.) A Properties window appears.

3. Click the Resources tab on the left side of the screen. The Resources editor appears.

4. Click the downward-pointing arrow on the Add Resource button. A pull-down menu appears.

5. Click Add New Text File. An Add New Resource dialog box appears, as shown in Figure 30-6.

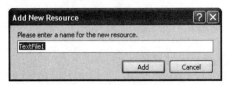

Figure 30-6: The Add New Resource dialog box lets you define a unique name to identify a resource.

6. Type a name for your resource and click Add. Visual Basic Express displays an icon representing your text file in the Resources editor, as shown in Figure 30-7.

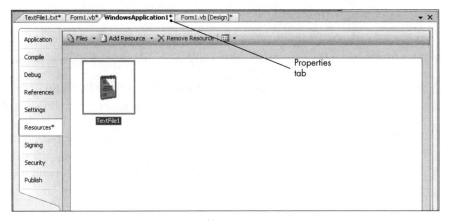

Figure 30-7: The Resources editor displays files as icons.

7. Double-click this icon to display a simple editor in which you can type a large amount of text.

8. Type your text, pressing ENTER at the end of each line, because lines won't wrap automatically as they do in a word processor.

9. Choose File ▸ Save Resources to save your newly created text file.

10. Click the Properties tab to view the Resources editor again.

Creating and Adding an Image to the Resources Folder

Graphics images can be used to display information in a PictureBox control or as an icon in a ToolStrip control. If you're artistically inclined, you can create a new graphics image from within Visual Basic Express by following these steps:

1. Load a Visual Basic project.

2. Choose Project ▸ *ProjectName* Properties. (The name of your project will appear in the menu.) A Properties window appears.

3. Click the Resources tab on the left side of the screen. The Resources editor appears.

4. Click the downward-pointing arrow on the Add Resources button. A pull-down menu appears (see Figure 30-4).

5. Either create an icon by clicking Add New Icon or, to create an image, click New Image and then choose the type of graphics file you want to create, such as GIF Image or BMP Image.

6. Visual Basic Express loads the Microsoft Paint program. Draw your image and choose File ▸ Save.

7. Choose File ▸ Exit to exit Microsoft Paint and return to Visual Basic Express. The Resources editor displays an icon to represent your newly created graphics file.

Adding an Existing File to the Resources Folder

If you want to add an audio file, a text file that you've created with another program, or a graphics file that you created with another program (such as Photoshop), you can add an existing file to your Visual Basic project.

To store an existing file into the Resources editor, follow these steps:

1. Load a Visual Basic project.
2. Choose Project ▸ *ProjectName* Properties. (The name of your project will appear in the menu.) A Properties window appears.
3. Click the Resources tab on the left side of the screen. The Resources editor appears.
4. Click the downward-pointing arrow on the Add Resources button. A pull-down menu appears (see Figure 30-4).
5. Click Add Existing File. An Add Existing File to Resources dialog box appears.
6. Click the file you want to use (you may have to search through drives and folders) and click Open. The Resources editor displays your file icon and includes your file in the Solution Explorer window under the Resources folder.

Using a Resource with BASIC Code

Once you've stored audio, text, or graphics files in the Resources editor, you can access that resource with this command:

```
My.Resources.ResourceName
```

where *ResourceName* is the unique name of the resource you want to use. For example, to use a resource named String1 and store its contents in the Text property of a label control, you could use the following code:

```
Label1.Text = My.Resources.String1
```

After you type `My.Resources.`, Visual Basic Express displays a pop-up menu that lists all the string resources you have stored in the Resources editor, as shown in Figure 30-8. At this point, you can either click the name of the resource you want to use or type the resource name manually.

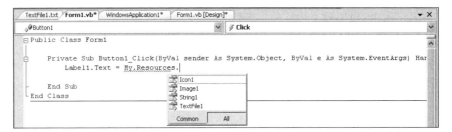

Figure 30-8: When you type the Visual Basic command to use a resource, a pop-up menu appears to list all the available resources in your Visual Basic project.

This tutorial shows you how to store strings in the Resources editor and retrieve them again in a label control.

1. Start a new project, then click OK. A blank form appears.
2. Choose Project ▸ *ProjectName* Properties. (The name of your project will appear in the menu.)
3. Click the Resources tab on the left side of the screen. The Resources editor appears.
4. Click the downward-pointing arrow on the Add Resource button. A pull-down menu appears.
5. Click Add New String. A grid appears with Name, Value, and Comments headings. The Resources editor should already display *String1* under the Name column.
6. Click in the Value column and type **This appears in Label1**.
7. Click in the next cell down in the Value column. Notice that the Resources editor automatically fills in *String2* under the Name column of the second row of the grid.
8. Type **This appears in Label2**, as shown in Figure 30-9.

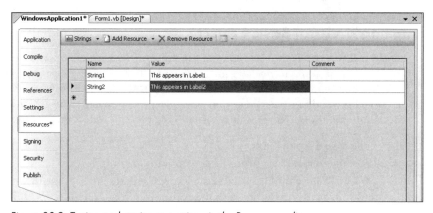

Figure 30-9: Typing and storing two strings in the Resources editor

9. Click the Form1.vb [Design] tab to view the blank form.
10. Choose View ▸ Toolbox to display the Toolbox, then choose Window ▸ Auto Hide to keep it visible.
11. Click the Label control in the Toolbox, mouse over the form, and click the left mouse button to create a label control.
12. Click the Label control in the Toolbox again, mouse over the form, and click the left mouse button to create a second label control.
13. Click the Button control in the Toolbox, mouse over the form, and click the left mouse button to create a new button control on the form.
14. Double-click the Button1 control on your form. The Code window appears.
15. Type the following between the `Private Sub` and `End Sub` lines of the `Button1_Click` event procedure:

```
Private Sub Button1_Click(ByVal sender As System.Object, ByVal e As_
System.EventArgs) Handles Button1.Click
```

```
     Beep
     Label1.Text = My.Resources.String1
   Label2.Text = My.Resources.String2
   End Sub
```

In this listing:

Line 1   Calls the Beep command to make a beeping noise.

Line 2   Takes the resource string named String1 and stores its contents into the Text property of the Label1 control.

Line 3   Takes the resource string named String2 and stores its contents into the Text property of the Label2 control.

16. Press F5. Your user interface appears.

17. Click the Button1 control. Your computer should beep and display the text you typed in steps 6 and 8 in the Text properties of the two label controls on your form, because the code you typed in step 15 stored the strings from the Resources editor directly in the Text property of both label controls.

18. Press ALT-F4 to stop your program. Choose File ▶ Close Project. A Close Project dialog box appears. Click Discard.

Compiling a Visual Basic Project

Once you've written your program, designed your user interface, and debugged your code, the final step is to *compile* your program so that other people can run your program on their own computers. Compiling turns your BASIC code into *machine code* and stores the machine code instructions in an *executable file* (often called an *EXE file*) that you can distribute to others. To compile a Visual Basic project, follow these steps:

1. Load Visual Basic Express.

2. Load the Visual Basic project that you want to compile.

3. Choose Build ▶ Build. Visual Basic Express creates an EXE file of your project and stores it in the folder with the rest of your Visual Basic project files.

Visual Basic EXE files will run only on computers that have Microsoft's .NET Framework files installed. To get a copy of the .NET Framework files, visit www.microsoft.com. (Note that any computer with Visual Basic Express installed automatically has the .NET Framework files installed.)

KEY FEATURES TO REMEMBER

Once you've written a program and debugged it to make sure it works, the final step is to add sound and graphics to make your program look more appealing.

- Visual Basic programs can play WAV files.

- The PictureBox control can hold and display a graphical image.

- Resources allow you to store external files in a single, easy-to-locate folder. You can store text, graphics, or audio files as resources.

- Compiling turns your Visual Basic project files into a single executable file. To run any Visual Basic EXE file, your computer must have the .NET Framework files installed as well.

INDEX

Symbols

&. *See* ampersand characters

* (asterisks) for multiplication, 248

\ (backslashes) for integer division, 248

^ (carets) for exponentiation, 248

... (ellipsis) for properties, 82

=. *See* equal signs

> (greater-than signs) for comparisons, 282

>= (greater-than-or-equal-to signs) for comparisons, 282

< (less-than signs) for comparisons, 282

<= (less-than-or-equal-to signs) for comparisons, 282

- (minus signs) for subtraction and negation, 248

<> (not equal operator) for comparisons, 282

() (parentheses) for precedence, 250

+ (plus signs) for addition, 248

/ (slashes) for division, 248

A

AbortRetryIgnore button style, 221, 224

Abs method, 251

Absolute size value, 202

ActiveLinkColor property, 179–180

Add Connection dialog box, 400

Add Existing Item dialog box, 44

Add method
  for collections, 320
  for hash tables, 339

Add New Item dialog box, 30, 43–44

addition operator (+), 248

aligning
  controls, 53, 120–123
  images, 98–99
  TabControls, 203
  text, 91

Alignment property, 203

All Windows Forms control category, 51

ALT key, 29

ampersand characters (&)
  for hot keys, 145
  for string concatenation, 254, 259

anchoring controls, 103–106

And operator, 284–285

AndAlso operator, 285

appearance
  of combo boxes, 173–174
  of controls, 87–88, 94–96
  of forms, 119
  for properties, 81

Appearance category. *See* appearance

Application Properties window, 114

ApplicationModal button style, 221

arranging
  menu titles and commands, 145–146
  tabs, 205
  ToolStrip commands, 154

arrays, 308
  clearing, 313–314
  copying hash table data to, 340–341
  copying queue data to, 333–334, 337–338
  initializing, 310–311
  multidimensional, 311–312
  searching, 315–316
  size, 309–310, 312–313

char data type, 238
characters
    comparing, 283–284
    in strings
        counting, 262
        deleting, 264
        retrieving, 265
        trimming, 262–263
Chars property, 265–266
check boxes, 163–164
check marks on menus, 149
CheckAlign property
    for check boxes, 163
    for radio buttons, 160–161
CheckChanged events, 128
checked list boxes, 170–172
Checked property, 135–136
    for check boxes, 163–164
    for radio buttons, 160–162
CheckState property, 163
CInt function, 254
classes and class files, 42
    libraries for, 43
    methods in, 247, 251
    for objects, 360–362, 364–365
Clear method
    arrays, 313–314
    hash table data, 342
    queues, 332
    stack data, 337
clearing. *See* Clear method
Click events, 128, 140
ClickOnClick property, 149
CLng function, 254
Close command, 114
closing
    forms, 114
    projects, 47
code snippets
    automatic insertion of, 21–23
    for event procedures, 131–132
    IntelliSense, 63–65
Code window, 20
    navigating, 67–69
    opening, 59–60
    searching in, 67–68
    as tabbed document, 38–39

typing in, 63–67
    viewing code in, 60–62
collapsing procedures, 61–62
collections, 319
    counting members in, 323
    deleting data from, 322–323
    For Each Next loops for, 323–324
    parts of, 319
    searching for data in, 321–322
    storing data in, 320–321
    working with, 324–327
color
    for controls, 92–93
    for link labels, 180–181
Color dialog box, 219–220
ColorDialog controls, 212–213
ColumnCount property, 200
columns
    for list boxes, 166
    for TableLayoutPanels, 201–202
ColumnStyles property, 200
combining conditional expressions,
        284–287
combo boxes, 172–173
    appearance of, 173–174
    filling, 173
    options for, 155
    sorting items in, 174
    on ToolStrips, 152
commands, 132–133
    menu, 27–30, 141
        adding, 143
        deleting, 143
        editing, 144–145
        hot keys for, 145
        rearranging, 145–146
    toolbar, 30–32
    ToolStrip
        deleting, 154
        grouping, 156
        rearranging, 154
    writing, 132–135
comments, 378–381
Common Controls category, 51
common properties, 82–84
Community menu, 29
Compare method, 269

Project menu, 29
projects, 41
  closing and opening, 47
  compiling, 434
  creating, 13–16, 42–43
  database files for
    binding, 400–403
    linking, 399–400
  files for
    adding, 43–45
    copying, 46
    deleting, 45
    managing, 41–42
    in resources folder, 432
    saving, 45–47
prompts
  for input boxes, 226
  for message boxes, 220
  for syntax, 63
properties, 79
  in class files, 361–363
  of controls, 55–57, 80
    appearance, 87–88, 94–96
    behavior, 106–112
    color, 92–93
    common, 82–84
    editing, 82
    images, 96–99
    layout, 101–106
    Properties window for, 80–81
    text, 88–92
    user interaction, 93–96
    viewing, 81
  for data, 135–136
  for objects, 359–360, 364–365
  retrieving data from, 363
  storing data in, 363–364
  for structures, 306
  variables for, 362
Properties window, 19, 33, 80–81
Public keyword, 233
pull-down menus, 27–30, 139
  check marks for, 149
  commands on, 141
    adding, 143
    deleting, 143
    editing, 144–145

hot keys for, 145
  rearranging, 145–146
  creating, 140–142, 151–152
  editing, 143–146
  icons on, 150–151
  separator bars on, 146–147
  shortcut key combinations for,
    147–148
Pulse Code Modulation (PCM) WAV
    files, 426
Push method, 335
pushing stack data, 335–336

Q

Question button style, 222
Question icon, 225
queues, 329–330
  adding data to, 330
  checking contents of, 330–331
  copying data to arrays from,
    333–334, 337–338
  counting contents of, 331
  deleting data from, 331–332
Quick Find searches, 67–68
Quick Watch dialog box, 384–385

R

R property, 220
radio buttons, 159–160
  grouping, 160, 162
  properties for, 160–162
ranges of values, 187
  in pattern matching, 271–272
  scroll bars for, 187–191
  in Select-Case, 291–292
readability, 379
ReadAllText command, 397
reading text file data, 397–399
ReadOnly property, 182
rearranging
  menu titles and commands, 145–146
  tabs, 205
  ToolStrip commands, 154
recently viewed projects, 47
records, database, 399
ReDim keyword, 309, 312

size
    arrays, 309–310, 312–313
    Code window, 60
    controls, 54–55, 83, 122
        anchored, 103–105
        AutoSize property, 107
        for layout, 101–102
        minimum and maximum, 105
    Font dialog box, 218
    forms, 117, 119
    TableLayoutPanel rows and columns, 201–202
Size property. *See* size
slashes (/) for division, 248
SmallChange property, 188
snaplines for controls, 53, 120
snippets
    automatic insertion of, 21–23
    for event procedures, 131–132
    IntelliSense, 63–65
Solution Explorer window, 33, 44–45
Sort method, 315
Sorted property. *See* sorting
sorting
    arrays, 314–315
    combo box items, 173–174
    list box items, 164–166
sound
    playing, 425–426
    resources for, 428
sources, database, 399–403
spaces, trimming, 262–263
spelling errors, 63–64
split buttons, 152, 154–155
SplitContainers, 205–207
SplitterDistance property, 206
SplitterIncrement property, 206
SplitterWidth property, 206
SQL Server database files, 400
Sqrt method, 251
stacks, 334
    clearing data from, 337
    contents of, 335–336
    popping data from, 336–337
    pushing data onto, 335–336
Start property
    for MonthCalendar controls, 193
    for SelectionRange controls, 136

StartPosition property, 117–118
Startup forms, 114–115
step increments in For-Next loops, 297–298
Step Into command, 387–388
Step Out command, 388
Step Over command, 387
Step property for progress bars, 156
stepping in debugging, 383, 387–388
Stop icon, 225
stopping debugging, 390
storing
    array data, 308–309, 317–319
    collection data, 320–321
    general procedures, 347–349
    property data, 363–364
    short strings, 429–430
    structure data, 307
    text file data, 396–399
StrComp function, 133, 268
Strikeout property, 218
String Collection Editor, 165
strings, 233–234, 259. *See also* text
    comparing
        Compare method for, 269
        conditional expressions for, 283–284
        Like operator for, 269–273
        StrComp for, 268
        tutorial for, 273–274
    concatenating, 254, 259–262
    converting to numbers, 254–255, 278–279
    counting characters in, 262
    deleting characters from, 264
    extracting, 276–278
    padding, 264–265
    replacing, 274–276
    reversing, 279
    searching, 265–268
    trimming, 262–263
Strings resources, 428
StrReverse function, 279
structures, 306
    arrays. *See* arrays
    collections, 319–323
    declaring and defining, 306–307
    hash tables. *See* hash tables

Electronic Frontier Foundation
Defending Freedom in the Digital World

Free Speech. Privacy. Innovation. Fair Use. Reverse Engineering. If you care about these rights in the digital world, then you should join the Electronic Frontier Foundation (EFF). EFF was founded in 1990 to protect the rights of users and developers of technology. EFF is the first to identify threats to basic rights online and to advocate on behalf of free expression in the digital age.

The Electronic Frontier Foundation Defends Your Rights!
Become a Member Today!
http://www.eff.org/support/

Current EFF projects include:

Protecting your fundamental right to vote. Widely publicized security flaws in computerized voting machines show that, though filled with potential, this technology is far from perfect. EFF is defending the open discussion of e-voting problems and is coordinating a national litigation strategy addressing issues arising from use of poorly developed and tested computerized voting machines.

Ensuring that you are not traceable through your things. Libraries, schools, the government and private sector businesses are adopting radio frequency identification tags, or RFIDs – a technology capable of pinpointing the physical location of whatever item the tags are embedded in. While this may seem like a convenient way to track items, it's also a convenient way to do something less benign: track people and their activities through their belongings. EFF is working to ensure that embrace of this technology does not erode your right to privacy.

Stopping the FBI from creating surveillance backdoors on the Internet. EFF is part of a coalition opposing the FBI's expansion of the Communications Assistance for Law Enforcement Act (CALEA), which would require that the wiretap capabilities built into the phone system be extended to the Internet, forcing ISPs to build backdoors for law enforcement.

Providing you with a means by which you can contact key decision-makers on cyber-liberties issues. EFF maintains an action center that provides alerts on technology, civil liberties issues and pending legislation to more than 50,000 subscribers. EFF also generates a weekly online newsletter, EFFector, and a blog that provides up-to-the-minute information and commentary.

Defending your right to listen to and copy digital music and movies. The entertainment industry has been overzealous in trying to protect its copyrights, often decimating fair use rights in the process. EFF is standing up to the movie and music industries on several fronts.

Check out all of the things we're working on at http://www.eff.org and join today or make a donation to support the fight to defend freedom online.

STEAL THIS COMPUTER BOOK™ 4.0
What They Won't Tell You About the Internet

by WALLACE WANG

This offbeat, nontechnical book examines what hackers do, how they do it, and how readers can protect themselves. Informative, irreverent, and entertaining, the completely revised fourth edition of *Steal This Computer Book* contains new chapters that discuss the hacker mentality, lock picking, exploiting P2P file sharing networks, and how people manipulate search engines and pop-up ads. Includes a CD with hundreds of megabytes of hacking and security-related programs that tie in with each chapter of the book.

APRIL 2006, 432 PP. W/CD, $29.95 ($38.95 CDN)
ISBN 1-59327-105-0

STEAL THIS FILE SHARING BOOK™
What They Won't Tell You About File Sharing

by WALLACE WANG

Steal This File Sharing Book tackles the thorny issue of file sharing networks such as Kazaa, Morpheus, and Usenet. It explains how these networks work and how to use them. It exposes the dangers of using file sharing networks—including viruses, spyware, and lawsuits—and tells how to avoid them. In addition to covering how people use file sharing networks to share everything from music and video files to books and pornography, it also reveals how people use them to share secrets and censored information banned by their governments. Includes coverage of the ongoing battle between the software, video, and music pirates and the industries that are trying to stop them.

NOVEMBER 2004, 296 PP., $19.95 ($27.95 CDN)
ISBN 1-59327-050-X

THE CULT OF iPOD

by LEANDER KAHNEY

Wired News editor and former Wired News reporter Leander Kahney follows up his best selling *The Cult of Mac* with *The Cult of iPod*, a comprehensive look at how Apple's hit iPod is changing music, culture, and listening behavior. *The Cult of iPod* includes the exclusive backstory of the iPod's development; looks at the many ways iPod's users pay homage to their devices; and investigates the quirkier aspects of iPod culture, such as iPod-jacking (strangers plugging into each other's iPods to discover new music) as well as the growing legions of MP3Js (regular folks who use their iPods to become DJs).

NOVEMBER 2005, 160 PP., $24.95 ($33.95 CDN)
ISBN 1-59327-066-6

THE BOOK OF™ VISUAL BASIC 2005
.NET Insight for Classic VB Developers

by MATTHEW MACDONALD

The Book of Visual Basic 2005 is a comprehensive introduction to Microsoft's newest programming language, Visual Basic 2005, the next iteration of Visual Basic .NET. A complete revision of the highly-acclaimed *Book of VB .NET*, the book is organized as a series of lightning-fast tours and real-world examples that show developers the VB 2005 way of doing things. Perfect for old-school Visual Basic developers who haven't made the jump to .NET, the book is also useful to developers from other programming backgrounds (like Java) who want to cut to the chase and quickly learn how to program with VB 2005.

MARCH 2006, 528 PP., $39.95 ($51.95 CDN)
ISBN 1-59327-074-7

IT'S NEVER DONE THAT BEFORE

by JOHN ROSS

It's Never Done That Before is a guide to troubleshooting Windows XP for people who use computers but don't necessarily feel comfortable poking around "under the hood" to make fixes. It includes basic troubleshooting techniques, specific instructions for solving the most common problems in Windows XP, and general tips for finding and fixing the more obscure ones. It also provides explanations of BIOS beep codes and blue screen errors; instructions for using the troubleshooting tools supplied with Windows XP, such as Safe Mode and the Recovery Console; and advice for dealing with device drivers, the ROM BIOS, and the Windows Registry. Viruses, spyware, and Internet connection problems are all discussed, along with hints for getting the most out of the Microsoft Knowledge Base and navigating help desks and technical support centers.

FEBRUARY 2006, 304 PP., $29.95 ($38.95 CDN)
ISBN 1-59327-076-3

PHONE:
800.420.7240 OR
415.863.9900
MONDAY THROUGH FRIDAY,
9 A.M. TO 5 P.M. (PST)

FAX:
415.863.9950
24 HOURS A DAY,
7 DAYS A WEEK

EMAIL:
SALES@NOSTARCH.COM

WEB:
HTTP://WWW.NOSTARCH.COM

MAIL:
NO STARCH PRESS
555 DE HARO ST, SUITE 250
SAN FRANCISCO, CA 94107
USA

UPDATES

Visit **http://www.nostarch.com/vbexpress.htm** for updates, errata, and other information.

COLOPHON

Visual Basic 2005 Express: Now Playing was laid out in Adobe FrameMaker. The font families used are New Baskerville for body text, TheSansMono Condensed for code text, Futura for headings and tables, and Dogma for titles.

The book was printed and bound at Malloy Incorporated in Ann Arbor, Michigan. The paper is Glatfelter Thor 60# Smooth, which is made from 50 percent recycled materials, including 30 percent postconsumer content. The book uses a RepKover binding, which allows it to lay flat when open.

WHAT'S ON CD1?

The first CD contains two different types of files to help you learn Visual Basic programming and learn how to use Microsoft® Visual Basic® 2005 Express:

Sample programs   These are short programs that demonstrate different concepts from each chapter. By running, examining, and tearing them apart, you can get a better idea of how to write programs in Visual Basic.

Flash movie tutorials   These movies let you see how Visual Basic Express works and how to write programs in Visual Basic. Watching these movies is the next best thing to peering over the shoulders of a Visual Basic programming expert.

Each chapter has its own folder on the CD. Within each chapter's folder you'll find the Flash movie tutorial files, along with additional folders that contain each sample Visual Basic program. To run a Flash movie tutorial, just double-click a file and it should start running.

 Throughout the book, you'll see the icon shown here to the left. Below the icon, you'll see the name of a movie file. The icon indicates that the text section it appears next to corresponds to a movie by that filename on the CD.

You can load and run the sample Visual Basic programs directly from the CD, but if you want to modify any of them, you'll need to save them off the CD and onto your hard drive.

WHAT'S ON CD2?

On the second CD, you'll find a full (non-evaluation) version of Microsoft® Visual Basic® 2005 Express Edition! You'll have everything you need to learn Visual Basic 2005 Express and begin writing your own programs.

To install your copy of Visual Basic Express, your system will need to have at least the following:

- 600MHz Pentium processor (but preferably a 1GHz Pentium processor)
- 192MB of RAM (256MB recommended)
- Up to 1.3GB of available hard drive space
- 800 × 600 display with 256 colors (16 bit, 1024 × 768 high color display recommended)
- A CD or DVD drive and a mouse

Visual Basic 2005 Express can be installed on the following operating systems:

- Microsoft Windows 2000 (Professional SP4, Server SP4, Advanced Server SP4, and Datacenter SP4)
- Microsoft Windows XP (Professional x64 [WOW], Professional SP2, Home SP2, Media Center 2002/4 SP2, Media Center 2005, Tablet PC SP2)
- Microsoft Windows Server 2003 (Standard SP1, Enterprise SP1, Datacenter SP1, Web SP1, Standard x64 SP1 [WOW], Enterprise x64 SP1 [WOW], Datacenter x64 SP1 [WOW])
- Microsoft Windows Server 2003 R2 (Standard, Standard x64 [WOW], Enterprise, Enterprise x64 [WOW], Datacenter, Datacenter x64 [WOW])
- Microsoft Windows Vista

Installation of Visual Basic 2005 Express is not supported on the Intel Itanium (IA64).

If either CD doesn't work or if you have any questions, please email us at info@nostarch.com.